ADVANCES IN PUBLIC INTEREST ACCOUNTING

Volume 5 • 1993

ADVANCES IN PUBLIC INTEREST ACCOUNTING

Editor: CHERYL R. LEHMAN
Hofstra University

Associate Editors: MARILYN NEIMARK
Baruch College
The City University of New York

BARBARA MERINO
University of North Texas

TONY TINKER
Baruch College
The City University of New York

VOLUME 5 • 1993

 JAI PRESS INC.

Greenwich, Connecticut   *London, England*

CONTENTS

LIST OF CONTRIBUTORS

A. Faye Borthick	The University of Tennessee
J. Ralph Byington	Louisiana Tech University
Al Y.S. Chen	North Carolina State University
Dan Davidson	Radford University
Charles R. Enis	The Pennsylvania State University
Martin Freedman	SUNY—Binghamton
Mary Anne Gaffney	Temple University
Leonard Goodman	Rutgers University
J.E. Harris	Penn State Harrisburg
Donald W. Hicks	Christopher Newport College
Rita P. Hull	Virginia Commonwealth University
H. Fenwick Huss	Georgia State University
Bud Lacy	Oklahoma State University
Ruth Ann McEwen	Virginia Commonwealth University
Nancy Meade	University of Louisville
Paul J. Miranti, Jr.	Rutgers University
Ramona L. Paetzold	Texas A&M

Robert L. Peace	North Carolina State University
Lynn M. Pringle	The Pennsylvania State University
M.A. Reynolds	Penn State Harrisburg
Zabihollah Rezaee	Middle Tennessee State University
Alan J. Richardson	Queen's University
Richard G. Schroeder	University of North Carolina at Charlotte
Bill Schwartz	Virginia Commonwealth University
Donna L. Street	James Madison University
Dan Subotnik	Touro College
Steve G. Sutton	Arizona State University West
Mary Jeanne Welsh	LaSalle University
Charlotte J. Wright	Oklahoma State University

AD HOC REVIEWERS

Charles Boynton
University of North Texas

Bruce Committe
University of Vermont

Dimitrios Ghicas
Baruch College—CUNY

O. Finley Graves
University of Mississippi

Ruth Hines
Macquarie University, Australia

Karen Hooks
University of South Florida

Chris Humphrey
University of Manchester, UK

Herbert Hunt
University of Vermont

H. Fenwick Huss
Georgia State University

Paul J. Miranti, Jr.
Rutgers University

Rob Nehmer
Georgia State University

Leslie Oakes
University of Alberta, Canada

Pekin Ogan
Indiana University

Ted O'Leary
University College—Cork, Republic of Ireland

David Pariser
West Virginia University

Lawrence Ponemon
Babson College

Sara Reed
Texas A&M

Sara Reiter
SUNY—Binghamton

Rob Ruland
Suffolk University

Terri Shearer
University of Iowa

Cynthia Simmons
University of Calgary, Canada

Paul Williams
North Carolina State University

THE FASB's RESCISSION OF STATEMENT 33 MAY RESULT IN INFORMATION ASYMMETRIES ACROSS INVESTORS

Charles R. Enis and Lynn M. Pringle

ABSTRACT

This paper reports on an experiment that investigated the influence of current value accounting information on the behavior of individuals towards capital intensive firms. Professional and nonprofessional investors provided their reactions to the performance of capital intensive firms based on the firm's historical cost and current value accounting numbers. Linear response models identified those who were the most likely to have used the latter numbers. Regardless of the data set, the professional investors displayed unfavorable reactions, while only those nonprofessional investors who used the current value data displayed this behavior. Nonprofessional investors who relied on historical cost data demonstrated much greater optimism concerning the profitability of

Advances in Public Interest Accounting, Volume 5, pages 1-30.
ISBN: 1-55938-496-4

the capital intensive firms. Because not all investors have equal access to information, the rescission of Statement 33 may result in information asymmetries whereby the needs of nonprofessional investors are not being served.

> "Cheshire-Puss," said Alice, "Would you tell me, please, which way I ought to go from here?"
> "That depends a good deal on where you want to get to," said the Cat.
> "I don't much care where—" said Alice.
> "Then it doesn't matter which way you go," said the Cat.
> —*Alice's Adventures in Wonderland*

INTRODUCTION

Although current value accounting (CVA) is not some "true accounting" because of its attachment to historical facts and "objective" market values, it may provide a better description of business reality than historical cost information by exposing possible earnings inadequacies or serious erosions of real capital employment. Hence, the introduction of inflation accounting systems may affect investment decisions and the way that resources are allocated. The purpose of this study is to examine the decision-making behavior of both professional and nonprofessional investors who are presented with disclosure of inflation accounting signals in tandem with historical cost signals. Beaver [1978, p. 48] noted that "from the outset, the [Securities and Exchange Commission] SEC has implicitly relied upon the existence of a professional community in order to justify its apparatus as an effective means of disclosure." Along the same line, he stated that "greater emphasis upon disclosure to the nonprofessional would appear to be counter to the current trend to recognize the central role of the professional in the disclosure process [p. 50]." Beaver, however, recognized that "there may be effects on resource allocation that are ignored when the investor setting is narrowly viewed" [p. 47] by the SEC and by the Financial Accounting Standards Board (FASB). According to Demski [1974, p. 232], the "fundamental questions of resource allocation and social choice appear to underlie the question of choice among financial reporting alternatives." May and Sundam [1976, p. 759] stated that for policymakers to predict consequences of financial reporting alternatives, "studies concerned with how individuals process information [as opposed to purely aggregate, investment decision making], and specifically, how they process accounting-type signals, takes on considerable potential relevance." Our study is thus motivated in an inflation accounting context since the FASB encourages but no longer requires a business enterprise to disclose supplementary information on changing prices.[1] Our investor setting was expanded to include both professionals and nonprofessionals. Results indicate that nonprofessional investors who used current value data modified their behavior. Potentially this investor group could move investment capital from industries which are most affected by price-level changes to those least affected.

CHANGING PRICES DISCLOSURES: A POLITICAL PROBLEM

Were required changing prices disclosures rescinded because the rate of inflation in the United States has subsided since the mid-1970s?[2] Even though a reduction in the inflation rate may be desirable from an economic and social viewpoint, total elimination of inflation will not solve our accounting problems. The relevance of historical values based on transactions that occurred during the oil crisis of 1973, for example, will continue to be eroded by inflation. Furthermore, even though general price inflation may be under control, relative or specific price changes cannot be eliminated. As noted by Mosso in his dissent to the issuance of Statement No. 89:

> The basic proposition underlying Statement 33—that inflation causes historical cost financial statements to show illusory profits and mask erosion of capital—is virtually undisputed. Specific price changes are inextricably linked to general inflation, and the combination of general and specific price changes seriously reduces the relevance, the representational faithfulness, and the comparability of historical cost financial statements.
>
> Although the current inflation rate in the United States is relatively low in the context of recent history, its compound effect through time is still highly significant.[3]

Given that inflation accounting models have the potential to bear directly on national economic policy issues such as capital formation and its corollary, productivity, why has the FASB decided that "it doesn't matter which way you go" with respect to disclosure of changing prices? Perhaps the answer lies in the conflicting interests of various groups of preparers and users of published financial statements. Consider the potential users of financial data as identified by the FASB in its December 29, 1977 exposure draft, *Objectives of Financial Reporting and Elements of Financial Statements of Business Enterprises:*

> owners, lenders, suppliers, potential investors and creditors, employees, management, directors, customers, financial analysts and advisors, brokers, underwriters, stock exchanges, lawyers, economists, taxing authorities, regulatory authorities, legislators, financial press and reporting agencies, labor unions, trade associations, teachers and students, and the public [para. 9, p. 4].

Any effort to reconcile the conflicting interests of these various user groups is essentially political. The politicization of the regulatory process due to heterogeneous interests was noted by Burchell et al. [1980, p. 21]:

Attention has had to be given to the origins of a diverse array of interests in the development
of accounting and, as this has happened, the roles [of regulatory organizations] embodied
in accounting change have been seen as being ever more implicated in the political pressures
[as opposed to simply writing technical standards] which have given rise to its emergence.[4]

Underlying these political pressures faced by accounting policymakers are
societal value judgments. Some parties perceive that they will benefit from
inflation accounting disclosures while other parties view such disclosures as
harmful.

VARIOUS PROTAGONISTS INVOLVED IN
THE INFLATION ACCOUNTING DEBATE

As already stated in note 1, the government through the SEC interposed ASR
190 which prompted the FASB to issue Statement No. 33 in order to avoid direct
action by Congress.[5] The motivation behind the government's intervention regards
the impact that inflation accounting systems can have on public interest issues
such as tax policy, price controls, capital investment, allocation of funds, tariffs,
wage bargaining, anti-trust regulation, rate regulation, and so forth.

Winn [1978] provided evidence of economic consequences resulting from
the lack of reported inflation-adjusted data. Relative to historical cost
measures, Winn found current cost earnings retention to be substantially lower
and current cost effective tax rates to be substantially higher. He concluded
[p. 31] that "the wisdom of anti-inflation policies (the 1968 corporate tax
increase, the repeal of the investment tax credit during 1969-1971, and the use
of price controls from 1971-1973)can be seriously questioned."

The accounting profession's ability to deal with the inflation accounting
problem has been hampered by the conflicting interests of various private sector
groups. Armstrong [1977], in a speech as chairman of the FASB, commented
that banks and insurance companies, public utilities and transportation
companies, and small public accounting firms were opposed to the Board's
inflation accounting project for reasons of pragmatic self-interest. Opinions
of the large accounting firms were split between favoring, opposing, and
deferring action on the project.

Other protagonists in the inflation accounting debate include trade unions,
corporate management, and businesses. Trade unionists who negotiate wage
and employment contracts may be skeptical of CVA since lower reported
profits could result in smaller pay awards.

Many corporate managers oppose CVA because it is in their best interest
to perpetuate the profit illusion.[6] Indeed, managerial rewards are often closely
tied to profitability measurements [Rappaport, 1978]. Also, some managers
may fear that their stockholders may react adversely to a set of financial data
that reflects poor profitability [Bryant and Mahaney, 1981].

On the other hand, some firms see an advantage in reactions to lower CVA net income numbers. The reported profits of capital intensive firms, ceteris paribus, are higher during periods of inflation than during periods of price stability. Because reported profits serve as the primary income tax base, capital intensive firms pay taxes on inflated earnings causing a capital erosion. As a result, some firms have drawn attention to CVA numbers in their annual reports to make a political point. For example, in the letter to shareholders, Alcoa's chairman referred to the replacement cost numbers in making a plea for tax reform and higher prices.[7] Furthermore, many large, capital intensive firms, because of their visibility, often favor financial disclosures that downplay profitability. Such firms fear that excessive profits invite public scrutiny and create a political climate that is ripe for divestiture, regulation, or taxation of an industry or corporation [Watts and Zimmerman, 1978]. The enactment of the Oil Windfall Profit Tax Act (P.L. 96-249) is an example of the imposition of a tax when profits are believed to be excessive. Sectors which are susceptible to such political pressures would have reason to embrace CVA disclosures if, in their view, the widespread dissemination of such data would provide the public with a more realistic perspective of profits, taxation, and capital formation.[8]

Obviously, the various participants in the debate advance arguments motivated by their own self-interest. Accounting policy decisions, however, should be "consistent with the public interest" (the view of the SEC as expressed by Burton [1973, p. 271] in a letter to the American Institute of Certified Public Accountants [AICPA]). Although the FASB (which succeeded the AICPA in 1973) has concurred with this view, noting [1976, p. 163] that disclosure practices should be guided by "a standard that specifies the public interest," the FASB has focused on the usefulness of information criterion (FASB Concepts Statement No. 1). This focus has resulted in the repeal of Statement No. 33 by Statement No. 89.

A NEED TO EXAMINE DISAGGREGATED BEHAVIOR OF INDIVIDUALS

In the exposure draft of Statement No. 89, the Board [1986, p. 6] stated that "the research studies and responses to the Invitation to Comment indicated that the Statement 33 information was not widely used." Most of the empirical research, however, has either focused on the properties of the numbers or on the stock market's reaction to the data. Typical of the former are studies that compare *CVA* numbers with their historical cost (*HC*) counterparts [e.g., Bates and Reckers, 1979; Davidson, Skelton, and Weil, 1979; Woo and Seth, 1978). Examples of market-based studies were those that examined the benefits of SEC-required replacement cost data as reflected by share prices [e.g., Gheyara and Boatsman, 1980; Beaver, Christie, and Griffin, 1980; Ro, 1980]. Beaver and Landsman (1983) reported on the information content of Statement No. 33 disclosures. The evidence generated by these market studies, each of which used a different methodological variation, suggests that no statistically significant stock price reactions were associated with the disclosure of CVA information. In short, these studies suggest that apprehensions concerning reactions to CVA disclosures by important economic actors such as management, creditors, shareholders, and so forth are unfounded.

Market-based studies are not the only frameworks within which to study financial disclosures. Such studies address the reaction of market participants in aggregate; thus, the findings of market-based studies may not necessarily be extended to individuals. The influence of accounting disclosures on individuals, especially if they are political participants such as law makers, congressional staffers, lobbyists, members of political action committees, ward patrons, and so forth, can have important consequences even if such disclosures failed to be associated with a market reaction. In addition, the conclusion that market participants in the aggregate did not react to CVA data says nothing concerning the behavior of those market participants who in fact did not ignore the *CVA* data. To sum up, the recent attention directed toward the political aspects of accounting treatment on the disaggregated behavior of individuals suggests that market-based studies by themselves do not address all of the issues that are germane to the disclosure of CVA data.

Scheiner and Morse [1979], have observed that research is needed to investigate the impact of CVA data on the decision behavior of individuals. The lack of this type of empirical research was also noted by Vasarhelyi and Pearson [1979] who surveyed more than five hundred sources involving inflation-accounting. According to Vasarhelyi and Pearson, "unfortunately, indepth analysis of field situations, user perception of value data, and experimentation with firms are not widely available in the literature." Some studies involving individuals' reactions to inflation-accounting [Heintz, 1973; McIntyre, 1973] were completed prior to Accounting Series Release No. 190. These studies were laboratory experiments that used students as surrogates for investors and the inflation-accounting data were created by the researchers.

The present study focuses on investment decisions of both professionals and nonprofessionals so as "to track through the effect of alternative financial reporting policies at the individual level . . . [enabling an evaluation] of the consequences that will follow from adopting one set of reporting policies as opposed to another" [Demski, 1974, p. 226]. The empirical work tests two general null hypotheses:

1. Sophistication level (as embodied in the classification of subjects as professional and nonprofessional investors) had no effect on subject judgments.

2. The usage of current value accounting data had no effect on subject judgments.

METHODOLOGY

General Description

After observing background information and specific data sets, 24 professional (sophisticated) and 24 nonprofessional (unsophisticated) investors were asked to indicate their expectations concerning the performance of the stock market and the performance of 40 unidentified firms from the chemical and drug industries. The chemical and drug industries were selected from which to draw the case observations because they are (1) capital intensive, (2) written of frequently in the financial press, and (3) have a relatively large number of firms that had both a calendar year reporting period and the requirement to disclose CVA information. The 40 firms represented virtually all of the chemical and drug firms traded on the major exchanges.[9]

Subject responses were made on a 9-point Likert scale with "9" as the most favorable expectation; that is, strongest "buy" recommendation and "1" as the least favorable expectation; that is, strongest "do not buy" recommendation. The primary factors under study were CVA usage and sophistication level. Their impact was examined by comparing the mean responses of four subject groups each consisting of 12 individuals—(1) sophisticated, high-CVA users; (2) sophisticated, low-CVA users; (3) unsophisticated, high-CVA users; and (4) unsophisticated, low-CVA users. Thus, the design of the present study was crossed and balanced.

Before responding to the chemical and drug firms, the subjects were asked to predict the one-year percentage change in the New York Stock Exchange (NYSE) Index. These predictions were used as a covariate to control for the subjects' general predispositions or expectations concerning the stock market as a whole (i.e., market outlook). In other words, the function of the NYSE covariate in the present study is analogous to the role of a market index in controlling for systematic risk in a market study using the capital asset pricing model.

Response Variable and Statistical Analyses

The task required the investors to recommend whether each of 40 stocks should or should not be bought. These recommendations were to be made for each stock based on its relative attractiveness as captured in the firm's financial profile. A firm's profile consisted of two sets of five financial ratios, one computed using HC numbers, the other using CVA numbers. A detailed discussion of the data set, research instrument and experimental setting is included in the Appendix.

The recommendations provided an indication of the subjects' decision behavior and served as the dependent variable. The analysis of the investors' responses consisted of comparing the mean responses of the four subject groups across the 40 firms. The Wilcoxon matched-pairs signed-ranks test was used to determine if the difference in mean responses between any two groups was statistically significant. Mean responses were examined because the "aggregation effect" diversifies out systematic and/or random variations in judgments [Wright, 1979]. Thus, a mean response is representative of the individuals in the group and hence associated with the characteristics upon which such individuals were assigned to the group.

The variances in the responses of the four subject groups across each of the forty firms were also analyzed in the same manner as the mean responses. Response variances were examined to determine if the subject groups differed in consensus; that is, the degree to which subjects within a group agree regarding their recommendations. Response variance is an inverse measure of consensus. Many behavioral studies in accounting measure consensus as a means of evaluating decision making in the absence of more objective criteria [e.g., Ashton, 1985; Keasey and Watson, 1989; Shields, 1983; Snowball, 1980].

An analysis of covariance (ANCOVA) was also performed. The dependent variable in the ANCOVA model was the mean responses given by each of the 48 subjects. The independent variables in the ANCOVA model were: (1) sophistication, two levels—professional and nonprofessional; (2) CVA usage, two levels—relatively high and low usage; (3) sophistication by CVA usage levels; and (4) the NYSE variable as the covariate.

Subjects and Sophistication Level

The voluntary subjects were 24 professional and 24 nonprofessional investors located in the Washington, D.C. area and were selected on the basis of referral and willingness to participate. The professional investors were considered sophisticated while the nonprofessional investors were considered unsophisticated. The professional investors were full-time stock brokers, financial analysts, and fund managers. The nonprofessional group consisted of those who have had some experience in making investment decisions other than in the capacity of a full-time occupation. In the latter group were individuals from a variety of situations—scientists, engineers, physicians, government employees, business persons, and so forth (see the Appendix for further discussion of the subjects participating in this research).

CVA Usage

One could estimate whether subjects were professional or nonprofessional investors before the research instrument was administered. However, the extent of *CVA* usage could not be determined until after the data collected by the instrument were analyzed. To classify subjects according to *CVA* usage, the twelve professional investors and the twelve nonprofessional investors who used *CVA* data the most were identified by analyzing human information processing models. Accordingly, standardized linear regression models were constructed for each subject as follows:

$$Y = \beta_1 X_1 + \ldots + \beta_5 X_5 + \beta_6 X_6 + \ldots + \beta_{10} X_{10}$$

where:

$$
\begin{aligned}
Y &= \text{a subject's recommendation response;} \\
X_1 \ldots X_5 &= \text{HC version of the 5 financial ratios;} \\
X_6 \ldots X_{10} &= \textit{CVA} \text{ version of the 5 financial ratios;} \\
\beta_1 \ldots \beta_{10} &= \text{Standardized linear regression coefficients.}
\end{aligned}
$$

Such linear models have been successful in capturing the impact of decision variables $(X_1 \ldots X_n)$ on the decisions (Y) of judges in diverse applications in such fields as finance, medicine, personnel management, law, political science, and so forth [Slovic, 1972].

The "usefulness" measure (U-score) was used to identify those subjects whose responses were likely to have been the most influenced by the *CVA* ratio set [Darlington, 1968]. The U-score of a variable set is the decrease in R^2 resulting from the elimination of that set from the model. The U-scores were tested for statistical significance as follows [McNemar, 1969, p. 321):

$$\frac{(R^2_{10} - R^2_5)/5}{(1 - R^2_{10})/29} = F; \quad df = 5, 29$$

where:

$$
\begin{aligned}
R^2_{10} &= R^2 \text{ of the full ten ratio model;} \\
R^2_5 &= R^2 \text{ of the five HC ratio model.}
\end{aligned}
$$

Because R^2 will always decrease or remain unchanged when variables are dropped from a linear model, the F-statistics associated with the U-scores were used to classify subjects according to *CVA* usage. As there is no accepted classification norm for *CVA* usage, the median F-statistic was used in this capacity. Accordingly, within each of the professional and nonprofessional investor groups the subjects with the twelve highest U-score F-statistics were considered relatively high *CVA* users (CVA_{Hi}), while the remainder were classed as relatively low *CVA* users (CVA_{Lo}) (see Table 1).

Table 1. Classification of Subjects According to CVA Usage

	Subject Number	R^2_{10}	R^2_5	U-Score	F
Professional Investors					
High CVA Users	14	.776	.575	.201	5.22**
	15	.656	.256	.400	6.75***
	18	.818	.732	.086	2.73*
	19	.604	.338	.266	3.90*
	20	.759	.472	.287	6.91***
	24	.736	.560	.176	3.87*
	29	.880	.779	.101	4.88**
	30	.641	.357	.284	4.11**
	31	.725	.433	.292	6.16***
	33	.703	.551	.152	2.97*
	34	.713	.329	.384	7.76***
	41	.774	.630	.144	3.70*
Low CVA Users	5	.543	.499	.094	1.19
	6	.481	.381	.100	1.12
	10	.430	.341	.089	0.91
	13	.817	.772	.045	1.43
	22	.591	.492	.099	1.40
	25	.428	.394	.034	0.34
	35	.392	.250	.142	1.35
	36	.699	.571	.128	2.46
	38	.668	.537	.131	2.29
	45	.546	.459	.087	1.11
	47	.470	.268	.202	2.21
	48	.403	.183	.220	2.14
Nonprofessional Investors					
High CVA Users	1	.838	.435	.403	14.43***
	2	.438	.056	.382	3.94*
	7	.621	.309	.312	4.77**
	11	.488	.243	.245	2.78*
	12	.802	.439	.363	10.63***
	16	.690	.217	.453	8.85***
	21	.745	.556	.189	4.30**
	28	.833	.729	.104	3.61*
	37	.839	.723	.116	4.18**
	40	.685	.527	.158	2.91*
	44	.713	.474	.239	4.83**
	46	.764	.352	.412	10.13***
Low CVA Users	3	.734	.641	.093	2.03
	4	.292	.201	.091	0.75
	8	.875	.847	.028	1.30

Table 1. (Continued)

9	.628	.499	.129	2.01
17	.602	.454	.148	2.16
23	.381	.264	.117	1.10
26	.712	.612	.100	2.01
27	.633	.563	.070	1.11
32	.721	.607	.114	2.37
39	.402	.297	.104	1.02
42	.582	.561	.021	0.29
43	.473	.316	.157	1.73

Notes: $*\alpha < .05$; $**\alpha < .01$; $***\alpha < .001$.

All CVA_{Hi} investors had U-scores significant at the .05 level; none of the CVA_{Lo} investors had U-scores significant at this level.[10] CVA_{Hi} subjects did not necessarily use CVA information to the exclusion of HC information. Likewise, CVA_{Lo} subjects did not use HC information to the exclusion of CVA information. However, one can say that CVA_{Hi} subjects were more likely to have used CVA information to a relatively greater degree than did CVA_{Lo} subjects.

The frequency of use of the individual ratios by CVA_{Hi} and CVA_{Lo} subjects is shown in Table 2. For example, the HC version of the GRO ratio was statistically significant at the .05 level in 11 and 9 of the response models of the CVA_{Lo} and CVA_{Hi} subjects, respectively. The ten ratios were presented to 48 subjects for a total of 480 possible significant variables. Table 2 shows 153 or 32 percent of this total as significant. This relatively broad representation of significant ratios suggests that the demand effect, a common problem in repetitive trial experiments whereby subjects become sensitized to a few ratios, may not have been severe.

According to Table 2, the CVA ratios in the CVA_{Hi} models were significant 52 of a possible 120 times (5 ratios $\times$ 24 subjects) for a frequency rate of 43 1/3 %) while only significant 22 times (18 1/3%) in the CVA_{Lo} models. This finding supports the classification procedure used to form the CVA_{Hi} and CVA_{Lo} groups. The CVA_{Hi} subjects also had a greater frequency rate with respect to the HC ratios. It should be emphasized that the responses of the CVA_{Hi} subjects were those in which the CVA data set explained variance in addition to variance explained by the HC data set. This concept reflects the nature of the financial reporting of CVA data. CVA numbers are disclosed to supplement and not to replace HC numbers. In short, the CVA_{Hi} subjects used the CVA ratios in addition to rather than instead of the HC ratios.

Table 2. Frequence of Variable Significance in the Subjects' Response Models

Subject Group[a]	HC						CVA					
	EPS	*DPO*	*EPR*	*ROA*	*GRO*	*Total*	*EPS*	*DPO*	*EPR*	*ROA*	*GRO*	*Total*
CVA$_{Lo}$	5	11	5	4	11	36	3	7	1	4	7	22
CVA$_{Hi}$	7	6	12	9	9	43	9	9	8	9	17	52
Total	12	17	17	13	20	79	12	16	9	13	24	74

Notes: *EPS* = Earnings Per Share; *DPO* = Dividend Payout Ratio; *GRO* = Growth in EPS; *EPR* = Earnings Price Ratio; *ROA* = Return on Assets.
[a]Each group consisted of 24 subjects.

12

Table 3.   Subjective Measures of Variable Set Importance

Variable Set	P-CVA$_{Hi}$	N-CVA$_{Hi}$	CVA$_{Hi}$	P-CVA$_{Lo}$	N-CVA$_{Lo}$	CVA$_{Lo}$
HC	56[a]	49	53	76	65	71
CVA	44	51	47	24	35	29
Total	100	100	100	100	100	100

Note: [a]These figures are group averages.

As an additional consistency check on the U-score *F*-test, the present study also employed a subjective measure of variable set importance [Cook and Stewart, 1975]. In the debriefing questionnaire, subjects were asked to allocate 100 points over the two ratio sets according to the relative importance they perceived each to have had in making their responses. The average number of points assigned to the *CVA* set by the *CVA*$_{Hi}$ (*CVA*$_{Lo}$) group was 47 (29) (see Table 3). This finding, significant at the .008 level using the binomial test [see Siegel, 1956, pp. 36-42], is consistent with the manner in which the investors were classified. Such agreement as to the measurement of variable set importance suggests that the importance measures were not dependent on the modeling technique [Kida, Cohen, and Paquette, 1990].

RESULTS

This section first presents the results of the ANCOVA model shown in Table 4 and supported by the diagrams in Figures 1 and 2. Next, the results of the Wilcoxon matched-pairs signed-ranks tests reported in Table 5 are discussed.

ANCOVA Model

The ANCOVA model shows the covariate (NYSE) as the most significant variable. This finding had a strong a priori expectation. Investors that had a favorable market outlook should also have responded favorably to the chemical and drug firms. This result was expected because these stocks move with the market as a whole as evidenced by their high systematic risk coefficients.[11]

The type III sum of the squares in Table 4 for the two main effects and the interactive effect gives the sum of the squares for these variables adjusted for the covariate. The most significant main effect is *CVA* usage. The other

Table 4.   Analysis of Covariance

Source	d.f.	Sum of Squares Type I	Sum of Squares Type III	F	Pr > F
Sophistication Level	1	1.219	1.729	3.96	.053
CVA-Usage	1	1.333	2.187	5.01	.030
Soph. Levl. × CVA-Use.	1	0.665	1.347	3.09	.086
NYSE Prediction	1	8.479	8.479	19.43	.001
Model ($R^2 = .384$)	4	11.696		6.70	.001
Error	43	18.762			
Total	47	30.458			

main effect, sophistication level, and the interactive effect are only marginally significant ($.05 < \alpha < .10$).

The substantial influence of the covariate is diagrammed in Figure 1. Represented on the x-axis are the subjects bifurcated according to market outlook; that is, the 12 highest and lowest predictions of the NYSE within the professional and nonprofessional groups. Mean responses are shown on the Y-axis. Two relationships are evident from an inspection of Figure 1. First, subject responses and sophistication level are inversely related in that the line representing the nonprofessional investors lies above the line representing the professional investors. Second, the NYSE variable is directly related to subject responses. The strength of the relationship is consistent across sophistication levels in that the nonprofessional and professional lines are almost parallel.

The significant main effect, *CVA* usage, is diagrammed in Figure 2. This diagram is similar to Figure 1 except that the x-axis shows the subjects bifurcated according to *CVA* usage within the professional and nonprofessional groups. As in Figure 1, the nonprofessional line lies above the professional line indicating an inverse relationship between investors' sophistication and their responses.

Figure 2 also shows that *CVA* usage is inversely related to subject responses of both professional and nonprofessional groups. However, this relationship is more pronounced with respect to the nonprofessional investors as indicated by the steepness of the slope.

The results of the ANCOVA model suggest that, although not as influential as one's belief concerning market movements, the usage of *CVA* data does influence one's judgments. In the present study, this influence was negative (i.e., associated with less favorable recommendations) because of the adverse effects of inflation on capital intensive firms as signaled by *CVA* ratios reflecting smaller profits than corresponding HC ratios. This signaling had a greater effect on the nonprofessional relative to the professional investors.

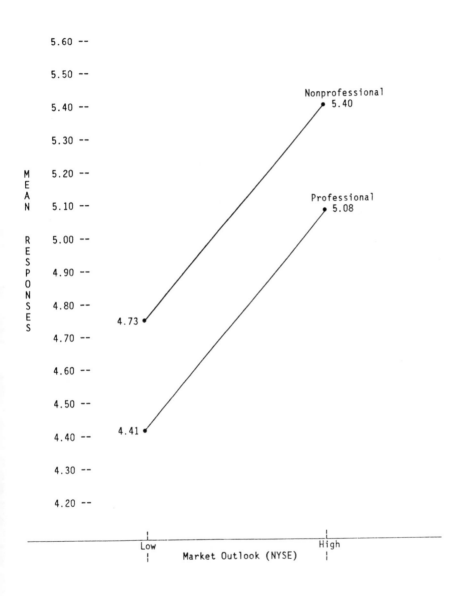

Figure 1. Diagram of the Influence of Market Outlook on the Difference in Average Responses Between Professional and Nonprofessional Investors

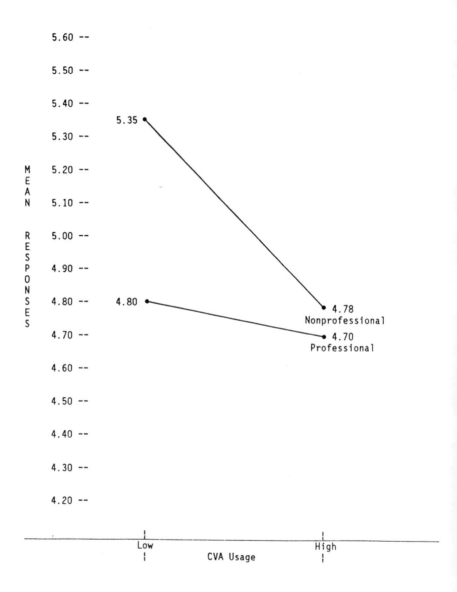

Figure 2. Diagram of the Influence of CVA Usage on the Difference in Average Responses Between Professional and Nonprofessional Investors

Matched-Pairs Tests

The present research design allowed for the segmentation of the 48 investors into four mutually exclusive subject groups consisting of twelve members each; that is, those investors who were (1) professional and high CVA users (P-CVA_{Hi}), (2) professional and low CVA users (P-CVA_{Lo}), (3) nonprofessional and high CVA users (N-CVA_{Hi}), and (4) nonprofessional and low CVA users (N-CVA_{Lo}). Six comparisons of the mean responses of these four subject groups averaged across the forty firms are shown in panel A of Table 5. Differences in mean responses were tested for statistical significance using the Wilcoxon matched-pairs signed-ranks test. The comparisons in panel B are the same as in panel A except that the forty matched-pairs in each comparison are variances rather than means.

Mean Responses

Three subject groups, P-CVA_{Lo}, N-CVA_{Hi}, and P-CVA_{Hi}, had mean responses that did not differ significantly from one another (Table 5, panel A); all three had unfavorable mean response scores (i.e., < 5). On the other hand, the favorable score (5.35) of the nonprofessional and low CVA users stands alone and is significantly greater than the unfavorable scores of the other three subject groups.[12] In short, all groups except the group consisting of the twelve nonprofessional investors who were relatively low users of the CVA data had unfavorable reactions toward the capital intensive firms in this experiment.

Table 5. Wilcoxon Matched-Pairs Signed-Ranks Tests for Differences in Subject Group Response Means and Variances Across the 40 Firms

Mean	Std Dev	Subject Group	Wilcoxon $|Z|$ Scores[a]		
			N-CVA_{Lo}	N-CVA_{Hi}	P-CVA_{Lo}
		A. Response Means			
4.70	1.46	P-CVA_{Hi}	3.92**	0.76	0.41
4.80	1.02	P-CVA_{Lo}	3.45**	0.29	
4.78	1.35	N-CVA_{Hi}	3.27*		
5.35	1.45	N-CVA_{Lo}	—		
		B. Response Variances			
2.16	1.15	P-CVA_{Hi}	3.51**	3.94**	3.72**
3.22	1.02	P-CVA_{Lo}	0.20	0.43	
3.16	1.13	N-CVA_{Hi}	0.19		
3.14	1.32	N-CVA_{Lo}	—		

Notes: [a] Test the null hypothesis that the response metric of the intersecting row and column subject groups did not differ; $n = 40$.
*Two-tailed $\alpha < .01$.
**Two-tailed $\alpha < .001$.

Response Variance

The six comparisons in panel B of Table 5 show which pairs of contrasted subject groups differed significantly in consensus. In each comparison, the group with the lower mean response variance is the group with the greater consensus. Three subject groups, $P\text{-}CVA_{Lo}$, $N\text{-}CVA_{Hi}$, $N\text{-}CVA_{Lo}$ had consensus that did not differ significantly from one another. However, the $P\text{-}CVA_{Hi}$ group had a significantly greater degree of consensus when compared to each of the other subject groups. In other words, CVA usage was associated with significantly greater consensus with respect to the professional investors, and no significant difference in consensus with respect to the nonprofessional investors.

To sum up, the matched-pairs component of the study suggests that CVA usage is associated with less favorable responses among unsophisticated subjects and greater consensus among sophisticated subjects.

Limitations

Several limitations concerning the present empirical work should be mentioned. To begin with, the subjects were a convenience sample rather than one selected using a scientific sampling procedure. This limitation exposes the experiment to self-selection bias. The research instrument was administered to the subjects over a 30-day period in various settings rather than to all subjects at the same time in the same controlled laboratory setting. This situation could also bias subject responses. In addition, to control for the influence of extraneous factors, the subjects were limited to the information contained in the instrument upon which to base their responses. Thus, the subjects did not have access to decision aids that they might have otherwise used, and hence made responses that might not be representative of those made in a more realistic setting.

Furthermore, in a repetitive trial experiment, within-subjects demand characteristics (such as subjects being sensitized to certain cases or ratios) can have confounding effects in the measurement of the response variable. Also, the results of the present study may have differed if some other set or presentation format of financial data was chosen to represent capital intensity. Finally, the classification of subjects according to sophistication levels may have differed if an alternative to occupational position was used as an indicator of expertise. In view of these limitations, extrapolation of the findings of the present study into the public policy domain should be done with caution.

CONCLUSIONS

The results reported in this paper are consistent with those of other behavioral studies in that sophistication level, as embodied in the professional and nonprofessional investors, was a factor in explaining differences in the reactions of individuals toward financial information. In addition, the observed response behavior was also consistent with portfolio theory. The strong positive relationship between subjects' market outlook and responses to chemical and drug stocks (i.e., typically high beta stocks) that was expected in the present study, was in fact observed.

Consistent with the findings of market studies, the results also suggest that level of CVA usage had little impact on the reactions of the professional investors. These sophisticated subjects, regardless of whether they were high or low CVA users, had relatively unfavorable reactions regarding their expectations as to the performance of capital intensive firms.[13] Two possibilities are offered to explain why the P-CVA_{Hi} and P-CVA_{Lo} subjects had similar mean responses despite their differences in CVA usage as shown in Table 3. Perhaps the P-CVA_{Lo} subjects, by integrating the economic and industry background information (discussed in the Appendix) with the more familiar HC ratio set, were able to "intuitively" adjust these numbers to obtain the same information as contained in the less familiar CVA ratio set; this possibility has been suggested by Bierman [1956], Horngren [1955], and Parker [1975]. Another possibility is that these subjects being skilled financial analysts had access to effective inflation rates from other sources and were able to detect sufficient negative signals which effected their unfavorable reactions.

In contrast to their professional counterparts, the nonprofessional investors did not have the same resources and were significantly influenced by CVA usage. Apparently the CVA ratios were able to influence the recommendations of the unsophisticated investors in the present study because these subjects were not as likely as the professional investors to be able to recall prototypical relationships between HC ratios and expected profitability. As expected, high CVA usage was associated with lower responses among the nonprofessional subjects. However, this finding does not appear to be descriptive of an oversimplified reaction such as translating the lower CVA ratios into lower recommendations. Indeed, high *CVA* usage by the unsophisticated subjects resulted in mean responses that did not differ significantly from those of the experts. Clearly, the nonprofessional subjects who were high CVA users displayed an unfavorable reaction similar to that of the professional investors. On the other hand, the nonprofessional low CVA users were the only subject group to have displayed a favorable reaction. Thus, CVA usage was apparently a factor in making the unsophisticated individuals have lower expectations concerning the profitability of the chemical and drug firms. In other words, CVA data were instrumental in tempering the optimism of the nonprofessional investors.

An important implication of these results is that the views of unsophisticated investors do not necessarily parallel those of professional investors. A similar observation was expressed by Brenner [1970] who mailed questionnaires to stockholders, brokers, and financial analysts to obtain responses regarding the inclusion of changes in current values in reported earnings per share. He noted that:

> In the past, many have assumed that the views of analysts were representative of the views of the stockholder. The [chi-square test] results of the present study however, suggest that the analysts may not be good surrogates for the stockholder. Comparison between the two groups resulted in statistically significant differences in responses to each question. [The stockholders more consistently desired a current value concept of earnings per share.] Future empirical research may have to give explicit consideration to the stockholder if the results are intended to reflect the views of the total investor group. [p. 164]

The present study considers both professional and nonprofessional investors and extends Brenner's work by demonstrating that the two groups react differently to CVA ratios. The linear response models indicated that CVA usage impacted the decision behavior of unsophisticated investors. For the sophisticated subjects, the CVA data, although associated with less favorable responses, were not a factor in imparting an unfavorable perception of capital intensive firms.

In their discussions of a collective choice rule for accounting policy decisions, May and Sundem [1976, p. 751] stated that "no satisfactory resolution of the issues will abandon completely the ethical judgment that *individual's preferences are to count*." Brenner's questionnaire responses indicated that nonprofessional investors desire *CVA* data and the present study suggests that this group can benefit from using such data. The FASB's decision, however, to rescind Statement No. 33 "confronts one of the most primitive notions of disclosure regulation—the concept of 'fair' disclosure, which is perceived [by the SEC] to mean equal access to information" [Beaver 1978, p. 51]. Clearly, as regards inflation-adjusted disclosures, the FASB has abandoned its own objective of symmetric distribution of information across investors as suggested in concepts Statement No. 1 (p. vii):

> The objectives [of general purpose external financial reporting by business enterprises] stem primarily from the needs of external users who lack the authority to prescribe the information they want and must rely on information management communicates to them.[14]

Concepts Statement No. 1 (para. 36) went on to state that "financial reporting should provide information that can be used by all—non-professionals, as well as professionals—who are willing to use it properly." CVA data cannot be used properly if it is not available. Therefore, Statement No. 89 results in information asymmetries that favor the interests of professional investors and "corporate protagonists over the rest of society" [Neimark, 1986, p. xi]. Lev [1988, p. 9] noted that such information asymmetries are "associated with a lower number of investors, higher transaction costs, lower liquidity of securities, thinner volumes of trade and it leads, in general, to decreased social gains from trade." To mitigate such undesirable social effects, Lev [p. 13] called for an equity objective whereby "the interests of the less informed investors should, in general, be favored over those of the more informed investors."[15] Perhaps the FASB should reconsider its rescission of Statement No. 33 even though "at present, government interest in any requirement to continue the disclosures required by Statement No. 33, as amended, seems to have diminished" (FASB, 1986a, para. 21]. Lack of political pressure is not justification for the Board's current position of "it doesn't matter which way you go"—that is, the Board's decision to make voluntary the supplementary disclosure of inflation-adjusted information.

APPENDIX

Settings and Subjects

The research instrument was administered in the homes and offices of the investors over a 30-day period. Experimental control was maintained by administering the research materials in person; thus, the researchers were assured that the subjects had no access to information other than that presented in the research instrument. The subjects, who were cautioned against discussing the experiment with colleagues, were from many different organizations; thus, they had little opportunity for interaction.

Data gathered in the debriefing questionnaire supported the notion that the professional subjects were in fact more sophisticated than the nonprofessional subjects in that the professional investors had a greater degree of experience and formal education in investment analysis. The professional subjects had considerably greater investing experience because the rendering of investment decisions is within the domain of their routine situational duties. The nonprofessional investors had varying investment experience. Two nonprofessional subjects described themselves as very frequent investors, 6 as frequent investors, 3 as somewhat frequent investors, and 13 as infrequent investors. Furthermore, the professional investors had substantially greater levels of formal education in financial fields than did the nonprofessional investors; 12(3) of the professional (nonprofessional) subjects had graduate degrees while 0 (5) of the professional (nonprofessional) subjects had no college level training in financial related areas. The nonprofessional investors with financial graduate degrees earned MBA degrees in preparation for middle and upper managerial opportunities.

The possibility that some of the nonprofessional subjects might have had greater investment expertise than some of the professional subjects can not be ruled out. For example, the two nonprofessional investors that described themselves as very frequent investors could have had investing skills superior to those of lesser experienced professional investors. Although one cannot claim with certainty that the professional group had an absolute advantage over the nonprofessional group with respect to investment decision making, the professional investors did have a comparative advantage in that these subjects were employed full-time in investment decision-making activities. Nevertheless, education and experience data compiled from the research instrument established the greater likelihood that the professional group as a whole was more sophisticated than the nonprofessional group.

A generally accepted goal of security transactions is to increase investor welfare from after-tax dividends and/or capital gains. Thus, in the normative sense, the investors should have aspired to respond with the highest or most favorable recommendations (i.e., buy recommendations) for those stocks that they evaluated as having excellent profit potential, and the lowest recommendations (i.e., do not buy recommendations) for those stocks that they evaluated as having poor profit potential. The subjects were requested to describe in the debriefing questionnaire "rule(s) of thumb" or decision technique(s) that may have aided their responses. Thirty-seven of the 48 investors related specific heuristics and/or decision-rules that came into play in making their responses. Statements such as "growth potential," "return on investment," "market appreciation," and so forth were common to most descriptions, and suggest that perceived profitability was in fact motivating the recommendations of the investors.

Research Instrument and Data Set

The research instrument consisted of two parts. Part I contained a description of the general conditions that actually existed during the first quarter of 1979. The background information was intended to add realism to the experimental task. The subjects were not informed of the actual time period from which the data were drawn. The background information included (1) a graph of the NYSE Index, (2) a table displaying the performance of leading economic indicators, and (3) a narrative discussion of inflation, interest rates, real economic growth and unemployment as reported in the financial press. Part I also contained background data on the chemical and drug industries obtained from *The Value Line Investment Survey*. This information included several paragraphs describing market conditions, product developments, median financial ratios, and so forth for each industry. A sample paragraph follows:

Cost of inputs other than wages will rise anywhere from 6% to 20% for the chemical industry. However, unit sales volume, growing faster than effective production capacity, will be up by about 5-7%.

Part II consisted of a booklet containing financial profiles for twenty chemical and twenty drug firms plus two repeat profiles.[16] The profiles were arranged randomly within each industry, one profile per page. Each page also included the 9-point scale on which the responses were made. The subjects were informed of each firm's industry classification, but not its identity.

Firm profiles contained two sets of five financial ratios presented in two columns, one computed using *HC* numbers and the other computed using CVA numbers. An attempt was made to select ratios which are (1) well-known to the investment community, (2) frequently used to evaluate common stocks, and (3) minimally correlated with each other. In selecting the five ratios, a list of 18 ratios that were differentially measurable in HC and CVA terms were compiled from annual reports and SEC 10-K filings for the year ended December 31, 1978. These ratios were ranked according to their cite frequency in textbooks, financial reporting services, professional and academic articles, and so forth. Factor analysis and three subjective criteria were employed to discriminate the five ratios chosen.[17]

The ratios chosen for the financial profiles are shown in Table A1. This table also shows the extent to which CVA-based ratios appear less profitable during inflation.[18] According to Wilcoxon signed-ranks tests, the CVA versions of the five ratios are significantly less favorable than the respective historic cost versions.

The ratios listed in Table A1 were used as independent variables in the construction of linear regression models that were used to classify subjects as relatively high or low CVA users [see p. 9]. Measurement problems could have resulted if multicollinearity is pervasive across the ratios; that is, the F-statistics for the HC ratio models could have been overestimated resulting in an underestimation of the explanatory power that was ascribed to the CVA ratios. Table A2 is a correlation matrix of the CVA and HC versions of the five ratios.

Table A1. Wilcoxon Signed-Ranks Tests for
Differences Between HC and CVA Versions
of the Five Financial Ratios

	Medians		Wilcoxon	
Ratios	*HC*	*CVA*	$|Z|$	$Pr>|Z|$*
Earnings Per Share (*EPS*)	3.12	1.88	4.248	.001
Dividend Payout (*DPO*)	.39	.50	3.403	.001
Earnings Price Ratio (*EPR*)	.10	.06	5.225	.001
Return on Assets (*ROA*)	.15	.11	3.589	.001
Growth in *EPS* (*GRO*)	.12	.06	1.704	.044

Note: *One-tailed test.

Table A2.   Correlation Matrix—HC and CVA
Versions of the Five Financial Ratios

	CVA Version					HC Version				
	GRO	ROA	EPR	DPO	EPS	GRO	ROA	EPR	DPO	EPS
HC Version										
EPS	−.10	−.02	.13	.32	.36	.18	−.05	.44	−.09	1
DPO	−.36	−.07	−.18	−.30	−.24	−.45	.03	.07	1	
EPR	−.37	−.55	−.08	.11	−.20	−.40	−.49	1		
ROA	.15	.86	.10	.25	.28	.53	1			
GRO	.59	.57	.26	.30	.55	1				
CVA Version										
EPS	.72	.66	.87	.14	1					
DPO	−.11	.19	.10	1						
EPR	.63	.56	1							
ROA	.46	1								
GRO	1									

Although multicollinearity is present, it does not appear pervasive as only four of the 25 intercorrelations between the HC and CVA versions of the respective ratios exceed .50.

The presentation of financial ratios in a separate profile for each firm facilitated the completion of the experimental task. However, this format also raised the possibility of demand characteristics influencing the results. For example, subjects could have become sensitized to certain ratios or profiles. This situation could have resulted in spurious recommendations for the remaining firms. The presentation of the firm profiles in a different random order for each subject and the inclusion of two repeat profiles was intended to mitigate demand effects [Harsha and Knapp, 1990].

The present study was structured in a manner in which the impact of CVA usage could be observed without varying the information load. Prior research has demonstrated that information load substantially influences decision behavior [e.g., Snowball, 1980; Slovic, 1972; Miller, 1972; Dickhaut, 1973; Jacoby, Speller, and Kohn, 1974]. Given that our main research objective is to determine the differences in responses that are attributable to the usage of CVA data given its availability (rather than determining response differences attributable to the presence of CVA data), all subjects were provided research instruments that did not vary with respect to the quantity or complexity of the information presented.

The Task

After reading the economic data each subject was asked to predict the percentage change in the NYSE index for the ensuing year. This information served as a covariate in subsequent analyses. Next, after observing each firm profile, the investors were asked to make investment recommendations utilizing a 9-point scale. A rating of one indicated a very strong do not buy or unfavorable reaction, a rating of 9 indicated a very strong buy or favorable reaction, and a rating of 5 indicated a neutral reaction.[19]

An important attribute of a repetitive trial task using a Likert scale is that the context of the experiment elicits responses that possess adequate variation. Figure 1A shows a histogram of the 1,920 responses obtained on the Likert scale. An inspection of Figure 1A shows that the experimental cases provided for a varied and balanced distribution over this 9-point scale.

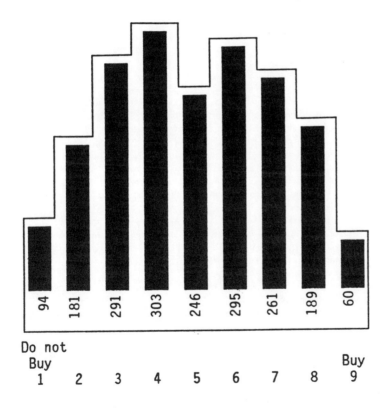

Note: The figures within the bars are frequencies (48 subjects × 40 firms = 1,920 responses).

Figure A1.   The Distribution of Subject Responses on the Nine Point Scale

After finishing the experimental task the subjects were administered a debriefing questionnaire which elicited responses concerning the subjects' perceived importance of the data sets, reactions to the task, recommendation strategies, and biographical data. Responses to the debriefing questions and observations by the researchers indicated that the investors were involved with the experimental task and found it interesting.

NOTES

1.   Effective for the financial reports issued after December 2, 1986, FASB Statement No. 89, *Financial Reporting and Changing Prices,* supersedes FASB Statement No. 33, *Financial Reporting and Changing Prices,* which, when issued in September 1979, required disclosure of constant dollar and current cost information. Prior to the issuance of Statement No. 33, Accounting Series Release No. 190 (ASR No. 190), *Disclosure of Certain Replacement Cost Data,* issued by the SEC in March 1976, mandated certain replacement cost disclosures. Once the requirements of Statement No. 33 became effective, Accounting Series Release No. 271, *Deletion of Requirement to Disclose Replacement Cost Information,* eliminated the requirements of ASR No. 190.

2.   It is not a novel idea that the level of interest in inflation accounting parallels the inflation rate. Tweedie and Whittington [1984, pp. 303-305] provide several references and examples consistent with this view.

3.   A 1980 study by Price Waterhouse & Co. indicated that a variety of financial performance measures are significantly different under historical cost, constant dollar, and current cost accounting. Thus, the materiality of Statement No. 33 disclosures is not in doubt.

4.   In *Statement of Financial Accounting Concepts No. 1,* "Objectives of Financial Reporting for Business Enterprises," the FASB (p. vii, 1978) recognized that accounting objectives "are not immutable—they are affected by the economic, legal, political, and social environment in which financial reporting takes place." May and Sundem (1976, p. 750) also described the development of accounting theory as a political process, noting that "in practice as well as in theory, the social welfare impact of accounting reports apparently is recognized. Therefore it is no surprise that the FASB is a political body and, consequently, that the process of selecting acceptable accounting alternative (sic) is a political process."

5.   International parallels include the Sandilands Committee in the United Kingdom, the Mathews Committee in Australia, and the Richardson Committee in New Zealand.

6.   See "The Profit Illusion" [1979, pp. 108-112].

7.   Aluminum Company of America, [1977, p. 1].

8.   See "Inflation Accounting" [1979, pp. 68-74].

9.   One chemical firm was not included because its very large size could have caused its identity to be revealed to the subjects.

10.   The criterion used to classify subjects according to CVA usage was a median split based upon the F statistics associated with the U-score. The occurrence of all CVA_{Hi} subjects having U-scores significant at the .05 level was coincidental.

11.   An accepted principle in portfolio analysis is that the performance of individual securities and market indicators are correlated [e.g., King, 1966; Beaver, 1973; Sharpe, 1964; Ball and Brown, 1967]. The systematic risk or beta coefficients for chemical and drug stocks usually range between .75 and 1.75. Betas for firms in the chemical and drug and other industries are reported by *The Value Line Investment Survey* [New York: Arnold Bernhard & Co., Inc.].

12.   It should be noted that only five of the twelve subjects who were both nonprofessional and low CVA users were among the investors who made the twelve highest predictions regarding

the NYSE. Therefore, a disproportionate number of N-CVA_{Lo} subjects with an optimistic market outlook was not a likely cause of this group having a favorable mean response.

13.   The use and nonuse of CVA data is consistent with Berliner's [1983] survey results of 190 members of the Financial Analysts Federation. Nearly half of the respondents (94) indicated that they used Statement No. 33 information while the remainder (96) indicated no use of such information.

14.   The AICPA [1973, p. 17] had also suggested a similar objective: "An objective of financial statements is to serve primarily those users who have limited authority, ability, or resources to obtain information and who rely on financial statements as their principal source of information about an enterprise's economic activities."

15.   The FASB [1976, p. 163] has recognized the need for a public interest criterion: "Since the arguments on both sides [of the inflation accounting debate] are often biased by self-interest or preconceptions about the public interest, it is necessary to air those differences of opinion and the arguments for and against them. But no objective solution is possible in the absence of a standard that specifies the public interest or the most desirable effect on the economy or society."

16.   Each industry group contained one repeat firm as a means of screening out unreliable respondents. A subject's responses were disqualified from the analysis if the sum of the squared differences between responses on the two sets of repeat cases exceeded nine. This standard resulted in the disqualification of three subjects in selecting the 48 investors whose responses were analyzed in the present study. This procedure also reduced the risk of demand effects.

17.   Factor analysis was performed on 36 variables (HC and CVA versions of 18 sample firm ratios). A limiting eigen-value of 1.5 was used and seven factors (explaining 85 percent of the total variance) were rotated using the veri-max procedure. The ratios were ranked according to the highest factor loadings on the ratios that represented each factor.

18.   Because the CVA data employed in this study were disclosures in compliance with Accounting Series Release No. 190, CVA and HC net income differed only with respect to cost of goods sold and depreciation; thus, holding and purchasing power gains and losses were not included in CVA net income.

19.   The use of 9-point scales to add gradations to otherwise dichotomous decision variables is common in human information processing studies. For example, Slovic [1969] used the same scale as in the present study to elicit from two stockbrokers buy/do not buy recommendations based upon various financial market cues ascribed to hypothetical stocks. Also see Savich [1977], Schultz and Gustavson [1978], and McGee, Shields, and Birnberg [1978].

REFERENCES

AICPA (American Institute of Certified Public Accountants), "Objectives of Financial Statements" [New York: AICPA, October 1973].

Aluminium Company of America, *1976 Annual Report* [Pittsburgh, PA: Alcoa, 1977].

Armstrong, M.S., "The Politics of Establishing Accounting Standards," *Journal of Accountancy* [February 1977], pp. 76-79.

Ball, R., and P. Brown, "Some Preliminary Findings on the Association Between the Earnings of a Firm, Its Industry and the Economy," *Journal of Accounting Research* [Supplement 1967], pp. 55-77.

Bates, H.L., and P.M.J. Reckers, "Does Replacement Cost Data Make a Difference?" *The Journal of Accountancy* [June 1979], pp. 42, 46, 48.

Beaver, W., "What Should be the FASB's Objectives," *The Journal of Accountancy* [August 1973], pp. 49-56.

_____, "Future Disclosure Requirements May Give Greater Recognition to the Professional Community," *The Journal of Accountancy* [January 1978], pp. 44-52.

Beaver, W., and W.R. Landsman, *Research Report: Incremental Information Content of Statement 33 Disclosures* [Stamford, CT: Financial Accounting Standards Board, 1983].

Beaver, W., A.A. Christie, and P.A. Griffin, "The Information Content of SEC Accounting Series Release No. 190," *Journal of Accounting and Economics* [August 1980], pp. 127-157.

Berliner, R.W., "Do Analysts Use Inflation-Adjusted Information? Results of a Survey," *Financial Analysts Journal* [March-April 1983], pp. 65-72.

Bierman, H., Jr., "The Effects of Inflation on the Computation of Income of Public Utilities," *The Accounting Review* [April 1956], pp. 258-262.

Brenner, V.C., "Financial Statement Users' Views of the Desirability of Reporting Current Cost Information," *Journal of Accounting Research* [Autumn 1970], pp. 159-166.

Bryant, M.J., and M.C. Mahaney, "The Politics of Standard Setting," *Management Accounting* [March 1981], pp. 26-28, 31-33.

Burchell, S., C. Clubb, A. Hopwood, and J. Hughes, "The Roles of Accounting in Organizations and Society," *Accounting, Organizations and Society*, 5, no. 1 [1980], pp. 5-27.

Burton, J.C., "The SEC and the Accounting Profession: Responsibility, Authority, and Progress," in *Institutional Issues in Public Accounting,* edited by R. Sterling [Scholars Book Co., 1973], pp. 265-275.

Cook, R.L., and T.R. Stewart, "A Comparison of Seven Methods for Obtaining Subjective Descriptions of Judgmental Policy," *Organizational Behavior and Human Performance* [February 1975], pp. 31-45.

Darlington, R.B., "Multiple Regression in Psychological Research and Practice," *Psychological Bulletin* [March 1968], pp. 161-182.

Davidson, S., L.B. Skelton, and R.L. Weil, "Financial Reporting and Changing Prices: Estimated Results of Applying the FASB Proposal," *Financial Analysts Journal* [May-June 1979], pp. 41-54.

Demski, J.S., "Choice Among Financial Reporting Alternatives," *The Accounting Review* [April 1974], pp. 221-232.

Dickhaut, J.W., "Alternative Information Structures and Probability Revisions," *The Accounting Review* [January 1973], pp. 61-79.

FASB, Discussion Memorandum: "Conceptual Framework for Financial Accounting and Reporting: Elements of Financial Statements and their Measurement," (Financial Accounting Standards Board: Stamford, Conn., December 2, 1976).

————, *Exposure Draft: Objectives of Financial Reporting and Elements of Financial Statements of Business Enterprises* [Financial Accounting Standards Board, December 1977].

————, *Statement of Financial Accounting Concepts No. 1: Objectives of Financial Reporting by Business Enterprises* [Financial Accounting Standards Board, November 1978].

————, *Statement of Financial Accounting Standards No. 33: Financial Reporting and Changing Prices* [Financial Accounting Standards Board, September 1979].

————, *Exposure Draft: Financial Reporting and Changing Prices* [Financial Accounting Standards Board, September 1986a].

————, *Statement of Financial Accounting Standards No. 89: Financial Reporting and Changing Prices* [Financial Accounting Standards Board, 1986b].

Gheyara, K., and J. Boatsman, "Market Reaction to the 1976 Replacement Cost Disclosures," *Journal of Accounting and Economics* [August 1980], pp. 107-125.

Harsha, P.D., and M.C. Knapp, "The Use of Within- and Between-Subjects Experimental Designs in Behavioral Accounting Research: A Methodological Note," *Behavioral Research in Accounting,* 2 [1990], pp. 50-62.

Heintz, J.A. "Price-Level Restated Financial Statements and Investment Decision Making," *The Accounting Review* [October 1973], pp. 679-689.

Horngren, C.T., "Security Analysts and the Price Level," *The Accounting Review* [October 1955], pp. 575-581.

"Inflation Accounting," *Business Week* [October 15, 1979], pp. 68-74.

Jacoby, J., D.E. Speller, and C.A. Kohn, "Brand Choice Behavior as a Function of Information Load," *Journal of Marketing Research* [February 1974], pp. 63-69.

Keasey, K., and R. Watson, "Consensus and Accuracy in Accounting Studies of Decision-Making: A Note on a New Measure of Consensus," *Accounting, Organizations and Society,* 14, 4 [1989], pp. 337-345.

Kida, T., J. Cohen, and L. Paquette, "The Effect of Cue Categorization and Modeling Technique on the Assessment of Cue Importance," *Decision Sciences* [Spring 1990], pp. 357-372.

King, B.F., "Market and Industry Factors in Stock Price Behavior," *Journal of Business* [January 1966], pp. 139-190.

Lev, B., "Toward the Theory of Equitable and Efficient Accounting Policy," *The Accounting Review* [January 1988], pp. 1-22.

May, R.G., and G.L. Sundem, "Research for Accounting Policy: An Overview," *The Accounting Review* [October 1976], pp. 747-763.

McGhee, W., M.D. Shields, and J.G. Birnberg, "The Effects of Personality on a Subject's Information Processing," *The Accounting Review* [July 1978], pp. 681-697.

McIntyre, E.V., "Current-Cost Financial Statements and Common-Stock Investment Decisions," *The Accounting Review* [July 1973], pp. 575-584.

McNemar, Q., *Psychological Statistics,* 4th ed. [Wiley, 1969].

Miller, H., "Environmental Complexity and Financial Reports," *The Accounting Review* [January 1972], pp. 31-37.

Neimark, M., "Marginalizing the Public Interest in Accounting," in *Advances in Public Interest Accounting,* Vol. 1, edited by M. Neimark [JAI Press, 1986], pp. ix-xiv.

Parker, R.C., "The Trueblood Report, An Analysts's View," *Financial Analysts Journal* [January-February 1975], pp. 32-41, 56.

Price Waterhouse, *Disclosure of the Effects of Inflation: An Analysis* [Price Waterhouse & Co., 1980].

"The Profit Illusion," *Business Week* [March 19, 1979], pp. 108-112.

Rappaport, A.E., "Executive Incentives vs. Corporate Growth," *The Harvard Business Review* [July-August 1978], pp. 81-88.

Ro, B.T., "The Adjustment of Security Returns to the Disclosure of Replacement Cost Accounting Information," *Journal of Accounting and Economics* [August 1980], pp. 159-189.

Savich, R.S., "The Use of Accounting Information in Decision Making," *The Accounting Review* [July 1977], pp. 642-652.

Scheiner, J.H., and W.J. Morse, "The Impact of SEC Replacement Cost Reporting Requirements: An Analysis," in *Inflation and Current Value Accounting,* edited by J.C. McKeown [Bureau of Economic and Business Research, College of Commerce and Business Administration, University of Illinois, Urbana, 1979], pp. 141-152.

Schultz, J.J., Jr., and S.G. Gustavson, "Actuaries' Perceptions of Variables Affecting the Independent Auditor's Legal Liability," *The Accounting Review* [July 1978], pp. 626-641.

SEC, *Accounting Series Release No. 190, Amendments to Regulation S-X Requiring Disclosure of Certain Replacement Cost Data* [SEC, March 1976].

_____, *Accounting Series Release No. 271, Deletion of Requirement to Disclose Replacement Cost Information* [SEC, October 1979].

Sharpe, W.F., "Capital Asset Prices: A Theory of Market Equilibrium Under Conditions of Risk," *Journal of Finance* [September 1964], pp. 425-442.

Siegel, S., *Nonparametric Statistics for the Behavioral Sciences* [McGraw-Hill, 1956].

Slovic, P., "Analyzing the Expert Judge: A Descriptive Study of a Stockbroker's Decision Processes," *Journal of Applied Psychology* [August 1969], pp. 225-263.

————, "Psychological Study of Human Judgment: Implications for Investment Decision Making," *Journal of Finance* [September 1972], pp. 779-800.

Snowball, D., "Some Effects of Accounting Expertise and Information Load: An Empirical Study," *Accounting, Organizations and Society*, 5, no. 3 [1980], pp. 323-338.

Tweedie, D., and G. Whittington, *The Debate on Inflation Accounting* [Cambridge University Press, 1984].

The Value Line Investment Survey [New York: Arnold Bernhard & Co., Inc.].

Vasarhelyi, M.A., and E.F. Pearson, "Studies in Inflation Accounting: A Taxonomization Approach," in *Inflation and Current Value Accounting,* edited by J.C. McKeown [Bureau of Economic and Business Research, College of Commerce and Business Administration, University of Illinois, Urbana, 1979], pp. 9-27.

Watts, R.L., and J.L. Zimmerman, "Towards a Positive Theory of the Determination of Accounting Standards," *The Accounting Review* [January 1978], pp. 112-134.

Winn, D., "The Potential Effect of Alternative Accounting Measures on Public Policy and Resource Allocation," *Economic Consequences of Financial Accounting Standards* [Financial Accounting Standards Board, 1978], pp. 3-37.

Woo, J.C., and S.B. Seth, "The Impact of Replacement Cost Accounting on Financial Performance," *Financial Analysts Journal* [March-April 1978], pp. 48-54.

Wright, W.F., "Properties of Judgment Models in a Financial Setting," *Organizational Behavior and Human Performance* [February 1979], pp. 73-85.

ACCOUNTING AND THE REPORTING OF POLLUTION INFORMATION

Martin Freedman

ABSTRACT

Environmental information needs to be made available to stakeholders so that they can make informed decisions about companies. It is argued in this paper that accountants are in a unique position to measure, compile, and generate pollution data. A case study using water pollution data from pulp and paper firms is utilized to demonstrate that accountants have the capabilities to generate, present, and audit these data.

The recent environmental disaster in Alaska caused by Exxon highlights the effect that corporations have on Earth's ecosystem. The reactions of stakeholders including customers, investors, governments, environmentalists, Alaskans, and the world community, indicate that concerns about the environment are not limited to fringe political groups. In Europe, the Green Parties (who are most associated with environmental issues) have scored major

Advances in Public Interest Accounting, Volume 5, pages 31-43.
ISBN: 1-55938-496-4

gains in parliamentary elections. Even the Soviet Union, with its economic difficulties, has decided that environmental concerns must be included in its economic decision making. People are recognizing that future planetary survival is dependent on maintaining our fragile ecosystem.

In order for people to make informed judgments about the environmental state of their community, environmental information must be made available to them in a way that is readily understood. Some environmental data are publicly available in the United States, where it is probably easier to obtain environmental data than it is in any other country. For example, water pollution data compiled by state or federal regional Environmental Protection Agencies (EPA) for each industrial plant that discharges into a navigable body of water are publicly available. The annual amount of toxic pollutants discharged by each industrial plant is available "on line" from the EPA through MEDLARS (a medical retrieval service). Unfortunately, these data are not compiled in a way that makes them easily understood by most people. Therefore, making the data publicly available is just the first step; somebody has to compile and interpret the data.

This paper presents a model for measuring and reporting water pollution data and argues that compiling and reporting such data are important roles for accountants and are in their realm of expertise. The paper is organized as follows: First, the literature review and rationale are provided. Second, the case of water pollution in the pulp and paper industry is presented including the methodology, generation of the data, and results. Third, conclusion and suggestions for improving the dissemination and compilation of pollution data are provided.

LITERATURE REVIEW AND RATIONALE

Environmental consciousness within the accounting profession is not a new phenomenon. In 1972, Robert Beyer, who was a managing partner with Touche Ross (a major accounting firm), wrote:

> Restrictions on the use of "free" air and water are also matters of social accounting. Society is now examining costs that have always existed—costs in terms of life and death, damaged buildings and art works, fouled beaches, ruined foliage, and all other noxious effects of pollution. The only difference is that now these costs are being transferred—to the extent that is feasible—from the community at large to those who cause and benefit from them. ... By defining costs and values, by dealing with emotion-charged issues such as oil coated ducks and the occupational diseases of coal miners in terms of double entry accounting we will make voters and legislatures aware of the social costs they are already bearing unwittingly [Beyer, 1972, p. 11].

However, it was the 1969 National Environment Policy Act and the Natural Resource Defense Council (NRDC) that actually forced accountants to become involved with pollution information. The act required the Securities and Exchange Commission (SEC) to mandate pollution disclosure in 10ks and the NRDC successfully sued the SEC to require more extensive disclosure [*Natural Resource Defense Council, Inc.* v. *SEC*, 1974]. Currently, the SEC requires that firms disclose the following pollution information in form 10K: any material effect from pollution abatement activities, estimated future capital expenditures for pollution abatement, any violations and potential violations of the pollution laws, and the extent of any fines [SEC, 1973, 1979].

As a result of the SEC pollution disclosure requirements, the 10k and the annual report to stockholders have become major sources of pollution information. Because these documents are prepared, for the most part, by accountants and are audited by accountants the accounting profession has been given a major role in providing pollution information.

Academic researches have questioned whether the information provided in these reports is useful, and have focused their investigations on two important questions. First, are the disclosures provided in these reports a surrogate for actual pollution performance? Second, do financial statement users utilize the pollution information in decision making?

Ingram and Frazier [1980], Freedman and Jaggi [1982], and Wiseman [1982] all content-analyzed pollution disclosures made either in annual reports or 10ks and correlated them with pollution performance, which was assessed by the Council on Economic Priorities (CEP). The Council on Economic Priorities is a nonprofit organization devoted to assessing the social implications of corporate activities. CEP did a number of studies analyzing the pollution performance of companies in highly polluting industries. Ingram and Frazier, Freedman and Jaggi, and Wiseman all independently concluded that there was no relationship between pollution disclosures made in annual reports or 10ks and pollution performance. The results of these studies indicate that it would be difficult to assess pollution performance based on the financial reports' pollution disclosures.

Although pollution disclosures do not mirror pollution performance it is possible that they do provide other information that is useful to people. A number of researchers have examined whether investors utilize these disclosures in decision making. Three studies have focused on the stock market reaction to financial statement disclosure of pollution information and the results have been mixed. Belkaoui [1976] found that pollution disclosure influenced investors' decision, and Jaggi and Freedman [1982] also found that disclosing pollution information in the 10k caused a stock market reaction. However, Freedman and Jaggi [1986a], in a paper reported in *AIPIA*, found that the extensiveness of the pollution disclosure made in the 10k did not alter investors' decision making. That is, the investors apparently reacted to the mere disclosure of the information and not to its content.

Although the last study was challenged both by Haw and Ro [1988] and by Cooper [1988] in the subsequent volume of *AIPIA*, Cooper's point that it is not useful to examine investors' reactions to social information really must be addressed. If the studies had shown that investors had not used the pollution information in decision making then that would not render the information useless. As was stated earlier, many different constituencies are interested in pollution information and if any of them found this information to be useful then it would be useful to produce it. There is also a normative question involved with this and any pollution information. It is possible that the information is inherently useful, but people are not aware of how it can be used and, therefore, it is necessary to educate these people. As far as investors are concerned, because they do find the information useful it is a justification for continuing to provide the information.

In addition to the financial reports, there are a few other sources of pollution data. The Department of Energy requires all electric utility plants to submit an annual report detailing their annual pollution emissions. As was stated previously, MEDLARS details annual toxic emissions (which do not include many of the elements of air and water pollution emissions) by plant. Finally, the EPA requires all industrial plants that discharge into a navigable body of water to obtain a pollution permit listing allowable emissions and to report their monthly emissions to the state or regional EPA.

Although all of this pollution information is publicly available, acquiring and compiling the data present a formidable task. However, because these data must be compiled by the appropriate industrial plant it would not be difficult within a company to acquire and compile the data. Furthermore, because pollution data are already available on the 10k and are often made available in the annual report why not include these data in these reports? In that way, people interested in utilizing pollution data would have companywide data made available to them. This would facilitate comparisons among companies and industries and it would facilitate the development of a pollution data base that could be utilized by researchers.

Assuming that the pollution data are included in the annual financial report should the accountant be responsible for compiling and reporting the data? Furthermore, is the accountant capable of dealing with pollution data? Finally, should the data be audited by accountants? Most of what is included in the financial reports is generated by the accountants and is audited by accountants. If the accountants are competent in understanding the pollution data and in the measurement system used to develop the data then there is no reason that the accountant should not feel comfortable compiling, reporting, and auditing the data.

In order to demonstrate that it is within the capabilities of the accountant to compile and report pollution data a case study of water pollution in the pulp and paper industry is provided. Water pollution data are utilized since they were relatively easy to acquire it from the state and regional EPAs. The industry chosen for the study is pulp and paper since it is one of the five largest water polluting industries in the United States [CEO, 1977].

THE CASE OF WATER POLLUTION IN THE PULP AND PAPER INDUSTRY

One of the goals of the 1972 Federal Water Pollution Act Amendments was to eliminate the discharge of pollutants into the nation's navigable waters by 1985 [*Federal Water,* 1972]. Originally, it was felt that the elimination of water pollution from industrial sources would do the most in achieving the 1985 goal. Therefore, a major thrust of the initial water cleanup campaign was focused on industrial polluters.

Included in the strategy of reducing industrial pollution was the development of the National Pollution Discharge Elimination System (NPDES). Entities that discharge pollution into the waterways must obtain a permit from the EPA or its state equivalent. As part of this procedure, monthly discharge reports must be filed with the EPA for each pipe discharging pollution into the water. Included in this report are the allowable discharge (permit condition) and the actual daily discharge for the month. The permits allowed a certain "acceptable" amount of pollution with the expectation that by 1985 the pollution discharge would be eliminated.

Pulp and Paper Industry Pollutants

Pulp and paper mills discharge a number of pollutants into the nation's waterways during the milling and manufacturing process. The EPA originally targeted three measures of pollutants that needed to be drastically reduced. These were BOD, TSS, and pH.

Biochemical Oxygen Demand (BOD) is the weight of oxygen needed to degrade and stabilize a discharge of waste materials. If the level of BOD is too high it can adversely affect the life chain in natural waters and ultimately cause death to aquatic life [EPA, 1976]. Total Suspended Solids (TSS) include the materials that are discharged in the papermaking process. These solids are suspended in the water and slowly sink to the bottom. Fish die from having their respiratory passages clogged by these solids [EPA, 1976]. pH is the measure of acidity or alkalinity of the water body. Changes in pH can cause harm to aquatic life.

Although there are a number of other pollutants discharged by pulp and paper mills, the EPA has consistently set permit conditions with pulp and paper mills using these three measures. Some mills are required to report other pollutants (e.g., fecal chloroform), but since the vast majority just report BOD, TSS, and pH that is all that will be focused on here.

Previous Studies

Most of the studies in which water pollution was measured on a plant basis were done under the auspices of CEP. CEP sponsored pollution studies for the pulp and paper, steel, oil refining industries, and electric utilities. The only study that relied on the NPDES discharge reports was a pulp and paper study published in 1988a [Freedman and Jaggi]. Except for the electric utilities study [White, 1977], all the other studies had difficulties in determining water pollution emissions since those data were acquired prior to the enforcement of the 1972 Act Amendments. The electric utilities study relied on a database based on annual pollution reports that electric utilities must file with the Department of Energy.

There have been two other studies in which water pollution on a plant basis has been measured. Both studies relied on the NPDES discharge reports in calculating pollution for the pulp and paper industry. One used data for 1978 [Freedman and Jaggi, 1986b] and the other used 1983 data [Freedman and Jaggi, 1988b].

Because pollution information on a plant and companywide basis has previously been provided in these studies, there may be some question as to whether stockbrokers have utilized this information. Both Shane and Spicer [1983] and Stevens [1984] examined the stock market reaction to the publication of a number of these studies. They both discovered a statistically significant market impact to the publication event. The accounting and management literature offers a number of examples of academics who have utilized the pollution databases in research studies. Ullmann [1985] summarizes a number of these studies in his article. Whether other stakeholders utilize this information is difficult to tell, but one can assume that CEP's willingness to fund these projects indicates that there is a demand for these data.

Pulp and Paper Firms

The data for this section of the paper are from the three Freedman and Jaggi studies [1986b, 1988a, 1988b] and the three years being reported are 1978, 1983, 1986. In 1978 only 13 firms were included in the study, because EPA data were not available for two of the firms. However, for 1983 and 1986 pollution data for 15 firms were reported. These 15 firms are among the largest producers of pulp and paper in the United States and the plants included in the studies produce about 45 percent of the total U.S. pulp and paper. However, by 1986 three of the companies included in the studies were acquired by other firms. St. Regis was acquired by Champion International in 1984, Hammermill by International Paper in 1986, and most of Crown Zellerbach's mills were acquired by James River in 1986. The 1986 pollution data for the acquired firms are comprised of plants that belonged to the firm before the firm was acquired.

Measurement of Pollutants

Freedom and Jaggi utilized a pollution measurement scheme that was adapted from the CEP study of the steel industry [Cannon, 1974]. This was considered to be the most sophisticated and best measure of water pollution of all the CEP studies since it utilized raw data and formulas to measure pollution. Most of the other studies utilized estimation techniques to determine if the companies were adequately controlling water pollution or not. Using the NPDES monthly discharge monitoring reports and the formulas adapted from Cannon, Freedman and Jaggi calculated BOD, TSS, and pH for each pipe that discharged waste from the mill.[1]

Once BOD or TSS is calculated per pipe, calculating it for the mill sharply requires summing the pollution by pipe. To assure that size does not distort the data, BOD per mill or TSS per mill can be divided by daily mill production resulting in daily BOD per ton of production or daily TSS per ton of production. This attempt at providing a relative measure of pollution is consistent with the approach that the EPA uses to determine the original permit conditions. That is, in general, the amount of gross pollution permitted by the EPA is a function of plant size. Companywide results can then be determined by summing the mill results.

Determining the pollution caused by excess acidity or alkalinity (pH) is a little more complicated, but once the pH per pipe is determined the remaining calculations are easy.[2] However, a major difference is that size is considered by using daily water flow. Calculating any of these measures should not be a challenge to any accountant.

Results

The calculations of companywide water pollution are presented in Table 1. From the standpoint of the company, BOD and TSS per ton of production and pH could be reported for a number of years so that the reader would be able to see comparative data. As the results in Table 1 indicate, even over a three-year period (1983-1986) the changes in measures of water pollution can be dramatic. An annual report user given the data provided in Table 1 would have a fairly good sense of how effective the firm has been in its water pollution abatement program

From a management accounting perspective, generating pollution data and having it audited would assure management that the data were reliable and it would help management assess the pollution performance of each plant. It might also aid management in determining potential future liabilities. Furthermore, this information could help the Board of Directors in assessing the pollution performance of the firm.

Users of financial statements could use this information to compare companies and to determine rankings for pollution performance. In one of the CEP's studies, *The Pollution Audit* [1977] the relative pollution performance of firms from industries studied by CEP were ranked by scoring performance by pollutant. Using water pollution in the pulp and paper industry

Table 1. BOD, TSS, and pH
1978, 1983, and 1986

	BOD/Ton of Production			TSS/Ton of Production			pH		
	1978	1983	1986	1978	1983	1986	1978	1983	1986
Boise Cascade	6.46	5.45	2.97	10.25	7.58	4.42	.009	.202	.0053
Champion International	3.95	.89	.81	5.66	1.56	.51	0	0	0
Crown Zellerbach	21.40	16.31	8.04	20.00	13.83	37.86	.182	.204	.1232
Georgia Pacific	16.22	10.83	6.92	6.04	13.91	8.22	2.678	0	0
Great N. Nekoosa	10.88	4.20	1.83	6.78	3.49	1.67	.061	2.030	.055
Hammermill	2.38	6.72	5.90	.53	3.39	2.29	.611	.090	0
International Paper	21.32	7.81	4.73	23.71	11.94	6.61	.099	.065	.063
Kimberly Clark		7.00	5.71		3.42	2.15		.038	.12
Mead	1.28	4.53	2.3	1.80	9.26	5.64	.1255	.010	0
Potlatch	11.98	4.63	2.36	9.00	5.45	4.87	.483	0	0
St. Regis	2.56	2.94	1.45	3.4	2.07	1.00	.615	.232	.144
Scott	8.03	11.26	5.92	13.82	10.76	8.27	1.489	.514	.10
Union Camp		4.24	3.61		2.09	3.11		0	0
Westvaco	1.51	1.62	1.92	.56	1.0	3.34	.413	0	.008
Wyerhauser	12.10	7.18	6.84	10.20	5.21	6.86	1.165	0	0

as an example, the three measures of pollutants would be ranked equally because they are equally detrimental to aquatic life [Freedom and Jaggi, 1986b]. Firms can be ranked by giving the firm with the greatest amount of a given pollutant a score of 100 and rank the remaining levels of that pollutant relative to the highest one. For example, Table 1 indicates that for BOD/ton of production Crown Zellerbach with a BOD/ton of production of 21.4 in 1978 is the highest level of BOD for any year and is therefore scored 100. Boise Cascade with BOD of 2.97 in 1986 receives a score of $2.97/21.4 \times 100 = 13.87$. These data are provided in Table 2 under the scaled index for BOD. This process is applied to each of the three pollution measures and each of the three measures is summed to arrive at a pollution ranking. The results for 1986 are provided in Table 2 and the comparative rankings for the three years are presented in Table 3.

An examination of Table 2 reveals that the range for BOD/ton of production is fairly narrow for 1986. Crown Zellerbach has the highest measure of 8.04 and Champion the lowest of .81. Because these scores are much lower than the 1978 high of 21.4 the score for BOD just ranges from 37.57 to 3.78. Overall there has been an improvement in BOD for the industry. The mean BOD/ton of production in 1986 for these firms amounted to 4.36 and a firm's performance can also be compared to that figure. Similar analyses can be made for TSS and pH.

Table 2. Pollution Emissions and Weighted Index—1986

Firm	BOD Per ton of Production	BOD Scaled Index	TSS Per ton of Production	TSS Scaled Index	pH Rawscore	pH Scaled Index	Total
Boise Cascade	2.97	13.87	4.42	18.64	.0053	.19	52.70
Champion							
International	.81	3.78	.51	2.15	0	0	5.93
Crown Zellerbach	8.04	37.57	37.86	159.67	.1232	4.60	201.84
Georgia Pacific	6.92	32.33	8.22	34.68	0	0	56.99
Great N. Nekoosa	1.83	8.55	1.67	7.04	.055	2.05	17.64
Hammermill	5.90	27.57	2.29	9.65	0	0	37.22
International Paper	4.73	22.10	6.61	27.87	.0634	2.36	52.33
Kimberly Clark	5.71	26.68	2.25	9.48	.12	4.48	40.64
MEAD	2.3	10.74	5.64	23.78	0	0	34.52
Potlatch	2.36	11.02	4.87	20.53	0	0	31.55
St. Regis	1.45	6.77	1.00	4.21	.144	5.37	16.35
Scott	5.92	27.66	8.27	34.87	.10	3.73	66.26
Union Camp	3.61	16.86	3.11	13.11	0	0	27.97
Westvaco	1.92	8.97	3.34	14.08	.008	.29	23.24
Weyerhauser	6.84	31.96	6.86	28.93	0	0	60.89

Table 3. Pollution Performance
1978, 1983, and 1986

Company	1978		1983		1986	
	Score	Rank	Score	Rank	Score	Rank
Boise Cascade	73.72	6	64.96	9	32.7	7
Champion International	42.35	4	10.71	1	5.93	1
Crown Zellerbach	180.14	11	142.14	15	201.84	15
Georgia Pacific	201.26	12	109.26	11	56.99	12
Great N. Nekoosa	81.71	7	109.53	12	17.64	3
Hammermill	36.6	3	49.05	6	37.22	0
International Paper	203.32	13	89.26	10	49.97	13
Kimberly Clark			140.64	14	40.64	10
Mead	18.24	1	50.89	7	32.52	8
Potlatch	111.97	8	44.60	5	31.55	6
St. Regis	49.15	5	20.32	3	15.35	2
Scott	151.42	10	117.18	13	66.26	14
Union Camp			28.57	4	27.93	5
Westaco	24.83	2	14.73	2	23.34	4
Weyerhauser	143.04	9	55.52	8	60.89	13

In Table 3 the rankings for the three years are presented. Ranking performance is important in determining how successful one firm's pollution abatement program is compared to another. Because all the companies in the industry can use the same technology in trying to abate pollution, a firm's claim that it is unable to achieve a given level of pollution can be disputed if other firms have been able to achieve that level.

CONCLUSION

As environmental consciousness increases, the demand for pollution information should increase. Pollution information is publicly available; the problem is that it is not easily accessible in a format that is readily understood by most of the potential users. Because pollution information must be included in a corporation's annual filing with the SEC it would make sense to incorporate other required pollution disclosures in this information set. Furthermore, because all the other required pollution information is generated from the industrial plant level, aggregating this information to a company level and also supplying it in the annual report should not be difficult tasks.

What the case study attempted to demonstrate was that it is possible for an accountant to utilize the raw pollution data from the plant and generate output that could be used by those interested in pollution data. Furthermore, this output could be used to develop a pollution database similar to COMPUTSTAT, which would be useful to pollution researchers.

The problem with having the accountant involved in compiling and generating pollution information is in whether the accountant is really competent to do this. Because accountants deal with measuring, compiling, and generating financial data, providing the same activities with pollution data should not be outside their area of expertise. Furthermore, if the internal accountant is competent in dealing with these data there is no reason that the external accountant should have difficulty in auditing these data.

Although companies are forced to provide pollution information to government agencies and this information then becomes publicly available, including the same information with the annual financial statements would be anathema to most corporations. Including it in the annual report and in a way that would be easily understood by financial statement readers would call attention to the company's pollution record. For companies in industries that have pollution problems this would provide unwanted publicity. Therefore, these companies will not provide pollution data unless forced to provide it.

Unless the public demands to know what corporations have done to the environment there will not be disclosure of pollution information in annual reports. Maybe the Exxon disaster will result in forcing firms to make public access to environmental data easier. Maybe it will encourage accountants to join in the fight to safe the ecosystem by becoming involved in compiling and reporting pollution data. In that way something positive can result from this environmental catastrophe.

ACKNOWLEDGMENT

The author acknowledges the comments and assistance of 2 anonymous reviewers.

NOTES

1. The formula used to compute the charge in BOD caused by the emissions from each pipe in the mill is as follows:

$$BOD_{ijk} = [1 - \frac{5}{BODC_{ijk}}] \times BODW_{ijk}$$

where: i = firm;
j = plant;
K = pipe;
BODC = BOD concentration which is in mg/l;
BODW = BOD weight which is in lbs/day.

Both measures of BOD are available from the monthly discharge reports. If not then the following formula can be used to compute the change in BOD from each pipe:

$$BOD_{ijk} = [BODC_{ijk} - 5] \times 8.3 \times F_{ijk},$$

where F_{ijk} represents the average water flow for pipe.

To calculate the change in TSS the same formulas are used except that TSSC + TSSW would be substituted for BOD and a 20 would be substituted for the 5 [Freedman and Jaggi, 1986b, p. 361].

2. The formula used to calculate pH requires using the average maxium and average minimum pH by pipe. A pH level greater than 8.5 or less than 6 is considered pollution. The level of pH pollution by pipe is computed as follows:

$$pH_{ijk} \left[\frac{1}{P} \sum_{K=1}^{P} (pH \max_{ijkt} - 8.5) + \frac{1}{P} \sum (6 - pH \min_{ijkt}) \right] \times F_{ijk,}$$

when F_{ijk} represents the average water flow for pipe. The calculation of pH pollution by mill is as follows:

$$\frac{pH_{ij1} + pH_{ij2} + \ldots + pH_{ijk.}}{F_{ij1} + F_{ij2} + \ldots F_{ijk}}$$

REFERENCES

Belkaoui, A. "The Impact of the Disclosure of the Environmental Effects of Organizational Behavior on the Market," *Financial Management* [Winter 1976], pp. 26-31.

Beyer, R., "Pilots of Social Progress," *Management Accountant* [July 1972], pp. 11-15.

Cannon, J., *Environmental Steel* [Praeger, 1974].

Cooper, D.J., "A Social Analysis of Corporate Pollution Disclosures: A Comment," *Advances in Public Interest Accounting*, Vol. 2, edited by M. Neimark [JAI Press, 1988].

Council on Economic Priorities (CEP), *The Pollution Audit* [CEP, 1977].

Council on Environmental Quality, *Environmental Quality 1977* [U.S. Government Printing Office, 1977].

Environmental Protection Agency (EPA), *Development, document for effluent limitation guidelines (BPCTA) for the bleached kraft. Sulfite, soda, de-ink, and non-intgrated paper plants segment of the pulp, paper, and paperboard point source category* [U.S. Government Printing Office, 1976].

Federal Water Pollution Control Act Amendments, U.S. Code, Vol. 33, Sec. 1251 [1972].

Freedman, M., and Jaggi, B. "Pollution Disclosure, Pollution Performance and Economic Performance," *OMEGA* (2nd quarter 1982), pp. 167-176.

————. "An Analysis of the Impact of Corporate Pollution Disclosure Included in Annual Finance Statements on Investors' Decisions," in *Advances in Public Interest Accounting*, Vol. 1, edited by M. Neimark [JAI Press, 1986a], pp. 193-212.

————. "Pollution Performance of Firms from Pulp and Paper Industries," *Environmental Management*, 10, 3 [1986b], pp. 359-365.

_____. "'Cleaning Up Their Act," *Council on Economic Priorities Research Report* [September 1988a].

_____. "Impact on Government Regulations on Pollution Performance of Pulp and Paper Firms," *Environmental Management*, 12, 3 [1988b], pp. 391-396.

Haw, I., and B. Ro. "An Analysis of the Impact of Corporate Pollution Disclosures: A Comment," in *Advances in Public Interest Accounting*, Vol. 1, edited by M. Neimark [JAI Press, 1988], pp. 187-192.

Ingram, R. and K. Frazier, "Environmental Performance and Corporate Disclosure," *Journal of Accounting Research* [Autumn 1980], pp. 614-622.

Jaggi, B., and M. Freedman, "An Analysis of the Information Content of Pollution Disclosures," *The Financial Review* [September 1982], pp. 142-152.

Securities and Exchange Commission (SEC), Securities Act Release No. 5386 [20 April 1973].

Securities and Exchange Commission (SEC), Securities Act Release Nos. 33-6130 and 34-16224 [27 September 1979].

Shane, P.B., and B. Spicer. "Market Response to Environmental Information Produced Outside the Firm," *The Accounting Review* [July 1983], pp. 521-538.

Stevens, W., "Market Response to Corporate Environmental Performance," in *Advances in Accounting*, Vol. 1, edited by B.N. Schwartz [1984], pp. 41-62.

Ullmann, A.A., "Data in Search of A Theory," *Academy of Management Review* [July 1985], pp. 540-557.

White, R.H., *The Price of Power Update* [CEP, 1977].

Wiseman, J., "An Evaluation of Environmental Disclosures Made in Corporate Annual Reports," *Accounting, Organizations and Society* [1982], pp. 53-63.

GENDER EFFECTS ON COMMITMENT
OF PUBLIC ACCOUNTANTS:
A TEST OF COMPETING SOCIOLOGICAL
MODELS

Mary Anne Gaffney, Ruth Ann McEwen,
and Mary Jeanne Welsh

ABSTRACT

This research investigates the effects of life events such as marriage and
parenthood on the professional and organizational commitment of women and
men working in public accounting. Three competing models of women's and
men's work-related attitudes were evaluated: the occupational approach,
differential socialization approach, and the role conflict approach. The study also
investigated gender differences in four needs thought to underlie commitment:
achievement, autonomy, affiliation, and dominance. Results supported the
differential socialization model, which predicts differences in men and women's
commitment attributable to early sex role socialization. There were no differences
in the professional and organizational commitment of women and men who did

Advances in Public Interest Accounting, Volume 5, pages 45-73.
ISBN: 1-55938-496-4

not have families. However, the study documents differences in the degree to
which family responsibilities impact the professional and organizational
commitment of both women and men accountants.

Women in accounting, as in other professions, face significant barriers to
advancement. For example, numerous studies have documented that despite
increased participation in the work force, women bear a disproportionate share
of domestic and parental responsibilities [Illich, 1983; Johnson, 1989; Chafetz,
1989]. Discriminatory practices in the work place, such as poor job
assignments, often push women out of public accounting early in their careers
[Gaertner, Hemmeter, and Pitman, 1987]. Some partners believe that men are
generally more dedicated than women to professional careers and that women's
commitment to quality of life is at the expense of their careers [AICPA, 1988].
Women may withhold commitment to a profession or limit career
aspirations based on their assessment of external and social barriers to success
[Shann, 1983; Eccles, 1987]. In addition, social pressure to conform to
stereotyped sex roles can affect career plans. Prior studies have not placed
gender differences in work attitudes among public accountants into a more
generalized sociological framework. The purpose of this research is to
investigate whether life events such as marriage and parenthood have different
effects on the professional and organizational commitment of women and men
working in public accounting. The analysis is framed in terms of competing
sociological models of women and men's career development: the occupational
model, differential socialization model, and the role conflict model.
Because there are many possible antecedents of professional and
organizational commitment, the research also examines other personal
influences besides gender, especially intrinsic needs. Presumably, professional
and organizational commitment are affected by how well the profession or
individual organizations are able to meet intrinsic needs. Yet, little empirical
evidence exists which relates individual need satisfaction to the accounting
profession.

REVIEW OF PREVIOUS RESEARCH

Professional and Organizational Commitment

Professional commitment is defined as dedication to work and long-term
career aspirations. It is considered an important factor in advancing the
professions' values as well as enhancing individual job performance, and among
accountants, a high degree of professional commitment is considered necessary
for independent professional judgments [Bartol, 1979; Aranya, Pollock, and
Amernic, 1981; Norris and Niebuhr, 1983]. Organizational commitment is
defined as the relative strength of an individual's identification with and

involvement in a particular organization [Steers, 1977]. High levels of organizational commitment have been positively associated with performance and job satisfaction, and may result in lower job turnover [Porter et al. Steers, Mowday, Boulian, 1974; Bartol, 1979; Norris and Niebuhr, 1983].

Professional/organizational commitment is indicated by a belief in the goals and values of a profession/organization, willingness to exert effort on behalf of a profession/organization, and a definite desire to maintain membership in the profession/organization [Porter et al., 1974]. Early research on commitment in the work place often assumed that professional and organizational commitment were incompatible; the higher an individual's loyalty to a profession, the lower his or her commitment to a particular organization [Gouldner, 1957; Merton, 1957]. However, later studies suggested the relationship of the two types of commitment is more complex, and that professional and organizational commitment may or may not be complementary, depending on the organization's willingness to reward professional behavior [Bartol, 1979]. Studies by Aranya, Pollock, and Amernic [1981] and Norris and Niebuhr [1983] found positive correlations between professional and organizational commitment in the public accountants. Lachman and Aranya [1986] found the level of professional commitment had a positive effect on organizational commitment among CPAs employed in accounting firms.

Prior research suggests that levels of organizational and professional commitment increase as accountants advance in a firm, although there may be a drop in average organizational commitment among accountants at the senior level [Aranya, Pollock, and Armenic, 1981; Norris and Niebuhr, 1983]. In a study by Lachman and Aranya [1986], organizational commitment was positively related to job satisfaction and negatively related to intent to leave the firm. The accounting studies cited did not test for gender differences in professional and organizational commitment.

Commitment Models

One persistent barrier facing women accountants in hiring and advancement is the belief that women are not committed to their careers [Westcott and Seiler, 1986, p. 117]. The traditional male model of professional and organizational commitment implies choosing the primacy of job over family, a choice women are presumed less willing to make than men, and the professional structure for success is based on what can be expected of male employees in a patriarchal society which allows them to resolve all conflicts between job and family in favor of the job [Diamond, 1988; O'Connell, Betz, and Kurth, 1989]. Public accounting, with expectations regarding overtime and travel, also conforms to a male model.

Whether men and women accountants are equally committed to their profession is an unresolved empirical question. There are several competing explanations for similarities or differences in women and men's work-related attitudes: the occupational approach, differential socialization approach, and role conflict approach [see O'Connell, Betz, and Kurth (1989) for a review of the literature]. No one theory has gained predominance and the theories provide conflicting predictions as to whether men and women accountants will display equal levels of professional and organizational commitment.

Occupational Model

The occupational model predicts there will be no difference in the professional commitment of men and women in the *same* occupation because the occupation structures an individual's work attitudes and behavior. If this model were true, there should be no differences in the professional and organizational commitment of women and men in public accounting.

Differential Socialization Model

The differential socialization approach asserts that men and women will differ in their professional and organizational commitment because of gender socialization, the process by which male and female children learn different gender-ascribed roles. There is substantial literature on the pervasiveness of sex-typing of behavior, and acceptance of stereotyped sex-roles could shape women and men's attitudes toward adult roles [Chodorow, 1978; England and McCreary, 1987; St. Claire, 1989]. (The impact of gender socialization on personality characteristics will be discussed further in the section on individual needs.) Schwartz [1989] suggests women are socialized to expect a job will not be needed as a lifetime source of support and will be much more casual than men in their professional commitment. Dexter [1985] also attributes women's difficulties in achieving upper management levels to differential socialization, although she explains its impact on work-related behavior differently. Men are taught status is achieved, but women are socialized to accept a subordinate status that is ascribed to them based on their role in the family. Once on the job, women lose time learning what male managerial candidates already know, including how to acquire organizational power and how to share in the (male) values of the organization.

Differential early socialization of women and men could affect their attitudes toward job versus family roles. For example, if men are socialized to define success as a parent as an extension of their jobs (i.e., being a good provider), they may respond to parenthood with increased professional and organizational commitment [Lorence, 1987]. However, if women are socialized to define success as a parent as a high level of involvement with their children, parenthood could be accompanied by a decrease in professional or organizational commitment, at least temporarily [Eccles, 1987].

Role Conflict Model

The role conflict model predicts that women's professional and organizational commitment will be different from men's, but only if women face family demands that conflict with work demands. This approach to commitment suggests that despite a woman's initial professional commitment, social expectations of her role as primary caretaker in the family will force a woman with children to abandon the male model of career development. However, the role conflict model also predicts there will be no differences in the professional commitment of women and men if women have no conflicting family roles (i.e., are single or childless).

The three models of gender-related work attitudes provide conflicting predictions as to whether there are differences in the professional and organizational commitment of men and women working in public accounting. Prior research is not sufficient to determine which model holds in accounting. Studies of accountants have not focused on gender differences, possibly because until recently women comprised a small proportion of public accountants [Norris and Niebuhr, 1983; Aranya, Pollock, and Amernic, 1981], and generalizations from research on subjects in other areas are difficult because results are inconsistent and appear sensitive to the organizational setting [Schuler, 1975; Brief, Rose and Aldag, 1977; Bartol, 1979, Chusmir, 1986].

Needs Theory and Commitment

The models of gender differences in work orientation illustrate two opposing directions of discussions of women in the work force. One view is that there are no differences in men and women's attitudes and behaviors, and that the barriers women face are the results of false stereotypes [Rohrbach, 1979; Breakwell, 1985; Morrison, White and Velsor, 1987]. However, there is another view that asserts that men and women do display different personality traits, primarily because they have been socialized to conform to a particular set of "masculine" or "feminine" characteristics. The problem is not that women are different from men, but that the difference is considered a deficiency [Gilligan, 1982; Case, 1988; O'Leary, 1988]. Under this view, the way to increase the upward mobility of women is not to make them behave like men, but to work toward increasing the social value of "feminine traits."

Research on work-related attitudes indicates that an employee's commitment to an organization is affected by the degree to which the organization is believed to be capable of satisfying individual needs [Steers and Braunstein, 1976]. Although individual needs represent general personality traits, they are influenced by a person's role orientation. The successful manager is usually described as being aggressive, forceful, independent, and achievement-oriented, traits typically identified as masculine [Warren, 1982; Rose and Larwood,

1988]. Women are supposed to be more people-oriented and less domineering [Eagly and Wood, 1985; Morrison, White, and Velsor, 1987]. The successful woman is expected to conform to the masculine stereotype, although she may be penalized for too great a departure from traditional feminine behavior.

Studies on individual factors associated with work attitudes and behavior have focused most frequently on four needs: achievement (n Ach), affiliation (n Aff), autonomy or independent (n Aut), and dominance or power (n Dom) [Murray, 1938; McClelland, Atkinson, Clark, and Lowell, 1953; Atkinson, 1958]. There should be a positive relationship between professional and organizational commitment and individual needs if an individual perceives public accounting and the firm as meeting his or her needs.

The most commonly studied psychological variable linked to career success is achievement. The need for achievement (n Ach) can be defined as the persistent tendency to strive for success with a standard of excellence [Bedeian and Touliatos, 1978]. Achievement connotes traditional masculine activity, and early validation studies provided evidence that neither women nor men considered achievement consistent with the female role [Sutherland and Veroff, 1985]. However, results of a study by Veroff [1982] suggest that there may be differences in how men and women channel their n Ach into various activities, rather than absolute gender differences in n Ach. Veroff found that for men, n Ach was positively associated with work attitudes, while high n Ach women seemed to define need fulfillment in terms of family and civic responsibilities.

If the model attitudes is correct, there should not be any differences in women and men accountants n Ach, or in any of the other intrinsic needs measured in this study. The implications of the differential socialization model and the role conflict model on n Ach are not as clear. Neither model precludes women evidencing a high n Ach; however both models suggest women may channel n Ach into family or civic roles, either because of internal socialization or external social expectations.

Generally, the differential socialization model implies men and women differ in the strength of various needs because of gender-role socialization. However, the implications of the role conflict model on intrinsic needs are more difficult to determine. The model has not been tested with respect to psychological variables. The role conflict model implies that women are differentially socialized than men, but that differences in work-related attitudes do not appear in the absence of conflicting family roles. However, the effect of socialization on underlying personality traits could exist even in childless or unmarried women. Differences between women's and men's intrinsic needs, regardless of family structure, support the differential socialization model and are not inconsistent with the role conflict model. However, differences in the strength of intrinsic needs among women with different family roles would more strongly support the role-conflict model.

Affiliation (n Aff) is the need to establish affective relations with others. There is a persistent theory that n Aff is stronger in women than in men [Gilligan, 1982; Sutherland and Veroff, 1985; Warren, 1982]. Gilligan's studies have convinced her that women are socialized to see their sense of self in their relations with others. The need for autonomy (n Aut), or independence, is a counter-drive to n Aff. Traditionally personal growth is considered the process of developing autonomy, which has been identified as a masculine trait. While personal autonomy is considered a strength, the presumed feminine concern with relationships is considered a weakness [Larsen, 1988].

Although the occupational model assumes men and women in the same occupations behave in the same way, the model may not hold true for n Aff. Some research has found sex differences in n Aff, consistent with predictions of the differential socialization model. Although high n Ach men tend to have low n Aff, high n Ach women have high n Aff. Sutherland and Veroff [1985] found high n Ach males are not especially concerned with making friends, but that high n Ach females are concerned with pleasing others. N Aff is expected to be positively related to professional and organizational commitment if accounting provides individuals with the opportunity to satisfy that need.

Independence, or N Aut, is more often identified as a masculine trait [Rose and Larwood, 1988], and hypotheses on gender differences in n Aut are in the opposite direction from hypotheses regarding n Aff. Although the occupational model predicts there will be no significant differences between women and men, differential socialization suggests men will display higher levels of n Aut. As noted previously, these results would not contradict the role conflict model. N Aut is expected to be negatively related to organizational commitment because high n Aut subjects can satisfy that need by remaining independent of the organization. However, a high degree of n Aut would not necessarily preclude strong professional commitment because professional commitment transcends the specific organization.

The need for dominance or power (n Dom) is part of the male model of a successful leader, because n Dom causes an individual to strive for increased responsibility and upward mobility [Bedeian and Touliatos, 1978, p. 64]. However, one of the most persistent barriers to women's advancement in accounting is the perception that women lack n Dom and are therefore not assertive enough with clients [Wescott and Seiler, 1986]. Whether men and women have inherently different needs for dominance has not been established, but managerial women are in a very difficult position when they exert power. N Dom is a part of the male model of success, but women are penalized for direct displays of power because such displays are a deviation from sex-role expectations [Morrison, White, and Velsor, 1987; O'Leary, 1988]. Although n Dom is expected to have a positive relationship to commitment, a woman who is strongly committed to success in the accounting profession might not display a high n Dom, having been socialized to expect negative sanctions from such behavior. Ample current evidence exists which documents negative sanctions for women in the form of sex discrimination [Burrell, 1987; Crompton, 1987; Hopwood, 1987; Lehman, 1989; Tinker and Neimark, 1987].[1]

Therefore, although the occupational model implies no differences for women and men in this study, the model may not hold true for n Dom even if women and men do not differ in professional or organizational commitment. Differential socialization predicts women display lower n Dom than men. As in the other needs discussed, the role-conflict model also predicts women will be affected by differential socialization, although the strength of the effect in unmarried or childless women has not been tested.

In summary, the occupational model predicts men and women working in public accounting will not differ in levels of intrinsic needs. The socialization model and role conflict model predict men and women will differ in intrinsic needs if general personality traits are influenced by a person's role orientation. The model predictions with regard to professional and organizational commitment and intrinsic needs are presented in Table 1.

Table 1.   Model Predictions

Sociological Models of Work-Related Attitudes		
	Professional Commitment	*Organizational Commitment*
Occupational Model	$F = M$	$F = M$
Differential Socialization	$F < M$	$F < M$
Role Conflict Model	$F_{snc} = M$	$F_{snc} = M$
	$F_{mc} < M$	$F_{mc} < M$

Intrinsic Needs			
Achievement	*Affiliation*	*Autonomy*	*Dominance*

	Achievement	Affiliation	Autonomy	Dominance
Occupational Model	$F = M$	$F = M$	$F = M$	$F = M$
Differential Socialization	$F ? M$	$F > M$	$F < M$	$F < M$
Role Conflict Model	$F_{snc} ? M$	$F > M$	$F < M$	$F < M$
	$F_{mc} < M$			

Notes: F = all female subjects;
   F_{snc} = single females with no children;
   F_{mc} = married females or females with children;
   M = all male subjects.

RESEARCH METHODOLOGY

Subjects came from the Philadelphia offices of two Big Eight public accounting firms. Questionnaires were distributed to 260 accountants, and 172 questionnaires were returned (a 66% response rate). Selected demographic data are presented in Table 2. Data were grouped into categories to simplify the table.

Table 2.   Descriptive Summary—Grouped
Data Accounting Professionals Sample

Variable	Grouping	Frequency	Percentage
Age	22-24 Years	58	33.7
	25-29 Years	60	34.9
	30-34 Years	31	18.0
	35-52 Years	20	11.6
	Missing	3	1.7
Gender	Male	118	68.6
	Female	52	30.2
	Missing	2	1.2
Marital Status	Married	80	46.5
	Not Married	88	51.2
	Missing	4	2.3
Child	No	123	71.5
	Yes	43	25.0
	Missing	6	3.5
Age of Youngest Child	Newborn (Less than 1)	14	8.1
	1 or Older	31	18.1
	None or Missing	127	73.8
Area of Professional Interest	Audit	145	84.4
	Tax	13	7.6
	MAS	10	5.8
	Other	3	1.7
	Missing	1	0.6
Number of Years with This Firm	Less Than 2	43	25.0
	2-4.9 Years	83	48.3
	5-10 Years	29	16.9
	Greater than 10	16	9.3
	Missing	1	0.6
Rank in Firm	First Year	29	16.9
	Second Year	25	14.5
	Senior/Supervisor	63	36.6

Table 2.   (Continued)

Variable	Grouping	Frequency	Percentage
	Manager	31	18.0
	Partner	14	8.1
	Missing	10	5.8
Highest Degree	Undergraduate	142	82.6
Held	Graduate	27	15.7
	Missing	3	1.7

Questionnaire

The subjects received a questionnaire that included scales to measure professional and organizational commitment, needs assessment scales, and demographic questions. The organizational and professional commitment scales were adapted from those used by Aranya, Pollock, and Amernic [1981] and originally developed by Porter et al. [1974]. Subjects responded to test items on a five-point Likert-type scale. Items were included on the subjects loyalty to the accounting profession and employer firm, pride in professional membership and intent to remain with the firm.[2] Measures of professional and organizational commitment for each subject were derived by computing a mean score on each set of items, which were recoded when necessary so that a high score represents high professional or organizational commitment. The internal consistency of each scale was measured using Cronbach's alpha [Cronbach, 1951]. The alpha coefficients for professional and organizational commitment for the entire sample were .80 and .79, respectively.

The four needs, n Ach, n Aff, n Aut, and n Dom were measured using the Manifest Needs Questionnaire (MNQ) developed by Steers and Braunstein [1976]. The MNQ measures the strength of the four needs in a work setting, and is brief enough to minimize completion time. The MNQ consists of 20 statements that describe activities people try to engage in while doing their jobs, based on the theory that asking people what they do, or attempt to do, on the job will elicit answers with less response bias than asking people what they think about their jobs. Responses were made on a 5-point Likert-type scale and coded so that the higher a mean score, the stronger a particular need.[3]

Variables

In addition to gender, other variables which might influence commitment were included in the design. Those variables were: *AGE,* martial status (*MARRIED*), whether or not the subject had children (*CHILD*), and age of

Table 3. Group Mean Scores

Variable	Grouping	nACH N	Mean	nAFF N	Mean	nAUT N	Mean	nDOM N	Mean	PC N	Mean	OV N	Mean
Age	22-24 Years	58	3.99	58	3.33	58	2.52	56	3.48	57	3.77	56	3.98
	25-29 Years	59	4.08	57	3.14	60	2.70	60	3.69	60	3.63	60	3.98
	30-34 Years	31	4.11	30	3.17	31	2.65	31	3.94	31	4.05	31	4.41
	35-52 Years	20	4.18	20	3.15	20	2.64	20	3.97	20	4.26	19	4.48
Gender	Male	117	4.08	116	3.21	118	2.66	117	3.74	118	3.81	118	4.14
	Female	52	4.03	50	3.23	52	2.52	51	3.58	51	3.87	49	4.06
Marital Status	Married	80	4.10	77	3.21	80	2.65	80	3.86	80	4.01	79	4.25
	Not Married	87	4.04	87	3.22	88	2.58	86	3.55	87	3.68	86	4.00
Child	No	128	4.05	127	3.21	129	2.61	127	3.65	128	3.76	127	4.07
	Yes	43	4.11	41	3.22	43	2.66	43	3.80	43	4.04	42	4.26
Age of Youngest Child	Less Than 1	14	4.04	13	3.18	14	2.72	14	3.77	14	3.80	14	4.10
	Greater than 1	31	4.14	30	3.24	31	2.63	31	3.81	31	4.14	30	4.32
Area of Professional Interest	Audit	144	4.07	142	3.22	145	2.60	144	3.69	144	3.81	144	4.10
	Tax	13	4.10	13	3.09	13	2.89	12	3.56	13	4.16	12	4.31
	MAS	10	4.00	9	3.20	10	2.50	10	3.90	10	3.76	9	4.28
	Other	3	3.93	3	3.13	3	3.13	3	3.40	3	3.20	3	3.40
Number of Years with This Firm	Less Than 2	43	4.01	43	3.34	43	2.52	42	3.54	42	3.72	42	3.96
	2-4.9 Years	82	4.05	80	3.19	83	2.64	82	3.60	83	3.74	81	4.04
	5-10 Years	29	4.11	28	3.13	29	2.71	29	4.00	29	3.99	29	4.33
	More Than 10	16	4.18	16	3.11	16	2.67	16	3.93	16	4.20	16	4.47
Rank in Firm	First Year	29	3.95	29	3.24	29	2.52	28	3.48	28	3.68	28	3.97
	Second Year	25	4.00	25	3.35	25	2.56	25	3.50	25	3.76	25	4.04
	Senior/Super	62	4.08	60	3.17	63	2.62	62	3.74	63	3.68	62	3.96
	Manager	31	4.18	30	3.13	31	2.72	31	3.97	31	4.20	30	4.43
	Partner	14	4.11	14	3.28	14	2.65	14	3.88	14	4.27	14	4.48
Highest Degree Held	Undergraduate	141	4.05	140	3.24	142	2.61	140	3.66	141	3.86	139	4.14
	Graduate	27	4.12	25	3.06	27	2.66	27	3.79	27	3.64	27	3.90

youngest child (*YOUNGEST*), number of years with the firm (*YEARS*), rank in the firm (*FIRST YEAR, SECOND YEAR, SENIOR, MANAGER, PARTNER*), highest degree held (*UNDERGRADUATE, GRADUATE*), and area of professional interest (*AUDIT, TAX, MAS*).

The subjects' age, marital status, family size and children's age were considered external factors affecting professional and organizational commitment. The differential socialization model predicts gender role stereotypes will have a stronger effect on the attitudes of older women (*AGE*). Although a male subject with a spouse and children (*MARRIED* and *CHILD*) is expected to display higher professional and organizational commitment because of the importance of the job to supporting the family [Chusmir, 1986, p. 91], both the differential socialization model and the role conflict model predict that married women, especially with children, will exhibit lower professional and organizational commitment because of conflicting family demands and traditional sex roles. Age of youngest child (*YOUNGEST*) is included because the effect of family responsibilities on commitment, if any, is expected to be more pronounced in subjects who have young children.

As discussed previously, professional and organizational commitment should increase as accountants advance in the firm. Professionals who advance in the firm to manager and partner should also have a higher n Dom and n Ach than entry level accountants as a group. Highest degree held and area of professional interest also were considered, even though prior research had not found this affected professional commitment [Norris and Niebuhr, 1983].

Multiplicative interaction variables were defined for each independent variable and *GENDER* [e.g., (*GENDER*) (*AGE*)] to test whether the independent variables had different effects on the attitudes of men and women. Table 3 presents group mean scores for professional and organizational commitment and the four manifest needs.

TESTS OF GENDER DIFFERENCES

Gender differences are assessed by regressing professional commitment, organizational commitment and each manifest need on all of the demographic variables. In each regression, forced entry of all of the demographic variables (including all the multiplicative interactions with gender) provides an evaluation of the differential attitudes of women and men on each dependent variable.[4] Because highly correlated independent variables tend to reduce the significance of regression coefficients [Neter, Wasserman and Kunter, 1985], the main effects variables were examined pair-wise for evidence of correlation. None of the comparisons yielded correlations above .80; thus multicollinearity was not considered to have affected the significance of the coefficients.[5]

In each regression, all of the demographic variables and all of the gender interactions were entered. Although the full regression models were tested, only the *significant* main effects and interactions are presented in Tables 4-9.

Professional and Organizational Commitment

The current study implicitly assumes that organizational and professional commitment will contribute to public accounting success. Group means on organizational and professional commitment presented in Table 3 show an increased level of commitment for the more successful respondents (managers and partners). The significance of the differences was tested using nonparametric Kruskal-Wallis One-Way ANOVAs on mean ranks. For organizational commitment, managers and partners exhibited mean ranks of 105.5 while lower ranked respondents displayed mean ranks of 71.5 (significantly different at an alpha of .000). In a similar manner, the mean rank for professional commitment of manages and partners was 102.8 while lower ranked respondents had a mean rank of 71.2 (significantly different at an alpha of .000).

Professional and organizational commitment are positively correlated (Pearson's correlation coefficient $= .7562, p = .000$), which is consistent with prior research on the commitment of public accountants. Generally, the results of the regression analyses on professional and organizational commitment are also consistent. *GENDER* is not significant as a main effect in either regression (Tables 4 and 5). However, there are significant interactions between *GENDER* and other independent variables. In both the professional and organizational commitment regressions, the interaction of (*GENDER*) (*MARRIED*) and (*GENDER*) (*CHILD*) are significant, and there was a significant interaction between (*GENDER*)(*YOUNGEST*) in the organizational commitment regression.

Significant interactions complicate the interpretation of the effect of gender on professional and organizational commitment because the *GENDER* effect is not constant across all levels of some of the other independent variables (e.g., *GENDER* does not have a constant effect on the professional and organizational commitment of married and unmarried subjects). To determine the effect of *GENDER* and *MARRIED* on professional and organizational commitment in the presence of significant interactions, one-way ANOVAS are performed using *GENDER* as the dependent variable while holding the level of the interacting variable constant.[6] For example, one-way ANOVAS are performed on the following classifications to test the relationship of *GENDER* and *MARRIED* on professional commitment: (1) married and unmarried men, (2) married and unmarried women, (3) married men and women, and (4) unmarried men and women (see Table 4).

If the occupational model holds, marriage is expected to enhance professional and organizational commitment for both sexes (i.e., there should be no differences between women and men). If, however, the role conflict or

Table 4. Professional Commitment

Regression

Significant Independent Variable	Coding	Coefficient	T-Statistic	Significance
Married	0 = No 1 = Yes	0.571	2.68	.0088
Tax	0 = No 1 = Yes	.0668	1.69	.0920
Degree	0 = Graduate			
	1 = Undergrad	0.508	2.41	.0176
Gender	0 = Male			
with	1 = Female			
Child	0 = No 1 = Yes	1.831	1.91	.0575
Gender	0 = Male			
with	1 = Female			
Married	0 = No 1 = Yes	−0.830	−2.15	.0333

One Way Anova: Interactions

Significant Independent Variable	Classification	Mean Score Dependent Variable	N	F	Significance
Gender	Male, Unmarried	3.51	54		
with	Male, Married	4.06	63	15.31	.0002
Married					
	Female, Unmarried	3.94	33		
	Female, Married	3.82	17	0.34	.5570
	Male, Unmarried	3.51	54		
	Female, Unmarried	3.94	33	6.25	.0143
	Male, Married	4.06	63		
	Female, Married	3.82	17	1.62	.2063
Gender	Male, No Children	3.71	82		
with	Male, with Children	4.05	36	4.59	.0341
Child					
	Female, No Children	3.86	45		
	Female, With Children	3.96	6	0.11	.7391
	Male, No Children	3.71	82		
	Female, No Children	3.86	45	1.03	.3121
	Male, with Children	4.05	36		
	Female, with Children	3.96	6	0.07	.7876

Notes: Dependent Variable: Professional Commitment R^2: .23091
Independent Variables: Age, Gender, Married, Child, Age of Youngest Child (Youngest), Audit, Tax, Number of Years with the Firm (Years), First Year, Second Year, Senior, Manager, Highest Degree Held (Degree), and Gender Interactions

Table 5. Organizational Commitment

Significant Independent Variable	Coding	Regression Coefficient	T-Statistic	Significance
Married	0 = No 1 = Yes	0.437	2.24	.0263
Degree	0 = Graduate 1 = Undergrad	0.538	2.79	.0060
Gender with Child	0 = Male 1 = Female 0 = No 1 = Yes	1.916	2.19	.0298
Gender with Married	0 = Male 1 = Female 0 = No, 1 = Yes	−0.698	−1.95	.0523
Gender with Youngest	0 = Male 1 = Female	−0.631	−1.171	.0883

One Way Anova: Interaction

Significant Independent Variable	Classification	Dependent Variable Mean	N	F	Significance
Gender with Married	Male, Unmarried	3.92	54		
	Male, Married	4.32	63	9.07	.0032
	Female, Unmarried	4.15	32		
	Female, Married	3.96	16	1.25	.2691
	Male, Unmarried	3.92	54		
	Female, Unmarried	4.15	32	1.84	.1780
	Male, Married	4.32	63		
	Female, Married	3.96	16	5.22	.0251
Gender with	Male, No Children	4.08	82		
	Male, with Children	4.27	36	1.61	.2057
	Female, No Children	4.06	44		
	Female, with Children	4.08	5	0.10	.9662
	Male, No Children	4.08	82		
	Female, No Children	4.06	44	0.01	.8888
	Male, with Children	4.27	36		
	Female, with Children	4.08	5	0.59	.4454
Gender with Youngest	Male, < 1 Year	4.22	7		
	Male, > 1 Year	4.31	30	0.13	.7134
	Female, < 1 Year	4.40	1		
	Female, > 1 Year	3.80	5	0.60	.4818
	Male, < 1 Year	4.22	7		
	Female, < 1 Year	4.40	1	0.05	.8302
	Male, > 1 Year	4.31	30		
	Female, > 1 Year	3.80	5	3.99	.0504

Notes: Dependent Variables: Organizational Commitment R^2: .21212
Independent Variables: Age, Gender, Married, Child, Age of Youngest Child (Youngest), Audit, Tax, Number of Years with the Firm (Years), First Year, Second Year, Senior, Manager, Highest Degree Held (Degree), and Gender Interactions

socialization models hold, marriage may affect men and women's commitment differently. An analysis of the effect of (*GENDER*) (*MARRIED*) for male subjects shows that marriage is associated with increased professional and organizational commitment; however, the same effect is not noted for women. The finding for the male subjects is consistent with the differential socialization model, which suggests that men respond to marriage with increased professional commitment [Eccles, 1987; Lorence, 1987]. However, contrary to the predictions of the differential socialization and role conflict models, marriage does not have a negative effect on women's professional or organizational commitment. There were no significant differences in the professional and organizational commitment scores of married and unmarried women.[7]

The effect of (*GENDER*) (*CHILD*) on professional commitment is similar to the effect of (*GENDER*) (*MARRIED*) (Table 4) and also supports the differential socialization model for men. The professional commitment of men with children is significantly greater than the professional commitment of men without children. *CHILD* does not have the same effect on the women subjects. Women with children exhibit about the same score for professional commitment as women without children.[8]

The other significant main effects on professional commitment are due to *TAX* specialists and subject's *DEGREE*. Overall, *TAX* specialists exhibit greater professional commitment than any other group, which is not consistent with prior research that found no differences in professionalism attributable to accountants area of specialization [Norris and Niebuhr, 1983]. Subjects with undergraduate degrees have significantly greater professional commitment scores than subjects with graduate degrees (Table 3).

The differential effect of marriage on the organizational and professional commitment of the men and women sampled does not appear to be due to the presence of children in the family. Although the interaction of (*GENDER*) (*CHILD*) is significant in the organizational commitment regression, none of the one-way ANOVAS are significant (Table 5). The interaction of (*GENDER*) (*YOUNGEST*) is also significant. Although there is no evidence overall that children have a negative effect on organizational commitment, organizational commitment is significantly lower for women with children older than one year than for men with children the same age.

The only main effect that is significant in the organizational commitment regression is *DEGREE*. Subjects with graduate degrees have significantly lower organizational commitment than subjects with just undergraduate degrees (Table 3). This is consistent with the effect of *DEGREE* on professional commitment.

The results of the professional and organizational commitment analyses document differences in commitment for men and women. Further evidence is provided by the individual regressions in which the manifest needs are regressed upon the demographic variables.

Manifest Needs

GENDER is significant as a main effect for n Aut and n Dom and is significant in interaction with other variables for all of the manifest needs. Tables 6 through 9 provide regression and Anova results.

The only significant effect of GENDER on n Ach is in the interaction of (GENDER) (CHILD) (Table 6). Men with children exhibit a significantly greater n Ach than women with children. There is no significant difference in n Ach between men with children and childless men and women. This is consistent with the role conflict model and with an earlier study by Baruch [1967], who found a temporal pattern in n Ach among women (men were not studied). In Baruch's study, n Ach was lower among women with young children, but increased as children grew older. These results also confirm Veroff's [1982] assertion that women with children may channel some of the need for achievement into family concerns.

GENDER was significant in the n Aff regression only in interaction with the second year professional level (Table 7). In this study, men who were in

Table 6. Achievement

Significant Independent Variable	Coding	Coefficient	T-Statistic	Significance
		Regression		
Gender with Child	0 = Male 1 = Female 0 = No 1 = Yes	−1.106	−1.181	.0734

Significant Independent Variable	Classification	Mean Score Dependent Variable	N	F	Significance
		One Way Anova: Interactions			
Gender with	Male, No Children	4.04	81		
	Male, with Children	4.16	36	1.45	.2302
	Female, No Children	4.06	46		
	Female, with Children	3.80	6	1.62	.2082
	Male, No Children	4.04	81		
	Female, No Children	4.06	46	0.01	.8985
	Male, with Children	4.16	36		
	Female, with Children	3.80	6	4.42	.0418

Notes: Dependent variable: Achievement R^3: .13769
Independent Variables: Age, Gender, Married, Child, Age of Youngest Child (Youngest), Audit, Tax, Number of Years with the Firm (Years), First Year, Second Year, Senior, Manager, Highest Degree Held (Degree), and Gender Interactions

Table 7. Affiliation

Regression

Significant Independent Variable	Coding	Coefficient	T-Statistic	Significance
Number of Years	N/A	−.032	−2.73	.0071
Degree	0 = Graduate			
	1 = Undergrad	0.184	1.69	.0925
Gender	0 = Male			
with	1 = Female			
Second	0 = No			
Year	1 = Yes	−0.644	−1.99	.0484

One Way Anova: Interactions

Significant Independent Variable	Classification	Mean Score Dependent Variable	N	F	Significance
Gender	Male, Not 2nd Year	3.17	100		
with	Male, 2nd Year	3.42	16	5.51	.0206
Second					
Year	Female, Not 2nd Year	3.23	41		
	Female, 2nd Year	3.22	9	0.01	.8969
	Male, Not 2nd Year	3.17	100		
	Female, Not 2nd Year	3.23	41	0.74	.3914
	Male, 2nd Year	3.42	16		
	Female, 2nd Year	3.22	9	2.92	.1009

Note: Dependent Variable: Affiliation R^2: .19238
Independent Variables: Age, Gender, Married, Child, Age of Youngest Child (Youngest), Audit, Tax, Number of Years with the Firm (Years), First Year, Second Year, Senior, Manager, Highest Degree Held (Degree), and Gender Interactions

their second year as staff accountants had a significantly higher n Aff than men at any other rank. This is not consistent with any of the explanatory models of work related attitudes since none of the models predicts an increase in n Aff for men.

The number of years the subject remains with the firm (*YEARS*) has a significant effect on n Aff. N Aff decreases as subjects advance in the firm. *DEGREE* also has a significant effect on n Aff. Subjects with only undergraduate degrees exhibit higher n Aff than subject with graduate degrees.

GENDER has a significant effect on n Aut (Table 8). Male subjects exhibit a higher average n Aut than female subjects, which appears to support the

Table 8. Autonomy

Significant Independent Variable	Coding	Regression		
		Coefficient	T-Statistic	Significance
Gender	0 = Male 1 = Female	−3.039	−3.22	.0381
Gender with Years	0 = Male 1 = Female	−0.147	−2.27	.0246
Gender with Age	0 = Male 1 = female	0.105	2.02	.0450

One Way Anova: Interactions

Significant Independent Variable	Classification	Mean Score Dependent Variable	N	F	Significance
Gender with Years	Male, < 2 Yrs.	2.56	26		
	Male, 2 to 4.9 Yrs	2.64	56		
	Male, 5 to 10 Yrs	2.81	21		
	Male, > 10 Yrs	2.73	15	1.69	.1729
	Female, < 2 Yrs	2.43	16		
	Female, 2 to 4.9 Yrs	2.62	27		
	Female, 5 to 10 Yrs	2.37	7		
	Female, > 10 Yrs	2.30	2	1.26	.2986
	Male, < 2 Yrs	2.56	26		
	Female, < 2 Yrs	2.43	16	0.99	.3235
	Male, 2 to 4.9 Yrs	2.64	56		
	Female, 2 to 4.9 Yrs	2.62	27	0.02	.8709
	Male, 5 to 10 Yrs	2.81	21		
	Female, 5 to 10 Yrs	2.37	7	7.22	.0124
	Male, > 10 Yrs	2.73	15		
	Female, > 10 Yrs	2.30	2	1.94	.1833
Gender with Age	Male, 22 to 24 Yrs	2.57	35		
	Male, 25 to 29 Yrs	2.75	41		
	Male, 30 to 34 Yrs	2.68	24		
	Male, > 34 Yrs	2.64	18	1.27	.2851
	Female, 22 to 24 Yrs	2.44	23		
	Female, 25 to 29 Yrs	2.58	19		
	Female, 30 to 34 Yrs	2.57	7		
	Female, > 34 Yrs	2.60	2	0.44	.7233
	Male, 22 to 24 Yrs	2.57	35		
	Female, 22 to 24 Yrs	2.44	23	1.57	.2149
	Male, 25 to 29 Yrs	2.75	41		
	Female 25 to 29 Yrs	2.58	19	1.70	.1964
	Male, 30 to 34 Yrs	2.68	24		
	Female, 30 to 34 Yrs	2.57	7	0.38	.5380
	Male, > 34 Yrs	2.64	18		
	Female, > 34 Yrs	2.60	2	0.01	.8912

Notes: Dependent Variable: Autonomy R^2: .19464
Independent Variables: Age, Gender, Married, Child, Age of Youngest Child (Youngest), Adult, Tax, Number of Years with the Firm (Years), First Year, Second Year, Senior, Manager, Highest Degree Held (Degree), and Gender Interactions

effect of differential socialization. However, the interaction of (*GENDER*) (*YEARS*) and (*GENDER*) (*AGE*) are also significant. When men and women are compared, holding *YEARS* constant, the only significant difference is a higher need for autonomy for men as compared to women with five to ten years experience.

In analyzing (*GENDER*) (*AGE*) on n Aut with one-way Anovas (Table 8), there are no significant differences between men and women when age is held constant. The interaction appears to be significant because n Aut increases with age for female subjects, but does not maintain a regular trend for male subjects. This result is not consistent with differential socialization, which predicts older women will show stronger effects of gender role socialization. However, results do support Dexter's [1985] theory that as women spend more time in the work force, they re-socialize toward more male organizational values.

GENDER is significant as a main effect in the n Dom regression (Table 9). Overall, women exhibit a lower n Dom than men, which is consistent with the effects of differential socialization. However, the interaction (*GENDER*) (*AGE*) is also significant. When (*GENDER*) is held constant, *AGE* has a significant effect on the n Dom of both male and female subjects. N Dom is expected to increase with age, and for the male subjects, n Dom did increase with age. The same effect is noted in the female subjects, but n Dom is lower for the oldest women in the sample. This result may indicate the presence of negative sanctions for dominant behavior in older women, but generalizations about the effects of *AGE* on n Dom of women accountants are difficult because only nine of the women in the sample were over 30.

When men and women were compared, holding age constant, the only significant difference in n Dom is among the subjects in the 22 to 24 year age range. Men in this age group exhibit a higher need for dominance.

The other significant variables in the n Dom regression are *MARRIED*, *CHILD*, and *MANAGER*. Married subjects of both sexes exhibit higher n Dom than single subjects, but *CHILD* is negatively related to n Dom. Subjects at the manager level have significantly higher n Dom scores than subjects in other ranks in the firm.

In summary, the results show some gender-related differences. *GENDER* is significant in the dominance and autonomy regressions and gender interactions are significant for professional commitment, organizational commitment and the manifest needs. These results clearly refute the occupational model of gender-related work attitudes which assumes that men and women in the same occupation do not differ in work attitudes.

The results also seem to reject the role conflict model, except with regard to n Ach. This model suggests that adding roles in the form of marriage and children should affect the professional and organizational commitment of women. Instead, no significant differences are found in professional and organizational commitment between married and unmarried women

Table 9. Dominance

Significant Independent Variable	Coding	Regression Coefficient	T-Statistic	Significance
Gender	0 = Male			
	1 = Female	−3.843	−2.49	.0140
Married	0 = No 1 = Yes	0.230	1.79	.0756
Child	0 = No 1 = Yes	−0.267	−1.90	.0595
Manager	0 = No 1 = Yes	0.527	2.81	.0058
Gender with Age	0 = Male 1 = Female	0.127	2.30	.0229

One Way Anova: Interactions

Significant Independent Variable	Classification	Mean Score Dependent Variable	N	F	Significance
Gender	Male, 22 to 24 Yrs	3.58	34		
with	Male, 25 to 29 Yrs	3.66	41		
Age	Male, 30 to 34 Yrs	3.91	24		
	Male, > 34 Yrs	4.01	18	4.88	.0031
	Female, 22 to 24 Yrs	3.31	22		
	Female, 25 to 29 Yrs	3.74	19		
	Female, 30 to 34 Yrs	4.02	7		
	Female, > 34 Yrs	3.60	2	6.00	.0015
	Male, 22 to 24 Yrs	3.58	34		
	Female, 22 to 24 Yrs	3.31	22	3.87	.0541
	Male, 25 to 29 Yrs	3.66	41		
	Female, 25 to 29 Yrs	3.74	19	0.47	.4944
	Male, 30 to 34 Yrs	3.91	24		
	Female, 30 to 34 Yrs	4.02	7	0.42	.5212
	Male, > 34 Yrs	4.01	18		
	Female, > 34 Yrs	3.60	2	1.73	.2044

Notes: Dependent Variable: Dominance R^2: .31782

Independent Variables: Age, Gender, Married, Child, Age of Youngest Child (Youngest), Audit, Tax, Number of Years with the Firm (Years), First Year, Second Year, Senior, Manager, Highest Degree Held (Degree), and Gender Interactions

or women with or without children. However, women with children may channel some of their n Ach away from their professional role.

The results do support the differential socialization model in that men seem to require a major life-event to attain the commitment that women have attained prior to marriage. The differential socialization model and role conflict model focus on the effects of socialization on women's attitudes regarding work and family roles and do not address the effect of life events such as marriage and children on men's attitudes. The results of this study suggest men also are affected by socialization to the traditional role of "bread winner." The higher level of professional commitment among married men and men with children could reflect their belief that they bear primary responsibility for financial support of their families. Their concern and anxiety over family support could lead to an increased emphasis on career success. The same effect of marriage and family on women is not observed because women have been socialized to view those events as an expansion of their role as care giver, not provider. However, contrary to predictions of the model, differential socialization does not have an adverse effect on women's professional or organizational commitment.

NEEDS THEORY AND COMMITMENT: EMPIRICAL RESULTS

Under the assumption of needs theory, the degree to which public accountants are committed to the profession or to individual organizations depends on the degree to which the entity is perceived as capable of satisfying needs. These perceptions can be tested by regressing professional and organizational commitment on the manifest needs. Regressions are performed and compared (1) across the entire sample, (2) for men only, and (3) for women only.

The regressions are joint tests of both the importance of the needs to the individual and of the entity's ability to satisfy each need. Regression coefficients are interpreted in the following manner: If the coefficient is positive and statistically significant, higher levels of the need enhance commitment and the respondents believe the profession or organization is capable of satisfying the need. Statistically negative coefficients imply that lower levels of the need enhance commitment and that the profession or organization is perceived as capable of satisfying the need. Insignificant coefficients imply either that there is no relation between the need and commitment, or that the entity is perceived as incapable of satisfying the need. Previous studies have suggested that higher achievement, dominance and affiliation needs will enhance commitment [Veroff, 1982; Bedeian and Touliatos, 1978]. A higher need for autonomy is expected to diminish organizational commitment. No prior study has investigated the gender effects of these relations for public accountants.

The results of the regressions are provided in Tables 10 and 11. For the entire sample, the R^2s for professional and organizational commitment were .22 and .20, respectively; however, needs theory is not expected to provide a full explanatory model of professional and organizational commitment. Although the models are not complete, an analysis of the attitudes of male and female respondents toward organizational and professional commitment provide insights into the importance of these components.

Table 10. Regressions Professional Commitment =
f (Achievement, Affiliation, Autonomy, Dominance)

Professional Commitment	Entire Sample			
	Achievement	*Affiliation*	*Autonomy*	*Dominance*
Coefficient	.5299	−.1235	−.5189	.1254
t-statistic	3.848	−.839	−3.807	.972
Significance	.0000	.4029	.0000	.3324
$R^2 = .22258$				
	Male Respondents Only			
Coefficient	.5410	−.1075	−.5232	.2231
t-statistic	3.155	−.636	−3.167	1.389
Significance	.0021	.5264	.0020	.1667
$R^2 = .25066$				
	Female Respondents Only			
Coefficient	.4985	−.3309	−.5355	−.1379
t-statistic	2.054	−.975	−1.948	−.584
Significance	.0462	.3354	.0481	.5626
$R^2 = .18232$				

Table 11. Regressions Organizational Commitment =
f (Achievement, Affiliation, Autonomy, Dominance)

Organizational Commitment	Entire Sample			
	Achievement	*Affiliation*	*Autonomy*	*Dominance*
Coefficient	.4754	−.0459	−.2296	.2435
t-statistic	3.745	−.338	−1.827	2.049
Significance	.0000	.7355	.0696	.0422
$R^2 = .20319$				
	Male Respondents Only			
Coefficient	.6004	−.0401	−.1944	.2322
t-statistic	3.706	−.251	−1.246	1.530
Significance	.0003	.8021	.2155	.1288
$R^2 = .23662$				
	Female Respondents Only			
Coefficient	.1933	−.1761	−.3635	.2052
t-statistic	.958	−.624	−1.590	1.044
Significance	.3435	.5360	.1193	.3026
$R^2 = .13469$				

Needs theory predicts a positive relation between the "masculine" need for achievement and commitment.[9] The results presented in Table 6 show only men and women with children differ in their needs for achievement, while men and women without families do not. This result holds for the relation between the needs theory and professional commitment (Table 10). For the entire sample, n Ach is positively related to professional commitment (coefficient = .53, p = .000). In the gender-specific regressions, both men and women exhibited statistically significant positive coefficients (.54 and .50, respectively). This result suggests that higher needs for achievement enhance professional commitment for men and women and that both groups perceive the profession as offering avenues to meet the need.

As documented in Table 11, n Ach is also positively related to organizational commitment across the entire sample (coefficient = .47, p = .000); however, there are gender differences in the relationship. Male respondents exhibit a positive, statistically significant relation between the need for achievement and organizational commitment while female respondents do not. This result implies that either women do not perceive the organization as capable of meeting needs for achievement or that women channel the need for achievement into areas other than the organization.

The need for affiliation has been characterized as "feminine" [Gilligan, 1982; Sutherland and Veroff, 1985; Warren, 1982], but in general, men and women in this study do not differ in n Aff [Table 7]. Needs theory posits a positive association between the need for affiliation and commitment. However, this relation was not confirmed for the entire sample or for women and men analyzed separately (Table 10). Either commitment is not related to a need for affiliation or respondents view neither the profession or the organization as meeting the need.[10]

Needs theory also predicts a positive relation between the "masculine" need for autonomy and professional commitment and a negative relation with organizational commitment. N Aut is significantly related to professional commitment for the entire sample, and for women and men separately (Table 10). However in each instance, the relation is negative. This result suggests that professional commitment of accountants is enhanced by lower n Aut. Differences in n Aut are not reflected by the organizational commitment regressions (Table 11). The relation between n Aut and organizational commitment is not significant for either men or women. The finding implies that in an organizational setting, commitment is independent of the need for autonomy or that neither group perceives the organization as meeting their need for autonomy.

Needs theory predicts a significantly positive relation between commitment and the "masculine" need for dominance. The relation with n Dom is not statistically significant for either men or women in either of the commitment regressions, and is significantly only at the aggregate level for organizational commitment (Tables 10 and 11). Either professional commitment is not related to n Dom or neither group perceives their needs for dominance are met by the profession. This finding has implications for a pervasive barrier to women's advancement in the profession. The need for dominance is assumed to be an important component of success, and men in this study exhibit a greater need for dominance than women. Yet, neither women or men associate a higher need for dominance with a greater degree of professional commitment.

The results of these empirical tests challenge the assumptions that commitment is enhanced by masculine traits and diminished by feminist traits. Achievement is the only "masculine" need associated with increased professional commitment. An increased need for autonomy diminishes professional commitment, and higher needs for affiliation and dominance either do not affect professional commitment or are not perceived as met by the profession.

LIMITATIONS AND CONCLUSIONS

Implications of the results are subject to limitations of this study. The questionnaire was not administered under the researchers' control and subjects were drawn from only two Big Eight firms in a single city.[11] An additional limitation was the inability in the present study to measure commitment of accountants who had left public accounting. This may be particularly important when studying gender effects. The demographic profile of the subjects in this study suggest that women working in public accounting are less likely than men to have children. One possible explanation for the lack of results to support the role-conflict model is that women who are most affected by family obligations are also the most likely to have interrupted their careers to care for children and these women were not included in the sample [O'Connell, Betz, and Kurth, 1989].

The study implicitly assumes that a single model can measure professional and organizational commitment among women and men. An untested alternative is that there are gender-specific models of commitment and success. This is a topic for future research.

Subject to the limitations, the results of this study provide empirical evidence that differential socialization affects work-related attitudes of public accountants. Traditionally, this model has been used to explain women's behavior with respect to a male "norm," but the results of the current study suggest that men's work-related attitudes also are affected. Men's commitment to their profession increases if they feel responsible for the financial support of a family. One possible explanation of the results of this study is that the construct "professional commitment" reflects anxiety and fear associated with increased financial responsibilities, which in turn leads men to place increased importance on their careers and career success.

The research did not find evidence of adverse effects of socialization on women's professional or organizational commitment. However, efforts to improve the position of women within the accounting profession cannot ignore the impact of socialization on men's attitudes toward women in the profession. Women in accounting, as in other professions, face significant structural and institutional barriers to advancement. Despite their professional and organizational commitment, women will have difficulty advancing if they are systematically excluded from the acquisition of organizational knowledge [Crompton, 1987]. State societies and public accounting firms should act on the recommendations of the AICPA's special committee, for example, providing conference sessions on issues such as discrimination and affirmative action. They can also provide a forum for exchange of information among employers on developing policies to remove discriminatory practices. Employers also need to develop constructive child care policies that will help female and male employees balance work and family responsibilities, without penalizing their professional advancement.

ACKNOWLEDGMENT

The authors appreciate the helpful comments of anonymous reviewers and the editor on drafts of this material. An earlier version of this paper was presented at the 1989 annual meeting of the American Accounting Association. Each author provided an equal contribution to this study.

NOTES

1. In a recent court case, Price Waterhouse was sued by a former female manager who was not elected to the partnership, allegedly because her "masculine" behavior was not consistent with the female stereotype [McCarthy, 1988]. In May 1990, the Federal Court directed Price Waterhouse to admit the manager to the partnership as of July 1, 1990. A Price Waterhouse representative stated that the case was currently under appeal.

2. A copy of the questionnaire is available from the authors upon request.

3. Cronbach's alpha scores for each of the needs were as follows: n Ach = .64, n Aff = .23, n Aut = .46, n Dom = .65.

4. OLS regression with multiplicative interaction variables was chosen instead of ANOVA because ANOVA required extensive collapsing of cells.

5. Judge, Griffith, Hill, and Lee [1980] suggest that correlations of .80 are usually considered evidence of potential multicollinearity.

6. For the purpose of preparing the ANOVA models, subjects were grouped into categories. Nonparametric Kruskal-Wallis ANOVAs confirmed the results of the one-way ANOVAs.

7. Statistical significance is defined at an alpha of .05.

8. Generalizations about this result are difficult because only six female respondents had children.

9. The designation of "masculine" and "feminine" traits was not supported by the regressions presented earlier in this study. Gender was not a main effect for either achievement or affiliation; however, men scored higher for both dominance and autonomy.

10. This result may also be due to a weakness in the measure of the affiliation need. N Aff had the lowest Cronbach's alpha of the four needs measures. Alpha coefficients for n Ach, n Aff, n Aut, n Dom, Professional Commitment and Organizational Commitment for each group were as follows: (1) the entire sample alphas were .64, .23, .46, .65, .80, and .79, respectively; (2) the male sample alphas were .62, .25, .44, .63, .80, and .81, respectively; and (3) the female sample alphas were .71, .18, .48, .69, .80, and .69, respectively. Pair-wise correlations were below .50 so multicollinearity probably did not affect the significance of the coefficients [Judge et al., 1980].

11. No significant differences were noted between the two firms in any of the empirical tests.

REFERENCES

American Institute of Certified Public Accountants, *Upward Mobility of Women: Special Committee Report to the AICPA Board of Directors* [AICPA, 1988].

Aranya, N., J. Pollock, and J. Amernic, "An Examination of Professional Commitment in Public Accounting," *Accounting, Organization and Society,* 4 [1981], pp. 271-280.

Atkinson, J.W., *Motives in Fantasy, Action, and Society* [Van Nostrand, 1958].

Bartol, K.M., "Professionalism As a Predictor of Organizational Commitment, Role Stress, and Turnover; A Multidimensional Approach," *Academy of Management Journal* [December, 1979], pp. 815-821.

Baruch, R., "The Achievement Motive in Women: Implications for Career Development," *Journal of Personality and Social Psychology* [March, 1967], pp. 260-267.

Bedeian, A.G., and J. Touliatos, "Work-related Motives and Self-Esteem in American Women," *Journal of Psychology* [1978], pp. 63-70.

Breakwell, G.M., *The Quiet Rebel: Women at Work in a Man's World* [Century Publishing, 1985].

Brief, A.P., G.L. Rose, and R.J. Aldag, "Sex Differences in Preferences for Job Attributes Revisited," *Journal of Applied Psychology* [October 1977], pp. 645-646.

Burrell, G., "No Accounting for Sexuality," *Accounting, Organization, and Society,* 12 [1987], pp. 89-101.

Case, S.S., "Cultural Differences, Not Deficiencies: An Analysis of Managerial Women's Language," in S. Rose and L. Larwood (eds.), *Women's Careers: Pathways and Pitfalls* [Praeger, 1988], pp. 41-63.

Chafetz, J.S., "Gender Equality; Toward a Theory of Change" in *Feminism and Sociological Theory*, edited by R.A. Wallace, [Sage, 1989], pp. 135-160.

Chodorow, N. *The Reproduction of Mothering* [University of California Press, 1978].

Chusmir, L.H., "Gender Differences in Variables Affecting Job Commitment Among Working Men and Women," *Journal of Social Psychology* [February, 1986], pp. 87-94.

Crompton, R., "Gender and Accountancy: A Response To Tinker and Neimark," *Accounting, Organization, and Society,* 12 [1987], pp. 103-110.

Cronbach, L.J., "Coefficient Alpha and the Internal Structure of Tests," *Psychometrika* [September 1951], pp. 297-334.

Dexter, C.R., "Women and the Exercise of Power in Organizations: From Ascribed to Achieved Status," in *Women and Work: An Annual Review,* Vol. 1, edited by L. Larwood, A.H. Stromberg, and B.A. Gutek [Sage, 1985], pp. 239-258.

Diamond, E.E., "Theories of Career Development and the Reality of Women at Work," in S. Rose and L. Larwood (eds.), *Women's Careers: Pathways and Pitfalls* [Praeger, 1988], pp. 15-27.

Eagly, A.H., and H. Wood, "Gender and Influenceability: Stereotype versus Behavior," in *Women, Gender and Social Psychology,* edited by V.E. O'Leary, R.K. Unger, and B.S. Wallston [Lawrence Erllbaum, 1985], pp. 225-226.

Eccles, J.S., "Gender Roles and Women's Achievement-Related Decisions," *Psychology of Women Quarterly* [June 1987], pp. 135-172.

England, P., and L. McCreary, "Integrating Sociology and Economics to Study Gender and Work," in *Women and Work: An Annual Review*, Vol. 2, edited by A.H. Stromberg, L. Larwood, and B.A. Gutek [Sage, 1987], pp. 143-172.

Gaetner, J.F., P.E.W. Hemmeter, and M.K. Pitman, "Employee Turnover in Public Accounting: A New Perspective," *CPA Journal* [August, 1987], pp.30-37.

Gilligan, C., *In a Different Voice: Psychological Theory and Women's Development* [Harvard University Press, 1982].

Gouldner, A.W., "Cosmopolitan and Locals: Toward an Analysis of Latent Social Roles—I," *Administrative Science Quarterly* [December 1957], pp. 281-306.

Hopwood, A., "Accounting and Gender: An Introduction" *Accounting, Organization, and Society* 12, [1987], pp. 65-69.

Illich, I., *Gender* [Pantheon Books, 1983].

Johnson, M.M., "Feminism and the Theories of Talcott Parsons," in *Feminism and Sociological Theory*, edited by R.A. Wallace [Sage, 1989], pp. 101-118.

Judge, G.W., R.E. Griffith, R.E. Hill, and T. Lee, *The Theory and Practice of Econometrics* [Wiley, 1980].

Lachman, R., and N. Aranya, "Job Attitudes and Turnover Intentions among Professionals in Different Work Settings," *Organization Studies*, 3 [1986], pp. 279-293.

Larsen, C.C., "The Treatment of the Sexes in Psychological Research," in *Gender Bias in Scholarship: The Pervasive Prejudice*, edited by W. Thomm and G. Hamilton [Wilfred University Press, 1988], pp. 25-43.

Lehman, C. "The Importance of Being Ernest: Gender Conflicts in Accounting," *Advances in Public Interest Accounting*, 3 [1989].

Lorence, J., "A Test of 'Gender' and 'Job' Models of Sex Differences in Job Involvement," *Social Forces* [September 1987], pp. 121-142.

McClelland, D.C., J.W. Atkinson, R.A. Clark, and E.L. Lowell, *The Achievement Motive* [Appleton-Century-Crofts, 1953].

McCarthy, M.J., "Supreme Court to Rule on Sex-Case," *The Wall Street Journal* [July 14, 1988], p. 37.

Merton, R.K., "Patterns of Influence: Local and Cosmopolitan Influentials," In R.K. Merton, *Social Theory and Social Structure* [Free Press, 1957], pp. 368-380.

Morrison, A.M., R.P. White, and E.V. Velsor, *Breaking the Glass Ceiling* [Addison-Wesley, 1987].

Murray, H.A. Explorations in Personality [Oxford University Press, 1938].

Neter, J., W. Wasserman, and M.H. Kutner, *Applied Linear Statistical Models* [Irwin, 1985].

Norris, D.R., and R.E. Niebuhr, "Professionalism, Organizational Commitment and Job Satisfaction in an Accounting Organization," *Accounting, Organization, and Society*, 1 [1983], pp. 49-59.

O'Connell, L., M. Betz, and S. Kurth, "Plans for Balancing Work and Family Life; Do Women Pursuing Nontraditional and Traditional Occupations Differ?" *Sex Roles* [January, 1989], pp. 35-45.

O'Leary, V.E., "Women's Relationship with Women in the Workplace," in *Women and Work: An Annual Review*, Vol. 3, edited by B.A. Gutek, A.H. Stromberg, and L. Larwood [Sage, 1988], pp. 189-213.

Porter, L.W., R.M. Steers, R.T. Mowday, and P.V. Boulian, "Organizational Commitment, Job Satisfaction and Turnover among Psychiatric Technicians," *Journal of Applied Psychology* [October 1974], pp. 603-609.

Rohrbaugh, J., *Women: Psychology's Puzzle* [Basic Books, 1979].

Rose, S., and L. Larwood, "Charting Women's Careers: Current Issues and Research," in *Women's Careers: Pathways and Pitfalls*, edited by S. Rose and L. Larwood [Praeger, 1988], pp. 3-21.

St. Clair, L., 'When is Gender a Handicap?: Towards Conceptualizing the Socially Constructed Disadvantages Experienced by Women," in *The Social Identity of Women,* edited by S. Skevington and D. Baker [Sage, 1989], pp. 130-151.

Schuler, A.P., "Sex, Organizational Level and Outcome Importance: Where Differences Are," *Personnel Psychology* [Autumn 1975], pp. 365-376.

Schwartz, F.N., "Management Women and the New Facts of Life," *Harvard Business Review* [January-February 1989], pp. 65-76.

Shann, M.H., "Career Plans of Men and Women in Gender-Dominant Professions, *Journal of Vocational Behavior* [June 1983], pp. 343-356.

Steers, R.M., "Antecedents and Outcomes of Organizational Commitment," *Administrative Science Quarterly* [March 1977], pp. 45-56.

Steers, R.M., and D.N. Braunstein, "A Behaviorally-Based Measure of Manifest Needs in Work Settings," *Journal of Vocational Behavior* [October 1976], pp. 251-266.

Sutherland, E. and J. Veroff, "Achievement Motivation and Sex Roles," in *Women, Gender and Social Psychology,* edited by V.E. O'Leary, R.K. Unger, and B.S. Wallston [Lawrence Erlbaum, 1985], pp. 101-128.

Tinker, T., and M. Neimark, "The Role of Annual Reports in Gender and Class Contradictions at General Motors: 1917-1976," *Accounting, Organizations, and Society,* 12 [1987], pp. 71-88.

Veroff, J. "Assertive Motivation: Achievement vs. Power," in *Motivation and Society*, edited by A. Stewart [Jossey Bass, 1982].

Warren, M.A., "Is Androgyny the Answer to Sexual Stereotyping?" in *"Femininity," "Masculinity," and "Androgyny,"* edited by M. Vetterling-Braggin [Rowman and Littlefield, 1982], pp. 170-186.

Wescott, S.H., and R.E. Seiler, *Women in the Accounting Profession* [Markus Wiener, 1986].

A BRIDGE BETWEEN KNOWLEDGE AND ACTION:

E.R.A. SELIGMAN AND THE NEW YORK STATE CORPORATE INCOME TAX, 1912-1917

Leonard Goodman and Paul J. Miranti, Jr.

ABSTRACT

This paper addresses the question of how expert knowledge in taxation was applied to promote growth and to achieve a more efficient allocation of economic resources in New York City. It focuses specifically on the role played by E.R.A. Seligman of Columbia University in formulating a state corporate income tax during the period 1912-1917.

After a week at sea, New York's upper harbor was a welcome sight to Professor Edwin Robert Anderson (E.R.A.) Seligman of Columbia University. It was July 1913, and he was returning after a year's travel in Europe. There he had counseled with leading academic and prominent officials in taxation and public finance. As the ship steamed ahead on the rising tide, the economist and his

Advances in Public Interest Accounting, Volume 5, pages 75-106.
Copyright © 1993 by JAI Press Inc.
All rights of reproduction in any form reserved.
ISBN: 1-55938-496-4

fellow passengers were soon confronted by a scene evocative of medieval triptychs he had seen overseas depicting the fruits of economic prosperity resulting from the good governance of society. But unlike work such as the Lorenzettis' in Siena, the wealth-creating activities in this modern panorama were neither allegorical nor pastoral. Instead, the unifying motif of this more dynamic scene involved the successful integration of complex and interdependent elements.

The horizon encompassed a range of economic activity of heroic proportions. The shores of the world's southernmost fjord were crowded with docks, shipyards and repair facilities which served the vast fleet of merchant vessels plying the seas between Europe and America. The waters were congested with barges, lighters and tugboats hauling cargoes between the ocean-going shipping and the giant railroad marshaling yards in the Bronx and adjacent New Jersey. The atmosphere was polluted by smoke and steam from hundreds of engines. The baritone horns and the raucous whistles of water craft as well as from the many light manufacturing plants ringing the harbor created a distracting cacophony. Although new buildings were being raised on every shore, construction activity reached its zenith on Manhattan. A solid granite rock bed, new designs and improved materials made it possible to erect skyscrapers like the recently completed Woolworth Building, then the world's highest. These structures housed not only thousands of commercial enterprises but also a growing number of advertising, banking insurance, law and accounting firms. And on the west, next to the Statue of Liberty, was Ellis Island, the point of debarkation for millions of European immigrants whose frontier of opportunity would in many instances center in this vibrant province.

The scene, as Professor Seligman well knew, reflected the state's impressive economic statistics. In 1910 New York's total population was nine million of which five million were concentrated in the five boroughs of the Greater City of New York (incorporated 1898). Although the state's population represented only ten percent of the national total, its overall economic contribution was far greater. The state's national banks held in 1913, 22 percent of the value of all outstanding loans for that class of financial institution; its corporations earned 25 percent of the taxable net earnings reported to the U.S. Internal Revenue Service; and its port facilities served as a conduit for 45 percent of the nation's foreign trade shipments [Department of Commerce, 1914, pp. 25, 55, 532-533, 595, 650-654].

Historians, however, have tended to ignore the study of the factors which contributed to this city's remarkable growth. Most, instead, have been interested in analyzing either political or social developments [Eager, 1977; Hammack, 1982; Herman, 1963; Lewinson, 1965; Prescott and Zimmerman, 1980; Zimmerman, 1981]. Others have dealt with the rise of the port and stressed the importance either of its location as an entrepôt for the Atlantic trade or as a national transportation hub [Albion, 1939; Condit, 1981].

Our study focuses on innovation in public finance and taxation. Specifically, it examines the role Seligman, a leader in the emerging professional subspecialization of tax economics, played in implementing a state corporate income tax in 1917. Besides alleviating a worrisome financial crisis, the reforms Seligman sponsored assured a more efficient allocation of economic resources. It was this concern about the allocational implications of public financial policies which contributed to the robust economic growth during this period of America's leading business center.

This study evaluates Seligman's contribution to financial reordering in New York in five steps. First, it discusses the key factors that shaped Seligman's social outlook and influenced his decision to pursue a career in tax scholarship. Second, it analyzes Seligman's misgivings about the prevailing modes of public finance at the beginning of the century. Next, it explains the economist's role in an initially unsuccessful effort to promote tax reform in New York City in 1914-1916. Fourth, it describes how success was ultimately achieved in corporate tax reform in 1917 after the focus of public policy debate was shifted to Albany. The study concludes with a consideration of what this experience tells us about the nature of innovation in public affairs.

PORTRAIT OF AN EXPERT AS A YOUNG MAN

E.R.A. Seligman's activism in tax reform in New York was conditioned by four elements in his world outlook: (1) family history, (2) education, (3) religion, and (4) sociopolitical commitment. Seligman's own family history served as a compelling parable to support his optimistic view of the potentials of American society. His father, Joseph, had emigrated in the 1850s from Baiersdorf in Bavaria, where he was unable to complete his studies because he was from an impoverished Jewish family. In America, Joseph and his two brothers prospered, initially as merchants in the Northeast, South, and West, and later, when they founded the private banking firm of J & W Seligman in New York [Birmingham, 1967, pp. 17-23; Dorfman, 1958].

Seligman's family experience also crystallized a close personal identification with the emerging American national executive state. The success of Joseph and his brothers had derived not only from business acumen but also from timely political alliances with leaders of the newly founded Republican Party. Chagrined by the religious discrimination experienced earlier in Germany, Joseph became a strong advocate of the Union cause and its commitment to racial emancipation. When war erupted in April 1861, he was elected vice president of the Unionist organizing committee in New York City [Kohler, 1958]. His patriotic exuberance became so strong that he named his recently born fourth son after Edwin Robert Anderson, the defender of beleaguered Fort Sumter [Birmingham, 1967, p. 132; Dorfman, 1958].

During the war the Seligmans rendered invaluable service to the Union cause not on the battlefield but rather in the corridors of financial and political power. During the dark early days when investor confidence in the Union was lowest, they succeeded in placing hundreds of millions of dollars of United States' treasury obligations in Frankfurt. Moreover, the brothers were strong supporters of their old friend from their merchant days, General Ulysses S. Grant. They encouraged President Abraham Lincoln to appoint Grant commander of the Army of the Potomac after General George S. Meade failed to exploit aggressively the victory won at Gettysburg in 1863. Later, the Seligman firm continued as major agents for the sale of federal debt securities in Europe during the subsequent Grant administration and helped it to weather the great financial panic of 1873 [Birmingham, 1967, pp. 101-105, 136-140; Kohler, 1935b].

E.R.A. Seligman was also influenced by his formal education which blended pragmatic training in law and economics with a conservative but sensitive social outlook. As a boy he and his brothers were encouraged by the parables of ambition and self-improvement of their tutor, Horatio Alger [Birmingham, 1967, p. 133; Scharnhorst, 1980, pp. 36, 39-43; Scharnhorst and Bales, 1985, p. 98-99, 108, 110-115 passim]. Later, at Columbia University Seligman excelled in the curriculum innovated by Dean John W. Burgess, a founder of professional political science. Burgess, one of the first American scholars to master the techniques of modern scholarship perfected in Germany during the 1870s, headed the mission to transform Columbia into a world-class center of scholarship along European lines as had been done earlier at the Johns Hopkins University in Baltimore [Burgess, 1934, Chapters 6-7].

Burgess's life like that of his good friend Joseph Seligman, had been influenced fundamentally by the Civil War. Brought up in a southern Whig family, Burgess first witnessed as a federal soldier the traumatic divisions within his home state of Tennessee, the result of bellicose rhetoric both of self-righteous abolitionists and of secessionist firebrands. Later, his unit's task was to keep open the tenuous supply line to General William T. Sherman's troops on their march through Georgia. Burgess eventually came to terms with these disturbing experiences by dedicating his life to the study of the nature of the modern state [Burgess, 1934, Chapters 2, 8].

Burgess's social schema, which he imparted to all his students including Seligman, intimately intertwined the concepts of sovereignty, nation, and state. In addition to a specific geographic locale, a nation was characterized by the fact that its inhabitants were unified by "language, custom, interest, and culture" and by a consensus of moral values. The state embodied the collective interests of all those composing the nation. Moreover, the state's sovereignty was ultimately "original, [and] underived and [it had] unlimited power to command to punish for disobedience." This power was channeled through the agency of government the authority of which was precisely defined in the formal body of law. The ultimate objective of state power was to preserve social order and tranquility [Burgess, 1934, pp. 246-255, 295-306].

Seligman's social outlook was conditioned, moreover, by exposure to the teaching of leading European scholars. Prior to taking his doctorate and law degree at Columbia in 1882, Seligman followed Dean Burgess's advice and spent four years rounding out his education through study and travel in the Old World. He spent three years at the University of Heidelberg in the seminar of Karl Knies, a leader in the German historical school of economics. There he was favorably impressed by the criticisms of the laissez faire doctrines of the Manchester School as being too abstract and insensitive to social welfare considerations. German scholarship, on the other hand, focused more on the problem of economic distribution and stressed the state's role in assuring social equity [Dorfman, 1958].

These themes seemed highly relevant to a young scholar from a nation beginning to undergo great change through industrialization, urbanization, and immigration. The old egalitarian America rooted in small towns and farms, which Tocqueville had described, was now in decline. It was being displaced by a society with great disparities in economic condition. The leisured opulence of Fifth Avenue and the grinding poverty of the Lowest East Side exemplified the extremes of the new social spectrum.

Seligman was also influenced during his European sojourn by the lectures of French aesthete and historian Hippolyte Taine at L'Ecole des Beaux Arts in Paris in 1883. Taine's then novel interpretation of the cataclysmic events of the French Revolution warned the young American of the dangers both of insensitive and effete leadership and of radical demagoguery for the maintenance of social order. He argued that the leaders of the ancien régime had failed to rectify the inequitable tax burdens that eroded the economic position of both the bourgeoisie and peasantry and, thus, drove them into revolt. Later, the unconstrained power of the Jacobins who eventually supplanted royal power, degenerated into a reign of terror relieved only by the emergence of the Napoleonic dictatorship [Weinstein, 1972, Chapter 6].

Seligman's involvement in the Ethical Culture movement was yet another influence on his moral development. The New York Ethical Culture Society had been formed by Felix Adler, who had received a doctorate from Columbia (1873) and had most lately been professor of Oriental languages at Cornell University. Adler's new sect sought to transcend religious particularisms and to achieve social coalescence by establishing a new moral order emphasizing ethical relationships between people. In 1905 Seligman played a key role in raising funds to finance a chair in ethical philosophy at Columbia for Felix Adler. He succeeded in soliciting generous contributions for this cause from a choice circle of the city's most prominent business leaders, including Jacob H. Shiff, Paul and Max Warburg, V. Everet Macy, George Foster Peabody, Robert W. DeForest, R. Fulton Cutting, Charles Stuart Smith, James Loeb and Otto Kahn [Birmingham, 1967, p. 149; Burgess, 1934, pp. 157-158; Golding, 1926, pp. 84-89].

The precepts of Ethical Culture encouraged an active participation in professional and public affairs. Adler's "religion of duty," with its emphasis on "deeds not creeds," promised fulfillment rather than redemption. It rejected spiritualism and counseled its adherents to find meaning in service to society. Nor did their belief in evolutionary social change lead to the pessimism characteristic of social Darwinism. Rather, they thought that the dedicated efforts of individuals could lead to social progress and uplift [Adler, 1903, pp. 1-17, 43-58; Adler, 1905, Chapters 4-6].

Seligman also embraced Ethical Culture's perception of the connection between knowledge and history. Felix Adler contended that man's experience was an evolutionary continuum during which patterns of belief changed in response to advances in human understanding. In his view all dogmas— whether religious, economic, or social—were merely rationalizations reflecting the level of mankind's knowledge at certain points in history [Adler, 1905, Chapters 1-2; Furner, 1975, pp. 97-99]. This penchant for viewing all social phenomena in this cool and detached manner became a hallmark of Seligman's scholarly style. It also helped him to avoid the trap of overzealous advocacy which was so damaging to the careers of several other contemporary American scholars who had also been trained in the German historicist tradition [Furner, 1975, pp. 109-110, 214, 244, 246-247].

Another dimension of Seligman's personality was his commitment to benevolent and political movements directed toward ameliorating social conditions in Greater New York. Although leaders in Ethical Culture were active in these endeavors, they also attracted representatives of all the city's major religious bodies. The tone of their activism, however, had first been established by preachers in local Protestant evangelical churches who extorted their flocks since the 1880s to create a city of God on earth within New York. Seligman, like many upper-middle-class idealists of this period, was attracted to philanthropies dedicated to improving the social, economic, and moral condition of the city's poor. And like many of his contemporaries he shared the belief that a new municipal order might operate as a strong engine for social regeneration [Hammack, 1982, pp. 77-78, 140-145].

Seligman and members of his family were leaders in many of these groups. The economist, for instance, worked for improved housing for the poor (the University Settlement and the Cooperative Social Settlement); better child welfare (New York Kindergarten Association and the National Child Labor Association); adult education (Peoples' Institute of Cooper Union); the curtailment of prostitution and other vices among the poor (Committee of Fifteen and American Society for Social Prophylaxis); more remedial penology (Prison Association and the New York Probation Association); and poor relief (State Charities Association); and the encouragement of the visual and plastic arts (Metropolitan Museum of Art, Municipal Art Society and the National Sculpture Society) ("Seligman, Edwin Robert Anderson," 1914).

The leadership of these groups were often not impractical visionaries but rather seasoned men of affairs skilled in pursuing their social goals through political action. The major focus of their political activism after 1900 was the Citizen's Union led by R. Fulton Cutting, president of the Charities Organization. Committed exclusively to New York politics, the Citizens' Union attracted independents who feared the consequences of machine-dominated rule on the city level by the Democratic Tammany Hall and on the state level by Boss Thomas C. Platt's "regular" Republicans. They viewed the machines as the natural allies of the criminal and corrupt elements thought chiefly responsible for the social ills they toiled to eradicate. To many proponents, the excesses of the Tweed Ring of the 1870s represented a breakdown that they never wished to see repeated. In 1903 the Citizens' Union demonstrated the broad appeal of their program among the city's middle classes by electing Seth Low, former president of Columbia University, mayor of New York. Later, this organization continued as a potent force in fusionist tickets led by liberals in their efforts to control municipal affairs [Cerillo, 1973, pp. 51-71; Hammack, 1982, pp. 116-119, 150-157; Mandelbaum, 1965; Callow, 1966; Herschowitz, 1977].

Seligman's influence within the Citizens' Union derived largely from his service as a trustee of its research affiliate, the Municipal Research Bureau (MRB). Besides its primary financial backer R. Fulton Cutting, its board of trustees also included Albert Shaw, a Johns Hopkins trained expert on municipal government and editor of *The Review of Reviews*, and railroad attorney Victor Morawetz [Harlow, 1958; Graybar, 1974, Dahlberg, 1966, p. 16]. Its research activities were directed by William A. Allen, Henry Bruere, and Frederick A. Cleveland [Cerillo, 1973, Dahlberg, 1966, p. 7]. Seligman enriched the MRB's efforts not only with his expertise in economics, law, and taxation, but also through his intimate contact with developments in several specialized associations devoted to enhancing the efficiency and effectiveness of municipal government. Seligman served as an important link between the MRB's research activities and the American Economic Association (AEA), the National Civic Federation, the National Municipal League (NML), the Civil Service Association, and the National Tax Association (NTA) ["Seligman, "Edwin Robert Anderson," 1914; "Seligman, Edwin, R.A., 1900].

In addition to the need for expertise in managing municipal affairs, the leaders of the Citizens' Union agreed that the achievement of their social goals depended directly on the continued expansion of the city's prosperity. Their thinking about the interdependence of social and economic goals is best illustrated in their attitudes about the desirability of improving municipal rapid transit. Beginning in the 1880s, they thought that such a system could alleviate the overcrowding in the lower Manhattan tenement districts, which they saw as a major cause of vice and crime. Better transportation would make feasible a diaspora of the city's laboring population to more hospitable districts envisioned for the then sparsely populated upper reaches of Manhattan and the outer boroughs. More salubrious and commodious housing was thought essential in raising public morality by weaning the working classes away from the damaging escapes afforded by gambling, prostitution, and substance abuse.

These pragmatic idealists, however, recognized that the financing necessary for their ambitious scheme for social improvement depended on the continued growth of the city's economy and tax base. Thus, to increase tax revenues from real estate, the primary source of local funding, liberal political leaders formulated a dual strategy; first to extend the city's leadership as a hub of international transportation; and, second, to promote a more intense utilization of the city's large tracts of undeveloped land [Felts, 1973, Hammack, 1982, Chapter 8].

The capital outlays necessary to achieve its transportation objectives placed heavy demands on the city's treasury. Although New York remained the nation's largest port, other locales made substantial inroads especially into its formerly dominant position as a grain exporting center. During the period 1870-1890, New York's share of the nation's wheat exports fell dramatically because of the competition from the expanding Gulf ports of New Orleans, Shreveport and Galveston. Distressed by this challenge leaders of the New York State Chamber of Commerce persuaded the city to undertake an ambitious construction program for docks and warehouse facilities and also to make capital improvements helpful to private transportation enterprises [Ripley, 1912, pp. 31-33].

The city's land development objective, like the social improvement plans of the Citizens' Union, depended on the extension of rapid transit. But constrained by a constitutional debt limit, the city had to rely on private enterprises to build the electrical traction systems which revolutionized local transportation beginning in the 1880s. As recompense for their valuable franchises, the rapid transit companies agreed to share profits with the city. The primary benefit to the city, however, was the opening of new districts for residential development that previously had been too remote from the downtown commercial and transportation centers. Besides the real estate and construction industries, these changes also provided profitable opportunities for the metropolis's large banking and insurance interests [Hammack, 1982, pp. 243-258].

It was these formative experiences that provided the background to E.R.A. Seligman's prodigious scholarly achievements. As we shall see in the following section, his writing were highly sensitive to the economic problems that contemporary governmental leaders were confronting in New York.

PROBLEMS AND PROSPECTS IN
PUBLIC FINANCE, 1890-1912

Seligman first became interested in taxation after completing his doctoral studies at Columbia University. His dissertation had been on the medieval guilds. His initial writings supported labor's organizing activities, federal railroad regulation, housing for the poor, and the Christian socialist movement. Eventually, however, he was persuaded to specialize in taxation by his old mentor John W. Burgess, who doubtless thought it a logical choice for a member of one of the country's leading banking families ["Seligman, Edwin R.A.," 1900].

Taxation was virgin territory for university-trained economists during the 1890s. Little research had been undertaken by trained scholars and opportunities abounded to advance one's career as a consultant to government. The leading American scholarly study at that time was Henry Carter Adams's *Public Debts: An Essay in the Science of Finance* [1887]. But Adams soon abandoned this field after taking charge of the Interstate Commerce Commission's statistics and accounting bureau [Shaw, 1927]. The resultant void was soon filled by Seligman and two other academic pioneers, Thomas S. Adams of the University of Wisconsin and, later, Yale University, and Charles J. Bullock of Harvard University [Fairchild, 1944; "Bullock, Charles Jesse, 1930]. This scholarly trinity dominated the field until World War I. Seligman's major contributions included *The Shifting and Incidence of Taxation* [1899], *The Income Tax* [1911], and *Essays in Taxation* [1931].

Seligman's scholarship was enriched through his extensive knowledge of the history of tax theory and practice. The first half of *The Shifting and Incidence of Taxation,* for example, analyzed the advance of tax theory from ancient to modern times [Seligman, 1926, Chapters 1-8]. Similarly, the introductory chapters of *The Income Tax* surveyed the major methods of taxation applied in the West since medieval times; the latter chapters contrasted earlier efforts to implement income taxation both in America and Europe [Seligman, 1911]. Seligman's writings were also tempered by knowledge gleaned through personal contact with contemporary theoreticians and practitioners. Many of these connections, such as those maintained with Thomas S. Adams and Charles J. Bullock, first flourished through his involvement in the affairs of the AEA and NTA. Former students were also a constant source of information, especially about public finance developments in particular states. He maintained close contact with Carl C. Plehn of the University of Nebraska, Louis F. Gephardt at Washington University in St. Louis, and Louis Levine at the University of Montana. Seligman also benefited through discourse over public financing matters with his older brother Isaac Newton Seligman, head of the family firm and long-term member of the Committee on Taxation of the New York State Chamber of Commerce, as well as fellow ethical culturists

Jacob H. Schiff, a vocal proponent of income taxation, and his young partner, Paul M. Warburg. Moreover, Seligman's access to membership on important governmental tax committees was enhanced because of the influence of his brother and Jacob Schiff in the affairs of New York's Republican Party. Through his membership in the NTA, on the other hand, he was able to cultivate the friendship of practitioners such as Lawson G. Purdy, president of the board of tax assessment in New York City, attorney Kent Kossuth Kennan (father of diplomat George Kennan) of Milwaukee, attorney Alfred E. Holcomb, assistant secretary of AT&T, and accountant Robert H. Montgomery of the firm of Lybrand, Ross Bros. & Montgomery. Moreover, Seligman was also intimate with many of Europe's leading economists and tax administrators including Josiah Stamp, Luigi Einaudi, and Joseph A. Schumpeter.

Seligman's scholarship was highly cognizant of the concerns of business and governmental leaders for improved modes of taxation that not only were more efficient and equitable but also were sensitive to the major social and economic developments which had transformed America since the last quarter of the nineteenth century. Industrialization and urbanization placed severe strains on the basic governmental mechanisms which had well served the country during its first century. The old nation of small and isolated agricultural communities had been held together primarily through a loose web of courts, legislative institutions, and political parties. Executive authority remained minimal except in time of war [Wiebe, 1967; Yearly, 1970, Chapter 1].

The impact of urbanization and industrialization on the costs of public administration were evident in the budgets of Seligman's home state and city. Expenditures mounted both for operating activities and for capital construction. In New York State, for instance, annual operating expenditures rose from $7.2 million in 1890 to $39.2 million in 1912. Education (23% of the 1912 operating budget), health and social welfare (26%), and administration, regulation, and judicial activities (14%) were the major factors driving the budgetary expansion. In addition, capital outlays also increased as the state bolstered its transportation infrastructure first by improving the Erie Canal and later after 1907 by undertaking an elaborate highway construction program. These outlays were financed primarily through the issuance of debt. Thus, the state's net funded obligations increased from a modest $1.8 million in 1890 to $86.3 million in 1912 [Department of Commerce, 1924, p. 14; Sowers, 1914, pp. 318-323].

In financial terms, the city tail wagged the state dog. The city's expenditures increased from $178.4 million in 1906 to $243.2 million in 1912. Its primary operating expenditures in 1912 were for education (15% of the 1912 total), public safety (11%), executive and judicial departments (7%), charities (4%), and sanitation (4%). Under the state's constitution the city was compelled to absorb over sixty percent of the Albany government's budgetary shortfall that year. In addition, it had to pay $41.3 million in interest charges (17%) on the $792.9 million in net outstanding debt incurred to finance an ambitious capital construction program. The city's debt mountain not only dwarfed that of the state but also represented 21 percent of the aggregate value of the nation's entire municipal, county, and state obligations [Department of Commerce, 1913, pp. 200-201, 208, 306-307; 1924, pp. 10, 14].

Cognizant of these great changes, Seligman advanced in his scholarly writing several economic propositions which he thought were critical in formulating effective tax policy. Foremost, was the belief that tax burdens should be allocated on the basis of "faculty" or simply the ability to pay [Seligman, 1908, Chapters, 2-3; 1911, pp. 6-9]. The justification for progressive taxation, however, was not rooted in what he believed to be the questionable notion that the rich should pay more because they extracted greater benefits from society. Instead, the rationale for tax progressivism was rooted in his perception of the organic nature of society. Because the state represented the primary social reality which provided meaning and order to its citizen's lives, its interests represented the ultimate moral imperative: "We pay taxes not because we get benefits from the state, but because it is as much our duty to support the state as to support ourselves or our family; because, in short, the state is an integral part of us" [Seligman, 1931, p. 73].

This scholar also stressed the need for rigorous economic analysis in policy formulation [Seligman, 1931, pp. 320-325]. Too often, he believed, legislators failed to recognize that the incidence of proposed taxes could be shifted to unintended social groups. Increases in real estate taxes, for instance, frequently did not affect landlords who passed them to tenants by raising rents. Similarly, tax on personal property, such as industrial assets could be shifted through higher prices to consumers [Seligman, 1926, pp. 217-254; 277-324, 328-337].

Greater sensitivity to economic analysis would also have debunked, he believed, the infatuation of many of New York City's voters for "single tax" proposals promoted by radical politicians such as Henry George and Daniel DeLeon [Ghent, 1930; Mitchell, 1931]. They had argued that both prosperity and equity could be best assured if public expenditures were financed exclusively by taxes on the unearned increment in land values resulting from metropolitan expansion. In their view it was unfair that favorably situated landowners should be enriched because of favorable demographic shifts. Taxing unearned increments was also favored because it discouraged speculative warehousing of tracts and provided an incentive for the construction of new housing [Barker, 1955, Chapter 10; George, 1880; Seligman, 1931, pp. 66-74].

Seligman, however, rejected these arguments. In his view the single tax was objectionable because it placed government finance on too narrow a revenue base. The tax was "inelastic" because the revenue it could provide was limited to the total value of land lease income. This feature was especially disadvantageous for farming districts or poorer communities, where land values were relatively static. Furthermore, administration was complicated by the problems of developing equitable assessments. A single tax also made it difficult for political leaders to use tax policy for promoting socially beneficial ends. Its use, for instance, would rule out the possibility of continuing the tariffs to protect infant industries. Nor did he believe that the Georgeite ideas would be effective in eradicating slums and urban congestion. Rather Seligman felt that improved transportation, adequate capital market conditions, and more comprehensive building codes were more important in solving this problem [Seligman, 1931, pp. 75-97].

The single tax was also wanting, Seligman believed, from a moral standpoint. It violated the principles of universality and equality so crucial to his organic social vision. The placement of the full burden on one class, he felt, only diminished the sense of obligation to the state among those citizens who were not taxed. Nor did he believe that the single tax represented a palliative for speculative abuses. Seligman felt that enrichment from personal sagacity and foresight was not necessarily immoral. Moreover, his own dabbling in real estate convinced him that this form of investment did not guarantee great riches. Finally, the possibilities for cornering markets and extracting monopoly rents were certainly not limited to real estate [Seligman, 1931, pp. 81-83].

Besides his misgivings about the single tax, Seligman abjured excises because they were regressive and violated the faculty principle by overburdening the poor [Seligman, 1926, Chapter 1]. The sole exception, however, was taxes that curbed socially disruptive consumption such as the one imposed on liquor sales in New York in 1896. Its proceeds were shared—one-third to the state and the remainder to the localities in which sales were made [McCormick, 1981, pp. 95-100, 120-121]. In 1912 the state's take amounted to $9.4 million or about 18 percent of its total revenues [New York State, 1925, p. 77].

Seligman also warned about the problems of personal property taxation. One drawback was the negative impact these taxes had on asset values and how that indirectly discouraged savings. A tax increase on intangible personal property such as bonds and stocks, for instance, effectively reduced their net returns and, thus, their resale values. In addition, administrative problems also often foiled the implementation of taxes on personalty as was amply demonstrated in New York City's long history of failure in applying this levy. Assessments were often assigned to untrained, inefficient and even corrupt officials. Moreover, intangibles were hard to assess because they could easily be spirited out of state. Lastly, wealthy individuals could also avoid these liabilities simply by living modestly [Seligman, 1926, Chapter 6; 1931, pp. 19-62; Yearly, 1970, pp. 31-96].

New York State planners had tried to overcome these problems by attaching the personal property of individuals through an array of inheritance, transfer, and recording taxes. Although they may not have contributed to economic efficiency, they were preferred by the state's tax bureaucracy because the information on which assessments were based was easily verifiable through public or business records. In 1886, the state imposed a limited inheritance tax which was substantially extended three years later. By 1912 this yielded about $12 million annually or 23 percent of total state revenues. It also taxed intangible personal property through a stock transfer tax (1905), a mortgage registration tax (1906), and a short-lived secured debt tax (1912) which collectively yielded $6.9 million in 1912 or 13 percent of state revenue [New York State, 1925, pp. 75-77; Seligman, 1908, pp. 112-117; 1931, pp. 126-145].

New York State also imposed a variety of personal property taxes on business corporations. Beginning in 1882 natural monopolies such as railroads and telephone and telegraph companies as well as state-chartered insurance companies were assessed based either on readily measurable gross earnings or equity capital balances. Later, in 1901 taxes on capital were also imposed on state-chartered trust companies and savings banks. In 1912 these corporate imposts raised $11 million representing 21 percent of state revenues [New York State, 1925, pp. 76-78].

Seligman also championed the income tax as the most equitable and efficient means for tapping wealth in America's complex economy and played a significant role in New York's ratification of the Sixteenth Amendment to the U.S. Constitution, which would pave the way for the adoption of a federal income tax in 1913.[1] Neither the excises, personal property taxes, nor the tariff used to finance federal operations was capable of attaching the income created by the nation's flourishing service sector. Nor were these mechanisms elastic. Instead, they acted as a drag on business in good times or bad. The income tax, on the other hand, was theoretically superior because it could be adapted to all forms of economic enterprise and grew proportionately with the expansion of the economy. This tax was also attractive because it was thought incapable of being shifted to other social groups [Seligman, 1931, pp. 15-18, 341-345, 375-385; 1908, pp. 310-315; 1911, pp. 15-23, 631-642].

But although Seligman recognized the positive potentials of income taxation, he feared that without proper administrative support it would be a failure. Critical were the existence of a well-organized cadre of trained bureaucrats, the availability of accurate economic and tax statistics, an uncomplicated compliance system based on standardized accounting, and the power to collect taxes at the source of income production [Seligman 1911, pp. 649-653; 1931, pp. 331-333].

Thus, Seligman had seen over the course of his then nearly 30-year professional career how in New York necessity had served as the mother of fiscal invention. Recurrent financial crises that were ultimately resolved by new taxes became a common pattern. As we shall see in the following section, the economist would be called on to serve as a bridge builder between the community of knowledge and action in efforts to chart a new course for state and city solvency during the crisis brought about by the outbreak of war in Europe in 1914.

THE CRISIS IN CITY FINANCE AND THE BARRIERS TO INNOVATION, 1914-1916

Since the 1880s proponents of new forms of expertise had participated in many New York public policy debates. Accountants, engineers, economists, social workers, and urban planners were eager to win acceptance by demonstrating that their specialties could cure weighty social problems. In their drive to affirm their relevancy, these savants often formed alliances with business and political leaders who appreciated the positive potentials of their knowledge. Moreover, the promise of progress and uplift deriving from expertise provided an appealing intellectual underpinning to the campaigns of reform-minded groups in their struggle to wrest power from the great political machines (Cerillo, 1973].

A major focus for this activism was the Citizens' Union, a local political party dedicated to civic reform. Its leadership followed a three-pronged strategy in its efforts to reform public finance. First, through its research arm, the MRB called for strengthening improved accounting, auditing, and budgeting procedures. Seligman, for instance, in his role as MRB trustee recruited personnel from Columbia's Faculty of Political Science to undertake assignments for improving municipal financial administration [Hoxie, 1955, pp. 70-71; *New York Times*, 1913a, 1913b, 1913c].

Second, the Citizens' Union pressed for a revision of the state constitution to increase municipal control over tax and budgetary matters. Two associates of Seligman's, Seth Low, former president of Columbia University who had served as mayor (1902-1903), and Professor Howard Lee McBain, were both advisers to Mayor John Purroy Mitchel (1914-1917) in the 1915 state constitutional convention. They wanted to limit the power of legislative committee chairmen to initiate appropriations by strengthening the governor's powers over the budgetary process. They also wanted to increase the city's home rule powers and, thus, avoid financing obligations over which the mayor exercised little control.

They pointed out, for example, that in 1914 about $14 million in municipal bond proceeds were set aside for governmental activities beyond the mayor's scope of authority; they wanted relief from the state's spending for education and highway construction, which provided few benefits to the city; they argued that the budget for Erie Canal improvement was padded to reward supporters of upstate political leaders; and they demanded that control over salary levels for many civic employees be transferred from the legislature to the mayor [Hoxie, 1955, pp. 268-269; Lewinson, 1965, pp. 129-132; Low 1915; McBain, 1915; Wallstein, 1914].

Third, the Citizens' Union's leadership influenced municipal governance by serving on advisory commissions formed to resolve pressing civic problems. By shaping committee agendas they often were able to direct the course of public debate and to delimit the policy choices available to political leaders. Through these forums they championed the notion that merit should displace patronage in civic affairs. They contended that the city's high taxes had resulted from the corruption and incompetence of the old machine-dominated regimes. The promise of efficient and honest government guided by specialists became a major plank in the fusionist platforms the Citizens' Union supported prior to World War I. This outlook drew support both from political independents and from business and professional groups [Cerillo, 1973, pp. 51-71].

In fact, the events that eventually led to the passage of New York State's corporate income tax law originated in the deliberations of such a special commission formed in February 1914 to advise fusionist Mayor John Purroy Mitchel about city finances and taxes. In forming this body the "Boy Mayor" was both extending the practice of previous administrations and responding to a promise made during his recent campaign to consider the proposals of Frederic C. Leubuscher, the leader of the politically active Society to Lower Rents and Reduce Taxes on Homes.

Leubuscher's followers were the intellectual heirs of Henry George's single tax movement. Their program was straight forward. They argued that the city could eliminate congestion in business districts and socially degrading conditions in the overcrowded Lower East Side through the simple expedient of cutting the taxes on buildings and improvements to half that on land. Besides discouraging the warehousing of undeveloped land, Leubuscher and his supporters believed that this reform would encourage the development of upper Manhattan and the outer boroughs [Leubuscher 1913a, 1913b, 1913c, 1913d].

But the politically sensitive Mitchel responded by forming a more broadly representative commission with a mandate to evaluate comprehensively city financial affairs. Besides his concerns about Leubuscher's ideas, the municipal leader, doubtless, sensed that such a controversial panacea might alienate many of his conservative business supporters. He appointed as chairman Alfred E. Marling of the real estate brokerage firm of Horace Ely and Company and as secretary economist Frederic C. Howe, a protégé of Leubuscher, who earlier had assisted Mayor Tom L. Johnson's efforts in Cleveland, Ohio, to introduce the single tax [Howe, 1925, Chapter 22].

Although Seligman served as vice chairman of the full committee, Mitchel selected him for the chairmanship of its executive subcommittee responsible for defining the scope of the inquiry. In addition, there were four subcommittees: new sources of tax revenues (chaired by Walter Lindner of the Title Guarantee and Trust Company), new sources of nontax revenues (chaired by Delos F. Wilcox of Columbia University, an expert on municipal franchises) [Wilcox, 1919], the administration of special assessments (chaired by attorney David Rumsey), and the city's debt (chaired by the economist Jeremiah Jenks of Cornell) [Commitee on Taxation, 1914].

For the Mitchel administration, however, Seligman was the key contact. Besides his demonstrated capabilities, other factors made him invaluable. Through the Ethical Culture movement, he was intimate with Jacob H. Schiff who, besides supporting Mitchel's candidacy, headed Kuhn, Loeb and Company, a major underwriter of city debt [Adler, 1975; Morris, 1934]. Additionally, Seligman's brother, Isaac Newton Seligman, head of the family's banking business, was a backer of the successful 1914 gubernatorial bid of Manhattan District Attorney Charles Seymour Whitman, a Republican [Kohler, 1935a; Logan, 1974; New York Times, 1915c]. Moreover, Issac Newton Seligman played a significant role in state politics as chairman of the committee on taxation for the city's influential Chamber of Commerce (New York Times, 1915b, 1915d, 1915e]. E.R.A. Seligman assisted Governor Whitman in drafting legislation that reorganizd the state's tax department [New York Times, 1915a]. An Albany connection was valuable to Mitchel, who surely foresaw the need for gubernatorial support in reforming the city's financing. Through the MRB, Seligman maintained close contact with two key Mitchel protégés, Frank L. Polk, the corporation counsel, and Henry Bruere, the city's chamberlain. Moreover, Seligman's influence on the advisory commission increased by recruiting several close associates. Besides Wilcox and Jenks, they included Seligman's young Columbia colleague, economist Robert M. Haig, and City Club secretary Robert Studebaker Binkerd [Hoxie, 1955, pp. 121, 124; Lewinson, 1965, p. 213]. He also tapped attorney and Citizens' Union secretary Seymour Arnold Tanzer, to replace Frederic Howe, who late in 1914 became the immigration commissioner at Ellis Island [Howe, 1925, Chapter 25; Tanzer, 1949, pp. 50-54]. Finally, Seligman's participation represented continuity with earlier state and city efforts to reform public finance. He, for example, had advised Governor Theodore Roosevelt, served on the tax advisory committee of Mayor George B. McClellan, Jr., and had written reports for Mayor William J. Gaynor's committee on new sources of city revenue [Commission on New Sources of City Revenue, 1913; Yearly, 1970, p. 158].

Although the war ultimately sparked an industrial boom, especially after the flotation of large Allied loans in 1915, it initially caused a panic. Uncertainties about international finance led to a 3-month closure of the New York Stock Exchange, a drying up of export credit and a slowing of port activity. Unemployment rose sharply. The costs of public construction programs also spiraled because of the war-induced inflation. Moreover, the crisis threatened the city with default on $80 million in gold obligations payable to European investors on 1 January 1915 [Carosso, 1970, pp. 193-200; Lewinson, 1965, p. 125-126].

The deterioration of city finances soon led to unpopular spending restrictions. The refunding loan to pay foreign creditors prepared jointly by

Kuhn Loeb, and J.P. Morgan and Company, prohibited capital projects that were not self-financing [Prendergast, 1914a, 1914b]. The "pay-as-you-go" plan immediately restricted the delivery of city services [Lewinson, 1965, pp. 125-127]. The city's efforts to provide relief for some 400,000 unemployed were meager, consisting primarily of coordinating private groups who operated emergency workshops [Lewinson, 1965, pp. 137-138; Richie, 1973]. It also impeded the city's efforts to alleviate serious classroom overcrowding by new school construction and induced the Mitchel administration to embrace a plan developed in Gary, Indiana, that introduced staggered school schedules and encouraged greater off-site vocational training [Lewinson, 1965, pp. 163-166]. Mitchel also supported charities commissioner John P. Kingsbury's investigation of the spending of grants received from private religious foundations [Lewinson, 1965, pp. 170-172].

The crisis also increased the importance of the tax commission's findings to the Mitchel administration. The deterioration of the budget was worrisome to Mayor Mitchel, whose career had advanced by exposing the managerial incompetence of several Tammany-connected officials [Lewinson, 1965, Chapter 2]. Recognizing that further financial deterioration was ammunition for his political foes, the mayor pressed Chairman Marling to issue a preliminary report in January 1915 to coincide with the debt refunding and the February financial planning report of City Controller William A. Prendergast's which marked the start of the 1916 budget deliberations. The mayor also needed guidance to prepare his testimony before a special state senate committee organized in February 1915 by Republican majority leader Elon R. Brown. The mayor, supported by State Senator Ogden L. Mills of Manhattan, wanted to use this forum to build support for new legislation to bolster municipal fiscal autonomy [Brown, 1915a, 1915b; Lewinson, 1965, pp. 131-132; Mills, 1915].

Although the tax committee deliberated for nearly a year, consensus formation came slowly as its members mulled over complex alternatives. These included the sale of surplus lands; the imposition of special assessments for public improvements; an extension of the personality tax to intangibles including bonds and stocks; Leubuscher's proposal to reduce taxes on buildings; and finally, an abilities tax in the form of a presumptive income tax estimated from rent data.

Seligman tried to guide the committee toward recommendations he believed were economically sound and politically beneficial to the Mitchel administration. From his perspective any new tax should be broadly based, easy of administration, economically elastic, and not overly onerous on any single class. In addition, he wanted to avoid solutions that would undermine the economic health of business institutions on which the city's continued growth and prosperity depended. In pursuing these goals he tried subtly to proselytize the committee through the sponsorship of research and the solicitation of expert opinion. He also privately advised the mayor about technical issues which the committee considered [Mitchel, 1915d].

The committee issued two preliminary recommendations on 13 January 1915 for providing additional revenue. First, it supported a 1 percent tax on any increases in city land values. The so-called incremental tax sponsored by Robert Binkerd was similar to levies adopted in Berlin and in London. It had also been unsuccessfully presented earlier both before the state legislature by the Citizen's Union and before the Gaynor administration's tax committee by Seligman. Although it was expected to net only an additional $600,000 in 1916, its advocates believed that the increment would grow steadily and provide an additional $15 million annually by 1921 [Committee on Taxation, 1915a, pp. 1-6; Seligman, 1931, pp. 491-492, 510-514].

The Binkerd proposal had broad support. Besides Seligman the other academic members, Wilcox and Jenks, favored this impost. In addition, Leubuscher and Howe viewed it as an acceptable substitute for their original proposal. Some building and real estate representatives including Leubuscher, Marling, and Robert E. Simon of M. Morgenthau and Company were willing to accept the incremental tax as a temporary expedient for an emergency. In addition, attorney Lawson Purdy, who also represented the New York Tax Reform Association, supported this change [Committee on Taxation, 1915a, pp. 6-9]. This latter group, led by William Low, brother of Seth Low, and attorney Arthur C. Pleydell, represented an elite business membership which included J.P. Morgan and Company, R.H. Macy and Company, Steinway and Sons, Brooks Brothers, H.D. Julliard and Company, and Yale and Towne Manufacturing Company. This group opposed levies on "mortgages and other capital engaged in production or trade," preferring, instead, to rely locally on real estate taxation [Pleydell, 1915].

The holdouts were representatives of the relatively undeveloped outer boroughs. This group included former Bronx Borough President Cyrus C. Miller, banker J.M. Francolini of Brooklyn, Mayor Mitchel's law partner George V. Mullan of the Bronx, and John J. Halleran, a Queens political leader who owned much of the Flushing Meadow on which the 1939 World's Fair would be situated [Lewinson, 1965, pp. 30, 36]. These dissidents argued that the incremental tax would unfairly shift taxes from Manhattan to the other boroughs and, thus, impede suburbanization [Committee on Taxation, 1915a, pp. 7-9].

A majority also affirmed Seligman's proposal for the presumptive income tax based on rents. The economist favored the rent tax because it had been successfully applied in Germany as a transitional mechanism that allowed the government the time necessary to organize a bureaucracy capable of servicing a full blown income tax. The rent tax was expected to generate about $25 million annually. Moreover, in a city of nearly five million residents which only had about 75,000 real estate taxpayers, most businesses and residents would be assessable under a rent-based tax. It was also believed superior to a net income tax because it did not require large cadres of attorneys and accountants to administer. Furthermore, it avoided the uncertain question of whether the city had the legal right to tax the income of nonresidents. Additionally, rent estimates were thought to be easily verifiable through real estate assessment records. The committee agreed that gross rents should approximate seven percent of full market valuation. Again the representatives of the middle classes in the outer boroughs objected, believing that their constituents would bear most of this burden [Committee on Taxation, 1915a, pp. 2-9; Seligman, 1931, pp. 474, 479, 607].

From the mayor's perspective, however, the preliminary report was unsatisfactory. It failed to address alternatives that intrigued some aldermen and members of the Board of Estimate including an expanded city personalty tax and a municipal income tax. Thus, on January 25, Mitchel again queried the committee about these matters [Committee on Taxation, 1915b, pp. 1-2].

Reluctant to propose any additional recommendations without more study, the committee appointed a working group to provide the mayor with a tentative recommendation based on a review of the existing literature. The subcommittee included George Mullan, Cyrus Miller, Walter Lindner, attorney Oscar R. Seitz, and Seligman. Burdened by the pressures of managing their own affairs, it is understandable that his busy colleagues deferred to Seligman in formulating the January 30 response to the mayor. The subcommittee's communiqué relied heavily on direct quotations from articles and minutes which previously appeared in National Tax Association meeting proceedings. Seligman also appended a separate memorandum which echoed the subcommittee's findings.

Besides providing the requisite factual data, neither document was very sanguine about the feasibility of the two taxes. The personalty tax was dismissed because of difficulties in administration and the relative ease of evasion. Even a low tax on such intangibles as stocks, bonds, and mortgages like the one New York State currently imposed would yield insufficient revenues. The income tax, on the other hand, was characterized as a dismal failure in virtually all other jurisdictions except Wisconsin [Brownlee, 1974, p. 93; National Industrial Conference Board, 1930, p. 26].

They reported mixed conclusions about whether a state or city income tax could succeed in New York. The Empire State's problems were thought more daunting than those of Wisconsin. New York businesses, for instance, operated to a greater extent out of state, creating an income tax allocation problem for assessors; and the legality of taxing its large nonresident work force was untested; the commentators were also generally in agreement that if the tax were to be successful, the government's administrative capabilities had to be materially expanded [Committee on Taxation, Report, pp. 1-23; Memorandum 1915, pp. 1-5].

After the January 30 preliminary report, the committee began to make decisions about three minor sources of revenue which various subcommittees had been pondering since 1914. First, a special report by Herbert S. Swan of the National Municipal League about the legal and administrative problems encountered by other communities in disposing of surplus land (i.e., excess condemnation) persuaded a majority that this promised little relief in alleviating New York's ills [Committee on Taxation, 1915e]. Second, Seligman also tabled the special assessments proposal and avoided offending its sponsor Jeremiah Jenks by persuading his colleagues to finance a research study by Robert Haig into the experience of some American and Canadian cities as a source of guidance [Committee on Taxation, 1915d, 1915f]. Third, Seligman also persuaded a majority to defer judgment about Leubuscher's original proposal. What was needed, he claimed, was research on the probable economic impacts of adjusting rates for land and buildings on real estate values, rents and mortgage holders [Committee on Taxation, 1915e].

After disposing of these matters Seligman scheduled a special meeting for 12 March 1915 in which several expert witnesses appeared to help resolve the thorny questions of income and personalty taxation. The personalty tax was discussed by Allan V. Girdwood, secretary of the Maryland State Tax Commission, who summarized his state's experience; Professor Charles J. Bullock of Harvard University, who reported on developments in Massachusetts and Pennsylvania; and W. Hastings Lyon, attorney for the recently organized Investment Banker's Association who analyzed Wisconsin and New Hampshire. Their testimony about the advisability of taxes on intangible personalty was mixed. Although they conceded that personalty taxes generally filed, Bullock and Girdwood were less dogmatic about the negative potential for a levy on intangibles which was set at a low rate [Committee on Taxation, 1915c, pp. 1-27].

Alfred E. Holcomb, assistant secretary of AT&T and secretary of the (NTA), on the other hand, introduced Robert H. Montgomery, a partner in the public accounting firm of Lybrand, Ross Bros. & Montgomery who argued that a municipal income tax was feasible provided that rates remained low, thus encouraging voluntary compliance. Although Holcomb in the past had advocated an intangible personalty tax, his support of a municipal income tax was not inconsistent. Either an income or intangible personalty tax seemed advantageous from the perspective of his firm. Both would shift the burden of local taxation away from the utility's heavy investment in real estate and tangible personalty [Committee on Taxation, 1915c, pp. 28-31].

But this attempt to solve these issues led to a sharp split within the committee a scant two weeks prior to Mayor Mitchels' scheduled appearance before Senator Brown's investigating committee in Albany. Although the majority affirmed in their report of April 2 the preliminary conclusions set down by Seligman on January 30, the subsequent testimony of experts had galvanized four dissenters representing middle-class interests in the outer boroughs to support a minority report calling for a low rate tax on both tangible and intangible personalty. These men, John J. Halleran, Frederick B. Shipley, Franklin S. Tomlin, the city's tax collector who was associated with fusionist groups in upper Manhattan, and Collin H. Woodward, a Brooklyn Republican, agreed with many of their constituents that wealthy individuals and business enterprises should bear a greater share of the burden of maintaining government [Committee on Taxation, 1915b, 1915c].

This embarrassing division in conjunction with other political setbacks experienced by Mitchel's regime influenced the future course of tax reform. Although the dissenters were a minority on a committee dominated by business and real estate interests. They represented a large political constituency vital to the fusionist coalition. The mayor was loath to alienate these voters whose support he needed for reelection in 1917. Moreover, his administration was also under heavy attack from teachers and the Board of Education, who strongly opposed the Gary educational experiment. In addition, revelations of the police wiretapping of two Roman Catholic priests as part of the charities investigation alienated the mayor from many of the large numbers of his coreligionists in the city. Finally, even Mitchel's advocacy of military preparedness and participation in the Plattsburgh reserve officer training program in 1916 distressed many voters who either identified with the central powers or simply favored continued American neutrality [Lewinson, 1965, pp. 166-169, 175-188, 198-205].

These local frustrations soon persuaded Mitchel that the solution to the financing problems could only come bout through greater cooperation with those in Albany who supported a more comprehensive state and city reform. This new direction eventually led to the passage of the state's first business income tax in 1917.

INNOVATION ACHIEVED: THE RATIFICATION OF A CORPORATE INCOME TAX, 1916-1917

The impasse in tax reform was ultimately resolved through the closer cooperation between the regular Republicans who dominated the Albany government and the urban progressives who were in the vanguard of Mitchel's fusionist regime. This transformation went through three stages. The first and least satisfactory had been the failure of the previously noted 1915 constitutional convention either to strengthen the governor's budgetary powers or to enhance the autonomy of city governments. Second and more satisfactory was the packet of new bills passed in 1916 in response to Mayor Mitchel's criticism before the special state legislative commission chaired by Senator Elton R. Brown. Last and most satisfying was the corporate income tax enacted in 1917 that provided substantial relief to the mounting pressures on state and city finances.

The reforms proposed in the constitutional convention of 1915 divided the upstate Republican regulars and the urban progressives. Legislative leaders opposed any efforts to curtail their powers and to increase those of the governor over state spending. Nor were they receptive to the proposals to bolster home rule powers of the cities. Specifically, the upstaters did not favor allowing the municipalities to write their own charters defining their scope of authority and, thus, curtailing the oversight powers of the legislature. They were also reluctant to accept proposed restrictions in the legislature's powers to enact bills that affected property, offices, or local governmental arrangements for any individual city. Lacking the support of either the Republican or Democratic machines the constitutional revision went down to defeat in a statewide referendum during November 1915 [Lewinson, 1965, pp. 130-131; Low, 1915; McBain, 1915].

The Brown committee, on the other hand, listened more sympathetically to the host of reforms that Mayor Mitchel called for in early 1915. The leaders of the powerful regular wing of the Republican party recognized that the city's financial condition was becoming severely strained. In addition, because of the refinancing brought about by war emergency, total city debt climbed by over $100 million in 1915 in spite of the spending restrictions imposed by the bankers. Part of the increase resulted from the politically unpopular $20 million direct tax imposed on all municipalities to close the state's deficit, of which about 70 percent was the city's allocable portion.

To cultivate the support of both urban progressive Republicans and independents for the forthcoming state and national elections in 1916 the Albany leadership accommodated the city in two ways. The legislature decided not to impose another burdensome direct tax on real estate but elected instead to finance its deficit through the issuance of more debt. In addition, Mitchel's testimony before the Brown committee persuaded a majority of legislators to enact several bills which provided New York City some measure of relief. Specifically, the legislature agreed to pay the costs of city normal schools and for highway construction in all boroughs except Manhattan. The state also assumed the costs of the Public Service Commission district encompassing the city and agreed to transfer its share of all proceeds on taxes for local banks and trust companies to the city [Lewinson, 1965, pp. 131-132].

By September 1915 Mitchel had conditionally decided to support a corporate income tax bill which would be introduced to the state legislature by Ogden L. Mills of Manhattan, chairman of the joint tax committee. Mills, a progressive Republican, enjoyed the support of the Citizens' Union and was revered by the city's business community. Banker Jacob H. Schiff was sufficiently impressed by his ideas on public finance to propose that Mills be selected as leader of the New York State Republican Party. Mills was also affiliated with the city's other major creditor, J.P. Morgan and Company, through his earlier membership in the firm of Stetson, Jennings and Russell, the banker's attorneys [*New York Times*, 1916a; Collins, 1958].

The state senator was also close to Mayor Mitchel. Besides helping to arrange the Brown committee's hearings in 1915, Mills agreed with the mayor about the need for the further development of New York harbor, particularly the dock and railroad facilities emerging along the Brooklyn waterfront. They were also drawn together by their mutual interest in the growing preparedness movement. In fact, Mitchel in 1917 used his influence with the Wilson administration to secure an army commission for Mills [Mitchell 1915a, 1917; Lewinson, 1965, pp. 200-202].

Mitchel's decision in September 1915 to support Mills's corporate income tax bill soon led to the appointment of Seligman as the city's representative to the legislature's joint tax committee. There he joined his colleague Professor H.A.E. Chandler of Columbia University, who had been engaged as the legislature's expert adviser. During October Mills held public hearings in Albany in which Seligman and others testified in favor of a business income tax. Two months later the support of the Mitchel regime for Mills's proposal further solidified when the state constitutional referendum was defeated at the polls. At its 13 December 1915 meeting the city's tax advisory commission at Seligman's urging voted to defer the abilities tax proposal in favor of the proposed corporate income tax and resolved to implement their original plan only if the state initiative ultimately failed [Committee on Taxation, 1915e, 1915f; Mitchell 1915b, 1915c; Prescott and Zimmerman, 1980, p. 363; Seligman, 1919, p. 528n].

Although Mills had garnered substantial support for tax reform during 1915, no legislation was enacted until the spring of 1917. The drive was doubtless purposely delayed because 1916 was an important election year both at the state and national levels. This pause and the temporary reliance on the debt markets proved propitious for the incumbent Republicans. In the November election they again won large majorities in both houses of the state legislature and returned Governor Whitman to office [Prescott and Zimmerman, 1980, pp. 363-367].

But the last development that assured the passage of a state corporate income tax was the growing threat of American involvement in the World War during early 1917. Although the European war had by 1915 sparked an economic boom, state and city revenues had not kept pace with the domestic expansion because they depended too heavily on a mix of relatively inelastic taxes. Thus, these governments were continually squeezed by higher material and labor costs. Rising international tensions during 1916 also necessitated additional public spending to place both the National Guard and Naval Militia on a war footing. Moreover, the recent heavy public borrowing precluded renewed reliance on the credit markets, especially if hostilities broke out, without first establishing new sources of public revenue. Neither civic nor state officials wanted to experience a repetition of the financial crisis of August 1914 [Prescott and Zimmerman, 1980, pp. 367-368].

The Mills tax plan progressed rapidly through the legislature after war was declared on April 8. Its sponsors encountered little opposition. A few representatives of upstate localities who would lose local personalty tax revenues under this new act objected. So too did Frederic Leubuscher and A.C. Pleydell. But in the new context of mobilization their disclaimers seemed peevish and eccentric. Leubuscher accused Mitchel of essentially selling out to land speculators; Pleydell, on the other hand, felt a corporate income tax was unconscionable in light of the recent imposition of the federal excess profits tax. A few businessmen also argued that the tax should also be extended as well to enterprises that had been organized as partnerships or proprietorships. But this legislation was finally ratified on May 10 (*New York Times*, 1917a, 1917b, 1917c, 1917d, 1917e].

The new tax of three percent on net income was imposed on all but public service corporations. Based on extrapolations from federal tax data, it was estimated that $32 million would be raised, two-thirds of which represented the state's share. The remainder went to the municipalities, 70 percent of which was New York City's estimated share. Although during its first year (1918) only $13.5 million was actually raised, this total increased to $42.9 million by 1921 (*New York Times*, 1917b, 1917c].

CONCLUSION

What then does this experience tell us about the relationship between taxation and economic growth in New York during this period? What does this experience tell us about innovation and expertise in the public sector?

With respect to economic growth, the corporate income tax diversified further the sources of revenue both to the city and the state. It was particularly advantageous to the city's real estate interests. Besides reducing future state deficits that municipalities had to fund, the growing revenues of the corporate tax helped city leaders to slow the advance of real estate tax rates. During the course of the 1820s the city was able to maintain a tax rate of about 2.5 percent of full valuation. This achievement was remarkable in light of the massive expansion of property development and growth of governmental services during this period.

This reform represented a step forward in establishing a more efficient allocation of economic resources. The shift in the distribution of taxation's burden under this legislation reduced the inherent subsidization of corporate enterprises that had previously prevailed. This trend was later reinforced in 1919 by a new state tax on personal income (whose proceeds were also shared with local governments). Thus, the significant broadening of the revenue base in New York during these years helped to promote balanced economic growth by reducing the distortions associated with unequal tax burdens.

The revenues from the corporate income tax and other public revenue sources also had a multiplier effect on economic growth. The public financing of a physical infrastructure of streets, bridges, docks, water systems, and public buildings complemented a growing private investment both in transportation facilities especially subways and railroad and in commercial and residential real estate. In addition, the expansion of the city's physical capital contributed to the increase in financial wealth in the form of bank deposits, mortgages insurance policies and state and municipal obligations. Moreover, strong public finances also made possible the investment in human capital in the form of spending on education and social services. Education supported the growth of the city's growing service industries. These social services helped to maintain the well-being of the city's laboring classes during periodic downturns in the business cycle.

The promoters of tax innovation in New York were sensitive to the need to keep welfare and economic development goals in harmony. In this drive to build a kinder and gentler society Seligman and his cohorts endeavored to maintain the major sources of economic strength for the state and city. In this view the fruits of good governance were only achievable as long as the city and state continued to grow and prosper. The corporate income tax structure that Seligman worked diligently to advance helped to maintain this essential balance between public and private interests.

With respect to our second question, on the other hand, the application of new forms of special knowledge depended in large part on the ability of experts to serve as bridges between the worlds of theory and practical affairs. In this sense the advance of taxation was similar to contemporary patterns in such dynamic and diverse fields as biochemistry, electrical power generation, and urban planning. Changes came about through the actions of those individuals who straddled more than one field of complementary knowledge or those who could effectively transfer knowledge in resolving the problems that frustrated leaders in government or business. Seligman did both. His achievement was to inculcate into the thinking of practical men of affairs how the ideas of leading tax economists and lawyers could be applied in modifying the institutional structure of public finance [Galambos, 1983; Hughes, 1983; Kohler, 1982; McCraw, 1984].

The success of the corporate income tax innovation was helpful in advancing the careers of some of its key architects. Seligman's sagacity and tact as the city's representative to the Mills's committee won the confidence of key leaders both in the legislature and the state tax commission. He continued as an adviser to these bodies for the next two decades and played an important role in the federal debate over war taxes [Brownlee, 1990]. Ogden Mills, after distinguished war service became for a time U.S. senator for New York and later served as secretary of the treasury under President Herbert Hoover [Collins, 1958]. Mayor Mitchel's future, however, was less fortunate. After failing to be reelected in 1917 he went on active duty with the Army's Air Service and died in the following year in a tragic accident in Louisiana [Lewinson, 1965, pp 253-258].

The pace of tax innovation in New York was rapid. The social and economic changes transforming the state were outstripping the capabilities of the limited governmental structures inherited from the nineteenth century. The pressure for expanded bureaucratic support for education, transportation, welfare, defense, and the other aspects of government affairs required substantial increases in funding beyond the levels that traditional forms of public finance could provide. These pressures were so acute as to overcome the usual aversion of legislative leaders to pursue the politically unpopular course of mandating taxes.

Tax innovation was also integral to a fundamental reordering of the structure of government. The judiciary and the political parties which during the nineteenth century had been the primary focuses of government were giving way to new executive bureaucracies manned by experts with special skills necessary for more efficient social ordering in a polity whose elements were becoming progressively more complex and interdependent. As early as the 1880s, for instance, New York's leaders recognized that tax administration required the services of permanent functionaries knowledgeable in accounting, auditing, economics, statistics, and law. The reliance of the state on these cadres increased as the number of new taxes in force increased and their individual requirements became more complicated [Galambos, 1982, 1983; Skowronek, 1982].

This episode suggests that special knowledge provided only temporary advantages to competitors for political power. Although urban liberals and practitioners of the new expertise worked together to create attractive platform for reform, their grasp on the levers of political power in the state and city was tenuous. This was most apparent in the city. There many within its polyglot immigrant population lived too closely to the economic margins to heed the hopeful appeals of better situated middle-class leaders for greater efficiency in government and lower real estate taxes. These voters often were influenced more by the informal welfare provided by local machines. Moreover, these urban groups were also separated by their differences in values, religion, and world outlooks. It was because of these basic incompatibilities that urban liberals pursued their political objectives by forming alliances with the upstate machines in the state legislature rather than with either the aldermen or Board of Estimate.

Nor would it be accurate to imply that experts were always in the Progressive vanguard. The experts were just too eager to find profitable outlets for their specializations to allow political particularism to limit too severely potential opportunities [Miranti, 1988, 1990, pp. 189-191]. Seligman's subsequent experience illustrates this point. He worked diligently to help advance the personal income tax enacted in 1919 during the regime of Tammany candidate Alfred E. Smith and to play a leading role in recognizing the New York State Tax Commission for that same regime [Comstock, 1921, pp. 104-135; Seligman, 1919].

Experts and political leaders approached the problem of innovation differently. Generally once they were persuaded of its effectiveness the politicians were willing to implement new proposals faster than the more cautious experts. Seligman, for example, impressed by European patterns, contemplated a habitation tax as a transitional arrangement which would allow sufficient time to create the bureaucracies necessary to support an income tax. But the political leaders ultimately were not impressed by this approach and decided to follow the examples of the federal government and the state of Wisconsin that directly adopted this tax. Unlike Seligman, politicians like Mills and Mitchel recognized that the circumstances necessary to obtain legislation were fleeting. Because their continuance in office depended on their ability to resolve pressing public problems, they were more willing to bear the risk.

Seligman's scholarship also provided a bridge connecting knowledge of the past with expectations about the present and the future. His optimism about the potentials for the continued advance of expertise in public finance doubtless encouraged many contemporaries who believed in progress. Moreover, history served as the substrate for building up theoretical frameworks useful in confronting the perplexing problems of taxation in a society growing steadily more complex. Lastly, these patterns of thought served as the intellectual foundations for the establishment of new governmental institutions of value which served New Yorkers well in the years ahead.

NOTE

1. In 1894 Congress passed a personal income tax and a year later the Supreme Court in *Pollock* vs. *Farmer's Loan and Trust Company* [155 U.S. 429c (1895)] declared it unconstitutional. The Supreme Court generally held that this levy was unconstitutional since it failed to meet the constitution's requirement that a direct tax be apportioned based on population. After Pollock other income tax bills were introduced by southern and western congressmen in an attempt to have the Supreme Court reconsider Pollock. They were led by Democrats and a group of insurgent Republicans upset by high protective tariffs. While they felt that the tariff was important in developing American resources and offered protection from foreign competition they also argued that the price paid for manufactured goods should be cut by reducing duty on these goods. They saw the income tax as a means to reduce heavy reliance on the tariff and wanted to modify the incidence of taxation so that it would be borne by those with the most ability to pay. They were strongly opposed by conservative Republicans who controlled both the House and Senate. The regular Republicans, while not wanting either an income tax on individuals or corporations, agreed

to support a corporate "excise" tax which was enacted in 1909. The Supreme Court upheld its constitutionality in 1911 in *Flint* vs. *Stone Tracy Company* [220 U.S. 108 (1911)] because it was considered a tax on doing business in corporate form with income only being a base for determining the amount of tax. This compromise which led to a corporate income tax was attributable to President Taft, who preferred that states approve a constitutional amendment allowing an income tax rather than risk a Supreme Court confrontation over Pollock [Ratner, 1967, pp. 196, 207, 271-297; Witte, 1985, pp. 70-75].

From 1909 to 1913 amendment supporters fought for ratification [Witte, 1985, p. 75]. The battle was critical in New York because it was the nation's wealthiest state and the amendment's most prominent supporters and opponents participated in the debate. Republican Governor Charles Evans Hughes strongly opposed the amendment because it granted Congress the power to tax income "from whatever source derived" and thereby could lead to the federal government's taxing the income earned on state and local borrowings. Hughes concern was echoed by other opponents of the amendment but was questioned by its supporters, most notably Seligman. Seligman, whose book on the income tax was published at the height of this controversy, was recognized as the nation's foremost authority on income taxation [Buenker, 1985, pp. 255-264]. In testimony on 21 May 1911 before the State Assembly's Judiciary Committee Seligman voiced strong support for a federal income tax. In regard to Hugh's concern Seligman doubted that the federal government would tax the income earned on federal obligations. He felt that it was not unfair even if the federal government did so if all debt securities were taxed in the same manner. And in a revenue-sharing theme similar to that endorsed in the political compromise which led to New York's enactment of its corporate income tax Seligman asks, "Why should not the Federal Government in ordinary times be content with the right to levy an income tax and distribute the bulk of the proceeds among the States, keeping only a small fraction for itself" [*New York Times*, 1911, p. 12].

REFERENCES

Adams, H.C., *Public Debts: An Essay in the Science of Finance* [1887].

Adler, C., "Schiff, Jacob Henry," in D. Malone (ed.), *Dictionary of American Biography*, Vol. 8, Part 2 [Scribner's, 1975], pp. 430-432.

Adler, F., *Life and Destiny or Thoughts from the Ethical Lectures of Felix Adler* [1903].

————, *The Religion of Duty* [1905].

Albion, R.F., *The Rise of New York Port,1815-1860* [1939].

Barker, C.A., *Henry George* [1955].

Birmingham, S., *"Our Crowd": The Great Jewish Families of New York* [1967].

Brown, E.R., Letter from J.P. Mitchel (April 12, 1915a) in J.P. Mitchel Papers, Library of Congress.

————, Letter to J.P. Morgan (April 15, 1915b) in J.P. Mitchel Papers, Library of Congress.

Brownlee, W.E., "Progressivism and Economic Growth: The Wisconsin Income Tax 1911-1929" [1974].

————, "Economists and the Formation of the Modern Tax System in the United States: The World War I Crisis," in *The State and Economic Knowledge: The American and British Experiences*, M.O. Furner and B. Supple (eds.) [1990].

Buenker, J., *The Income Tax and the Progressive Era* [1985].

"Bullock, Charles Jesse," s.v. *National Cyclopedia of American Biography*, Vol. C [J.T. White & Co., 1930], pp. 104-105.

Burgess, J.W., *Reminiscences of an American Scholar: The Beginnings of Columbia University* [1934].

Callow, A.B., *The Tweed Ring* [1966].

Carosso, V.P., *Investment Banking in America: A history* [1970].

_____, *The Morgans: Private International Bankers* [1987].

Cerillo, A. Jr., "The Reform of Municipal Government in New York City: From Seth Low to John Purroy Mitchell," *The New-York Historical Society Quarterly*, 57 [1973], pp. 51-71.

Collins, E.H., "Mills, Ogden Livingston," in R.L. Schuyler and E.T. James (eds.), *Dictionary of American Biography*, Supp. 2, [Scribner's, 1958], pp. 459-460.

Commission on New Sources of City Revenue, *Report* ERA Seligman Papers, Columbia University [1913].

Committee on Taxation of New York City, *Minutes* [February 1914]. ERA Seligman Papers, Columbia University.

_____, *Minutes* [January 13, 1915a)]. ERA Seligman Papers, Columbia University.

_____, *Minutes* [January 27, 1915b)]. ERA Seligman Papers, Columbia University.

_____, *Minutes* [March 12, 1915c)]. ERA Seligman Papers, Columbia University.

_____, *Minutes* [July 13, 1915d)]. ERA Seligman Papers, Columbia University.

_____, *Minutes* [September 1, 1915e)]. ERA Seligman Papers, Columbia University.

_____, *Minutes* [December 13, 1915f)]. ERA Seligman Papers, Columbia University.

_____, "Memorandum Submitted to his Honor Mayor Mitchel by ERA Seligman, Chairman of the Executive Committee and the Mayor's Tax Committee." ERA Seligman Papers, Columbia University.

_____, *Report of Subcommittee to Prepare Answers to Questions in the Mayor's Letter of January 25, 1915*. ERA Seligman Papers.

_____, *Report of Majority Opinion* (April 2, 1915g) in ERA Seligman Papers, Columbia University, pp.1-8.

_____, *Report of Minority Opinion* (April 2, 1915h) in ERA Seligman Papers, Columbia University, pp. 1-7.

Comstock, A., *State Taxation of Personal Income* [1921, reprinted 1969].

_____, *Taxation in the Modern State* [1929].

Condit, C.W., *The Port of New York: A History of the Rail and Terminal System from the Grand Central Electrification to the Present* [1981].

Dahlberg, J.S., *The New York Bureau of Municipal Research: Pioneers in Government Administration* [1966].

Department of Commerce, *Financial Statistics of Cities 1912* [1913].

_____, *Statistical Abstracts of the United States 1913* [1914].

_____, *Financial Statistics of Cities 1915* [1916a].

_____, *Financial Statistics of States 1915* [1916b].

_____, *Financial Statistics of States 1916* [1917].

_____, *Wealth, Public Debt and Taxation 1922* [1924].

Dorfman, J., "Seligman, Edwin Robert Anderson," in R.L. Schuyler and E.T. James (eds.), *Dictionary of American Biography*, Supp. 2 [Scribner's, 1958], pp. 606-609.

Durand, E.D., *The Finances of New York City* [1898].

Eager, R.C., "Governing New York State: Republicans and Reform, 1894-1904." Ph.D. dissertation, Stanford University [1977].

Fairchild, F.R., "Adams, Thomas Sewell," in H.E. Starr (ed.), *Dictionary of American Biography*, Supp. 1 [Scribner's, 1944], pp. 9-10.

Felts, J., "Vice Reform as a Political Technique: The Committee of Fifteen in New York, 1900-1901," *New York History*, 54 [1973], pp. 24-51.

Furner, M.O., *Advocacy and Objectivity: A Crisis in the Professionalization of American Social Science, 1865-1905* [1975].

Galambos, L., *America at Middle Age: A New History of the United States in the Twentieth Century* [1982].

————, "Technology, Political Economy and Professionalization: Central Themes of the Organizational Synthesis," *Business History Review*, 57 [Winter 1983], pp. 471-493.

George, H., *Progress and Poverty: An Inquiry into the Cause of Industrial Depressions and of Increase of Want with Increase of Wealth: The Remedy* [1880].

Ghent, W.J., "DeLeon, Daniel," in A. Johnson and D. Mallone (eds.), *Dictionary of American Biography*, Vol. 3, Part 1, [Scribner's, 1930], pp. 222-224.

Golding, H.J., ed. *The Fiftieth Anniversary of the Ethical Movement 1876-1926* [1926].

Graybar, L.J., "Shaw, Albert" in J.A. Harraty and E.T. James (eds.), *Dictionary of American Biography*, Supp. 4 [Scribner's, 1974], pp. 738-739.

Hammack, D.C., *Power and Society: Greater New York at the Turn of the Century* [1982].

Harlow, A.F., "Morawetz, Victor," in R.L. Schuyler and E.T. James (eds.), *Dictionary of American Biography*, Supp. 2, [Scribner's 1958], pp. 470-471.

Hays, S.P., "The Upper Class Takes the Lead," in *The Progressive ERA: Major Issues of Interpretation*, ed. Arthur Mann, [1975], pp. 79-83.

Herman, H., *New York State and the Metropolitan Problem* [1963].

Herschowitz, L., *Tweed's New York: Another Look* [1977].

Howe, F.C., *The Confessions of a Reformer* [1925, Reprinted 1967].

Hoxie, R.G. et al. *A History of the Faculty of Political Science of Columbia University* [1955].

Hughes, T.P., *Networks of Power: Electrification in Western Society, 1880-1930* [1983].

Hunter, M.H., "The Development of Corporation Taxation in the State of New York." Ph.D. dissertation, Cornell University [1917].

Johnson, A., *Pioneer's Progress: An Autobiography* [1952].

Keynes, J.N., *The Scope and Method of Political Economy* [1987, 1990].

Kohler, M.J., "Seligman, Issac Newton," in D. Malone (ed.), *Dictionary of American Biography*, Vol. 8, Part 2, [Scribner's, 1935a], pp. 570-571.

————, "Seligman, Joseph," in D. Malone (ed.), *Dictionary of American Biography*, Vol. 8, Part 2 [Scribner's, 1935b], pp. 571-572.

Kohler, R.E., *From Medical Chemistry to Biochemistry: The Making of a Biochemical Discipline* [1982].

Leubuscher, F.C., Letter to J.P. Mitchel (July 17, 1913a) in J.P. Mitchel Papers, Library of Congress.

————, Letter to J.P. Mitchel (July 21, 1913b) in J.P. Mitchel Papers, Library of Congress.

————, Letter to J.P. Mitchel (July 29, 1913c) in J.P. Mitchel Papers, Library of Congress.

————, Letter to J.P. Mitchel (August 1, 1913d) in J.P. Mitchel Papers, Library of Congress.

Lewinson, E.R., *John Purroy Mitchel: Boy Mayor of New York* [1965].

Logan, A., "Whitman, Charles Seymour," in J.A. Garraty and E.T. James (eds.), *Dictionary of American Biography*, Supp. 4, [Scribner's, 1974], pp. 884-886.

Low, S., Letter to William A. Prendergast (July 2, 1915) in J.P. Mitchel Papers, Library of Congress.

McBain, H.L., Letter to George V. Mullan (September 7, 1915) in J.P. Mitchel Papers, Library of Congress.

McCraw, T.K., *Prophets of Regulation: Charles Francis Adams, Louis Brandeis, James M. Landis, Alfred E. Kahn* [1984].

McCormick, R.L., *From Realignment to Reform: Political Change in New York State1893-1910* [1981].

Mandelbaum, S.J., *Boss Tweed's New York* [1965].

Meriam, C.E. "Burgress, John William," in H.E. Starr (ed.), *Dictionary of American Biography*, Supp. 1 [Scribner's, 1944], pp. 132-134.

Mills, O.L., Letter from J.P. Mitchel (April 5, 1915) in J.P. Mitchel Papers, Library of Congress.

Miranti, P.J., Jr. "Professionalism and Nativism: The Competition for Professional Licensing in New York During the 1890s," *Social Science Quarterly*, 69 [June 1988], pp. 361-380.

_____, "The Mind's Eye of Reform: The ICC's Bureau of Statistics and Accounts and a Vision of Regulation, 1897-1940," *Business History Review*, 63 [1989], pp. 469-509.

_____, *Accountancy Comes of Age: The Development of An American Profession, 1886-1940* [1990].

Mitchel, J.P., Letter to J.H. Schiff (January 2, 1914) in J.P. Mitchel Papers, Library of Congress.

_____, Letter to Ogden L. Mills (April 5, 1915a) in ERA Seligman Papers, Columbia University.

_____, Letter to Alfred Marling (August 6, 1915b) in J.P. Mitchel Papers, Library of Congress.

_____, Letter to Alfred E. Marling (August 25, 1915c) in J.P. Mitchel Papers, Library of Congress.

_____, Letter from ERA Seligman (December 23, 1915d) in J.P. Mitchel Papers, Library of Congress.

_____, Letter to Newton D. Baker (June 14, 1917) in J.P. Mitchel Papers, Library of Congress.

Mitchell, B, "George, Henry," in A. Johnson and D. Malone (eds.), *Dictionary of American Biography*, Vol. 4, Part 1 [Scribner's, 1931], pp. 215-216.

Morris, R.B., "Mitchel, John Purroy," in D. Malone (ed.), *Dictionary of American Biography*, Vol. 7, Part 1 [Scribner's 1934], pp. 37-38.

Muzzey, D.S., *Ethics as a Religion* [1951].

National Industrial Conference Board, Inc. *State Income Taxes, Income Taxes, Volume I, Historical Development* [1930].

_____, *State and Local Taxation of Business Corporations* [1931].

New York State, *Annual Report of State Tax Commission-1924* [1925].

New York Times, [May 21, 1911]12:1.

_____, July 18, 1913a] 9:2.

_____, [November 9, 1913b]VIII:5.3.

_____, [December 29, 1913c] 6:7.

_____, [January 16, 1915aB11:3.

_____, [February 17, 1915b]6:2.

_____, [February 22, 1915c]4:3.

_____, [October 14, 1915d]9:2.

_____, [December 16, 1915e],10:3.

_____, [August 9, 1916a]5:1.

_____, [April 27, 1917a]17:2.

_____, [April 28, 1917b]14:3.

_____, [April 29, 1917c]I:14:1.

_____, [May 6, 1917d]IV;5:1.

_____, [May 11, 1917e]10:8.

Pleydell, A.C., Letter to ERA Seligman (April 12, 1915) in ERA Seligman Papers, Columbia University. ,

Prendergast, W.A., Letter to John Purroy Mitchel (September 4, 1914a) in J.P. Mitchel Papers, Library of Congress.

_____, Letter from Kuhn Loeb and Company and J.P. Morgan and Company (September 4, 1914b) in J.P. Mitchel Papers, Library of Congress.

Prescott, F.W., and Zimmerman, J.F., *The Politics of the Veto of Legislation in New York State*, 2 Vols. [1980]. .

Ratner, S., *Taxation and Democracy in America* [1942, 1967].

Ripley, W.Z., *Railroads: Rates and Regulation* [1912].

Ritchie, D.A., "The Gary Committee: Businessmen, Progressives and Unemployment in New York City 1914-1915," *The New-York Historical Society Quarterly*, 54 [1973], pp. 327-347.

Scharnhorst, G., *Horatio Alger, Jr.* [1980].

Scharnhorst, G., and J. Bales, *The Lost Life of Horatio Alger, Jr.* [1985].

Seligman, E.R., *Essays in Taxation* [1895, Revised 1931].

————, *The Shifting and Incidence of Taxation* [1899, Reprinted 1926].

————, *Progressive Taxation in Theory and Practice* [1908].

————, *The Income Tax: A Study of the History, Theory and Practice of Income Taxation at Home and Abroad* [1911].

————, "The New York State Income Tax," *Political Science Quarterly,* 34 [December 1919], pp. 521-545.

————, *The Shifting and Incidence of Taxation* [1899, 1926].

————, *Studies in Public Finance* [1925].

"Seligman, Edwin R.A.," s.v. *National Cyclopedia of American Biography,* Vol. 10 [J.T. White & Co., 1900], p. 49.

"Seligman, Edwin Robert Anderson,," s.v. in W.F. Mohr (ed.), *Who's Who in New York City and State-1914* [L.R. Hamersly Co., 1914], p. 644.

Shaw, W.B., "Adams, Henry Carter," in A.Johnson (ed.), *Dictionary of American Biography,* Vol. 1 [Scribner's, 1927], pp. 67-69.

Skowronek, S., *Building a New American State: The Expansion of National Administrative Capacities,* 1877-1920 [1982].

Sowers, D.B., *The Financial History of New York State From 1789 to 1912* [1914].

Strassman, W.P., *Risk and Technological Innovation: American Manufacturing Method during the Nineteenth Century* [1959].

Tanzer, L.A., *The Reminiscences of Laurence Arnold Tanzer,* Columbia University Oral History Project [1949].

Wallstein, L.M., "Mandatory Expenditures Not Reflected in the Budget and Miscellaneous Revenues Diverted from the General Fund, 1914," in J.P. Mitchel Papers, Library of Congress.

Weinstein, L., *Hippolyte Taine* [1972].

Weiss, M.A., "Richard T. Ely and the Contribution of Economic Research to National Housing Policy, 1920-1940," *Urban Studies,* 26 [1989], pp. 115-126.

Wesser, R.F., *Charles Evans Hughes: Politics and Reform in New York, 1905-1910* [1967].

Wiebe, R.H., *The Search for Order, 1877-1920* [1967].

Wilcox, D.F., "The Franchise Policy of New Municipal Program," in C.R. Woodruff (ed.), *A New Municipal Program* [1919], pp. 173-198.

Witte, J.F., *The Politics and Development of the Federal Income Tax* [1985].

Yearly, C.K., *The Money Machines: The Breakdown and Reform of Governmental and Party Finance in the North, 1860-1920* [1970].

Zimmerman, J.F., *The Government and Politics of New York State* [1981].

FORMAL CODES:

THE DELINEATION OF ETHICAL DILEMMAS

J.E. Harris and M.A. Reynolds

ABSTRACT

The inherent existence of ethical dilemmas within codes of conduct is revealed by extending the environmental perspective and the exchange theory of professions to professional codes of ethics. Evidence is developed relevant to four propositions by applying a three step investigative process to five codes of conduct. This examination demonstrates that: (1) codes of ethics contain inherent conflicts, (2) the elements in conflicts represent competing expectations about professional conduct by various interests, (3) these conflicts are common to a broad range of accounting professionals, and (4) the codes of conduct do not provide adequate guidelines for dilemma resolution. Guidelines for assigning priority to conflicting claims are proposed.

Given the current attention to ethical issues within the accounting profession, it is appropriate to consider the utility of formal codes of ethics. Although codes are intended to facilitate the resolution of ethical dilemmas, it will be assumed that codes also may magnify ethical dilemmas. This paper analyzes the codes of ethics peculiar to various organizations of professional accountants,

Advances in Public Interest Accounting, Volume 5, pages 107-120.
Copyright © 1993 by JAI Press Inc.
All rights of reproduction in any form reserved.
ISBN: 1-55938-496-4

identifies ethical dilemmas revealed by this analysis, and proposes guidelines for the resolution of these dilemmas.

This analysis of formal codes of ethics for professional accountants is guided by three critical questions:

1. What are the elements of each ethical code?
2. What dilemmas, if any, are inherent in these codes of ethics?
3. What guidance is applicable for resolving these dilemmas?

In seeking to answer these questions an environmental perspective is assumed. This involves the consideration of the expectations directed to individual accountants by various interests such as the professional organization, employer organization, client (public accounting), government, and society in general.

INTRODUCTION

Codes of ethics are a distinguishing characteristic of professions. Such codes appear to define the conduct expected of professionals. Newton [1982, p. 41] argues that "to be a profession is to have a professional ethic." The specification of desired conduct is so much a part of the concept of profession that codes of ethics are identified as a professional characteristic [Lambert and Lambert, 1979]. Toulmin [1977] emphasizes that it is the exclusive privilege accorded professions which creates the social responsibility for observing ethical standards of performance and conduct.

The motivation for codes of ethics is related to the function of professions in society [Newton, 1982; Luegenbiehl, 1983]. There are two schools of thought on the role of professions in society. The power theorist school contends professions form to exercise power over social territory in such a way as to benefit the profession. Accordingly, this school presupposes codes are unilaterally produced by professionals to enhance the power of the profession acting in its own interests. In contrast, the exchange school contends professions bargain with society for the right to perform unique functions requiring special education [Cullen, 1978]. Accordingly, this school presupposes that professionalism and codes of ethics are a bargain struck between society and professionals.

This paper assumes an exchange view that codes of ethics are bargains struck between professionals as a group and interests in the environment external to the profession. This assumption is consistent with the environmental perspective assumed by Pfeffer and Salancik [1978] and Dermer [1986] in examining organizational behavior. The argument for an external environmental perspective is based on the assertion that definitions of ethical conduct arises from interaction between professions and other interests in the environment. Whereas codes of ethics may be produced by a consensus of professionals, it is assumed that such consensus reflects a response to the interests of others.

The problematic in an exchange view that includes multiple environmental interests is that these interests will project conflicting claims. Because all conflicts will not be resolved, the presence of conflicting claims is unavoidable [Freedman, 1975]. Unless the professional code includes guidelines for assigning priority to conflicting claims, the resulting dilemma may be unsolvable within the structure of a code of ethics [Toulmin, 1977]. Not only are there external conflicts but there is also an inherent conflict between the actual profession and the ideal for the profession. The code itself can serve to evolve the profession closer to the ideal. However, in this case the divergence of foci of accounting professionals, that is, auditors, management accountants, governmental accountants, and so forth, make a broad professional ideal difficult to define.

The dilemma of conflicting demands falls on the individual professional. Codes of ethics by incorporating conflicting demands aggravate the dilemma, but provide no guidance for mediating the dilemma. Absent professional guidance, the professional is forced to apply his or her internal ethic in mediating the dilemma. Newton [1982] describes a fundamental dichotomy in professional ethics. She divides professional ethics into two categories: (1) internal ethics and (2) external ethics; thereby distinguishing personal ethics from professional ethics. She describes an internal ethic as being unique to the individual and characterizes it as, "more of a set of professional feelings than a set of examinable rules" [Newton, 1982, p. 45]. In contrast, an external profession-specific ethic results from a political process. Such an external ethic is represented by logically coherent sets of rules: codes of ethics.

It is our contention, that the incorporation of conflicting demands within codes of ethics, creates dilemmas for professionals forcing them to rely on an internal ethic to mediate the dilemmas. Both benefit and cost result to accounting professions from this process. A benefit and cost result to accounting professions from this process. A benefit is avoidance of the cost of negotiating the resolution of conflicting demands. A cost is the application of diverse internal ethics to the mediation of professional behavior.

In a general sense rather than a professional sense, Dewey [1891] discusses conduct (behavior) as being manners or customs that incorporate judgment. Ethics are not prescriptive. The ethical province is meant to, "detect the element of obligation in conduct, to examine conduct to see what gives it its worth" [Dewey, 1891, p. 1]. He further notes that each individual must develop ethical conduct out of respect for the societal whole. Davis [1900] elaborates this complex social relationship and provides a listing of the various systems to which these obligations apply. These systems are: man (the individual), family, community, state, and church. Subsumed under the rubric of community were applications of common law, contracts, capital, and labor issues. The state, so it was held, has regulatory and enforcement obligations. To promote the good of the whole, it was argued that ethical conduct was essential in interactions between these various interests. Professions, like individuals, are subject to the expectations of multiple interests, and must develop ethical conduct with respect to the environmental whole. It will be assumed in this paper that the professional codes project the expectations of known interests.

Professionals participate in various spheres or activity within society. These interests may have different functions and values resulting in a diversity of expectations being placed on professionals. Westra [1986] and Loeb [1978] discuss the conflict characteristic to accounting professionals from having to serve multiple interests. When these interests are sufficiently powerful, their values and expectations may be incorporated in codes of professional ethics. The incorporation into codes of ethics of conflicting expectations from powerful interests creates potential dilemmas for professionals.

Dilemma, as used in this paper, refers to the problem caused whenever multiple and conflicting expectations are supported within one and the same code of ethics. Dilemmas of this nature generate extreme internal conflict (i.e., stress) for the professional confronted by them because explicit demands are brought to bear upon the professional by the multiple interests. Such a dilemma is not a moral weakness, but rather a conflict caused by diverse interests seeking to influence the individual professional's conduct. Examples of those with interests in the accounting professions are: (1) the individual professional, (2) the employer organization, (3) the client (public accounting), (4) the government, and (5) the society. Among the interests listed only the individual has an internal ethic, while the remaining four interests have sociopolitically determined ethics. The profession itself and many other interests exist, but the five identified are adequate to investigate the nature of dilemmas inherent within codes of ethics applicable to professionals in the field of accounting.

One function of a professional code of ethics is to provide guidance for the resolution of ethical issues. Whenever these formal codes incorporate elements that reflect conflicting expectations, ethical dilemmas are rendered visible. The professional organization when originally drafting the code may have failed to recognize the potential of such dilemmas. When such a dilemma does arise, it may be addressed in the code by the provision of some explicit guideline or it may be ignored. In addition to providing guidance codes also define parameters. In this sense the codes may serve to limit ethical deliberation.

The purpose of this paper is to investigate the codes of ethics of professional accounting organizations to determine what kinds of dilemmas, if any, are inherent in them. Research is conducted in relationship to four specific propositions:

1. Codes may contain elements that are in conflict, or self-contradictory.
2. To the extent that a code incorporates elements that are in conflict, fundamental ethical dilemmas for a profession may arise.
3. The ethical dilemmas for a profession represent the divergent conduct expected of professionals by conflicting interests.
4. The conflict inherent in the ethical dilemmas of a profession is more than simply the conflict between internal (individual) and external ethics. Ethical dilemmas of a profession also represent conflict among interests and between the various interests and the accounting profession.

METHODOLOGY AND RESULTS

In order to examine these propositions, published codes of ethics were obtained from: the American Institute of CPAs (AICPA), the National Association of Accountants (NAA)[1], the Institute of Internal Auditors (IIA), the Government Finance Officers Association (GFOA), and the Financial Executives Institute (FEI). Using a three-step approach, three matrices were constructed as primary analytical tools.

Step 1

The first matrix (Table 1), lists professional organizations and elements (provisions) of the selected codes. Professional organizations are designated in columns and elements are designated in rows. The cells identify the presence of elements (rows) in the codes of respective professional organizations (columns). The elements in each code were identified by both authors working jointly. Each code was reviewed, and lists of distinct elements were prepared. Then, in repetitive fashion, each code was reviewed a second and third time to exact a complete and uniform classification. After listing all elements, two subsets of elements were identified. One subset consisted of elements that were common to most codes. Another subset of elements that were unique to some codes was identified. The presence or absence of elements helped to reveal the manner in which each of the professional organizations perceived the boundaries of ethics.

Results 1

The frequency table revealed a number of elements that commonly occurred in the codes. Three elements appeared in all of the five codes analyzed:

1. confidentiality,
2. no acts discreditable to the profession, and
3. competence.

Table 1. Code Elements

Code Elements	Organizations				
	AICPA	NAA	IIA	GFOA	FEI
Serve the public interest	x			x	
Integrity	x	x		x	x
Objectivity	x	x	x		x
Independence	x				
Due care	x		x		
Service scope	x				
Confidentiality	x	x	x	x	x
Contingent fees, commissions	x				
Acts discreditable	x	x	x	x	x
Advertising	x				
Form of practice	x				
Competence	x	x	x	x	x
Reporting					
1. Full disclosure		x	x	x	x
2. Respect the laws		x		x	x
3. Reporting responsibility		x		x	x
Honesty	x		x	x	x
Loyalty			x	x	
Conflict of interest	x		x	x	
No bribes			x		
Informed					
1. Observe professional standards	x	x	x	x	
2. Continuing education			x	x	x
Dignity			x		
Fairness					
1. Energy to office				x	
2. Respect colleagues				x	
3. Impartial				x	

Four of the five codes included elements relating to:

1. integrity,
2. objectivity,
3. full disclosure,
4. honesty, and
5. conformity to professional standards.

These eight elements taken together reflect core tenets of accountants' ethical codes.

The analysis of extant elements further revealed that public accountants (AICPA) and governmental accountants (GFOA) each perceived an additional unique dimension to ethics. Public accountants (AICPA) alone, included the elements of independence, service scope, advertising, form of practice, and contingent fees. Thus, public accountants (AICPA) perceive operational concerns, in addition to behavioral concerns, as being ethical issues. Only governmental accountants (GFOA) included personnel practices, rights of colleagues, and devotion to duty in the code. Hence, it is apparent that the governmental accountants (GFOA) perceive administrative trust issues as additional ethical concerns. Two elements unique to the internal auditors (IIA) were nonacceptance of gifts and maintenance of personal dignity.

Several elements emerge as being shared by only two codes. These elements include: service in the public interest (AICPA/GFOA), exercise of due care or diligence (AICPA/GFOA/IIA), and loyalty to employer (IIA/GFOA). These same three organizations are also the only ones that showed unique code elements.

Further analysis revealed that the absence of elements common to the other codes points to a commonality between NAA and FEI. This commonality may result from similar constraints characterizing the NAA and FEI. These two organizations have fewer divergent interests to satisfy than do the other accounting organizations undergoing consideration. Consequently, NAA and FEI responsibilities are more directed to the expectations of the employer organization than to the expectations of other interests. Differences in code elements may also reflect an audit versus nonaudit function as an activity of the professional accounting organization. For example, both the AICPA and the IIA (organizations that bear an audit responsibility) stressed exercise of due care and absence of conflict of interest, but omitted reporting responsibility. Thus it appears that the audit function requires certain virtues for its practice and may influence an accountant's perception of ethics.

Step 2

The second matrix (Table 2) lists professional organizations and attributes of professional codes. Professional organizations are designated in columns and code attributes are designated in rows. The empty cells illustrate the absence of some code attributes (rows) in the codes of the respective professional organizations (columns). The attributes listed include: source of code, premises, enforcement, conflict resolution and elements.

In the row labeled elements, the elements listed in the appropriate cell for each code were described as stated in the published codes. No attempt was made to interpret the text of each code. For every code analyzed, the membership of the professional organization was responsible for writing the code.

Table 2. Code Attributes

| Code | Organization | | | | |
Attributes	AICPA	NAA	IIA	GFOA	FEI
Source	x	x	x	x	x
Premises	x				
Enforcement	x		x		
Conflict resolution	x	x			
Elements	x	x	x	x	x

Results 2

The empty cells of the matrix are especially useful for revealing code attributes which although anticipated in fact turned out to be absent. Premises on which the codes are based are left unstated in the text. Enforcement is mentioned only in the audit directed codes of the AICPA and IIA. Enforcement provisions in these two codes emphasize that membership and compliance remains voluntary. The AICPA code lists peers, public opinion, and disciplinary proceeding as part of the enforcement mechanism. Both codes include enforcement as an attribute. The AICPA code refers to court settlements, and the IIA code to forfeiture of membership and certification. The other codes do not cover enforcement as an attribute associated with noncompliance.

Although one should be able to look to ethical codes for guidance pertaining to an ethical conflict, only two codes specifically provided guidance for conflict resolution. The AICPA code advises taking into consideration the public interest first, and relying on standards of personal integrity second. The NAA advises giving first consideration to organization policy bearing on resolution, second consideration to seeking counsel from succeeding hierarchical levels of management in the employer organization, and third, consideration to tendering a personal resignation. The NAA code also adds that even in the face of resignation, no external whistle blowing is sanctioned. In effect, both codes ultimately avoid assigning priority to the claims of conflicting interests, by pushing resolution down to the ethic of the individual professional.

Step 3

A third matrix (Table 3) was constructed to examine elements of the codes which are associated with various interests that result in dilemmas. Professional codes are designated in the columns, and interests are designated in the row. The cells identify different elements associated with conflicting interests (rows) by professional codes (columns). Interests are an extension of parties identified by Westra [1986] and Loeb [1978]. Elements were associated with interests by

Table 3.

Social Systems	Organizations				
	AICPA	*NAA*	*IIA*	*GFOA(1)*	*FEI*
Individual Organizational/Professional vs. Societal/Governmental	Service scope vs. Independence a no conflict of interest				
Commercial vs. Societal	Confidentiality vs. Full disclosure				
Organizational vs. Individual/Societal		Confidentiality vs. Reporting responsibility and disclosure			
Organizational vs. Organizational			(1) Loyalty vs. Objectivity and independent attitude		
			(2) Loyalty and confidentiality vs. Full disclosure		
Organizational vs. Societal				(1) Information management vs. Information issuance	Confidentiality vs. Full disclosure
				(2) Loyalty vs. Independence objectivity and public service	
Organizational/Governmental vs. Societal				Confidentiality vs. Full disclosure	
Organizational vs. Organizational/Societal					Policy formulation vs. Reporting responsibility

asking, which of the interests would have the strongest stake in the adoption of a given element. Interests considered included the following: individual professional, profession, employer organization, client (public accounting), government, and society. Analysis of this matrix shows the presence or absence of conflict. It also illustrates an interest may exert conflicting demands. For example, internal auditors appear to experience conflicting demands from different stakeholders within the employer organization: audit committee and operating divisions. Both stakeholder groups are external to the internal auditing profession. Such intra-organizational conflict may exist for other accounting professionals, but is explicit in the code of internal auditors.

Results 3

This analysis reveals five basic conflicts causing dilemmas. These are listed in Table 4. The conflicting interests which bring pressure to bear on accountants also create dilemmas. These dilemmas result from the incorporation of conflicting elements within codes.

These five elemental conflicts pose significant ethical dilemmas. The first of these dilemmas (service scope/independence) is unique to public accounting. The critical issue in this dilemma is how to balance the potential conflict between dependence created by receiving compensation for nonaudit services and the need for the auditor (CPA) to be independent in fact and appearance. This is a particularly complex dilemma because it involves the interaction of multiple interests. It is an intense dilemma, too, because the interests of the certified public accountant (CPA) as an individual and also as a professional are directly in conflict with the public demand for independence. In this instance, the profession becomes the direct locus for the conflict. There is pressure by the individual professional and by the organization in which the professional functions (CPA firm) to provide nonaudit services. Simultaneously there are conflicting pressures exerted by the government and by society, to restrict the provision of the services thereby enhancing independence.

Table 4.

Elementary Dilemmas		
1. Service scope	vs.	Independence
2. Confidentiality	vs.	Disclosure
3. Loyalty	vs.	Objectivity
4. Information management	vs.	Information issuance
5. Policy formation	vs.	Reporting responsibility

The remaining four dilemmas are more general, and the accountant is caught between the demands of competing interests. The dilemma between confidentiality and full disclosure appears in all five of the codes examined. Thus, this dilemma seems to be inherent in the accounting function. The accountant experiences this dilemma because pressures from two interests exert conflicting demands. Although the interest varies, the elements in this dilemma remain constant. Irrespective of the elements in a dilemma, conflict is created by one interest wishing to contain information, particularly negative information, and another interest seeking to obtain information, particularly negative information.

The third dilemma involves the balancing of organizational loyalty and objectivity. It is explicitly a concern for the IIA and the GFOA. It represents both intra-organizational and extra-organizational conflict.

The fourth and fifth dilemmas are closely related and will be discussed jointly. The issue of information management versus information issuance is noted explicitly in the GFOA code. This dilemma represents a conflict between employer organization and society. The core concern in this conflict is whether one who produces accounting information should have responsibility for independently selecting information to be distributed. This is the same core concern that emerges in the fifth dilemma between formulating policy and reporting responsibility. Here however, the critical concern is whether one who formulates policy should have responsibility in producing accounting information. The underlying concern in these two dilemmas is that the accounting information reported may be biased to support a specific policy.

PROPOSED PRIORITIES

In the absence of the formal consideration of ethical dilemma, one must question the adequacy of codes of ethics. If guidance about the resolution of an inherent dilemma is lacking, the profession, by default, "pushes down" the resolution to the individual. Although not adequately addressed in professional codes, the resolution of such dilemma requires that the accountant assign higher priority to the claims of one interest than another. Professional codes failing to provide such guidance merely define the boundaries of conduct while avoiding the reality of the ethical dilemma faced by professionals.

Three proposed priorities for resolving such dilemmas merit consideration. These are that it is the accountant's obligation to assign the highest value to:

1. the expectations of society, when the profession has accepted an exclusive societal privilege, because such conduct provides the strongest protection for maintaining the privilege;

2. the interest of those receiving information, rather than to those generating the information, because such conduct best protects the integrity of information flows; and
3. information receivers with the least direct access, because such conduct best provides information to those who are the most dependent on the accountant for information.

The first priority applies to certified public accountants because only they have an exclusive societal privilege, the right to sign audit opinions. The second and third priorities apply to all accounting professionals. An accountant conveys information to others who often have little or no interaction with the accountant. Consideration of the interests and needs of the users is a fundamental responsibility of accountants. Finally, it must be recognized that these priorities are ideals.

CONCLUSIONS

The three-step analysis process supports the interpretations as follows:

1. For accountants the utilization of information is at the core of conflicts creating dilemma.
2. Two interests may incorporate the same principle (element) with conflict arising in the larger environment as a consequence of the competing expectations of multiple interests.
3. The specific professional role the accountant performs may influence the nature of the ethical dilemma..
4. In the absence of professional code guidance, dilemma resolution is dependent on the internal ethic of the individual accountant who must assign priority to the claims of competing interests.

The content of information to be conveyed is at the core of professional accounting dilemmas. The function of the accountant is to provide information about the social activities of one or more interest to other interests in the environment. Given this function, it is inevitable that conflicting information transmittal demands are placed on accountants. As accountants are in the middle of these competing demands they may assume the role of mediators. Competing information demands are really demands for accountability. Who is accountable and to whom? Although the accountant is in a position central to mediating this conflict, guidance from the profession is often lacking.

The expectations of conflicting interests over information transmittal may create an ethical dilemma for professionals. The dilemma is significant because the expectations of each interest have been legitimized by their incorporation into a professional code of ethics. Thus, inherent dilemmas result.

The specific role of an accountant as a professional may influence the nature of such an inherent dilemma. The dilemma between independence and scope of services is unique to auditors (CPAs). This is a particularly complex dilemma. It involves (1) the interaction of multiple interests. In addition, the interests of the auditor (CPA) are in direct conflict with the societal demand for auditor independence. Society having granted auditors (CPAs) the exclusive right to issue audit opinions on financial statements, has a strong independence expectation. Four other dilemmas are common to all accountants regardless of their specific professional role. In these dilemmas, at least two interests are in conflict over the structuring of information by accountants.

In summary, five codes of conduct were examined. This examination demonstrated that: (1) the codes of ethics contain inherent conflicts, and (2) the elements in conflict represent competing expectations about professional conduct by various interests. Specific elements in conflict were identified as examples of inherent dilemmas. It was determined that: (1) most of these conflicts are common to a broad range of accounting professionals, and (2) that codes do not provide adequate guidelines for dilemma resolution. Consequently, guidelines for assigning priority to conflicting claims are proposed.

The strength of this paper is that it extends the environmental perspective and an exchange theory of professions to professional codes of ethics. The analysis is restricted to one activity, accounting, and is based on using formal codes of ethics of various accounting organizations to reveal concerns dominant to those organizations. The major weakness is the authors' reliance on their judgement to define the association of code elements with interests.

NOTE

1. The National Association of Accountants (NAA) recently has adopted the new name Institute of Management Accountants (IMA).

REFERENCES

"Blowing the Whistle on Accountancy," *Economist* [December 22, 1990], p. 15.

Cullen, J.B., *The Structure of Professionalism: A Quantitative Study* [A Petrocelli Book, 1978].

Davis, N.K., *Elements of Ethics* [Silver, Burdett, 1900].

Dermer, J.D. and Lucas, R.G., "The Illusion of Management Control," *Accounting, Organizations and Society*, 11, No. 6 [1986], pp. 471-482.

Dewey, J., *Outlines of a Critical Theory of Ethics* [Hillary House, Inc., 1891].

Fannin, W.R., and C.J. Hill, "Professional Ethics in a Competitive Environment," *Businesss Forum* [Summer 1988], pp. 4-7.

Freedman, M.H., *Lawyers' Ethics in an Adversary System* [Bobbs-Merrill, 1975].

Lambert, J.C., and S.J. Lambert, III, "The Evolution of Ethical Codes in Accounting," *Working Paper Series,* Vol. 2 [Academy of Accounting Historians, 1979], pp. 33-69.

Larson, M., *The Rise of Professionalism* [University of California Press, 1977].

Loeb, S., *Ethics in the Accounting Profession* [Wiley, 1978].

Luegenbiehl, H.C., "Codes of Ethics and the Moral Education of Engineers," *Business & Professional Ethics Journal* [Summer 1983], pp. 41-61.

Newton, L.H., "The Origins of Professionalism: Sociological Construction and Ethical Implications," *Business & Professional Ethics Journal* [Fall 1982], pp. 41-57.

Pfeffer, J., and G.R. Salancik, *The External Control of Organizations* [Harper & Row, 1979].

Toulmin, S., "The Meaning of Professionalism: Doctors' Ethic," in *Knowledge, Value and Belief,* edited by H.T. Englehardt, Jr. and D. Callahan [Hastings Center, 1977], pp. 254-278.

Westra, L.S., "Whose "Loyal Agent?" Toward an Ethic of Accountancy," *Journal of Business Ethics* [April 1986], pp. 119-128.

LANGUAGE AND GENDER:
THE PERVASIVENESS OF SEXISM
IN ACCOUNTING AND BUSINESS
PUBLICATIONS

Rita P. Hull and Donald W. Hicks

ABSTRACT

This paper examines the discriminatory impact of sexism in language both by exploring the origin of sexist language and by discussing its consequences for women. Within this framework, the paper reports the results of a survey of journal editors as well as a content analysis of accounting and selected business journals to determine policies and practices regarding nonsexist language in professional journals. Results of the study suggest that sexist language in professional journals is pervasive, possibly because journal editors are unreflective, insensitive, or unaware of the consequences of sexist language. This may reflect the pervasiveness of gender bias in our society and its many manifestations, including language and social discourse. Given the importance of language, recommendations for specific nonsexist guidelines, similar to those existing in other professions, are proposed. However, it is recognized that changes in attitudes

Advances in Public Interest Accounting, Volume 5, pages 121-143.
Copyright © 1993 by JAI Press Inc.
All rights of reproduction in any form reserved.
ISBN: 1-55938-496-4

occur slowly and that these changes will not occur as a result of linguistic reforms alone. Substantial challenges to other institutional structures that perpetuate inequalities are also imperative if the barriers that reinforce sexist thinking and practice are to be dislodged.

Since the passage of the Civil Rights Act of 1964, considerable gains have been made in eliminating blatant sex discrimination in the workplace. However, as Lehman has observed, "If equal opportunity in the accounting profession is measured by promotion, women have not been able to break the ideological and institutional barriers enabling them to reach upper level positions" [Lehman, 1990, p. 149]. Evidence exists that, while prejudice against women in the workforce may be diminishing, it has not been eliminated.

BACKGROUND

During the past two decades, considerable empirical research concerning sexism has emerged. In what is now considered a classic study, Goldberg [1968] asked female subjects to rate identical manuscripts. For each article, a female's name appeared on half the manuscripts and a male's name appeared on the other half. Results showed that the women rated a manuscript more favorably when they believed the author was a male. Goldberg concluded that the author's name prejudiced the women's judgment concerning the quality of the manuscript. Later extensions of this study included both male and female subjects [Paludi and Bauer, 1983] and an additional author with a sexually neutral name [Paludi and Strayer, 1985]. The results of these studies provided further support to the idea of prejudicial belief in male superiority.

Dayhoff [1983] manipulated linguistic factors in simulated newspaper articles about candidates for political office. The independent variables were sex of the candidate, the gender appropriateness of the elective office (e.g., sheriff, town clerk, or President of the League of Women Voters), and the degree of sexism of language (e.g., lady candidate, gal, and girl). Dayhoff found linguistic sexism affected the evaluation and perception of candidates for office depending on the sex of the candidate being evaluated and the gender appropriateness of the office being sought.

Lipton and Hershaft [1984] investigated the effects of sexist labeling by asking male and female subjects to evaluate an artist by viewing a series of paintings. Other variables, in addition to the sex of the subjects, were the sex of the artist and the status of the artist (e.g., man, guy, or person as opposed to woman, girl, or person). The findings were consistent with the other studies in demonstrating prejudice against women by both men and women. In addition, the study further supported the Dayhoff findings that language tends to reinforce and perpetuate sex stereotypes. For example, the neutral label *person* tended to upgrade the evaluation of the female artist in comparison to the *woman* or *girl* labels whereas the neutral label *person* tended to downgrade the male artist in comparison to the *man* or *guy* labels.

SEXISM AND ITS CONSEQUENCES FOR WOMEN

Sex differences are primarily the result of social pressures which socialize women and men into differing gender roles. Unfortunately, "society constructs male and female roles as different and unequal" [Coates, 1986, p. 160]. The sexual caste system which devalues women and their contributions is painfully apparent in the findings of the studies cited above.

Smith explains the prominence of sex as a focal point of social discrimination as follows: "From the moment of birth, genital anatomy is a cue for all sorts of discriminative beliefs, expectations and behaviors [1985, p. 22]. Smith further argues that this sexual subculture, created by a simple binary classification, ensures that gender identity hinges upon the masculine ideals of masculinity and femininity. The impact of this ideology is to misrepresent the nature and extent of sex differences and to foster the notion of male supremacy.

Why is it that one-half of the population is able to define the beliefs, attitudes, standards, values, and perceptions for the entire population? Sex-role dominance is the result of a long process of patriarchy which has existed for centuries and which is dependent upon the use of physical and economic power to maintain women in a subordinate role. "To obtain special privilege and to maintain a stigmatized group over which power is exerted, the movement of the 'inferior' person through time and space must be controlled" [Roberts, 1976, p. 15]. Hence, sex-role dominance is necessary so long as white males are unwilling to give up favored positions of power. As Bernard explains: "In a society where money means power, most of the money must come to the dominant group if it is to maintain the status quo" [1975, p. 239]. Sadly, women have been excluded from the power structure for so long their absence seems "natural" [Roberts, 1976, p. 42].

Some negative real-world consequences of this sexual caste system are that women are powerless in politics and government, discriminated against in law, and economically deprived. Men are paid more because work performed by men is deemed more important than work performed by women. "In a masculist society, poverty is a woman's problem" [Roberts, 1976, p. 34]. Women's disadvantaged position in the economy is reflected by the fact that men earn 90 percent of the world's wages and own 99 percent of the world's resources [Spender, 1985, p. 4].

Another consequence of sexism is that we perceive men as active achievers seeking career success as a major goal at the same time we view women primarily as wives, girlfriends, mothers, and daughters [Hall and Sandler, 1984, p. 3]. If social rejection is perceived as the consequence of role-violating behavior (i.e., becoming a professional in one of the fields usually reserved for males), some women may avoid seeking career success. Evidence to support this theory exists. Horner investigated achievement motivation and role-violating behavior in an interview study and concluded: "The attitude of male peers toward the appropriate role of women, which they apparently do not hesitate to express, appears to be the most significant factor in arousing the motive to avoid success [in these women]" [Horner, 1972, p. 65].

Patriarchy also causes human beings to accept male behavior as the norm and to expect and to perpetuate "dominant" communication styles from men, but "submissive" ones from women. Thus, "the language of apology belongs predominantly to the female. Women are always being sorry or asking pardon for something. Whether or not they are to blame for something is not the issue. Men also say "I'm sorry" or "excuse me" occasionally but it is a way of life for females [Key, 1975, p. 37].

The damaging effect on women of being viewed as subordinate is summarized by Ruth [1980, p. 96]:

> The patriarchal images of women ... all say that women as human beings are substandard: less intelligent; less moral; less competent; less able physically, psychologically, and spiritually; small of body, mind, and character; often bad or destructive.

> These other stereotypical images of women are destructive to us. In their positive aspects, impossible to meet; in their negative, deprecatory and ugly, they flourish in the minds of women, who are forced to live them. Functioning in large part as social norms, they have great power to direct attitudes and behavior, among the group stereotyped as well as in the larger community. The tragedy of the female stereotype is that it impels women not only to appear substandard, but to become substandard; it moves to form us into the loathed monster.

SEXISM IN THE LANGUAGE

"Every language reflects the prejudices of the society in which it evolved" [Miller and Swift, 1980, p. 3]. The existence of sexism in the English language is well documented. Linguist Ethel Strainchamps [1971] argues sex bias in language is one of the primary means by which sexism is manifested in our society. Sociologist Jessie Bernard asserts that "American-English not only is sexually denigrating of women but is also a vehicle for asserting male superiority" [1981, p. 377]. Linguists Thorne and Henley observe that "language helps enact and transmit every type of inequality, including that between the sexes; it is part of the 'micropolitical structure' that helps maintain the larger political-economic structure [1975, p. 15].

"Language not only reflects social structures but, more importantly, sometimes serves to perpetuate existing differences in power" [Frank, 1989, p. 109]. Language socializes people into perceptions and attitudes. By excluding, subordinating, or stereotyping women, language influences the way people perceive and evaluate women and, in turn, results in discriminatory attitudes.

The Invisible Woman

"An importance of words is their power to exclude. Man, mankind, and the family of man have made women feel left out" [Steinem, 1983, p. 157]. The use of *he, his, man,* or compounds using *man* (e.g., mankind) as generic words are primary examples of the invisibility of women in our language.

Male nouns used to refer to both sexes assume the equivalence of maleness with humanness. The use of the pronoun "he" both as specifically male and generically human results in a nonparallelism between the male and female pronoun. Commenting on this inequity in the language, Miller and Swift wrote:

> Those who have grown up with a language that tells them they are at the same time men and not men are faced with ambivalence—not about their sex, but about their status as human beings [1976, p. 37].

"The rationalization that 'man embraces woman' is a relatively recent one in the history of our language. It was a practice that was virtually unknown in the fifteenth century" [Spender, 1985, p. 147]. Prior to 1000 AD, the term *man* was used as a generic noun to denote the human species and the gender specific terms *wer* and *wif* were used to refer to males and females respectively [Smith, 1985, p. 49]. Eventually, the noun *man* assumed its modern function of performing the ambiguous semantic duty of referring to males only while, at the same time, retaining its original generic function.[1]

The use of masculine pronouns to refer to people in a general sense probably correlates with the dual usage of the meaning of the noun *man*. Until the 1800s, it was common practice to use *he or she* and singular *they* for indeterminable sex references. The prescriptive grammarians of the nineteenth century condemned these practices arguing that *he* should be used when the sex is unknown. Insisting on absolute adherence to this rule in the name of proper grammar, these male grammarians succeeded in obtaining passage of the 1850 Act of Parliament which legalized the use of *he* as a generic pronoun. This action, according to Spender, was the result of a "deliberate policy . . . consciously intended to promote the primacy of the male as a category [1985, p. 151].

Although many people are aware of the humanistic arguments against usage of male terms as gender-neutral terms, critics of language and gender research fail to realize the relationship of sexist language to discrimination and, therefore, tend to trivialize it as being unimportant relative to other issues. As Smith observed, "This kind of denial assumes that sexism must be active and deliberate in order to be considered unfair [1985, p. 179]. For this reason, it is important that more people become aware of the considerable research evidence substantiating the fact that "the masculine 'generic' does not really function as a generic" [Thorne, Kramarae, and Henley, 1983, p. 10].

Research Evidence

In their study, Schneider and Hacker [1973] asked college students to illustrate titles such as "political man" and "urban man" and found that so-called generic male nouns or pronouns are not gender-neutral at all; rather these supposedly neutral referents tend to elicit only male images by a majority of both sexes.

Martyna [1978] investigated the generic *he* when referring to sex-unspecified persons by asking students at Stanford University to complete sentence fragments. After examining the pronouns in the completed sentences, Martyna concluded that "he" is an ambiguous term which, rather than serving as a generic function, results in male-related imagery. Moulton, Robinson, and Elias studied the impact of male terms in a gender-neutral sense on college students and concluded "male terms sometimes fail to be gender-neutral and may therefore be a cause of sex bias [1978, p. 1032].

Observing that elementary and secondary science textbooks usually referred to cavemen or early men in discussions of human evolution, Harrison [1975] asked 503 junior high science students to draw pictures of early humans. Three forms of a survey, identical except for the terms referring to people, described specific situations. Survey I used the terms *man, men, mankind,* and *he.* Survey II used the terms *humans, people,* and *they.* Survey III used the terms *men and women* and *they.* Harrison found that an overwhelming majority of the students receiving Survey I were unable to conceptualize female images (and, therefore, female contributions to early civilization) when asked to draw pictures of early man.

Fiske [1985] investigated the manner in which language initiates or reinforces sex-role bias in children. Fiske found evidence to suggest that children, as early as age six or seven, respond to the pronoun *he* as a male referent rather than a generic *he.*[2]

Sexist Language—A Public Issue

Sexist language "includes any usage that unfairly delimits the aspirations or attributes of either sex [Nilsen et al., 1977, p. 182]. Although awareness of the link between sexism and language existed at least as far back as the late 1890s when Elizabeth Cady Stanton criticized the use of masculine generics in the Bible as a symbol of the oppression of women [Stanton cited in Moulton et al., 1978, p. 1032], it was not until the late 1960s when, spurred on by the women's movement, the inequality of our language became a public issue.[3]

One of the major objectives of The National Organization for Women (NOW), founded in 1966, was to achieve equality in the educational system. As a result, many women's organizations began to monitor language in educational literature and to pressure publishing houses to develop nonsexist educational materials. Further stimulus for eliminating sex-role stereotyping in educational institutions came from Title IX of the Educational Amendments of 1972, which outlawed sex discrimination in educational institutions receiving government funding, and the Women's Educational Equity Act of 1974, which, among other things, provided funding to develop gender-neutral educational materials.

In 1975, amendments to Title IX clarified public policy on the issue by mandating the removal of gender-discriminatory language in textbooks and other educational materials. During that same year, both the American Psychological Association and the National Council of Teachers of English published guidelines for nonsexist language. Since then many other professional organizations [e.g., American Press Women, 1976; Association for Education in Journalism, 1980; International Association of Business Communicators, 1982; and the Society of Automotive Engineers, 1984] and book publishers [e.g., John Wiley and Sons, Inc., 1977; Harper and Row, 1976] have adopted similar guidelines for nonsexist language.[4]

Despite the fact that these guidelines have been available for some time, continued evidence of gender bias has been reported in various communication media including magazine fiction [Lazar and Dier, 1978], introductory college textbooks [Bertilson et al., 1982], social work journals [Else and Sanford, 1987] and corporate annual reports [Kuiper, 1988].

PURPOSE OF STUDY

The accounting profession has stated the following commitment to nondiscrimination in Interpretation 501-2 of the *Code of Professional Conduct:*

> Discrimination based on race, color, religion, sex, age or national origin in hiring, promotion or salary practices is presumed to constitute an act discreditable to the profession in violation of Rule 501 [AICPA, 1992c, Vol. 2, p. 4831].

The Upward Mobility of Women Special Committee of The American Society of Certified Public Accountants acknowledged the negative effect that language may have on women in the committee's following recommendation:

> Employers should review and update their organization's written material to ensure that no sexist or gender references exist that might have a negative impact on female employees. Inappropriate use of gender references is discouraging and demotivating to female staff members [1988, p. 4].

However, the AICPA's apparent lack of sensitivity to the discriminatory impact of the use of masculine nouns and pronouns in professional literature may be found in the definitions sections of the Bylaws where it is stated: "masculine terms shall be understood to include the feminine" [AICPA, 1992a, p. 23]. As McConnell-Ginet argues in her essay [cited in Frank, 1989, p. 49], "A footnote explaining one's generic intentions does not suffice, since some readers will doubt the sincerity of that announcement and others will forget it." Thus, the unfortunate disclaimer in the Bylaws of the AICPA only serves to reinforce the concept of woman as a subspecies in the accounting profession

Based on the assumption that many members of the accounting profession may be unreflective, insensitive, or unaware of the discriminatory impact of certain unquestioned semantic customs, this study was motivated to determine to what extent, if any, sexist language exists in our journals. Specifically, the study investigates both the extent of gender bias in professional journals and the state of awareness among journal editors as to what constitutes sexist language. To accomplish these objectives, the authors performed a content analysis of professional journals and surveyed journal editors.

METHOD

Content Analysis

Target journals included accounting journals as well as selected business journals in which accountants frequently read and publish. These were identified by reference to a recent study listing nonacademic and academic journals in which accounting faculty publish [Milne and Vent, 1987] and another study reporting accounting educators' quality rankings of accounting and business journals [Hull and Wright, 1990].

Forty-five journals were common to both of the studies referred to earlier. From these 45 journals, a stratified random selection was accomplished by separating the selected journals into two groups—nonacademic and academic—and then statistically sampling 15 journals from each group. From each of these 30 journals,[5] four feature articles were randomly selected from the period July 1, 1988, through June 30, 1989. Using "Guidelines for Nonsexist

Use of Language" [APA, 1975] as a standard, a comprehensive content analysis for all forms of stylistic sexist language was performed for each of the 120 articles in the 30 journals.

APA guidelines are grouped into two broad categories: stylistic and substantive. The latter category is concerned with sex differences in research methodology and content (e.g., using subjects of one sex and generalizing results to all people or not reporting research results yielding sex differences). Only the stylistic guidelines were applied in this study because neither the content analysis nor the survey would necessarily reveal instances in the other category. While a comprehensive listing of specific forms of sexist usage is beyond the scope of this paper, some examples of sexist language, common to all of the guidelines mentioned previously, may be found in Appendix B.

The two forms of sexist language primarily identified in the sample were the use of the personal pronoun when the sex of the antecedent was unknown and the use of the generic male term to indicate homo sapiens. In other words, we found frequent usage of masculine pronouns to refer to accountants, managers, and business executives. We also found terms such as chairman, workman, manmade, grandfathered, manpower, workmanship, assemblyman, businessman, Scotsman, vestryman, middlemen, salesman, medicine men, and master of ceremonies. More than 37 percent of the articles in our sample (representing 11 of the academic and 13 of the professional journals) included at least one of these two forms of sexist language. The frequency count for all journals is summarized in Table 1.

As indicated in Table 1, six of the articles in academic journals and ten of the articles in professional journals were classified as sexist on the basis of one instance of sexist language. At the other end of the spectrum, one article contained 95 examples of masculine pronouns and nouns when referring to sex-unspecific persons.

In performing the analysis, sex-specific pronouns were not included as sexist language when they were appropriate (i.e., the sex of the referenced person was known). Also, we did not include generic nouns or pronouns in direct quotations. However, because there may be a difference of opinion as to whether inappropriate sex-specific references in quotes should be considered sexist without an accompanying *sic,* the number of articles in this category were recorded. Two instances were found in academic journals and four instances were found in professional journals.

Illustrations that arbitrarily assign roles to people on the basis of sex are also sexist. We found no evidence of this in our content analysis of academic journals, but then, illustrations are rarely used in academic journals. This type of gender bias was observed in one article in our sample of professional journals; an article on accounting and health care issues included several illustrations depicting all physicians as male and all nurses as female.

Table 1. Frequency Count of Sexist Nouns and Pronouns Identified In the 120 Sampled Articles*

Journal	0	1	2-5	6-10	11-25	26-50	More then 50
				*Number of Instances Observed per Article***			
Academic Journals							
1		1				1(47)	2(95,64)
2	1			1(6)	1(12)	1(31)	
3	1		2(3,4)	1(10)			
4	2	1	1(3)				
5	2	2					
6	3					1(47)	
7	3				1(12)		
8	3		1(4)				
9	3		1(2)				
10	3	1					
11	3	1					
12	4						
13	4						
14	4						
15	4						
Total	40	6	5	2	2	3	2
Professional Journals							
			3(2,2,3)			1(27)	
2	1		1(2)	1(7)		1(38)	
3	1	2		1(10)			
4	2	1					1(51)
5	2		1(3)		1(12)		
6	2	2					
7	2	2					
8	2	1	1(2)				
9	3			1(10)			
10	3		1(3)				
11	3		1(3)				
12	3	1					
13	3	1					
14	4						
15	4						
Total	35	10	8	3	1	2	1
Total all Journals	75	16	13	5	3	5	3

Notes: *Chi-square test revealed no significant differences between academic and professional journals at the .05 level.

**Numbers in parenthesis represent the actual number of instances in which sexist language was used in one article.

Table 2. Number of Sampled Articles in Which at Least One Instance of Sexist Language Was Observed

	Number	*Percent*
Accounting Journals		
Academic (*n = 36*]	13	36
Professional [*n = 36*]	18	50
Total	31	43
Business Journals		
Academic [*n = 24*]	7	29
Professional [*n = 24*]	7	29
Total	14	29

Note: *Both the academic and professional classifications included nine accounting and six business journals.

Because the sample included non-accounting journals, a chi-square test was used to determine whether the use of sexist language differed between business journals and accounting journals in the sample. Substantial, but not statistically significant, differences were found. Sexist language was more prevalent in accounting journals—and particularly in professional accounting journals— than in business journals. A summary of findings of sexist language when the sample is classified according to business and accounting journals may be found in Table 2.

Males were clearly more visible than females in the accounting and business journals. Eighty-six percent of the editors of academic journals and 67 percent of the editors of professional journals were males. In the 120 articles analyzed (many of which were coauthored), there were 144 male authors, 26 female authors, and 30 whose gender could not be determined by name alone.

Male pronouns were referred to 7.4 times as often as female pronouns. While the majority of these pronouns were gender specific, and, according to the guidelines used, not labeled sexist for purposes of this study, this ratio does serve to illustrate how the male sex continues to dominate the professional literature. In fact, it might be argued that, although it may be unintended, male omnipresence in our literature sends a subtle message to women that males have more opportunities in the profession.

The analysis also revealed some evidence of sensitivity to sexist language. Uses of plural pronouns or phrases such as *he or she, his or her,* or *husband and wife* to avoid masculine generics were observed. However, the convention of placing males first when both sexes are referenced is so deeply embedded in linguistic customs that not one instance of placing the female first (e.g., she or he) was found in the sample.

The use of the gender-neutral word *person* was common. Unfortunately, however, some inconsistencies were also noted. For example, sometimes

Table 3. Editorial and Review Boards by Gender

	Entirely Male	Entirely Female	Primarily Male	Primarily Female	About Even	N/A*	N/R**
Editorial Boards							
Total							
Number	17	0	39	3	3	5	1
Percent	25	—	57	4	4	7	1
Academic							
Number	12	0	20	2	0	2	1
Percent	32	—	54	5	—	5	3
Professional							
Number	5	0	19	1	3	3	0
Percent	16	—	61	3	10	10	—
Review Boards							
Total							
Number	5	0	33	1	12	14	3
Percent	7	—	49	1	18	21	4
Academic							
Number	3	0	24	0	7	2	1
Percent	8	—	65	—	19	5	3
Professional							
Number	2	0	9	1	5	12	2
Percent	7	—	29	3	16	39	6

Notes: *No editorial/review board.
**No response.

gender-neutral nouns or pronouns were used only to be subsequently referenced in the article by the generic word *he*.

The Survey

The authors also designed and pretested a questionnaire for the purpose of obtaining information about editorial policies and practices regarding the use of nonsexist language. This questionnaire was mailed to the editor of each of the 30 journals originally selected for content analysis; it was also mailed to the editors of 70 additional accounting and business journals selected from *The Author's Guide to Accounting and Financial Reporting Publications* [Vargo, 1988-1989]. This resulted in a total sample of 100 journals. (See Appendix C for the complete list.) Initially, 45 responses were received. Second requests were mailed one month later which brought the total number of responses to 68 for a 68 percent response rate.

There were two parts to the questionnaire. The first provided background information about both the journal and the individual responding to the questionnaire. The second part, consisting of a five-point Likert-type response scale, addressed the respondents' understanding of their journals' policies and practices regarding specific examples of sexist language.

Survey Results

Overall, 87 percent of the respondents were either editors or managing editors; 60 percent were male. Written editorial policies were reported by 91 percent of the respondents from academic journals and 57 percent of the respondents from professional journals. The same percentage of respondents (i.e., 91% from academic and 57% from professional journals) reported anonymous reviews of manuscripts.

The majority of both editorial and review boards were composed of men. In fact, as shown in Table 3, 82 percent of the editorial boards were composed of all or predominately all men whereas none of the editorial boards was entirely women and only 4 percent were predominately women.

All respondents indicated they published articles authored by both sexes. Most reported a higher frequency of articles by male authors. This response was usually followed with a written notation to the effect that men submitted more articles and/or constituted a greater proportion of the readership.

Table 4 lists condensed versions of the questions asking whether, in the respondents' opinion, actual practice permits the use of sexist language in their journals. Data received from the respondents are summarized, both by the type of journal and by the gender of the respondent, using means and standard deviations (in parentheses).

Discussion of Survey Results

The results of the survey seem to reinforce an observation made in the content analysis section. That is, there appears to be some evidence that editors attempt to be sensitive to sexist language (e.g., questions 1-3 and 8-10); however, responses to questions 4-7 and 11 suggest some confusion among respondents as to what constitutes sexist language. Responses to question 11, for example, suggest that a significant number believe if sexist language is used "only once" then it is not really sexist. Clearly, these respondents are unfamiliar with the guidelines for nonsexist writing which have been extant for several years.

Questions 12 and 13 dealt with situations not classified as sexist language in existing guidelines (and therefore not treated as such in this study) but which the authors believe should be avoided because such practices result in a domination of space by males which contributes to the invisibility of women in professional literature.

As shown in the first two columns of Table 4, statistical differences between respondents from professional and academic journals were found for questions 5, 6, 7, and 12. The last two columns in Table 4 show the results when analyzed

Table 4. Perceptions of Respondents Relating to Treatment
of Specific Sexist Language

		Mean Attitudinal Scores°				
		Professional	Academic	Both	Male	Female
1.	We review manuscripts to ensure that gender references that may have a negative impact are removed.	1.933 (.96)	1.750 (.92)	1.820 (.94)	1.850 (1.06)	1.777 (.74)
2.	We try to avoid sexism entirely.	1.866 (.92)	1.583 (.95)	1701 (.95)	1.725 (1.09)	1.666 (.67)
3.	Our process checks for statements presenting or implying a stereotyped image of any person or group or persons.	1.933 (1.00)	1.833 (.93)	1.865 (.96)	1.900 1.04)	1.814 (.82)
4.	Both sexes are represented in equal numbers in photos and illustrations.	2.321 (.92)	2.675 (1.00)	2.459 (.97)	2.655** (.99)	2.175** (.85)
5.	In photos and illustrations, we are careful not to assign roles to people on the basis of sex.	2.409** (.78)	2.916** (.92)	2.621 (.87)	2.863** (.92)	2.342** (.73)
6.	We avoid the use of generic pronouns when referring to nonspecific persons.	2.689*** (1.17)	2.194*** (1.27)	2.393 (1.25)	2.450 (1.38)	2.307 (1.03)
7.	We avoid gender-specific terminology such as mankind, chairman, etc.	2.566** (1.15)	2.000** (1.04)	2.287 (1.14)	2.307 (1.24)	2.259 (.97)
8.	We avoid sex stereotype phrases such as woman accountant.	1.533 (.72)	1.771 (1.04)	1.651 (.91)	1.641 (.97)	1.666 (.82)
9.	Last names, first names and titles are used consistently for both sexes.	1.333 (.54)	1.472 (.80)	1.402 (.69)	1.450 (.77)	1.333 (.54)
10.	We stry to avoid the terms "girl" and "boy" when referring to adults.	1.206 (.48)	1.232 (.43)	1.222 (.45)	1.162 (.37)	1.307 (.54)
11.	One generic "he" or "she" would be considered sexist language in our review.	3.071 (l.16)	2..914 (1.34)	3.00 (1.26)	2..950 (1.40)	3.083 (1.00)
12.	We try to avoid personal pronouns even when the sex of the antecedent is known.	3.857** (1.16)	3.300** (1.21)	3.570 (1.22)	3.333** (1.36)	3.940** (.83)
13.	When a pronoun referring to a nonspecific person is used in quotes, we note it with a "sic."	4.1333 (1.09)	3.843 (.97)	3.984 (1.03)	3.972 (1.05)	4.000 (1.00)

Notes: * Means (and Standard Deviations) based on a 5-point scale where 1 = strongly agree and 5 = strongly disagree; ** Significant at 5%; *** Significant at 10%.

by gender; this analysis shows significant differences between groups for questions 4, 5, and 12. Because further analysis indicated that two variables (i.e., the type of journal and the gender of the respondent) were not independent, they are discussed together.

Of the 68 respondents, 37 were from academic journals and 31 were from practitioner journals. Males accounted for 73 percent of those from academic journals and 45 percent of those from practitioner journals. Thus, the majority of respondents in the "academic" group were male and the majority in the "practitioner" group were female.

Questions 4 and 5 concerned illustrations and photographs. The difference between academic and professional journal responses is probably irrelevant since most academic journals do not use illustrations or photographs. However, detailed analysis showed these differences were not caused by journal affiliation but rather by the gender of the respondents. Whereas male respondents were primarily indifferent (neutral) regarding stereotyping in photos and illustrations, women respondents were more sensitive to illustrations that may be degrading to either sex.

The differences between affiliation groups observed in questions 6 and 7 suggest that academics are more willing to avoid masculine pronouns and nouns when referring to homo sapiens than practitioners. These differences were also observed in the content analysis as reported in Table 1. As indicated in the last two columns of Table 4, responses for these two questions did not differ much between male and female respondents.

Gender—not the type of journal—appears to explain the significant differences observed for questions 12. This question referred to the use of gender-specific pronouns when the sex of the antecedent is known. An analysis of the range of responses revealed a pattern of diversified views from male editors indicating no clear consensus on this question. Conversely, there was a much narrower range of responses from female editors who clearly believed it is unnecessary to avoid gender-specific pronouns.

Overall, the range of responses from women editors tended to be narrower e.g., 1-3 on questions 1, 2, 8, 9, and 10) than those from men editors who utilized the full 1-5 range for all questions except 9 (1-4) and 10 (1-2). These findings would suggest that women are somewhat more sensitive to avoiding sexist language than men. Unfortunately, however, the responses also suggest that many of the respondents—both male and female—are unaware of what constitutes sexist language.

CONCLUDING REMARKS

The authors are not suggesting that sexual inequality exists because of sexist language. Nor are we arguing that the eradication of sexist labeling would eliminate the injustices that exist in real life. At the same time, we agree with Lakoff that "linguistic imbalances are worthy of study because they bring into sharper focus real-world imbalances and inequities" (1975, p. 43). Our study clearly demonstrates both the pervasiveness of sexist language in journals in which accountants read and publish and the general insensitivity or unawareness of journal editors as to what constitutes sexist language.

Sexist language is a reflection of sexism in our society and is not, by any means, limited to the accounting profession. On the other hand, the fact that sex discrimination is embedded in our language is not justification for its continued usage in our professional literature. "Whether language merely reflects existing societal practices or contributes significantly to them, sexist language by its existence reinforces sexist thinking and practices" (Frank, 1989, p. 125). If women are to reach their full potential and men are to develop an image of women as equal, it seems we, as accountants, must pay closer attention to the findings of those in other disciplines who have conducted research on language and the sexes. In other words, we must rethink the effects of conventional models of language use in terms of its potential effect on women's careers.

Based upon this research several recommendations are offered. First, the accounting profession should adopt formal guidelines, similar to those which already exist in many other professions, establishing clear and equitable standards for nonsexist language. These guidelines should apply to all professional and academic literature and not be limited to professional journals.[6]

Second, more accountants, sensitive to sexist language, need to be appointed as journal editors or need to become members of editorial boards where they can delete sexist language in the editorial process and encourage editorial policies prohibiting its usage entirely. Perhaps the approach used by one editor, James McCroskey, could be used as an example. On the editor's page of *Human Communication Research,* McCroskey stipulated that manuscripts failing to use alternatives to masculine generics would not be accepted. Regarding this policy, Todd-Mancillas observes, that "during and since [McCroskey's] editorship, only articles have been published in HCR which, in fact, used alternatives to masculine generics" [Todd-Mancillas, 1981, p. 114].

Finally, educators must educate students as to the importance of using nonsexist language in both written and oral communication. By serving as role models and prohibiting the use of sexist language in the classroom, educators can have a strong impact on future language patterns.

Change is already occurring. The use of sexually discriminatory language is on the wane. We must work to speed the process. While linguistic reforms may not in themselves eliminate sexist conduct, liberating the language is one step toward greater equality. There is power in words. "The powerful of the earth, both male and female, are word merchants, and words are the base of their power" (Havens cited in Persing, 1977, p. 15).

APPENDIX A

Journals Selected for Content Analysis

Academic Journals

Accounting and Business Research
Decision Sciences
Financial Management
Journal of Accounting, Auditing and Finance
Journal of Accounting and Economics
Journal of Accounting Education
Journal of Accounting Research
Journal of Business
Journal of Business Research
Journal of Finance
Journal of Financial and Quantitative Analysis
National Tax Journal
The Accounting Historians Journal
The Accounting Review
The International Journal of Accounting

Professional Journals

Business Horizons
CPA Journal
Datamation
Financial Analysts Journal
Government Accountants Journal
Government Finance Review
Harvard Business Review
Journal of Accountancy
Journal of Corporate Taxation
Journal of Taxation
National Public Accountant
Tax Adviser
Taxation For Lawyers
The Tax Executive
The Woman CPA

APPENDIX B

Selected Stylistic Guidelines for Nonsexist Language

Avoid generic pronouns:

Incorrect	Correct
The average student is worried about his grades.	The average student is worried about grades.

Avoid terms such as man, mankind, the suffix -man, and other man compounds when referring to humans:

Incorrect	Correct
man or mankind	women and men, people
man-made	synthetic, manufactured
chairman	chair, coordinator, head
businessman	business manager

Use parallel language when referring to persons by sex:

Incorrect	Correct
men and ladies	men and women
man and wife	husband and wife

Refer to women and men equally:

Incorrect	Correct
Bob Cook and Mrs. Jones	Bob Cook and Mary Jones
Mr. Cook and Mary	Cook and Jones or Bob and Mary

Avoid patronizing or trivializing terms, nouns, adjectives, and suffixes:

Incorrect	Correct
Gal Friday	Assistant
libber	feminist
Faculty wives	Faculty spouses
the little lady	wife, partner
The girls (for females Over 18)	The women

Avoid Stereotypic terms:

Incorrect	Correct
The chimpanzees received mothering.	The chimpanzees received nurturance.
The emergency room must be manned at all times.	The emergency room must be staffed at all times.

Avoid unnessary sex qualifiers which demean the person described:

Incorrect	Correct
woman accountant	accountant
male nurse	nurse
lady doctor	doctor

Avoid sexist job titles. Different titles should not be used for the same job when it is held by both men and women.:

Incorrect	Correct
stewardess	flight attendant
seamstress	sewer, mender

Avoid the convention of always placing males first whenever reference is made to people of both sexes:

Incorrect	Correct Alternative
husband-wife team	wife-husband team
he/she	she/he

Avoid pictures or illustrations that stereotype either sex:

Incorrect	Correct Alternative
Illustrations depicting all accountants as men	Illustrations depicting both men and women as accountants
Illustrations depicting all secretaries as women	Illustrations depicting both men and women as secretaries

APPENDIX C

Journals Surveyed

Abacus
Accountancy
Accounting and Business Research
The Accounting Educators' Journal
The Accounting Historians Journal
Accounting, Organizations and Society
The Accounting Review
The Accounting Systems Journal
Advances in Accounting
Advances in International Accounting
Advances in Public Interest Accounting
Advances in Taxation
Akron Business and Economic Review

Auditing: A Journal of Practice and Theory
Behavioral Research in Accounting
Business
Business & Economic Review
Business & Professional Ethics Journal
Business and Society
Business Horizons
CA Magazine
CMA–The Management Accounting Magazine
The CPA Journal
Cashflow

Columbia Journal of World Business
Compensation Planning Journal
Computers in Accounting
Connecticut CPA
Contemporary Accounting Research
Datamation
Data Management
Decision Sciences
The EDP Auditor Journal
Estate Planning
Estates
Financial Analysts Journal
Financial Executive
Financial Management
The GAO Journal
Georgia Journal of Accounting
Government Accountants' Journal
Government Finance Review
Harvard Business Review
Internal Auditor
The International Journal of Accounting
International Journal of Government
    Auditing
International Tax Journal
Issues in Accounting Education
Journal of Accountancy
The Journal of Accounting, Auditing
    and Finance
Journal of Accounting and EDP
Journal of Accounting and Economics
Journal of Accounting Education
Journal of Accounting Literature
Journal of Accounting & Public Policy
Journal of Accounting Research
The Journal of the American Taxation
    Association
Journal of Applied Business Research
Journal of Business
Journal of Business Finance and
    Accounting
Journal of Business Forecasting:
    Methods and Systems
Journal of Business Research

The Journal of Corporate Taxation
The Journal of Cost Management
Journal of Economics and Business
Journal of Finance
Journal of Financial Economics
Journal of Financial and Quantative
    Analysis
Journal of Information Systems
Journal of International Business Studies
Journal of Petroleum Accounting
The Journal of Real Estate Taxation
Journal of State Taxation
Journal of Systems Management
Journal of Taxation
Kent/Bently Review
MIS Quarterly
Management Accounting
Management Science
Massachusetts CPA Review
Mergers and Acquisitions
Michigan CPA
National Public Accountant
National Tax Journal
The Ohio CPA Journal
Oil & Gas Quarterly
The Practical Accountant
Public Finance and Accountancy
Quarterly Journal of Business and
    Economics
The Review of Taxation of Individuals
The Southern Collegiate Accountant: A
    Research Annual
The Tax Adviser
The Tax Executive
The Tax Lawyer
Tax Management International Journal
Taxation for Accountants
Taxation for Lawyers
Taxes—The Tax Magazine
Trust and Estates—The Journal of
    Estate Planning and Administration
The Woman CPA

NOTES

1.   Spender argues that this evolutionary process occurred when women were denied access to education and not included in the production of grammatical rules [1985, p. 147].

2. Other studies reporting similar results include Bem and Bem [1973]; Kidd [1971], and Pincus and Pincus [1980].

3. For further reading on this topic, see Friedan [1963] and Deckard [1975].

4. All of these guidelines are quite specific regarding the avoidance of masculine nouns or pronouns in a gender-neutral sense.

5. A listing of these journals is included in Appendix A.

6. The Canadian Institute of Chartered Accountants and the Institute of Chartered Accountants of Ontario have revised their respective bylaws to provide for amending the language in all handbooks in the course of updating them to make them gender neutral.

REFERENCES

American Institute of Certified Public Accountants (AICPA), *Bylaws of The American Institute of Certified Public Accountants* [AICPA, as amended January 14, 1992a].

_____. *Code of Professional Conduct* [AICPA, January 14, 1992b].

_____ *Professional Standards* [AICPA, 1992c].

American Press Women, "Guidelines to Eliminate Sexism in the Media," *Press Women* [January 1976], p. 6.

American Psychological Association (APA), Task Force on Issues of Sexual Bias in Graduate Education, "Guidelines for Nonsexist Language," *American Psychologist* [June 1975], pp. 682-684.

Association for Education in Journalism, Public Service Committee, Theory and Methodology Division, *Guidelines for Journalists: Equal Treatment of the Sexes* [1980].

Bem, S., and D. Bem, "Does Sex-biased Job Advertising 'Aid and Abet' Sex Discrimination?" *Journal of Applied Social Psychology* [1973], pp. 6-18.

Bernard, J., *The Female World* [The Free Press, 1981].

Bernard, S., "Women's Economic Status: Some Clichés and Some Facts," in *Women: A Feminist Perspective,* edited by J. Freeman [1975].

Bertilson, H.S., D.K. Springer, and K.M. Fierke, "Underrepresentation of Female Referents as Pronouns, Examples, and Pictures in Introductory College Textbooks," *Psychological Reports,* 51 [1982], pp. 923-931.

Coates, J., *Women, Men and Language* [Longman Group UK Limited, 1986].

Dayhoff, S.A., "Sexist Language and Person Perception: Evaluation of Candidates from Newspaper Articles," *Sex Roles,* 9 [1983], pp. 527-539.

Deckard, B.S., *The Women's Movement: Political, Socioeconomic, and Psychological Issues* [Harper & Row, 1975].

Else, J.F., and M.J. Sanford, "Nonsexist Language in Social Work Journals: Not A Trivial Pursuit," *Social Work* [January-February 1987], pp. 52-59.

Fiske, W.R., "Responses to 'Neutral' Pronoun Representations and Development of Sex-biased Responding," *Development Psychology,* 21 [1985], pp. 481-485.

Frank, F., and P. Treichler, *Language, Gender, and Professional Writing: Theoretical Approaches and Guidelines for Non-sexist Usage* [The Modern Language Association of America, 1989].

Friedan, B., *The Feminine Mystique* [Dell, 1963].

Goldberg, P.A., "Are Women Prejudiced Against Women?" *Transaction* [April 1968], pp. 28-30.

Hall, R., and B. Sandler, *Out of The Classroom: A Chilly Campus Climate for Women* [Association of American Colleges, Project on the Status and Education of WOMEN, 1984].

Harper and Row Publishers, Inc., College Department, *Harper and Row Guidelines on Equal Treatment of the Sexes in Textbooks.* [1976].

Harrison, L., "Cro-Magnon Woman—In Eclipse," *The Science Teacher,* 42 [1975], pp. 8-11.

Horner, M., "The Motive to Avoid Success and Changing Aspirations of College Women," in J. Bardwick (ed.), *Readings on the Psychology of Women* [Harper & Row, 1972].

Hull, R., and G. Wright. "Faculty Perceptions of Journal Quality: An Update," *Accounting Horizons* [March 1990], pp. 77-98.

International Association of Business Communicators, *Without Bias: A Guidebook for Nondiscriminatory Communication* [Wiley, 1982].

Key, M.R., *Male/Female Language* [Scarecrow Press, 1975].

Kidd, V, "A Study of the Images Produced Through the Use of the Male Pronoun as the Generic, " *Moments in Contemporary Rhetoric and Communication* [1971], pp. 25-30.

Kuiper, S., "Gender Representation in Corporate Annual Reports and Perceptions of Corporate Climate," *The Journal of Business Communication* [Summer, 1988], pp. 87-94.

Lakoff, R. *Language and Woman's Place* [Harper & Row, 1975].

Lazar, C. and S. Dier, "The Labor Force in Fiction," *Journal of Communication, 28* [1978], pp. 174-182.

Lehman, C.R., "The Importance of Being Ernest: Gender Conflicts in Accounting," in *Advances in Public Interest Accounting,* Vol. 3, edited by M. Neimark [JAI Press, 1990], pp. 137-158.

Lipton, J.P., and A.M. Hershaft, " 'Girl,' 'Woman,' 'Guy,' 'Man': The Effects of Sexist Labeling," *Sex Roles* 10 [1984] pp. 183-194.

Martyna, W., "What Does 'He' Mean?" *Journal of Communication 28* [Winter, 1978], pp. 131-138.

Miller, C., and K. Swift, "One Small Step for Genkind," *New York Times Magazine,* 36 [April 16, 1976], pp. 99-101, 106.

_____. *The Handbook of Nonsexist Writing* [Lippincott and Crowell, 1980].

Milne, R.A. and G.A. Vent, "Publication Productivity: A Comparison of Accounting Faculty Members Promoted in 1981 and 1984," *Issues In Accounting Education* [Spring 1987], pp. 94-102.

Moulton, J., G. Robinson, and C. Elias, "Sex Bias in Language Use," *American Psychologist* [November 1978], pp. 1032-1036.

National Council of Teachers of English, *Guidelines for Non-sexist Use of Language in NCTE Publications* [NCTE, 1975].

Nilsen, A.P., H. Bosmajian, H.L. Gershuny, and J.P. Stanley, *Sexism and Language* [National Council of Teachers of English, 1977].

Paludi, M.A., and W.D. Bauer, "Goldberg Revisited: What's in An Author's Name?" *Sex Roles* 3 [1983], pp. 387-390.

Paludi, M.A., and L.A. Strayer, "What's In An Author's Name? Differential Evaluations of Performance as A Function of Author's Name," *Sex Roles,* 12 [1985], pp. 353-361.

Persing, B., "Sticks and Stones AND Words: Women in the Language," *Journal of Business Communications, 14* [1977], pp. 11-19.

Pincus, A.R.H., and R.E. Pincus, "Linguistic Sexism and Career Education," *Language Arts* [January 1980], pp. 70-76.

Roberts, J., *Beyond Intellectual Sexism: A New Woman, A New Reality* [David McKay Company, 1976].

Ruth, S., *Issues in Feminism* [Houghton Mifflin, 1980]

Schneider, J.W., and S.L. Hacker, "Sex Role Imagery and Use of The Generic 'Man' in Introductory Texts," *American Sociologist* [February 1973], pp. 12-18.

Smith, P.M., *Languages, The Sexes And Society* [Basil Blackwell, 1985].

Society of Automotive Engineers, Inc., *Communication Alternatives: Guidelines for the Use of Non-sexist Language"* [SAE, 1984].

Spender, D., *Man Made Language,* 2nd ed. [Routledge & Kegan Paul, 1985].

Steinem, G., "Words and Change," in *Outrageous Acts and Everyday Rebellions* [Holt, Rinehart and Winston, 1983].

Strainchamps, E., "Our Sexist Language," in *Woman in Sexist Society: Studies in Power and Powerlessness,* edited by V. Gornick and B.K. Moran [Basic Books, 1971].

Thorne, B., and N. Henley, *Language and Sex: Difference and Dominance* [Newbury House, 1975].

Thorne, B., C. Kramarae, and N. Henley, "Language, Gender and Society: Opening A Second Decade of Research," in *Language, Gender and Society* [Newbury House, 1983].

Todd-Mancillas, W.R., "Masculine Generics—Sexist Language: A Review of Literature and Implications For Speech Communication Professionals," *Communications Quarterly* [Spring 1981], pp. 107-115.

Vargo, R.J., and J. Agudelo, *The Author's Guide to Accounting And Financial Reporting Publications* [John Wiley & Sons, 1988].

John Wiley and Sons, Inc., College Editing Department, *Wiley Guidelines on Sexism in Language* [New York, 1977].

THE FRAUD-ON-THE-MARKET THEORY:

ITS LEGAL EVOLUTION AND IMPLICATIONS FOR AUDITING

H. Fenwick Huss, Ramona L. Paetzold, and
A. Faye Borthick

ABSTRACT

Judicial forces are rapidly changing the independent accountant's attestation environment. The emergence of the fraud-on-the-market theory has relaxed the burden of proof for plaintiffs seeking recovery under the Securities Exchange Act of 1934. Under this theory, auditors may be deemed liable to investors who may not have even seen the audited financial statements. This paper examines the evolution of the fraud-on-the-market theory, the 1988 Supreme Court decision that endorsed the theory, and the theory's recent application in accounting and auditing cases. Implications of the theory for the profession's public interest responsibility are discussed, and suggestions for rethinking accounting concepts and processes are made.

Advances in Public Interest Accounting, Volume 5, pages 145-157.
Copyright © 1993 by JAI Press Inc.
All rights of reproduction in any form reserved.
ISBN: 1-55938-496-4

Judicial developments are expanding the independent accountant's potential liability. These changes present an immediate challenge to the profession to rethink the audit process in light of the independent accountant's increased vulnerability from a larger set of potential plaintiffs. The impetus for the expanded liability is a new legal concept, the fraud-on-the-market theory, which "has been used to enable purchasers and sellers of securities who have never read, much less relied on, any financial statements audited by an accountant ... to sustain an action under section 10(b) and Rule 10b-5"[Craco and Cooper, 1987, p. 72].

The fraud-on-the-market theory holds that in an active, impersonal securities market, material misrepresentations and nondisclosure will defraud market traders even if the traders do not rely directly on the information. Already, the theory has contributed to a growing number of class action lawsuits against independent accountants. Moreover, in recognition of the possible effects of the theory on the profession, the American Institute of Certified Public Accountants (AICPA) and the largest accounting firms (the then Big Eight) have been active amici curiae even when accounting firms were not defendants. The continued adoption by the courts of the fraud-on-the market theory could dramatically extend the auditor's liability under federal securities laws.

This paper examines the fraud-on-the-market theory and its recent application in accounting cases. Implications for the profession are explored and suggestions are made for rethinking attestation concepts and processes. In order, we describe the evolving legal environment, discuss the implications for auditing, and state conclusions.

LEGAL ENVIRONMENT

The fraud-on-the-market theory assumes that markets are efficient. Accounting researchers have previously debated the potential effects of market efficiency on auditors' legal liability. For example, Anderson [1977] hypothesized that if common law courts took efficient markets research into account, the class of potential plaintiffs would grow. On the other hand, Largay and Paul [1983] argued that such expansion of liability under common law was unlikely but noted that market efficiency arguments had already been accepted by some courts applying the Securities and Exchange Act of 1934 [for the reply, see Anderson and St. Pierre, 1983].

Today, the effects of market efficiency arguments on legal reasoning are indeed most apparent in cases brought under the federal securities statutes. As previously indicated, the profession has been active as amicus curiae in fraud-on-the-market cases brought against accountants and other professionals under these statutes. To date, the profession's position has not been accepted by the courts. For example, the AICPA, in its amicus curiae brief, argued in the 1988 Supreme Court case *Basic Inc.* v. *Levinson* that the fraud-on-the-market theory is "bad law, bad logic, bad economic theory, and bad public policy" [Brief of the AICPA, 1986, p. 20]. Nevertheless, the Supreme Court adopted the fraud-on-the-market theory, and federal courts have continued to consider its general applicability. In these modern cases, the courts have recognized the changing nature of securities trading in established, impersonal markets where the price reflects available information, and have reevaluated how an investor can be "harmed" by information of which he or she is not even aware at the time of trading.

Fraud-on-the-Market Theory

Fraud-on-the-market cases have been brought under section 10(b) of the Securities and Exchange Act of 1934 as implemented by Rule 10b-5. Section 10(b) and the rule are generally considered to be "catch-all" provisions in the law, which were intentionally worded in the broadest possible terms to be all-inclusive [Huss and Leete, 1987]. Since no specific provisions are included in the section or the rule concerning when proceedings may be brought or by whom, the application of Rule 10b-5 to various market participants has been the result of judicial evolution.

The adoption of the fraud-on-the-market theory is a recent development in the evolution of Rule 10b-5's applicability. In cases alleging that the defendants' actions have caused damages, plaintiffs have traditionally been required to demonstrate knowledge of the information and actions based on it. Plaintiffs' demonstration of their direct reliance created the necessary connection between the defendant's behavior and the plaintiffs' injuries.

The direct reliance requirement was first relaxed in cases involving omission of material facts. In 1971 the U.S. Supreme Court held in *Affiliated Ute* that, when an obligation to disclose exists, nondisclosure of the material information establishes causation. Although the Supreme Court did not describe its position then in terms of a "presumption of reliance," the case was soon referred to as having established a presumption of reliance in nondisclosure cases.

Subsequently in several lower court cases involving material misrepresentations rather than omissions of material facts, the traditional direct reliance requirement was also relaxed. For example, a Ninth Circuit case, *Blackie* v. *Barrack* [1976, p. 906], determined that "causation is adequately established in the impersonal stock exchange context by proof of purchase and materiality of misrepresentations, without direct proof of reliance." The *Blackie* decision has often been cited as supporting a generalized fraud-on-the-market theory [Note, 1982]. The market participant should be able to rely on the integrity of the market and the processes that establish the market price.

Many cases have been filed against independent accountants in which recovery was sought based on the fraud-on-the-market theory. For example, in a Second Circuit case, *Panzirer* v. *Wolf* [1981], which preceded *Basic* by several years, the plaintiff did not see the allegedly false annual report issued by the corporation and audited by the accounting firm named as a defendant, but rather had purchased stock after reading a *Wall Street Journal* article. She claimed that the article would have described the company less favorably if the annual report had been correct. The court stated that a material misrepresentation or omission should be "presumed to affect the information 'heard on the street' that led Zelda Panzirer to make her losing investment" [*Panzirer* v. *Wolf*, 1981, p. 368].

Prior to the Supreme Court's 1988 *Basic* decision, some lower courts defined the right to rely on the integrity of the market more restrictively than others, and not all circuits accepted that a presumption of reliance was appropriate in misrepresentation cases, distinguishing them from the nondisclosure case of *Affiliated Ute*. The next sections describe the context of the *Basic* case, the accounting profession's arguments against the theory, and the Court's support for it, and post-*Basic* cases[1] against accountants and auditors.

Basic and the Presumption of Reliance

When the management of Basic, Inc. began merger negotiations, trading volume of the stock increased dramatically and the price of the stock rose. During negotiations, Basic either denied that any negotiations existed or issued "no corporate development" statements. After many months, Basic announced acceptance of a tender offer.

Basic stockholders who sold during the period of the merger negotiations and corporate denials sued the company. The plaintiffs claimed that stock prices were artificially depressed because of the false statements made by Basic management. Plaintiffs requested class certification, to include those who may not have heard the corporate denial, by invoking the presumption of reliance based on the fraud-on-the-market theory. The District Court granted, and the Court of Appeals affirmed, class certification on that basis. The Supreme Court granted certiorari to resolve, inter alia, whether the fraud-on-the-market theory could support a presumption of reliance for the purpose of class certification.

Briefs Filed by the Accounting Profession

Although independent accountants were not defendants in *Basic*, the accounting profession nevertheless recognized the importance of the Supreme Court's consideration of the fraud-on-the-market theory in material misrepresentation situations and the possible effects on the legal environment for independent accountants. Amicus curiae briefs were filed by both the AICPA and the then Big Eight (as a group).

A primary argument presented by the AICPA in its brief was that the earlier *Affiliated Ute* nondisclosure decision did not support the lower courts' position in a material misrepresentation such as *Basic*. The AICPA argued that the evidentiary problems justifying the presumption in nondisclosure cases do not exist in misrepresentation cases. The AICPA also argued that congressional intent based on a reading of the hearing reports does not support the relaxation of the reliance requirement. Finally, the AICPA in its amicus curiae brief maintained that "[t]he fraud-on-the-market theory is premised on a misunderstanding of how the financial markets function" [Brief of the AICPA, 1986, p. 19].

The Big Eight branded the fraud-on-the-market theory an investor insurance scheme [Brief Amici Curiae of Arthur Andersen et al., No. 86-279, 1986]. The AICPA questioned whether the theory is consistent with the efficient market hypothesis. And, in arguments similar to those of the AICPA, the Big Eight challenged the theory in light of their interpretation of Congressional intent in writing section 10(b), arguing that no recognition of market efficiency existed when the statute was enacted.

The Decision

The Supreme Court addressed whether the fraud-on-the-market theory could be the basis for a plaintiff invoking the presumption of reliance in material misrepresentation situations. In its decision the Court [*Basic*, quoting *Peil* v. *Speiser*, 1986, pp. 1160-1161] adopted the following description of the theory:

> Misleading statements will ... defraud purchasers of stock even if the purchasers do not directly rely on the misstatements.... The causal connection between the defendants' fraud and the plaintiffs' purchase of the stock in such a case is no less significant that in a case of direct reliance on misrepresentations.

The Court held that the presumption of reliance was appropriate and consistent with congressional intent in writing the securities laws. The Court, in accepting the fraud-on-the-market theory, noted [quoting *In re LTV Securities Litigation*, 1980, p. 143] that the trading markets today are very different from those of just a few decades ago when the securities laws were drafted:

> In face-to-face transactions, the inquiry into an investor's reliance upon information is into the subjective pricing of that information by that investor. With the presence of a market, the market is interposed between seller and buyer, and ideally, transmits information to the investor in the processed form of a market price.

POST-*BASIC* CASES AGAINST ACCOUNTANTS

Numerous cases involving the fraud-on-the-market theory have been filed against accountants since the 1988 *Basic* decision (e.g., *Cammer* v. *Bloom* [1989], *Freeman* v. *Laventhol & Horwath* [1990], *In re ZZZZ Best* [1990]).

In this section some of those cases are discussed. The major issues addressed by the courts in these cases include (1) rebutting the presumption of reliance, (2) trading contexts in which the presumption is logical, and (3) the possible extension of the theory to common law cases.

Rebutting the Presumption

The fraud-on-the-market theory creates a rebuttable presumption of reliance. The burden of rebutting the presumption is on the defendant accountant, who, to successfully rebut the presumption, must sever the "link between the alleged misrepresentation and either the price" received (or paid) by the plaintiff, or his decision to trade at a fair market price" [*Basic*, 1988, p. 248]. It is insufficient to rebut the presumption by merely alleging (1) the absence of actual reliance or (2) actual reliance on other specific sources of information.

For example, in a 1990 case, *In re Consolidated Capital Securities*, the federal district court denied Laventhol and Horwath's motion for summary judgment on the issue of reliance. Laventhol and Horwath claimed that an absence of actual reliance was in itself insufficient to rebut the presumption of reliance created by the fraud-on-the-market theory. In rejecting Laventhol and Horwath's motion, the court stated:

> In the present case, the only claim by Laventhol is that a number of the plaintiffs did not rely upon any statements or recommendations by Laventhol. As such, Laventhol asserts, they have successfully rebutted the presumption of a fraud-on-the-market theory.
>
> Laventhol apparently misunderstands both the nature of the presumption and the burden upon the party seeking to rebut the presumption.... Laventhol has not shown that other information was available in the market which counteracted the omission and/or misstatements by Laventhol [*In re Consolidated Capital Securities*, 1990, p. 96, 055].

In a decision in late 1990, Main Hurdman was unsuccessful in rebutting the presumption in a case [*Fine* v. *American Solar King*] in which the plaintiffs alleged that Main Hurdman had violated section 10(b) and Rule 10b-5 by issuing a materially false auditor's opinion. The district court had held that the fraud-on-the-market theory controlled the reliance issue. In granting summary judgment for Main Hurdman, the district court had also "found that Main Hurdman rebutted the presumption of reliance, ... because the deposition testimony, read as a whole, indicated that the named Plaintiffs did not rely on Main Hurdman's report ... " [Fine v. *American Solar King*, 1990, p. 298]. The Fifth Circuit reversed, stating [p. 299] that "misleading statements defraud purchasers of stock even if the purchasers do not rely directly on such misstatements." Main Hurdman argued that it rebutted the presumption by proving that the plaintiffs relied on other information with which Main Hurdman had no connection, but the court [p. 299] rejected this allegation:

Under the fraud on the market theory, however, the Plaintiffs did not need to show that they actually relied on Main Hurdman's report rather than on other materials. Main Hurdman had the burden of showing that the plaintiffs knew of the omitted or misstated facts, or that they would have traded at the same price had they known. They offered no such evidence. The evidenced upon which Main Hurdman relies demonstrates only that the plaintiffs had their own investment strategies and motives in purchasing the...stock.

Types of Markets Where Presumption Is Logical

The trading context in which the presumption of reliance is logical is an issue before several courts. For example, Peat Marwick Main & Co. filed a motion to dismiss a case, *Cammer* v. *Bloom* [1989], because the shares were not traded "actively in an 'open and developed' securities market, such as the New York or American Stock Exchanges," but were traded over-the-counter [p. 1264]. The court decided that the issue to be decided is not whether the whole market is efficient, but rather whether the market for a particular security is efficient. In denying Peat Marwick's motion for dismissal of the Rule 10b-5 claim, the court concluded:

> It is not logical to draw bright line tests—such as whether a company is listed on a national exchange or is entitled to register securities on SEC form S-3—to assist fact finders in determining whether a stock trades in an "open and efficient market." A well established and widely followed company may choose for any number of unrelated reasons not to list itself on a national exchange. Furthermore, there may be a company whose stock trades in an efficient market, but which just missed or recently failed to meet the qualifications for S-3 registrants [*Cammer* v. *Bloom*, 1989, p. 1287].

The Sixth Circuit Court of Appeals (where *Basic* was heard) examined a case, *Freeman* v. *Laventhol & Horwath*, in 1990 and concluded that the fraud on-the-market theory could not be extended to securities traded in inefficient markets. The specific question in the case was whether the primary market for newly issued tax-exempt municipal bonds is efficient. The court concluded that, as a matter of law, it is not. The court cited five factors that would be useful in proving that a security traded in an efficient market:

> (1) a large weekly trading volume; (2) the existence of a significant number of reports by securities analysts; (3) the existence of market makers and arbitrageurs in the security; (4) the eligibility of the company to file an S-3 Registration Statement; and (5) a history of immediate movement of the stock price caused by unexpected corporate events or financial releases [*Freeman* v. *Laventhol & Horwath*, 1990, p. 199].

Based on these criteria, the court concluded that "securities traded in national secondary markets such as the New York Stock Exchange, as was the case in *Basic* v. *Levinson*, are well suited for application of the fraud on the market theory" [p. 1991].

A complaint against Laventhol & Horwath, *Stinson* v. *Van Valley Development Corporation* [1989], was dismissed when the court determined that the plaintiffs had failed to show that securities were offered in an open and developed market. Although the plaintiffs alleged that the "bonds were publicly offered throughout the United States in a diverse market," the court explained that allegations must support an inference of a developed market, that is, a "secondary market with a relatively high level of trading activity and for which trading information such as price and volume were readily available" [*Stinson* v. *Van Valley*, 1989 p. 137]. The plaintiffs also argued that a "fraud-created-the-market" theory should be applied to their case, but the court rejected the argument, claiming that such a theory should apply only in a case involving theft or hoax, which had not been alleged.

In *In re Bexas County Health Facility Development Corporation* [1989], Laventhol and Horwath had prepared a financial feasibility study that was included in an official offering. Laventhol and Horwath argued that the fraud-on-the-market presumption could not apply since the mortgage revenue bonds involved were not traded in an open, developed market. Acknowledging a fraud-created-the-market theory, the court held narrowly that the plaintiffs had alleged sufficient facts entitling them to a presumption of reliance for the purpose of class certification. In *Longden* v. *Sunderman* [1990], Arthur Andersen's motion for summary judgment on the reliance issue was denied because of the fraud-created-the-market theory. According to the court, the theory required that the securities be "patently worthless" when sold. The investor is allowed to rely on the integrity of the market "to the extent that the securities [the market] offers to him for purchase are entitled to be in the market place" [*Longden* v. *Sunderman,* p. 979, citing *Shores* v. *Skilar*, 1981, pp. 470-471]. The court concluded that the plaintiffs had presented sufficient evidence that Arthur Andersen know that many of the projects were valueless from the beginning.

Fraud-on-the-Market and Common Law Cases

The fraud-on-the-market theory is generally limited to cases brought under federal securities statutes and is unavailable in common law cases (see, for example, *Keller* v. *E.F. Hutton* [1990], *Wolfson* v. *Ubile* [1990], *In re 3COM* [1990], *In re Wyse Technology* [1990]). In a recent decision in the U.S. District Court for the Northern District of California, in a case involving Laventhol & Horwath, the court stated [*In re Consolidated Capital*, 1990, p. 95,238]:

> In light of the judicial expansion and liberalization of the necessary elements of federal securities law, and the Supreme Court's repeated warning that this liberalization is uniquely applicable to federal securities claims, this court is hesitant to mechanically apply an important and unique concept found in federal securities litigation to state common law claims. Accordingly, plaintiff's request to apply the doctrines enunciated in the Supreme Court's decision of *Basic, Inc.* and *Affiliated Ute Citizens* and the Ninth Circuit decision of *Arthur Young* to the two common law claims is denied.

However, at least in California, the issue of the presumption of reliance in common law cases is unsettled. The U.S. District Court for the Central District of California, in *In re ZZZZ Best* [1990], rejected Ernst & Young's motion for summary judgment on the issue of whether the fraud-on-the-market theory could be substituted for actual reliance in common law fraud cases. The court stated [p. 95,416] that it "continued to abide by its previous stand...that the plaintiffs may plead fraud-on-the-market" or "reliance on the integrity of the market" to allege reliance.

POLICY IMPLICATIONS

The purpose of the federal securities laws was to restore and maintain investor confidence in the integrity of the securities markets. Section 10(b) and Rule 10b-5 were written using broad, general wording so as to cover a variety of market activities that change as trading mechanisms develop. The evolution of the applicability of Rule 10b-5—and the fraud-on-the-market theory in particular—suggests that in the future the courts will readily apply the rule to changing reporting and auditing environments.

The responsibility of independent auditors to help preserve the fairness of the securities markets is often underscored by the courts and other public policy makers. For example, in the *United States* v. *Arthur Young* [1984], the U.S. Supreme Court, in dicta, stated:

> [T]he independent auditor assumes a public responsibility transcending any employment relationship with the client. The independent public accountant performing this special function owes ultimate allegiance to the corporation's creditors and stockholders, as well as to the investing public [p. 817].

This now-famous quotation from the Supreme Court describes a somewhat vague concept of the independent auditor's "public responsibility." The fraud-on-the-market theory helps to clarify the profession's public responsibility.

The removal of the direct reliance requirement under the fraud-on-the-market theory underscores the accounting profession's *public* responsibility and suggests the importance of profession's attempts to close the "expectations gap" by meeting rather than trying to change society's expectations. In commenting on the expectations gap, Kaplan [1987, p. 8] noted that "[t]o rail against the public's misconceptions may be great fun, but when those misconceptions are consonant with the historical and statutory mission of the accountants' function, such a response is as self-defeating as it is delusional." The fraud-on-the-market theory suggests the need for the profession to adapt concepts and definitions to the changing environment. Rethinking concepts such as materiality in the context of the current legal environment seems an appropriate first step.

Materiality

The concept of materiality is crucial for both generally accepted accounting principles and for generally accepted auditing standards. By *SAS 47*, "[t]he auditor's consideration of materiality is a matter of professional judgment and is influenced by his perception of the needs of a *reasonable* person *who will rely* on the financial statements" [AICPA, 1983]. Recall that under the fraud-on-the-market theory, the plaintiff would not even be required to demonstrate *actual* reliance on any piece of information produced or examined by the auditor or accountant in order to recover money damages. Thus, the plaintiff also need not demonstrate that any reliance was *reasonable*. Given this environment, the independent accountant's enhanced vulnerability to users requires incorporation of a business risk component into an expanded notion of materiality judgments.

In the future, materiality judgments might be broadened so as to encompass nonfinancial factors relevant to audit planning such as the number of users, the extent of users' reliance (direct or indirect), audit sampling decisions, audit risk, and the consequences of auditor errors. This "macromateriality" concept should also entail a much broader view of audit risk than exists today. The aggregate of the potential losses (by direct or indirect users) would represent the auditor's Type II error losses. In this environment, the context of the auditor's decisions and the consequences of audit failure are very complex. The complex and competitive legal and business challenges that independent accountants will face in the future suggest that the guidance provided by existing standards such as *SAS 47* is, at best, limited.

The legal developments described earlier are especially critical in light of the effects of technology on the reporting environment and thus the audit function. The adoption of the fraud-on-the-market theory could dramatically extend the scope of the independent accountant's responsibilities to information users. As the attestation time shortens, the theory could extend the independent accountant's duties to all those market traders affected by an omission or misstatement. By recognizing the changing nature of the securities trading— from face-to-face transactions to an impersonal market—the judiciary accepted that buyers and sellers are affected through the market price by information omissions or misstatements, whether or not particular market participants actually relied on the disclosure. Seen in this light the shortcomings of existing audit risk models [see for example, Kinney, 1989] and risk containment procedures for accounting firms require immediate attention.

Risk Containment

Procedures to contain risks, such as in the selection and retention of clients, are of increasing importance in the changing and uncertain reporting environment. All possible sources of information—prior financial statements, personal knowledge of the client, prior auditor input, input from bankers, checks of management character—need to be evaluated before a firm bids on a prospective client or retains an existing one. More extensive codification of these procedures by the profession should (1) reduce the legal exposure of individual accounting firms and (2) raise the overall quality of attestation, thus maintaining the integrity of the securities markets--an obligation the law will not let the profession avoid. The fraud-on-the-market theory underscores the importance of the recent expectation gap standards [AICPA, 1988], especially those related to detection of fraud and illegal acts and the evaluation of internal control. And, in such a reporting environment, traditional disclosure and attestation concepts based on an individual user's actual reliance require reexamination.

CONCLUSIONS

Various theories of responsibility to information users have made the independent accountant vulnerable to more parties. While the *Basic* case pertained to merger negotiations, the effect of the decision on the accountant's legal environment is evident from several post-*Basic* cases against accountants. Several points are important for the accounting profession. First, the fraud-on-the-market theory has been endorsed by the Supreme Court in situations involving nondisclosure and misrepresentations. Second, the Court was not convinced by the profession's arguments that direct reliance is always a requisite for establishing causation between action and injury. Indeed, the direct reliance argument has been rejected in many accounting and auditing cases. The implications of this evolution in the law require the profession's attention since the accounting firms are viewed as "deep pocket," even though peripheral, defendants.

Could it be that the independent auditor's duty in the future will be presumed to include all possible users of real-time information disclosures? And, might users be defined to include those relying (1) directly on the information and (2) indirectly through the market mechanism? These are questions the profession ought to consider now since the legal system may be doing so soon.

NOTE

1.   See also the Brief of the AICPA, Supreme Court 86-279, at page 26 for a summary of cases filed against independent accountants before *Basic* in which recovery is sought based on the fraud-on-the-market theory.

REFERENCES

Affiliated Ute Citizens v. *United States,* 406 U.S. 128 [1971].

American Institute of Certified Public Accountants, [AICPA], Auditing Standards Board, Statement on Auditing Standards No. 47, *Audit Risk and Materiality in Conducting An Audit* [AICPA 1983].

————, Auditing Standards Board, Statements on Auditing Standards No. 53, *The Auditor's Responsibility to Detect and Report Errors and Irregularities,* No. 54, *Illegal Acts by Clients,* No. 55, *Consideration of the Internal Control Structure in a Financial Statement Audit* [AICPA, 1988].

Anderson, J. A., "The Potential Impact of Knowledge of Market Efficiency on the Legal Liability of Auditors," *The Accounting Review* [April 1977], pp. 417-426.

Anderson, J.A., and K.E. St. Pierre, "Market Efficiency and Legal Liability: A Reply," *The Accounting Review* [October 1983], pp. 833-836.

Basic Inc. v. *Levinson,* 485 U.S. 224 [1988].

Blackie v. *Barrack,* 524 F2d 891 [1975], cert. denied, 419 U.S. 816 [1976].

Brief of the American Institute of Certified Public Accountants as Amicus Cursiae in Support of the Petitioners in *Basic, Inc.* v. *Levinson,* Supreme Court of the United State, No. 86-279 [1986].

Brief Amici Curiae of Arthur Andersen & Co., Arthur Young & Company, Coopers & Lybrand, Deloitte, Haskins + Sells, Ernst & Whinney, Peat Marwick Main & Co., Price Waterhouse, and Touche Ross & Company in Support of Petitioners in *Basic, Inc.* v. *Levinson,* Supreme Court of the United States, No. 86-279[1986].

Cammer v. *Bloom,* 711 F. Supp. 1264 [D.N.J. 1989].

Craco, L. A., and D. E. Cooper, "The Institute as Amicus Curiae: The Key to the Courthouse," *Journal of Accountancy* [November 1987], pp. 70-74.

Fine v. *American Solar King.,* 919 F.2d 290 [5th Cir. 1990].

Freeman v. *Laventhol & Horwath,* 915 F.2d 193 [6th Cir. 1990].

Huss, H. F., and B. A. Leete, "Insider Trading Regulations: A Comparison of Judicial and Statutory Sanctions," *American Business Law Journal* [Summer 1987], pp. 301-322.

In re Bexas County Health Facility Development Corporation, 125 F.R.D. 625 [E.D. Pa. 1989].

In re 3COM, Fed. Sec. L. Rep. (CCH) P95,270 [N.D. Cal. 1990].

In re Consolidated Capital Securities, Fed Sec. L. Rep. P95,238 [N.D. Cal. 1990].

In re LTV Securities Litigation, 88 F.R.D. 134 [N.D. Tex. 1980].

In re Wyse Technology, Fed. Sec. L. Rep. (CCH) P95,509 [N.D. Cal. 1990].

In re ZZZZ Best, Fed. Sec. L. Repp. P95,416 [C.D.Cal. 1990].

Kaplan, R. L., "Accountants' Liability and Audit Failures: When the Umpire Strikes Out," *Journal of Accounting and Public Policy* [Spring 1987], pp. 1-8.

Keller v. *E.F. Hutton,* 558 So. 2d 144 [Fla. 1990].

Kinney, W. R., Jr., "Achieved Audit Risk and the Audit Outcome Space," *Auditing: A Journal of Practice and Theory,* 8 [Supplement, 1989], pp. 67-84.

Largay, J. A. III, and J. W. Paul, "Market Efficiency and the Legal Liability of Auditors: Comment," *The Accounting Review* [October 1983], pp. 820-832.

Longden v. *Sunderman,* 737 F. Supp. 968 [N.D. Tex. 1990].

Note, "The Fraud-on-the-Market Theory," *Harvard Law Review* 95 [1982], at p. 1148.

Panzirer v. *Wolf,* 663 F.2d 365 [2d Cir. 1981], vacated as moot sub nom., *Price Waterhouse* v. *Panzirer,* 459 U.S. 1027 [1982].

Peil v. *Speiser,* 806 F.2d, 1154, 3d Circuit [1986].

Shores v. *Siklar,* 647 F.2d 462 [5th Cir. 1981], cert. denied, 459 U.S. 1102 [1983].

Stinson v. *Van Valley Development Corporation,* 714 F. Supp. 132 [E.D. Pa. 1989].
United States v. *Arthur Young,* 465 U.S. 805 [1984].
Wolfson v. *Ubile,* 78 A.D. 2d 612, 432 N.Y.S.2d 393 [1990].

PUBLIC POLICY IMPLICATIONS OF THE EFFECTS OF TAX ACCOUNTING ON PUBLIC UTILITY RATE MAKING

Robert L. Peace and Al Y.S. Chen

ABSTRACT

Congress, through the Internal Revenue Code, encourages public utilities to use the normalization method of tax accounting for rate-making purposes. Normalization accounting generally increases the cost of service to utility customers by allowing a current charge for deferred federal income taxes. This cost increase is justified by the expectation that normalization will improve the financial health and integrity of companies in the industry. This paper attempts to evaluate the effect of normalization accounting on the financial attributes of electric utility companies. In a statistical analysis included herein, normalization accounting is compared with the flow through method of accounting, a method that allows the tax benefits of accelerated depreciation to flow through to ratepayers. The analysis examines the growth rate of revenues from residential customers, interest coverage, dividend payout, the market value of common stock and the price-to-earnings (PE) ratio of companies that changed from flow through to normalization during the period between 1973 and 1980. The results of the data analysis indicate no statistically significant improvement in financial data for companies adopting normalization within the test period, when compared to the improvement in the financial data of utilities that consistently normalized. This is troubling from a public policy standpoint because the expected results of normalization were not apparent from the data analyzed.

Advances in Public Interest Accounting, Volume 5, pages 159-178.
Copyright © 1993 by JAI Press Inc.
All rights of reproduction in any form reserved.
ISBN: 1-55938-496-4

INTRODUCTION

The electric utility industry operates within the jurisdiction of state and federal regulators. The objective of utility rate regulation is to establish reasonable rates to utility customers while providing a fair return to utility investors. This is a balancing act involving a distribution of wealth and resources between publicly owned utilities' customers and investors using accounting information [Neimark, 1990]. Accounting has public policy significance in this area of wealth distribution. Moreover, the effect of tax law on regulated accounting has particular importance as a determinant of resource allocation between large corporate utilities and society.

The Internal Revenue Code (IRC) denies public utilities the use of favorable tax depreciation methods unless the utilities use a normalization method of accounting for rate-making purposes.[1] That prescribed method of accounting for rate-making generally increases the cost of service to utility customers because customers are charged currently for an income tax liability that a utility is able to defer.

Utility regulators and Congress, through the IRC, have justified normalization accounting and consequently higher utility rates on the basis that utility companies will become more competitive in financial markets and develop greater financial integrity under normalization. In short, the conventional regulatory wisdom is that it is a benefit for consumers, in the long run, to pay more currently to assure the financial health of an important public industry. This justification raises public policy concerns: First, does normalization work as expected so that the additional cost to consumers improves the financial attributes of utilities? Second, does promoting capital accumulation through the tax law intrude on the role of state and federal regulatory agencies in their rate-making capacity? These issues were litigated in cases after the Tax Reform Act of 1969 and argued before the United States Supreme Court in 1973.[2]

The Supreme Court in *FPC* v. *Memphis Light* acknowledged the aim of regulators to promote financial integrity in utility companies in order to maintain their credit and to enable them to attract capital. In this 1973 decision the court also reversed an earlier opinion by the United States Court of Appeals, District of Columbia Circuit, written in 1972,[3] that held that the limited nature of the IRC election provision deprived the Federal Power Commission (FPC) of authority in regard to certain tax depreciation decisions regarding normalization. In the 1973 decision, the Supreme Court determined that the language of the IRC, on the normalization requirement, did not amount to a congressional deprivation of the authority of the Federal Power Commission.

In *FPC* v. *Memphis Light, Gas and Water Division, et al.,* the Supreme Court summarized prior court decisions and utility commission orders on the benefits or normalization. The summary mentioned rate stability for utility customers, improved before tax coverage of interest, the enhanced quality of utility securities, and public confidence in the financial integrity of the utilities to allow them to attract capital.

As a matter of law, therefore, the IRC does not deprive regulators of their discretion regarding the rate-making treatment of utilities' federal income tax costs. As a matter of fact, a majority of state commissions adopted normalization accounting for federal income taxes prior to 1981, to allow companies under their jurisdiction to use accelerated tax depreciation.

Critics of normalization accounting argue that a Federal mandate under the Internal Revenue code is an unnecessary intrusion into a matter better left to state regulators. This argument concludes that state regulators, entrusted to establish fair and reasonable rates balanced with the financial needs of the utilities in their jurisdictions, are better equipped to make rate policy decisions. This argument would exclude the Congress from rate-making policies [Foley, 1987].

In the period between 1969 and 1981 state and federal regulators allowed a majority of investor-owned electric utilities to adopt normalization accounting for rate purposes. However, some utilities were not allowed to adopt normalization. Consumer advocacy departments or commissions were created in this period within each state's utility commission or as an arm of the state attorney general's office. These new advocacy groups addressed the normalization issue, and were charged with the mission of advocating the consumer's position in rate hearings. Consumer advocates have been generally opposed to normalization accounting. But when the Internal Revenue Code introduced the Accelerated Cost Recovery System of tax depreciation in 1981 *all* of the investor-owned electric utilities adopted normalization.

This paper attempts to evaluate the influence of normalization accounting on the financial attributes of electric utility companies. In a statistical analysis included herein, normalization accounting is compared with the flow through method of accounting, a method that allows the tax benefits of accelerated depreciation to flow through to ratepayers.

The normalization/flow through consequences to investor-owned electric utilities is analyzed for utilities that have operated on both sides of the issue. The analysis measures the growth rate of revenues from residential customer rates, interest coverage, dividend payout growth, market value of common stock growth and price-to-earnings (PE) ratio of utilities that changed from flow through to normalization during the period between 1973 and 1980. Each of these financial factors is compared with the same factor in utilities that used normalization consistently throughout this test period. Companies changing from flow through to normalization are paired, in this paper, with comparable companies that normalized consistently. The pair matching was done on the basis of comparable net sales and similarity of the fuel sources used by both utilities in each pair.

The results of the data analysis indicate that there is no statistically significant improvement in financial data for companies adopting normalization within the test period, when compared to the improvement in the financial data of utilities that consistently normalized. This is troubling from a public policy standpoint. A legislated tax accounting method may substantively intrude on commission discretion and increase customer costs under the rationale that the accounting method will result in a public utility industry with enhanced financial integrity. The expected positive results of normalization were not apparent from the data analyzed in this paper.

BACKGROUND ON UTILITY RATE MAKING

A public utility's income tax expense is a cost of providing service to its ratepayers. There is a clear consensus that a just and reasonable rate charged to utility customers should cover a regulated public utility's costs, including income tax, and provide an adequate return on capital.[4]

The amount of federal income tax appropriately charged to a utility's customers has been an issue in rate hearings before State utility Commissions as well as the Federal Energy Regulatory Commission (FERC) which was previously the Federal Power Commission (FPC). At issue in these rate hearings was the accounting method used by a utility to determine tax expense for rate-making purposes. Since income taxes are a major cost of operating a regulated utility the accounting methods involved in calculating tax depreciation, for instance, complicate state utility regulation[5]

Utilities can elect to use accelerated depreciation methods or the straight-line method for federal income tax reporting purposes and for purposes of most state income tax report. Most utilities choose to accelerate tax depreciation and realize the consequent current tax savings. Most utilities will also depreciate plant and equipment using the straight-line method for financial reporting purposes and for calculating depreciation as a cost of service in a rate case [Hahne and Aliff, 1989, pp. 6-29].

The difference between income tax currently payable (using accelerated depreciation to determine taxable income) and income tax expense reflected on a utility's financial statements (assuming straight-line depreciation) is accounted for with a deferred tax expense accounting entry. Total tax expense is then a combination of current tax payable and deferred tax. Deferred tax is payable in the future when accelerated tax depreciation expires. A utility may charge the deferred tax expense to ratepayers as a cost of service, without making a current tax payment, in rate-making jurisdictions that allow tax normalization.

Normalization, as a rate-making concept, is designed to adjust a utility's operating expenses in a test year, by eliminating abnormal, nonannual events which are known and certain to change in a regularly recurring manner [Cawley and Kennard, 1983 pp. 150-153]. Normalizing tax benefits related to accelerated tax depreciation is intended, in theory, to spread the tax benefits from depreciation deductions ratably over the life of the asset being depreciated. As a result, the tax expense as a cost of service in the last year of depreciation should be the same of the tax expense in the first year the asset was depreciated. This would provide a comparable rate treatment of tax benefits from depreciation to a range of ratepayers being served by the utility over the life of an asset. In theory the taxes currently collected under normalization will also be used to minimize the requirement for outside capital.

The IRC encourages the adoption and use of normalization accounting, but the decision to allow normalization rests with federal and state utility commissions. Throughout the 1970s there was inconsistency among the states' regulatory commissions on normalizing taxes related to tax depreciation and other book/tax timing differences. The Asset Depreciation Range (ADR) System provided significantly accelerated tax depreciation for assets placed in service after December 31, 1970.[6] The ADR system's shortened tax depreciation lives, and the use of vintage accounts provided regulators with a discrete and identifiable accounting source of depreciation-related deferred taxes to evaluate for either normalization or flow through treatment. A majority of states' regulators opted to normalize the deferred taxes assignable to ADR depreciation, but some states flowed the current tax benefits, from ADR, through to ratepayers.

Income taxes collected from a utility's ratepayers but not remitted to the government are accumulated in a deferred tax account on the utility's balance sheet. The funds in the deferred tax account are available to the utility as working capital free of any charges for interest or dividends. As such, these funds are either eliminated from a utilities rate base or assigned a zero cost capital component status in the ratemaking process. Both of these options will result in a rate reduction that partially mitigates the deferred tax expense cost of a service rate increase [Hahne and Aliff, 1989, pp. 3-13].

It is useful to analyze the federal regulatory treatment of normalization in establishing background. The IRC of 1954 enacted Section 167 which introduced the use of accelerated depreciation for tax purposes. The FPC recognized the congressional goal of encouraging capital accumulation and industrial expansion, and initially allowed utility normalization of the tax benefits of rapid depreciation.[7] The FPC later decided, in the mid 1960s, that the power industry would expand faster in response to greater consumer demand created by lower rates. This lead to a commission decision to use taxes actually paid as a cost of service for rate-making purposes.[8] Normalization gained favour again with the introduction of the Asset Depreciation Range (ADR) System of tax depreciation in 1971.

THE INTERNAL REVENUE CODE
EVOLUTION ON NORMALIZATION

IRC section 167 generally prohibits a utility from claiming tax deductions for accelerated depreciation expense unless the utility normalizes the tax benefit of accelerated depreciation in excess of a straight-line depreciation. There are some exceptions to the general rule. As to utility property placed in service after 1969 (both post-1969 replacement property and post-1969 expansion property), accelerated tax depreciation may be used, and a state commission can direct the use of a flow through method of accounting, This treatment is available if the company was flowing through tax benefits to its customers, while taking accelerated depreciation on pre-1970 public utility property, on its latest federal income tax return filed before August 1, 1969.[9]

The exception for post-1969 expansion and replacement property permitted certain state commissions to insist on flow through accounting for tax benefits from depreciation without fear of the utility losing the ability to use accelerated depreciation for tax return filing purposes. Some states with this option chose to continue to use flow through on the tax benefits associated with the Asset Depreciation Range System (ADR) introduced as a part of the Revenue Act of 1971, while other states adopted normalization. During the 1970s the issue of flow through verses normalization was addressed in several FPC orders and in a number of court cases.

ARGUMENTS IN FAVOR OF NORMALIZATION

The financial well-being of an electric power or a gas utility is a public concern. The courts and the FPC or FERC have evaluated the normalization/flow through issue from a public interest perspective in developing a rationale for federal income tax normalization.

The U.S. Court of Appeals for the Fifth Circuit found that Congress expected accelerated depreciation to aid the expansion of industrial capacity and to assist modernization, resulting in economic growth, increased production, and a higher standard of living. [10] The court in *Alabama-Tennessee Natural Gas Co.* went on to cite congressional reports on Section 167 of the IRC, to the effect that the stated purpose of rapid depreciation is to increase working capital and to materially aid businesses in financing their expansions.[11]

In an earlier fifth circuit case the court of appeals emphasized that tax benefits are available to regulated companies to make it easier for them to compete with other industries seeking the investor's dollar and to earn a return that is adequate for exploration and development. The court specifically mentioned the tax benefits of rapid depreciation in this analysis. At the same time, the court noted that there is nothing in Section 167 that dictates treatment of depreciation to regulatory commissions.[12]

The issue of whether depreciation-related normalization involves a permanent tax saving or a true deferral has been argued on both side of the normalization/flow through issue. The FPC issued Order No. 530 on June 18, 1975, which prescribed regulatory accounting for deferred taxes.[13] This order was clarified by Order No. 530A on March 18, 1976.[14] The clarification was issued pursuant to applications arguing that, in Order No. 530, the commission did not require a utility to show that normalization was appropriate because taxes were to be deferred and not saved.

In response to the applications, the FPC cited a court of appeals decision to the effect that courts have required a finding that a tax deferral will occur rather than a permanent tax savings.[15] The FPC went on to state, "We of course would require a showing by the utility requesting normalization of a class of items covered by Order No. 530 ... that a tax deferral rather than a tax saving would occur and that tax normalization, with respect to the class of items, is therefore appropriate." Thus, prior to receiving normalized rate treatment with respect to a class of items, a showing of tax deferral must be made with respect to the class of items.

The FPC went on to state in Order No. 530A that mandatory normalization will benefit future ratepayers. This will occur at the time a crossover point is reached, when straight-line depreciation on an item exceeds the remaining tax depreciation available on an item subject to earlier accelerated depreciation. The order went on to mention, in this context, that normalization will offer a greater chance for rate stability for ratepayers over time.[16]

An additional argument favoring normalization was made, in Order No. 530A, on the basis of generally accepted accounting principles. A utility group supporting normalization cited Accounting Principles Board Opinion No. 11 to the effect that comprehensive interperiod tax allocation (deferred tax accounting) provides a better matching of revenue with expense and a less distorted view of an entity's income from period to period.[17]

A second application for rehearing of Order No. 530 resulted in Order No. 530B, an order revising prior orders. The commission had, in order 530A, accepted the requirement that a utility requesting normalization show that a tax deferral rather than a tax savings would occur.[18] In Order No. 530B, the commission announced its policy to permit normalization "upon a showing that the tax effect being normalized relates only to timing differences between book and tax differences."[19]

The commission, in Order No. 530 B, restates the reasons given in Order 530 for allowing normalization and stated that these reasons amply support the general policy of the commission.[20] The commission's statement of reasons was on P. 2127 of Order No. 530 *Supra.,* and follows:

The adoption of normalization of income taxes for rate purposes will contribute to the health of the electric and natural gas industries by increasing cash flow and by reducing internal financing requirements. In addition, normalization will contribute to the financial stability of companies and improve fixed charge coverages ... we believe that the cash flow which would result from the use of normalization for rate purposes would be a benefit and in the public interest.

ARGUMENTS AGAINST NORMALIZATION

The principle argument against normalization is founded in the rate-making doctrine that customers are to be charged for actual expenses. Ratepayer advocates testifying against normalization contend that, under normalization, consumers pay "phantom" taxes.[21] With the knowledge that their payments for service are not used to cover current tax charges to a utility using normalization accounting, consumers could lose confidence in the rate-making process. Under the flow through treatment of liberalized depreciation, ratepayers reimburse the utility for federal income taxes actually paid, and this puts flow through in accord with established principles consistently held by the Federal Power Commission.[22]

Flow through advocates argue that deferred taxes are not actual expenses and that normalized tax benefits are a utility company's permanent benefits. Unless tax benefits are passed on to the ratepayers, the utility will reap a permanent tax saving as long as the cost of assets subject to accelerated tax depreciation and tax deferral remain stable or increase. Assuming growth over time and normal asset replacements, current tax deferrals will continue to grow and exceed current tax liability attributable to the reversal of previously deferred taxes. This proposition is strengthened in periods of inflation when the costs of replacement assets increase, which in turn generates higher tax depreciation and new tax deferrals. Simply stated, as new and replacement assets are acquired, accelerated depreciation on such assets will continue to postpone tax lilability.[23]

Deferred tax liabilities are not subject to discounting under GAAP and as a consequence the magnitude and accuracy of deferred tax balance sheet provisions is controversial. Foley [1987] showed that deferred tax balances of the nation's major utility companies have routine, substantial increases of 20 percent per year on average. Foley further estimated that ratepayers have supplied more than $60 billion of interest-free funds to the nation's utilities over the period of three decades or so.

Other arguments include the point that normalization forces ratepayers to become involuntary investors. This is based on the fact that tax funds generated by normalization are available for any proper business purpose. Consumer advocates also point out that normalization may produce an inequity because the ratepayer who pays in the first part of an asset's life may not be the one who realizes the benefit of underpaying in the latter part of the asset's life.[24] An argument is also made that capital generated by tax normalization and accelerated depreciation encourages new construction and overbuilding of plant facilities. Conservation and other so-called soft path options may be a neglected alternative to construction when funds are available for expansion [Bradford, 1987].

The Tax Reform Act of 1986 reduced the maximum federal corporate income tax rate from 46 percent to 34 percent, effective July 1, 1987. The rate reduction created excess deferred tax reserves to the extent reserves provided at 46 percent can never totally reverse at a lower tax rate. The estimate of excess electric utility industry reserves at the end of 1986 is $9.3 billion [Keifer, 1987]. The Internal Revenue Code directs that excess reserves flow back to ratepayers, as a decrease in deferred tax expense, over a period equal to the remaining regulatory lives of the asset creating the excess reserve.[25] This is considered a favorable treatment for the utilities that retain these excess funds at no cost. This circumstance gives substance to the argument that normalization accounting is fraught with ambiguity and creates ample opportunities for excessive pricing by utilities [Tinker, 1985). Critics of normalization also point out that the extended flow back period under the Tax Reform Act of 1986, together with the time value of money, yield an expected return to ratepayers of about 50 cents on the dollar [Foley, 1987].

Proponents of normalization argue that there is equity in spreading tax benefits from depreciation evenly among ratepayers throughout the productive life of a utility's capital assets. Flow through advocates counter with the argument that normalization creates an intergenerational transfer of wealth from today's ratepayers, who should benefit from rapid tax depreciation, to future ratepayers [Tinker, 1985].

In summary, the theoretical battle on normalization/flow through was won by advocates of normalization so that the tax benefits of ACRS depreciation, and most other book/tax timing differences, have been normalized since 1981. The mix of treatment among the states in the 1970s provides an opportunity for a comparative study of the variables that would appear to be affected by the change from flow through to normalization. The effect of a change from flow through to normalization in a rate-making jurisdiction should be manifest in such theoretically dependent factors as increased revenue, interest coverage, dividend payout growth, growth in the market value of common stock and a healthy price-to-earnings ratio. Significant increase in these variables, as utilities switched from flow through to normalization, could be viewed as evidence that normalization promotes the financial integrity and stability of utilities. This postulate is tested in the following section.

RESEARCH METHOD

The analysis employs a repeated-measures design. Financial data were collected for firms before and after their adoption of normalization, after identifying those utilities that changed to normalization during the period 1973 through 1980, the test period. The National Association of Regulatory Utility Commission (NARUC) *Annual Report* for years 1973 through 1980 was used to identify depreciation-related deferred tax treatments for rate-making purposes in electric and combined electric utilities.

Because of lags in the rate-making process and the potential lag in investor response to the new accounting method, data from the year of change and the year following the change were excluded from the study. The study uses average values for the financial variables of the test firms over a pre-period, the three-year period before the adoption of normalization, and over a post-period, the three-year period after the adoption of normalization. Three-year mean measures of financial variables were used to mitigate the potential misleading effects of outliers.

The electric and combined gas and electric utilities employed in the study were subject to the following selection criteria:

1. Net sales, common stock dividends, interest expense, pretax income, year-end common stock closing price, year-end common shares outstanding, primary earnings per share excluding extraordinary items and standard industrial code (SIC) were available in *Compustat II* data base for during the pre- and post period.
2. Sales in Kilowatt-hour and revenue from sales of electricity to residential customers were available on the *Financial Statistics of Selected Electric Utilities* data base.
3. Net energy generated from steam, nuclear and other sources was available on the *Financial Statistics of Selected Electric Utilities* data base.

A total of 147 pure electric and combined gas and electric utilities in *Compustat II* met these criteria. As might be expected, other factors besides income tax normalization could cause changes in utilities' financial status. For example, economic cycles and the oil embargo may have caused utility rates to fluctuate between the pre- and post-periods. Environmental protection concerns and the regulatory climate after the Three-Mile Island nuclear accident may have delayed new plant investments and rate increases. In order to control for the effects of extraneous factors such as changes in the economy and the regulatory environment, a pair-marching process based on utilities' size and power generation sources was adopted for this study.

Electric utilities were divided into two groups, those that changed from flow through to normalization in the test period (the test-utility group) and those that consistently normalized during the test period (the control-utility group). Test utilities were paired with control-utilities by using most comparable net sales in dollars and the mix of energy sources (i.e, steam nuclear, and others). The pair matching process ultimately yielded 38 sample firms (19 pairs). Table 1 lists the matched pairs of utility firms. Candidate utilities were removed from the study because of missing data and/or no-match. Table 2 presents the distribution by state of test-utilities and control-utilities.

Table 1.   Matched-Pair Sample Utilitity Firms

Pair No.	Test Utility Firm	Control Utility Firm
1	Cleveland Electric	Gulf State Utilities Co.
2	Cincinnati Gas & Light	Florida Progress Corp.
3	DPL Inc.	Duquesne Light Co.
4	Ohio Edison Co.	Pennsylvania Power & Light
5	IPALCO Enterprises Inc.	Public Service Co. of New Mexico
6	NIPSCO Industries Inc.	Long Island Lighting
7	PSI Holdings Inc.	New York State Electric and Gas
8	Southern Indiana Gas & Electric	Nevada Power Co.
9	Pinnacle West Capital Corp.	Oklahoma Gas & Electric
10	Potomac Electric Power	Illinois Power Co.
11	Public Service Co. of Colorado	Union Electric Co.
12	Tucson Electric Power Co.	Kansas Gas & Electric
13	Black Hills Corp.	St. Joseph Light & Power
14	Northwestern Public Service Co.	Empire District Electric Co.
15	Pacific Gas & Electric	Niagara Mohawk Power
16	Southern California Edison Co.	Public Service Enterprise GP
17	San Diego Gas & Electric	Northern States Power-Minnesota
18	SCANA Corp.	Wisconsin Energy Corp.
19	United Illuminating Co.	Central Hudson Gas & Electric

Table 2.   State Membership of Sample Firms

Panel 1

State	Number of Test Firms	Change in Deferred Tax Accounting for Rate Making Purposes
Arizona	2	Stopped flow-through in 1976
California	3	Stopped flow-through in 1981
Colorado	1	Stopped flow-through in 1976
Connecticut	1	Stopped flow-through in 1981
District of Columbia	1	Stopped flow-through in 1976
Indiana	4	Stopped flow-through in 1978
Ohio	4	Stopped flow-through in 1978
South Carolina	1	Stopped flow-through in 1981
South Dakota	2	Stopped flow-through in 1981

Panel 2

State	Number of Control Firms	Note
Florida	1	Control firms used
Illinois	2	normalization consistently
Kansas	1	throughout the test period.
Louisiana	1	
Minnesota	1	
Missouri	1	
Nevada	1	

(Continued)

Table 2. (Continued)

New Jersey	2
New Mexico	1
New York	4
Oklahoma	1
Pennsylvania	2
Wisconsin	1

Table 3. Financial Variables of Pairwise Comparisons
Between Test and Control Utility Firms

Financial Variable	Definition/Formula
Revenue Growth Rate (GW)	Growth in the utility's Net Sales ($SALES$): $$\frac{\text{Net Sales}_t}{\text{Net Sales}_{t-1}}$$
Interest Coverage (CVR)	Measure of the relationship between interest (CVR) expenses and the earnings available to meet such expenses: $$\frac{\text{Interest Expenses}_t + \text{Pretax Income}_t}{\text{Interest Expenses}_t}$$
Dividend Payout Growth Rate (DIV)	Growth in the total dollar amount of dividends (DIV) (other than stock dividends) declared on the common stock of the company during the year: $$\frac{\text{Common Stock Cash Dividends}_t}{\text{Common Stock Cash Dividends}_{t-1}}$$
Market Value of Common Equity Growth Rate (MKV)	Growth in the market value of common equity: $$\frac{(\text{Year-end Close Price} * \text{Number of Common Shares Outstanding})_t}{(\text{Year-end Close Price} * \text{Number of Common Shares Outstanding})_{t-1}}$$
Price-to-Earnings Ratio (PE)	Measure of the Multiple at which the market is capitalizing the earning per share of a utility: $$\frac{\text{Year-end Close Price}_t}{\text{Primary Earnings per share before Extraordinary Items}_t}$$

The study measures the effect of normalization on financial variables of the test companies. If the growth rate and other financial variables after normalization for the test companies are significantly greater than the pair-matched control companies in the postnormalization test period, the financial status justification for normalization would seem to be supported. Table 3 includes the following five financial variables chosen for the study:

1. Revenue Growth Rate
2. Interest Coverage[26]
3. Dividend Payout Growth
4. Market Value of Common Equity Growth
5. Price-to-Earnings Ratio.

Each test utility is compared to a matching control utility using the following relative financial measures:

$$RGW_{p,d1} = \frac{GW_{t,d1}}{GW_{c,d1}} \qquad\qquad RGW_{p,d2} = \frac{GW_{t,d2}}{GW_{c,d2}}$$

$$RCVR_{p,d1} = \frac{COVER_{t,d1}}{COVER_{c,d1}} \qquad\qquad RCVR_{p,d2} = \frac{COVER_{t,d2}}{COVER_{c,d2}}$$

$$RDIV_{p,d1} = \frac{DIV_{t,d1}}{DIV_{c,d1}} \qquad\qquad RDIV_{p,d2} = \frac{DIV_{t,d2}}{DIV_{c,d2}}$$

$$RMKV_{p,d1} = \frac{MKV_{t,d1}}{MKV_{c,d1}} \qquad\qquad RMKV_{p,d2} = \frac{MKV_{t,d2}}{MKV_{c,d2}}$$

$$RPE_{p,d1} = \frac{PE_{t,d1}}{PE_{c,d1}} \qquad\qquad RPE_{p,d2} = \frac{PE_{t,d2}}{PE_{c,d2}}$$

Where:
$GW_{t,d1}$, $COVER_{t,d1}$, $DIV_{t,d1}$, $MKV_{t,d1}$, $PE_{t,d1}$

> denotes the mean revenue growth rate, interest coverage, dividend payout growth rate, market value of common equality growth rate and PE ratio for test utility t in the pre-period, d_1

$GW_{t,d2}$, $COVER_{t,d2}$, $DIV_{t,d2}$, $MKV_{t,d2}$, $PE_{t,d2}$

> denotes the mean revenue growth rate, interest coverage, dividend payout growth rate, market value of common equity growth rate and PE ratio for test utility t in the post-period, d_2

$GW_{c,d1}$, $COVER_{c,d1}$, $DIV_{c,d1}$, $MKV_{c,d1}$, $PE_{c,d1}$

> denotes the mean revenue growth rate, interest coverage, dividend payout growth rate, market value of common equity growth rate and PE ratio for control utility c in the pre-period, d_1

$GW_{c,d2}$, $COVER_{c,d2}$, $DIV_{c,d2}$, $MKV_{c,d2}$, $PE_{c,d2}$

> denotes the mean revenue growth rate, interest coverage, dividend payout growth rate, market value of common equity growth rate and PE ratio for control utility c in the post-period, d_2

The following null hypothesis, *Ho,* was tested against the alternative, *Ha*:

Ho: Relative financial measures did not improve with the adoption of deferred tax normalization.

Ha: Relative financial measures improved significantly with the adoption of deferred tax normalization.

If deferred tax normalization was to be associated with improvements in relative financial measures, including: revenue growth ratio, dividend payout, interest coverage, PE ratio and market value of common equity, it was expected that:

1. for a significant number of relative revenue growth ratios:

    Ha: $RGW_{d1} < RGW_{d2}$

2. for a significant number of relative dividend payout ratios:

    Ha: $RDIV_{d1} < RDIV_{d2}$

3. for a significant number of relative interest coverage ratios:

    Ha: $RCVR_{d1} < RCVR_{d2}$

4. for a significant number of relative PE ratios:

    Ha: $RPE_{d1} < RPE_{d2}$

5. for a significant number of relative market value of common equity:

    Ha: $RMKV_{d1} < RMKV_{d2}$

The nonparametric Wilcoxon Signed-Rank Test was used to test these hypotheses. The test results are provided in the next section.

EMPIRICAL RESULTS

Table 4 provides descriptive statistics of financial measures of interest for the 19 firm pairs. As noted in Table 4, these statistics suggest very little change in the financial measures for the test and control groups between the pre- and post-periods. In the pre-period, the financial attributes of the test utilities were higher than those of control utilities. Test firms also maintained better financial attributes than control firms in most financial measures, except for dividend payout growth ratio, during the post-period. In neither the pre- nor the post-

Table 4. Descriptive Statistics

	Pre-period		Post-period	
	Mean	Median	Mean	Median
Revenue Growth				
Test-Utilities	1.193	1.209	1.104	1.108
Control-Utilities	1.170	1.162	1.091	1.115
Dividend Payout Growth				
Test-Utilities	1.169	1.170	1.144	1.138
Control-Utilities	1.149	1.112	1.167	1.146
Interest Coverage Ratio				
Test-Utilities	2.987	2.684	3.405	3.244
Control-Utilities	2.936	2.955	3.340	3.102
Market Value of Common Equity Growth				
Test-Utilities	1.110	1.078	1.186	1.225
Control-Utilities	1.102	1.068	1.186	1.139
Price-to-Earnings Ratio				
Test-Utilities	8.160	8.089	8.005	8.336
Control-Utilities	8.058	7.315	7.587	7.785

Table 5. Test of Change in Relative Financial Strength
Measure from Pre-period to Post-period

Test Statistic	Declines	Increases	p Level of Wilcoxon Matched-Pair Signed Rank Test
RGW	8	11	.245
RCVR	9	10	.330
RDIV	11	8	.150
RMKV	9	10	.390
RPE	8	11	.245

period, was there a statistical significant difference in the increase in the means of the variables of the test utilities compared with the control utilities.

The growth ratio of the mean market value of common equity and the mean interest coverage increased from the pre-period to the post-period for both test and control firms. Conversely, Table 4 indicates that mean revenue and mean dividend payout growth ratios declined for both test and control firms from the pre-period to the post-period.

Additional tests results on an increase/decrease basis are reported in Table 5. Of financial data reported by the companies, revenue growth ($RGWp$) and

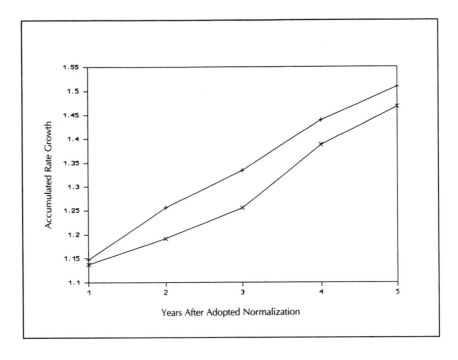

Notes: + Control utilities that used normalization consistently
            x Test utilities that changed from flow through to normalization

Figure 1.   Average Accumulated Rate Growth

interest cover ($RCVR_p$), increased in 10 of 19 pre-period of post-period comparisons, respectively. However, dividend payout growth declined in 11 of 19 pre-period to post-period comparisons. These results are inconsistent with expectations that the effect of changing to normalization would be an increase in electric rates and a relative improvement in the test statistics reported by the companies.

Using a Wilcoxon Signed-Rank Test, the increases in the three financial variables reported by the companies are not statistically significant at a probability level of .05. This is some evidence that the adoption of deferred tax normalization did not lead to a significant change in revenue growth, interest coverage or dividend payout for the test firms relative to the control firms.

The absence of a statistically significant improvement in these three financial variables is curious. Under the assumption that the test period was affected by regulatory lag, a subsequent study was made for a five-year period after the adoption of normalization by test utilities. Figure 1 presents a graph comparing growth rates of test and control utilities in the five-year study which shows that test companies continued to trail behind control utilities in the growth rate of the financial variables reported by the companies.

The growth rate of the market value of common equity and the price-to-earnings ratio were tested to gauge market perceptions of the change to normalization. These test results are also presented in Tables 4 and 5. Once again, the test results do not indicate a statistically significant increase in the test companies' market variables. The results do, however, show more frequent increases than decreases in the market value and price-to-earnings ratios of test companies.

LIMITATIONS AND CONCLUSION

The results of the statistical analysis are subject to certain limitations. Data collection constraints resulted in a sample size of only 38 firms (19 pairs). These 38 utilities are relatively large, public companies, but it can be argued that the small sample size limits the significance of the evidence on deferred tax normalization. In addition, the small sample size may restrict the general applicability of the study's results.

Although the data are not decisive it offers some evidence that normalization may not accomplish what was intended. The public policy issue on the autonomy of regulators in regard to normalization was addressed as a matter of law by the Supreme Court in 1973. It appears, however, that Congress and the courts have been content to allow IRC section 167 to dictate regulatory policy under the rationale that normalization served to protect and enhance the financial integrity of public utilities. This positive purpose is referenced in court cases, congressional reports and federal commission orders, with specific mention of the financial attributes measured in this paper. The data analysis reported in this study however, does not support the position that federal income tax normalization is a significant factor in promoting or maintaining financial quality in the utility industry.

SOCIAL IMPLICATIONS

Electric utilities are regulated monopolies because they provide a service that is " ... one of deep public interest and vital to the welfare of the general public."[27] The nature of the industry is such that it has broad reaching economic consequences since power costs become a factor in product and service pricing throughout the American economy. As a consequence, utility costs influence what people buy in the market place and how they live.

Utility rates charged to consumers are based on a utility's costs plus a regulated return on rate base. Accounting provides the mechanisms for establishing a cost of service and determining rate base. Income tax accounting is of particular significance since tax expense is greater than all other expenses, except for fuel, on most electric utility income statements.

As we have discussed, normalization tax accounting generally results in higher rates. This cost to consumers is being justified by the proposition that normalization improves financial health and integrity of the companies in this industry, thus making it easier to attract capital and provide power more reliably and efficiently. At the same time, however, a distortion of capital resource allocation in the economy may be the result when deferred tax expense is reflected as a current charge to ratepayers under normalization accounting. The empirical evidence in this study does not support the theoretical justification of greater financial health; the putative benefits from normalization are not readily apparent.

One important implication of this study's results pertains to the question of the balance of authority between federal and state government. When using accounting to implement policy, it is important to consider whether it is appropriate for federal public policymakers to impose accounting rules, like normalization accounting on state public utility commissions, in the absence of adequate evidence of the benefits of restricting state regulators' options.

A second implication is the importance of giving more explicit consideration to evaluating the condition of fairness created by accounting procedures [Williams, 1987]. The fairness of normalization to consumers is an issue raised by this study's results. As discussed previously, normalization requires today's ratepayers to provide subsidies which may involve both intra- and inter-generational wealth transfers. The results indicate that the positive factors justifying such transfers may not have materialized. Since many accounting policies initiated by the Financial Accounting Standards Board or Securities and Exchange Commission also likely have resource distributional consequences, it would seem appropriate that analyses similar to this analysis of normalization accounting policy become more common in order to provide a better basis for evaluating the fairness of other accounting policies. Information content is not the only relevant phenomenon associated with an accounting policy's evaluation. Accounting methods make a difference in many ways. Evaluating them from many perspectives seems, therefore, a legitimate undertaking for accounting researchers.

NOTES

1.   Internal Revenue Code Section 168 (e) (3) (A) and (B) provide that the term "recovery property" (meaning property subject to Accelerated Cost Recovery for federal income tax purposes) does not include public utility property if the public utility does not use a normalization method of accounting. Consequently, a utility can only use accelerated cost recovery if it normalizes, that is, charges it customers/ratepayers for deferred tax expenses recorded as a cost

of service. Section 168 (e) (3) (A) refers to the definition of public utility property under section 167 (1) (3) (A), which allows utilities to calculate depreciation using Asset Depreciation Range, accelerated depreciation methods, on post 1969 utility property, only if the utility normalizes.

2.   *FPC* v. *Memphis Light, Gas and Water Division, et al.,* 411 U.S. 458 [1973].

3.   *Memphis Light, Gas & Water Div.* v. *FPC,* 149 U.S. App. D.C. 238, 462 F.2d 853.

4.   *FPC* v. *United Gas Pipeline Co.,* 386 U.S. 237, 244-45. 87 S. Ct. 1003 [1967].

5.   "Accelerated Depreciation and State Ratemaking Policy: The Case of California," *Stanford Law Review* 31 [1979], p. 265.

6.   IRC Regulations 1.167 (a) (11). In June 1971, the U.S. Treasury Department approved the ADR System which combined some parts of depreciation guidelines with new class lives authorized by the Revenue Act of 1971.

7.   *Amere Gas Utilities Co.,* 15 FPC 760.799, [1956]; *El Paso Natural Gas Co.,* 22 FPC 260, 267 [1960].

8.   *Alabama-Tennessee National Gas Co.,* 31, FPC 208, 218-219 [1964]; *Public Systems* v. *Federal Energy Regulatory Commission,* 606 F.2d 973, at 977 [1979].

9.   IRC Section 167 (1) (1) and 167 (1) (2).

10.   *Alabama-Tennessee Natural Gas Co.* v. *Federal Power Commission,* 359 F.2d 318, at 322, [5th cr. 1966].

11.   S. Rep. No. 1622, 83rd Cong., 2d sess. 26 [1954]U.S. Code Congressional and Administrative news, p. 4656.

12.   *El Paso Natural Gas Co.* v. *Federal Power Commission,* 281 F.2d 567 at 571 [5th cr. 1960].

13.   53 FPC 2123.

14.   55 FPC 162.

15.   *Memphis Light, Gas and Water Division, et al,* v, *FPC,* 500 F.2d 798 [CADC, 1974].

16.   Order No. 530 A at 167.

17.   *Accounting Principles Broad Opinion No. 11* cited in order No. 530 A at 163.

18.   Order No. 530 B, 56 FPC 44, issued July 6, 1976.

19.   Id. at 45.

20.   Id. at 47.

21.   *Public Systems* v. *Fed. Energy Regulatory Commission,* 606 F.2d 973 [1983].

22.   *Alabama-Tennessee Natural Gas Co.* v. *Federal Power Commission, Supra.,* at 327 [1966]. *United Fuel Gas Co.,* 12 FPC 251, 264-65 (1953).

23.   *Barash* v. *Pennsylvania Public Utilities Commission,* 507 Pa. 496 at 508 [1985].

24.   *Barash* v. *Pennsylvania Public Utilities Commission, Supra,* at 505 [1985].

25.   IRC Section 168(F)(2) and (i)(9)-(10). Failure to normalize excess reserves over remaining regulatory lives results in a loss of eligibility to use accelerated depreciation for federal income tax purposes.

26.   There is an important limitation of interest coverage ratio as a measure of long-term solvency risk. That is, interest coverage ratio uses earnings rather then cash flows in the numerator (see Table 2). It should be noted that net income is not the same thing as cash provided by operations. As a result, some analysts suggest that some measures of cash flows should be used in the numerator [Bernstein, 1989, pp. 594-595].

27.   *Munn* v. *Illinois,* 94 U.S. 113 [1877].

REFERENCES

"Accelerated Depreciation and State Ratemaking Policy: The Case of California," *Stanford Law Review,* 31 [1979], p. 265.

Bernstein, L., *Financial Statement Analysis: Theory, Applications, and Interpretations* [Irwin, 1989].

Bradford, P. "Federal Income Taxes: The 'Expense' Utilities Love to Hate," *Public Utilities Fortnightly* [November 26, 1987], pp. 13-18.

Cawley, J.H., and N.J. Kennard *Rate Case Handbook* [1983], pp. 150-53.

Foley, M., "Flowbacks and Deferrals Under the 1986 Tax Reform Act: Normalization or Confiscation," Graduate School of Business Administration, Michigan State University [1987], pp. 602-631.

Hahne, R., and Aliff, G., eds. *Accounting for Public Utilities* [Matthew Bender, 1989].

Kiefer, D. "The Effects on Public Utilities of the Tax Reform Act of 1986," Graduate School of Business Administration, Michigan State University [1987], pp. 583-601.

Neimark, M. "Accounting Doesn't Matter Does it?" in *Advances in Public Interest Accounting,* Vol. 3, edited by M. Neimark [JAI Press, 1990], pp. ix-xvi.

Tinker, T. "The Role of Accounting in Public Utility Pricing," in *Paper Prophets: A Social Critique of Accounting* [Praeger, 1986].

Williams, P. "The Legitimate Concern with Fairness," *Accounting Organizations and Society* [1987], pp. 169-189.

CIVIL RIGHTS AND PUBLIC ACCOUNTING:
CONSTITUTIONAL CHALLENGES TO ACCOUNTING REGULATION IN CANADA

Alan J. Richardson

ABSTRACT

The Canadian Constitution was enacted in 1982, replacing the British North America Act as the foundational document of Canadian society. The constitution contains within it the Charter of Rights and Freedoms, the first statement of enshrined civil rights for Canadians. This paper examines recent uses of the Charter to challenge the structure of accounting regulation in Canada. In particular it has been claimed that aspects of the current regulatory regime violate (1) the freedom of speech, (2) the right to mobility among Canadian jurisdictions, (3) the right to liberty and security of the person, (4) the presumption of innocence, and (5) the right to equality before and under the law. Following the format of a constitutional court case, the paper examines the argument that there is a prima facie violation of rights, then considers the evidence that any violations which do exist are "justified in a free and democratic society." Under Section 1 of the Charter such justifications are sufficient to override individual rights and freedoms. Finally, the paper considers the remedies, that is, changes in the structure of accounting regulation, which would overcome the violations of civil rights claimed in these cases. It is argued that these court cases and recent voluntary changes in accounting regulation reflect the changing pattern of political values in Canada.

Advances in Public Interest Accounting, Volume 5, pages 179-200.

As a legacy of its colonial beginnings, Canada became a sovereign nation through an act of the British Parliament—The British North America Act of 1867 (BNA Act). This document served to provide the administrative framework for justice and legislative action in Canada but was deficient as a guide to civil rights and responsibilities. In particular, following British tradition, civil rights were a matter of common law rather than being specified as "inalienable rights." Furthermore, under the BNA Act, the legislature must retain supreme authority and may not make binding commitments which would restrict the authority of future legislatures. Thus laws could not guarantee future rights, and any right could be rescinded at the will of the legislature.

In 1982, the Canadian Constitution was repatriated as the Constitution Act, removing British control of Canadian constitutional affairs and enshrining within it certain rights fundamental to a "free and democratic society."[1] The Charter of Rights and Freedoms (contained within the Constitution Act), hereafter referred to as the Charter, marks a dramatic turning point in Canadian legal and social history. As will be clear in the discussion below, the Charter focuses on individual rights and serves, as the U.S. Constitution and Bill of Rights do, to protect the individual against collective demands. Yet it has been recognized that, historically, the values of the Canadian and American people have not been closely aligned.

> Americans do not know but Canadians cannot forget that two nations, not one, came out of the American Revolution. The United States is the country of the revolution, Canada of the counter revolution. These very different formative events set indelible marks on the two nations ... Government is feared in the south; uninhibited popular sovereignty has been a concern in the north. [Lipset, 1990, p. 1]

The Charter adds a new dimension to debates over the structure of accounting regulation in Canada. It allows practitioners to claim that they are "entitled" [Weaver, 1985] to practice as a public accountant as a result of constitutionally guaranteed civil rights. This logic is distinct from the arguments used in previous challenges to accounting regulation in Canada. Typically, regulatory reform has been couched in terms of the state seeking to overcome "market failures," or as tests of the lobbying strength of various groups, or, finally, as attempts by the state to establish corporatist structures to contain conflict within the profession [Richardson and McConomy, 1992]. Each of these interpretations assumes the primacy of the state and/or organized interests in the evolution of accounting regulation. The Charter is thus a potentially revolutionary document. It enumerates a set of concerns for individual rights which may not have been considered in the design of existing Canadian institutions. It also provides a mechanism for individuals to seek relief from the demands of these institutions [Axworthy, 1986].

In recent years the provisions of the Charter have been used to question the validity of certain statutes used to regulate the practice of accountancy in

Canada.[2] The purpose of this paper is to sketch the issues raised by these court cases and to identify the changes in accounting regulation which might be necessary to overcome these issues. The courts have yet to lease their decisions on these cases; thus the legal validity of these challenges is unresolved and the consequences for accounting regulation in Canada are uncertain.

The paper is organized as follows. The first two sections provide brief overviews of the structure of accounting regulation in Canada and of the aspects of the Charter which it is claimed are violated by these regulations. The third section then elaborates on the connection between specific constitutional rights and accounting regulation to establish a prima facie case that these rights are violated. The fourth section examines elements of the argument that these violations are reasonable in a "free and democratic society." The paper concludes with some speculation on the type of regulation of accounting practice which would be consistent with the Charter.

ACCOUNTING REGULATION IN CANADA: AN OVERVIEW

Canada is a federation of ten provinces and two territories. Under the BNA Act, and now under the Constitution Act, state powers were divided between the federal and provincial governments. The regulation of the professions falls under provincial/territorial jurisdiction but laws created at this level are subject to the provisions of the Charter (subject to certain exemptions provided in Section 33).[3]

There is considerable variation in the structure of accounting regulation among these jurisdictions. All provinces allow the incorporation of professional associations of accountants and authorize the use of distinctive titles and designations for members of the association. Typically, these Acts also allows the association to establish and enforce Codes of Ethics subject to appeal to the Provincial courts. Currently there are three associations of accountants represented federally and in all provincial jurisdictions: Chartered Accountant (CA), Certified General Accountant (CGA), and Certified Management Accountant (CMA). The key point of difference among provinces is the extent to which a restricted area of practice is recognized and the means by which those who will be given access to this market are identified.

In five Canadian jurisdictions there are no general restrictions on the practice of accountancy (i.e., Saskatchewan, Manitoba, New Brunswick, Northwest Territories, and the Yukon). In five jurisdictions licensing boards have been established to restrict access to specific types of practice (i.e., Alberta, British Columbia, Ontario, Nova Scotia, and Newfoundland). In the remaining two jurisdictions (Prince Edward Island and Quebec) one association of accountants (the Institute of Chartered Accountants) has been given privileged access to particular types of practice. Generally, the area of restricted practice involves adding credibility to financial information for use by third parties (for convenience I shall refer to this as auditing). The scope of practice included in this definition is variable; for example, in Quebec the restriction on audit practice does not apply to school boards, municipalities, or credit unions, while in Ontario all actions which signify that an individual acts as an independent expert accountant or auditor fall under the Public Accountancy Act.

The variation in accounting regulation across Canada reflects local solutions to issues and interest group pressures at particular points in each provinces' history. These arrangements are political compromises which reflect the nature of the Canadian legislative process prior to the enactment of the Charter. For example, Richardson [1989a] has described accounting regulation in Ontario as a form of corporatism involving close linkages between the profession and the state. The substance of the legislation emerged from negotiations among the dominant groups in the profession and provided them with the means to control access to public accounting. Individuals or groups adversely affected by this regulation could change their status by lobbying the government or by negotiating with the ruling coalition. This process put particular emphasis on the organized expression of interests and historically specific outcomes. The Charter provides a set of standards against which each province's regulation is compared and provides, for the first time, a means for individuals to challenge the "social compact."

CONSTITUTIONAL CHALLENGES TO ACCOUNTING REGULATION: AN OVERVIEW

Various aspects of the current regulatory regime in Canada have been challenged as violating five provisions of the Charter of Rights:

1. freedom of speech (S.2.6),
2. the right to mobility (S.6),
3. the right to liberty and the security of person (S.7),
4. presumption of innocence (S.11.d), and
5. the right to equality before and under the law (S.15).

These violations, however, may be constitutionally valid, if their violation is owing to "such reasonable limits prescribed by law as can be demonstrably justified in a free and democratic society" (S.1).

This clause may be decomposed in order to specify the conditions that must be met [*The Impact of the Canadian Charter, 1986*]. First, any restriction of rights must be "reasonable," which implies that the violation serves the common good *and* the extent of restrictions imposed is proportional to the benefit achieved. The courts (particularly in *Regina* v. *Oakes*) have defined "reasonable" to mean that the state can demonstrate that a "pressing and substantial objective" existed at the time the legislation was enacted. In addition, the challenged legislation must pass three "proportionality" tests. Specifically, (a) the measures must have a rational connection to the objective; (b) the measures should impair the right or freedom as little as possible; and (c) there must be proportionality between the effects of the impugned measure on the protected right and the benefits of attaining the objective. I will return to an assessment of accounting regulation in Canada with regard to these criteria in a later section of the paper.

Second, the restriction must be "prescribed by law," which implies that the circumstances under which rights are to be violated must be *precisely* specified and included in statute law or regulations, or be a necessary implication of that law (*Regina* v. *Therens*). Third, the requirement that violations of rights be "demonstrably justified" creates an onus of proof. An individual must demonstrate that his or her rights have been violated but then the onus of proof shifts to the state to justify this restriction. The final phrase, "in a free and democratic society," sets the basis for comparative evidence allowing, for example, experience with the U.S. Constitution to be entered as evidence in Canada.

Within the context of the Canadian Constitution, the validity of accounting regulation can be challenged by demonstrating that a behavior being restricted is protected by the Charter of Rights and, then, it falls on the state to demonstrate that the restriction meets all aspects of the override clause discussed earlier (Peck [1987] provides an extended discussion of the analytical framework which has emerged in judicial rulings on the Charter). The next section presents the arguments used to demonstrate that accounting regulation violates specific rights.

CONSTITUTIONAL RIGHTS AND ACCOUNTING REGULATION

Freedom of Speech

The Charter, in Section 2(b), provides that "everyone has the following fundamental freedoms: freedom of thought, belief, opinion and expression, including freedom of the press and other media of communication." In the case of *Irwin Toy* v. *The Attorney General of Quebec*, the Supreme Court ruled that the guarantee of freedom of expression extended to commercial advertisements aimed at persons under 13 years of age. The court held that any activity which "attempts to convey meaning" is protected by Section 2(b) provided that the form of expression is legitimate and inoffensive. The latter clause recognizes that violence may convey meaning, but that particular form of expression is not protected by the Charter. The Court thus found that the legislation violated the company's freedom of speech but was valid, under Section 1, owing to the purpose of the legislation.

The Irwin Toy ruling has been used in *Regina* v. *Walker and Robertson* v. *P.E.I.* to claim that the expression of an opinion on the credibility of financial disclosures by a company falls within the protection of the Charter. The ruling also suggests that an opinion does not have to be given verbally or in words to be protected; any action[4] that conveys the same meaning is also protected. In other words, because public accounting practice adds credibility to accounting information, that practice represents an attempt to "convey meaning" which is protected by the Charter.

The applicability of these rulings to accounting regulation can be demonstrated with the Ontario Public Accountancy Act. In this Act, "public accountant" is defined in part as "a person ... where by reason of the circumstances or of the signature, stationary or wording employed, it is indicated that such person ... purports to act ... as an independent accountant or auditor." This definition clearly indicates that the role of "public accountant" is primarily exercised through "expression" both verbally and through action. *Any* restrictions on who may practice as a public accountant under the act, prima facie, violates the constitutional guarantee of freedom of speech for at least some people.

The counter argument is that the act does not prevent anyone from expressing an opinion on the credibility of financial information; it merely restricts who may charge for that service. This argument relies on the lack of protection of economic rights under the Constitution. For example, in the case of *Wilson and Maxson* v. *Medical Services Commission of British Columbia*, the British Columbia government had enacted a policy restricting access to the Medical Services Plan, which reimburses doctors for services to insured persons. Access to reimbursement by the plan is essential to earning a livelihood in private practice as a physician in the province. A group of qualified doctors who were denied access to the plan argued that the policy denied them a "livelihood" which is protected under Section 7 of the Charter. The Court ruled that the Charter does not protect economic rights but allowed that the "liberty" to pursue a profession was protected. The policy was allowed to stand, on the basis of Section 1, owing to the state's need to ration health care funding.

The Right of Mobility

Section 6.2.6 states that "Every citizen of Canada and every person who has the status of a permanent resident of Canada has the right to pursue the gaining of a livelihood in any province." This guarantee read in the context of the diversity of accounting regulation across Canada may mean that an accountant's rights are violated where he or she is free to practice in one province but denied that right in other provinces. Two examples of this problem follow.

The Ontario Securities Commission is the body that regulates financial disclosure by companies listed on the Toronto Stock Exchange (TSE). As the largest stock market in Canada, the TSE attracts listings from companies operating in all provinces. The Ontario Securities Act and the national policies established by the provincial securities commissions require audited statements by listed companies, but do not specify the individuals qualified to conduct audits (National Policy Statement #3 specifies "Unacceptable Auditors"). The result is that a company operating in British Columbia could use an auditor to submit statements acceptable to the TSE but if the company moved to Ontario or had operations in Ontario, that same auditor would be prohibited from providing the service under the Ontario Public Accountancy Act. The Act, thus, violates the individual's freedom to pursue a livelihood in all provinces.

In the case of *Walker and Robertson* v. *P.E.I.,* the plaintiffs are partners in a public accounting firm with offices in Prince Edward Island and New Brunswick. In New Brunswick they may legally act as public accountants and have developed a practice that includes firms with operations in both Prince Edward Island and New Brunswick. In Prince Edward Island, the right to practice as a public accountant is restricted to Chartered Accountants by S.15 of the Public Accounting and Auditing Act. The plaintiffs hold the Certified General Accountant designation and, therefore, are unable to service their clients in Prince Edward Island. The plaintiffs claim that this constitutes a violation of their right to mobility.

The typical counter argument to this objection is that such statutes seek to regulate quality and do not discriminate on the basis of residency. Any individual, regardless of the place of residence, is free to apply for a license. It has also been argued that where knowledge of local circumstances is a prerequisite to effective professional performance, then residency requirements may be a reasonable mechanism for ensuring that an individual possesses the knowledge (*Black* v. *Law Society of Alberta* and *Law Society of British Columbia* made similar arguments for the use of citizenship as a requirement). Furthermore, there have been several rulings that, with the exception of criminal law, regional differences in laws which do not have an "invidious purpose" are constitutionally valid under the distribution of federal and provincial powers (e.g., *Regina* v. *Ushkowski*).

Liberty and Security of Person

Section 7 states that "everyone has the right to life, liberty and security of person and the right not to be deprived thereof except in accordance with the principles of fundamental justice." There are two issues of interpretation within this Section: the scope of the terms "life, liberty and security" and the meaning of "fundamental justice." On the first issue there have been rulings (e.g., *Wilson and Maxson* v. *Medical Services Commission of British Columbia*) that "security of the person" does not include economic security. This would seem to imply that the right to work is not guaranteed but the courts have also adopted the idealist notion that a profession is a "calling" which people should be at liberty to pursue [Grey, 1990]. In *Walker and Robertson* v. *P.E.I.,* it was claimed that the plaintiffs' right to liberty had been violated in that they were prohibited from practicing the profession for which they were qualified in Prince Edward Island. The counter argument on this point is to allow people to follow their calling as long as they do not charge for their services.

On the second issue, the meaning of "fundamental justice" is still developing in case law. "The Impact of the Canadian Charter of Rights and Freedoms on Canadian Business Law" [1986] suggests that the phrase may have been used to avoid a strict procedural interpretation (for example, as implied by the "due process of law" phrasing of the equivalent section of the Canadian Bill of Rights) and to encourage the courts to inquire into the substance of each case. This interpretation was used in *Regina* v. *Morgentaler et al.* but typically it has been used in addition to the procedural requirements rather than as a separate doctrine. In other words, Section 7 rights may be violated if improper procedures are followed or if the substance of the matter precludes justice being done.

A violation of Section 7 freedoms is contemplated under the following scenario cited in *Regina* v. *Kitchen*. The Ontario Public Accountancy Act provides for the prosecution of individuals who may be fined if found guilty of practicing public accountancy without a license. If this fine is not paid, the Provincial Offenses Act (S.70) provides for action leading to possible imprisonment. The risk of imprisonment was ruled to constitute an infringement of the right to liberty in *Regina* v. *Vaillancourt* whether or not actual imprisonment was involved. The loss of "liberty" possible under the Act requires that the procedures followed and outcomes rendered by the Public Accountants' Council in prosecuting a charge of practicing as a public accountant without a licence must be in accord with "fundamental justice." The primary objection in this regard is that the definition of "public accounting" under the Act is too vague for individuals to be certain of the circumstances under which they may be charged, (*Regina* v. *Raynor* allowed an appeal on this basis). The inability of individuals to recognize the offense precludes the possibility of fundamental justice being achieved in a prosecution

Presumption of Innocence

Section 11 (d) states that "Any person charged with an offence has the right to be presumed innocent until proven guilty according to law in a fair and public hearing by an independent and impartial tribunal." This section is violated by any statute that places the burden of proof on the individual rather than on a regulatory authority. In fact, it is very common for professional statutes to create such a "reverse onus" requiring that individuals prove that they have the qualifications to enter practice rather than requiring a regulatory body to give cause why an individual should be denied a livelihood.

In the case of *Regina* v. *Kitchen*, for example, the defense argued that the Ontario Public Accountancy Act establishes a reverse onus by defining public accountancy largely by providing exemptions from prosecution for practicing as a public accountant without a license under Section 34. This section states that:

> Nothing in this precludes a registered member of the Society of Industrial and Cost Accountants of Ontario, or any other person, from practising as an industrial accountant, cost accountant or cost consultant, from, designating himself as such or from issuing statements, opinions, reports or certificates in connection with such practice.

In essence, Section 34, in conjunction with the definition of public accounting in the act, means that individuals can avoid prosecution if they can prove that "statements, opinions, reports or certificates" prepared by them were not intended for use by third parties. These "statements," however, may be identical to those that would be prepared for external users. Given that a prosecution is only likely where such statements have become public, the accused is put in the impossible position of proving lack of foreknowledge of the client's intended use. The existence of a reverse onus is explicitly recognized in *Regina* v. *Rayner*.

The Right to Equality Before and Under the Law

Section 15 states that "every individual is equal before and under the law and has the right to equal protection and equal benefit of the law without discrimination and, in particular, without discrimination based on race, national or ethnic origin, colour, religion, sex, age or mental or physical disability." The terminology of "before and under the law" implies that Section 15 guarantees apply both to the process of lawmaking and to law enforcement. There are two types of regulatory actions that have been cited as violations of Section 15.

First, in several provinces, public accountancy laws have used specific accounting designations as the basis for restricting access to audit practice. These provisions are regarded as discriminatory to the extent that they exclude from practice those who, but for this designation, have the necessary skills (e.g., *Walker and Robertson* v. *P.E.I.*). More generally, to the extent that membership in different organizations reflects differences in any of the criteria listed in Section 15 (Richardson [1989b] provides some historic evidence on this possibility), then membership may be regarded as an "analogous category" (*Andrews* v. *Law Society of British Columbia*[5]) and its use regarded as discriminatory. Second, in several cases where regulation was introduced, existing practitioners were licensed regardless of their qualifications (grandfathering). It has been argued that this represents discrimination on the basis of age (*Walker and Robertson* v. *P.E.I.*).

The former argument probably has greater validity than the latter which would effectively preclude social change. The counterargument to the former assertion is that those who possess the necessary qualifications must merely

Table 1.   Constitutional Challenges to Accounting Regulation

Charter Section	Violation Claimed	Defense
Freedom of Speech (Section 2)	Restriction on the right to express an opinion on the credibility of financial information	The freedom of expression is not restricted only the ability to charge for this service
Right of Mobility (Section 6)	Provincial variations in accounting regulation restrict the ability of practitioners to practice in all jurisdictions	Accounting regulation does not include residency requirements but legitimately sets provincial quality standards
Right to Liberty and the Security of Person (Section 7)	Accounting regulation denies a livelihood to some practitioners and violation of regulations can lead to fines and imprisonment	Guarantees of liberty and security do not extend to economic security
Right to Be Presumed Innocent (Section 11)	Accounting regulation creates a"reverse onus" by requiring that practitioners prove competence and/or that their actions fall outside the definition of public accounting	This point has apparently been conceded
Right to Equality before and under the Law (Section 15)	Accounting regulation has used designations (private certification) as a basis for regulation resulting in discriminatory access	Individuals wishing to be licensed can become a member of the certifying body

present themselves to the competent authority in order to qualify for membership in that association whose designation is used as the basis for licensing. This argument cannot be countered with the claim that this would violate the guarantee of freedom of association. This approach is ruled out by the judgment in *Professional Institute of the Public Service [PIPS]* v. *Commissioners of the North West Territories Public Service Association.* In this case, PIPS acted as the bargaining unit for a group of nurses employed by the federal government in the Northwest Territories. These nurses were transferred to the employ of the territory and were required by law to be represented by a bargaining unit incorporated in the territory. PIPS sought incorporation in order to continue representing these nurses. This application was denied leading to the claim that the nurses' freedom of association had been violated.

The Supreme Court of Canada ruled that legislative restrictions on which organizations can represent workers do not violate the Charter. The nurses were still free to belong to PIPS. Although PIPS could no longer act as their bargaining agent, this right was not protected by the Charter. This ruling suggests that accounting practitioners' rights are not violated by licensing laws based on membership in a particular association if licensing itself does not violate the Charter.

Summary: Is Public Accounting an Activity Protected by the Charter?

The arguments sketched earlier, and summarized in Table 1, claim that accounting regulation violates certain protected civil rights. These arguments vary in validity and it is unlikely that all will be upheld by the courts. Certain aspects of these challenges are likely to succeed. For example, the reverse onus provisions of numerous statutes have been ruled unconstitutional by virtue of violating Section 11d. This would suggest that at least this aspect of accounting regulation will have to be reexamined by the legislature. This, and most of the other claims discussed above, concerns the violation of a constitutional right which occurs due to the specific *form* of regulation. The argument that public accounting regulation violates the freedom of speech probably holds regardless of the form that regulation takes. There is, therefore, a prima facie case that certain aspects of the accounting regulation violate protected rights of freedoms.

REASONABLE LIMITATIONS IN A FREE
AND DEMOCRATIC SOCIETY

As stated earlier, even if it can be demonstrated that accounting regulations violate the Charter, this does not imply that such regulation is unconstitutional. All rights (with the possible exception of S.28—sexual equality) are subject to reasonable limitations which serve the greater good. This raises three questions: (1) what purpose(s) does accounting regulation serve, (2) what means are available to achieve this purpose, and (3) how can that purpose be achieved with the minimum violation of civil rights?

The question of the purpose of accounting regulation must be approached careful. In particular, the teleology of inferring purpose from current effect has been recognized by the courts [*Irwin Toy* v. *Quebec*] as insufficient grounds to uphold existing legislation. Similarly, Merino and Neimark [1982] have taken accounting researchers to task for criticizing disclosure regulation for failing to address the objectives of current accounting theory. The purpose of accounting regulation in cases of constitutional law is the purpose explicitly recognized by the legislature at the time the Act was approved. Current research and theory may be relevant in upholding existing legislation to the extent that it demonstrates that a valid objective is still a "pressing and substantial" concern and that the measures undertaken have the intended effect.

In the case of the Ontario Public Accountancy Act, a review of the legislative debates[6] indicates that the primary purpose of the Act was to prevent the formation of new associations of accountants and to resolve disputes among existing groups [Richardson, 1989a]. While the concept of the "public interest" was used in passing, no discussion of the public benefits of the legislation appears in the debates (Falk [1989] finds a similar situation with respect to the introduction of audit requirements into the U.S. 1934 Securities Act). In fact, on several occasions during the debates the Premier of Ontario expressed indifference to the Act claiming that it represented a compromise among the various groups of accountants and as such had the support of government. In essence, the debates in this instance fail to provide a "pressing and substantial" objective which the state was attempting to achieve through this legislation. A plausible interpretation of statements made in the legislature is that public legislation was being used to achieve the private purposes of the accounting groups which existed at that particular point in history.

The lack of any *realized* public concern over the quality of public accounting services is also reflected in other statutes. By and large, Canadian legislation has emphasized disclosure requirements and is silent on the qualifications of auditors. For example, the Canada Business Corporations Act specifies that the CICA Handbook shall be regarded as GAAP for the purposes of financial disclosure but the Act does not require that auditors be licensed nor does it specify the qualifications of auditors [Dickerson, n.d.]. A similar situation exists with respect to the Ontario Securities Act which governs financial reporting by companies listed on the Toronto Stock Exchange. This approach is consistent with academic models of the disclosure process which suggest that the market is capable of interpreting information—provided that it is available—and that "adverse selection" pressures will lead management to ensure that disclosures are regarded as credible.

In the absence of evidence of real public concern about the quality of public accounting, most justifications of accounting regulation rely on the theoretical existence of information asymmetries between the client and practitioner or the existence of externalities which impose costs on third parties [Trebilcock, 1989].[7] If a market failure in accounting exists primarily because of information asymmetries, then the appropriate remedy is the creation of certification processes to signal the quality of practitioners [Young, 1988]. This, in essence, is the current state of affairs with multiple designations in use. The residual question is whether or not the consumer is able to interpret the quality signals provided by these designations. The extent of information asymmetries between the client and practitioner is generally not considered to be great. Public accounting services are used primarily by sophisticated corporate clients with well-specified needs and the market appears to be successful in choosing public accountants consistent with their needs [Young, 1988; Lazar, Sievers, and Thornton, 1978]. This evidence is particularly important in light of the ruling in *Regina* v. *Keegstra*[8] that restrictions on the freedom of speech must prevent real harm and not the possibility of harm. If the organization and conduct of the market is such to overcome these harms, then there is no basis for the restriction of freedom of speech. The client, therefore, is not seen as requiring protection beyond that provided by certification processes operating through the market.

The case for the use of regulation to protect third parties who rely on audited financial information in making consequential decisions is similarly ambiguous. The concern has been addressed through minimum disclosure requirements, the expansion of auditors' legal liability to include third-party effects [Johnson and Terando, 1990] and, to a lesser extent, by licensing auditors. The latter step of restricting access to practice to those who meet some minimum standard of competence seems logically connected to the objective of protecting third parties but the evidence on the effect of licensing is less supportive. Young [1987, 1988], for example, finds that licensing increases the cost to consumers without appreciable increases in service quality, restricts access to service at the low end of the market, and restricts mobility among jurisdictions resulting in a mismatch of the supply and demand of practitioners. In light of the evidence on the cost of licensure, the consensus is that its use should be restricted to those cases where potential third-party losses are greatest and/or ex post mechanisms of redress (e.g., the courts) are inadequate. There is, to date, little literature to provide guidance on this issue.

If we accept the premise (unproven here) that there is an aspect of public accounting practice that severely affects either first-party or third-party interests, and accept that these interests cannot be protected through the markets or the courts, then it is reasonable that the legislature acts to protect those interests. Following the doctrine of proportionality established by the courts, the impact of regulation on the civil rights of current and future practitioners must be proportional to the benefit to society. This suggests that the scope of restricted practice must be narrowly defined to capture only those areas of practice where the vulnerability of those parties warrants the curtailment of rights, and the nature of the restriction must be the minimum necessary to achieve this protection. Implementing each of these criteria is problematic.

In Ontario, the definition of public accounting has been subject to legislative and judicial consideration which has been gradually reducing the scope of licensed practice. The term *public accounting* was originally used to refer to the location and form of practice, serving to distinguish those who offered their services to the public on a fee-for-service basis from those who provided services as a salaried employee. In the Public Accountancy Act of 1950, there was an attempt to specify public accounting in terms of task rather than form of practice as "the investigation or audit or the preparation of or reporting on balance sheets, profit and loss accounts or other financial statements." This was a very broad definition including many routine procedures. In 1962, the Act was revised and the definition of public accounting was restated in terms of "causing to be prepared" rather then preparing financial statements, and with an emphasis on the "independence" of the "expert accountant or auditor." The revision envisions the licensed public accountant in a supervisory role with respect to other accounting practitioners and independent of management. In 1980, a Report commissioned by the Ontario Attorney-General's Office recommended that the definition of licensed practice be restricted to those audits required by statute [Trebilcock, Tuohy, and Wolfson, 1979]. This would require that the legislature give individual consideration to each area of practice which is to be restricted. Finally, in the case of *Regina* v. *Manuel*, an appeal of a conviction of practicing as a public accountant without a licence in Ontario was allowed on the grounds that "public accounting" within the Act properly referred only to the preparation of financial information *intended* for third party use. This history indicates that the range of restricted practice is decreasing but precisely where the limits should be drawn is uncertain.

The requirement that licensing should establish *minimum* standards for the protection of third parties is a major departure from the usual operations of the professions. Although the increase in professional standards over time can be interpreted as either part of a strategy of closure or as an integral aspect of the professional ethic, there can be no doubt that the level of education requirements and the complexity of technical knowledge in each of the professions has increased. The minimum standard used for licensing clearly must be tied to the changing knowledge of the professions but herein lies a dilemma. The public interest is served by the contradictory imperatives of a minimum standard for licensing and an ideal standard of professionalism. Collectively, the profession is expected to maintain and advance the standards of practice but, individually, it is counterproductive to expect or require that all practitioners should be trained and practice at the highest levels of technical prowess. This approach suggests that there needs to be a continuum of skills in the profession, or a highly branched network with specialization accompanying technical elaboration, truncated at a level that protects vulnerable interests.

Summary: Is Accounting Regulation Justified under Section 1?

The justification for the regulation of public accounting practice rights appears to hinge on hypothesized third-party effects and the failure of market and legal mechanisms to mitigate these effects. In the development of regulation in Canada, evidence on these effects was not discussed in the legislature nor does current regulation appear to be designed to address these concerns with minimal violation of the civil rights of those affected. Furthermore, general evidence on the effects of licensing suggest that this form of regulation imposes costs on consumers without commensurate benefits. Overall, the protection of third-party interests may constitute a "pressing and substantial" objective but considerable doubt may be raised about the proportionality between the restrictiveness of current regulation and the benefits to be achieved.

The current structure of much accounting regulation emerged from negotiations between accounting associations and the state to bring "order" to the market for accounting services. In Ontario, control of the Public Accountants' Council, which grants licenses to practice public accounting, was given to representatives of the existing associations in spite of the fact that the majority of public accountants at that time were unaffiliated with these associations [Richardson, 1989a]. In the legislature, this state of affairs was justified pragmatically in terms of the difficulty of negotiating with unorganized accountants. Once the legislature had restricted the rights of accountants, there was no process through which an individual could challenge that action. Under these conditions, the lack of concern with individual rights in current legislation is understandable. The Charter, however, emphasizes the rights of the individual over those of organized interests and provides a mechanism for the individual to seek redress of violations of civil rights.

ACCOUNTING REGULATION UNDER THE CHARTER OF RIGHTS AND FREEDOMS

The challenges to accounting regulation in Canada sketched above will ultimately be decided by the courts. If these cases are successful, those portions of existing law which violate the Charter will be struck down and will be unenforceable (of "no force or effect," S.52.1). The issues touched upon in these challenges—the right to sign opinions, the definition of the boundaries of restricted practice, the criteria for licensing and the mechanisms for enforcement of restrictions—are the essence of accounting regulation. Given that some form of regulation of accountancy is in the public interest, a ruling that current provisions are unconstitutional would thus force a thorough revision of these statutes.

In this section I wish to speculate on the nature of accounting regulation under the Charter. It should be immediately apparent that there is no necessary relationship between the specifics of accounting regulation and the constitutional issues discussed earlier. Achieving a degree of congruence between constitutional values and legislative actions is an art [Richardson and Dowling, 1986]. The discussion that follows combines the concerns raised in current court challenges with observations on recent voluntary changes in accounting regulation in Canada in order to project the forms of accounting regulation that will emerge in response to changing legal and social values.

Private Regulation of Accounting Practice

In five Canadian jurisdictions there are no general restrictions on practice rights. In these jurisdictions it may be possible to avoid the issue of civil rights in accounting regulation altogether. The Charter applies only to government actions and not to private arrangements. The current test of applicability of the Charter is whether or not the state has "direct routine control" over the contested action. In a dissenting opinion expressed in *KcKinney* v. *University of Guelph* a more complete set of criteria were suggested. Specifically:

1. Does the legislative, executive or administrative branch of government exercise general control over the entity in question?
2. Does the entity perform a traditional function which in modern times is recognized as a responsibility of the state?
3. Is the entity one that acts pursuant in statutory authority specifically to enable it to further an objective that the government seeks to promote in the broader public interest?

If these broader criteria are adopted, even private action which implements a state function will be affected by the Charter.

As the Charter is currently interpreted, however, if a system of accounting regulation could be established without legislative sanction, then it would be immune from challenges under the Charter. Individual accounting associations, for example, are free to conduct their operations within the limitations of statute law unencumbered by constitutional considerations. On many occasions in Canadian accounting history, attempts have been made to establish a single professional association. One justification for these mergers was that they would allow the creation and enforcement of a single standard of competence and, thereby, reduce the need for government intervention. The current regime of accounting regulation in Canada can be attributed, in part, to the failure of competing accounting associations to achieve voluntary agreements. This factor is particularly evident in the history of the profession in Quebec [Collard, 1980] and Ontario [Creighton, 1984]. These attempts have reduced the number of distinct association but have failed to adequately address the diverse interests within the profession resulting in continuing rifts.

Preventing Regulatory Capture

The essential rationale for the creation of self-governing professions is that only a member of the profession can evaluate the competence and performance of other members. The potential for individual malfeasance is to be overcome by holding the profession collectively responsible for the quality of service provided to clients. Traditionally, when regulatory boards have been established in accountancy, the same logic has been used to appoint members of the profession to those boards. The challenges to existing regulation under Section 7 (right to liberty and security) and Section 15 (right to equality under the law) have arisen because the regulatory apparatus is perceived to have been "captured" by a particular group of accountants.

In regulation created recently in Canada, for example in Alberta, attempts have been made to overcome this problem by appointing members of the board from outside the profession and by ensuring that the board represents organized interests within the profession. This structure appears to meet the concerns for political accountability. It is not clear, however, whether these boards will also result in definitions of the boundaries of restricted practice and appropriate levels of qualifications which would minimize the extent of violation of Section 2 (freedom of speech) rights. These boards reflect the interests of groups with incentives to engage in exclusionary practices. It may be possible to overcome this concern if third parties have a greater say in the operation of regulatory regimes.

Identifying Third Party Interests

The problem identified above reflects the need to tailor accounting regulation to protect vulnerable third parties. The concept of third parties must be defined broadly to include two classes: those individuals who would be harmed through the reliance on a poor quality of public accounting service, and those individuals (clients and practitioners) who would be harmed through the creation of a restrictive regulatory regime. The research on accounting regulation to date has not identified the extent of third party effects nor the relative magnitude of the two types of costs involved. The existing regulation is structured as if the protection of the first group of third parties was the sole issue. The costs to individuals excluded from the regulated market or the extra costs to clients due to regulation are not explicitly considered.

If it were possible to better segment and identify third party interests, one way of incorporating their concerns into accounting regulation would be to provide them with representation on regulatory boards. This does not appear to have been tried. A more common suggestion [e.g., Aucoin, 1979], and one which is being used in Quebec and Alberta, is to establish an executive oversight mechanism independent of the profession being regulated. For example, in Quebec there is an Office of the Professions which monitors the way in which delegated powers are used by the professions and this office has been active in suggesting modifications to the professions' educational programs and entrance procedures.

The challenges to accounting regulation based on Section 6 (right to mobility) identifies another group adversely affected by current regulations: those accountants engaged in transborder practices. With the advent of the Free Trade Agreement between Canada and the United States, there has been renewed lobbying to reduce trade restrictions between the provinces of Canada. One aspect of this might be the creation of uniform regulation of public accounting practice. Unfortunately, Canada has historically been characterized by extreme regionalism, with each province or group of provinces experiencing conditions that demand local solutions. This is reflected in the operations of the professional bodies. Although each of the accounting association has some form of national uniform final examination, other requirements vary considerably among provinces depending on the educational resources available and on the political environment in which the association operates. It seems unlikely given these circumstances that uniformity at this level is possible.

Reconciling Professional Idealism with Individual Civil Rights

The Charter represents a marked change in the values that have traditionally guided action in Canadian society [Lipset, 1990]. The Charter emphasizes individual rights and is largely silent on the communal values that have guided the development of Canadian society, creating the potential for challenges that strike at the core of current institutional structures. The structure of accounting regulation in Canada reflects traditional values. For example, standard-setting in Canada is unique in that it remains a private-sector activity and its output has legislative authority without any oversight mechanism.[9] The profession operates on an informal standard of "noblesse oblige" rather than formalizing their duty to the public purpose. In many respects, this structure has served Canada well, and there is no question that the Canadian profession is held in high regard in the international community. The potentially revolutionary impact of the Charter arises because of the limited recognition of individual rights within this structure.

In order to design a system of regulation that establishes minimum competencies in public accounting while encouraging the development of the highest professional standards, it is necessary to separate the licensing function from the credentialing function of professional associations. In several jurisdictions in Canada, the credentials of specific associations have been adopted as the standard for licensing, this has lead to a continual escalation of licensing standards as those associations, rightly, seek to improve the qualifications of members. In an environment where there are multiple associations competing for the accounting market, the separation of licensing and credentialling would provide consumers with a minimum level of quality while allowing them to select the qualifications beyond this minimum that suits their needs. The competing professional associations would then have incentives to improve their skills to the extent that there was a market for a particular level of service (Thornton [1991] reaches similar conclusions arguing from economic rather than constitutional grounds).

CONCLUSION

The enactment of the Charter of Rights and Freedoms has created a new dimension to the debate over the legitimacy of accounting regulation in Canada. Historically, the structure of accounting regulation has reflected the pattern of coalitions within the profession and the success of lobbying efforts by these groups. Those individuals adversely effected by regulation could attempt to improve their status only through collective political action. The Charter guarantees rights and freedoms which can be invoked by an individual to challenge legislation even where such legislation has the support of the majority or of the dominant groups in society. The Charter, thus, introduces the logic of "entitlement" to the debate over accounting regulation.

In this paper I have examined the way in which the Charter has been used to challenge the legitimacy of accounting regulation. Specifically, it has been claimed that existing regulations violate one or more of the freedom of speech, the right to mobility, the right to liberty and the security of person, the right to be presumed innocent and the right to equality before and under the law. These violations may be constitutional if it can be shown that such violations serve the common good and the costs are proportional to the benefits. Although these challenges have not been definitively resolved in the courts, this paper presents an analysis which suggests that at least some aspects of current accounting regulation will be ruled unconstitutional and will have to be reconsidered by the legislature.

The final part of the paper speculates on the changes in accounting regulation which would be necessary to accommodate the constitutional issues raised in these cases. The primary conclusions are the (1) regulatory bodies will have to become more representative of interests within the profession, (2) third-party interests affected by accounting regulation need to be better identified and represented, in particular those adversely affected by regulation (as opposed to those adversely affected by poor quality of the service being regulated) need to be brought into the process, and, (3) licensing regimes should be constructed that parallel rather than intersect credentialing regimes to minimize barriers to entry to regulated fields while encouraging competition among a diversity of levels of practitioner qualification. These changes are consistent with recent voluntary changes to accounting regulation in several Canadian jurisdictions. Such changes may anticipate the changing legal environment in Canada or be concurrent reflections of the changing values of Canadian society.

ACKNOWLEDGMENTS

An earlier version of this paper was presented to the Second Annual Critical Perspectives Symposium: Ethics, Regulation and Professionalism in Accounting New York, March 23-24, 1991. The Paper has benefited from the comments of Bruce McConomy, Dean Neu, and Dan Thornton. The author, who is not a lawyer, retains responsibility for the interpretations offered.

NOTES

1. These rights were presaged in the Bill of Rights (S.C. 1960, *c* 44) but are not identical with them [Carson, 1988].

2. This has taken various forms. In *Walker and Robertson* v. *Prince Edward Island* (P.E.I.), the Act regulating public accounting has been challenged by individuals seeking to enter practice. This case is being heard by the Supreme Court of Prince Edward Island. In *R.* v. *Kitchen* in Ontario, the law has been challenged as part of a defense of a charge of practicing as a public accountant

without a license in a case heard in the Provincial Court Trials Division. Other cases are pending in Nova Scotia and Newfoundland.

3. Section 33 allows any province to enact laws which violate the Charter but requires that a five-year sunset clause be included in the legislation. This is referred to as the "not withstanding" clause. It has been invoked by the Province of Quebec to enact legislation requiring the use of French as the province's working language.

4. For example, printing a financial statement on the letterhead of an accounting firm may convey the same message as a signed auditor's report.

5. It was ruled in this case that the use of citizenship to deny entry to the Bar resulted in discrimination on the basis of categories specifically listed in Section 15. The use of citizenship was, therefore, ruled to be analogous to these categories.

6. The minutes of meetings leading to draft legislation were not preserved. These debates provide the only written evidence of the legislature's intent.

7. In *Walker and Robertson* v. *P.E.I.* the Crown's Section 1 defense rested entirely on the need to protect third party interests.

8. Keegstra was convicted of using his position as a school teacher to promote anti-semitism. On appeal, the Court considered the conditions under which Section 1 of the Charter could be used to overrule the freedom of speech. The court concluded that it could be applied only to prevent *actual* harm but not the *risk* of harm. This implies that arguments about the statistical likelihood of audit failure can not override the freedom to express an audit opinion.

9. There is no appeal mechanism for individual standards created by the CICA but, of course the legislature could repeal those sections of the Canada Business Corporations Act which recognize the Handbook as GAAP. This all-or-nothing approach does not provide an effective oversight procedure.

REFERENCES

Andrews v. *Law Society of British Columbia, Canada Law Book,* case 089037001 [February 2, 1989].

Aucoin, P., "Public Accountability in the Governing of Professions: A Report on the Self-Governing Professions of Accounting, Architecture, Engineering and Law in Ontario," working paper prepared for the Professional Organizations Committee, Ministry of the Attorney General, Toronto [1978].

Axworthy, T.S., "Colliding Visions: The Debate Over the Charter of Rights and Freedoms 1980-81," in J.M. Weiler and R.M. Elliot (eds.), *Litigating the Values of a Nation: The Canadian Charter of Rights and Freedoms* [Carswell, 1986].

Black v. *Law Society of Alberta, Canada Law Book,* case 089122019 [April 20, 1989].

Carson, B., "Charter of Rights and Freedoms and the Bill of Rights: A Comparison," Research Branch, Library of Parliament Background paper BP-180 [May 1988].

Cohen, D. "Can it Really Be Unconstitutional to Regulate Product Safety Information?" *Canadian Business Law Journal,* 17 [1990, pp. 55-74].

Collard, E.A., *First in North America* [Ordre des Comptables Agrees du Quebec, 1980].

Creighton, P., *A Sum Of Yesterdays* [Institute of Chartered Accountants of Ontario, 1984].

Cunningham, B.C., R. Tondkar, and E.N. Coffman, "Trust or Antitrust for the Profession of Accountancy?" in *Research in Accounting Regulation,* Vol. 4, edited by G.J. Previts [JAI Press, 1990], pp. 111-128.

Dickerson, R.W.V., *The Canada Business Corporations Act: Implications for Management and the Accountant* [The Society of Industrial Accountants of Canada, n.d.].

Falk, H., "A Comparison of Regulation Theories: The Case for Mandated Auditing in the United States," in *Research in Accounting Regulation,* Vol. 3, edited by G.J. Previts [JAI Press, 1989], pp. 103-123.

Grey, J.H., "Does Section 7 of the Charter Protect the Right to Be a Professional?" *Les Cahiers de Droit,* 31 [1990, pp. 933-943].

The Impact of the Canadian Charter of Rights and Freedoms on Canadian Business Law [Davies, Ward & Beck, January 1986].

Irwin Toy v. *Quebec* (A-G), 58 DLR(4th)577 [April 27, 1989].

Johnson, O., and W.D. Terando, "From Contract to Tort: The Evolution of Accountants Legal Liability For Negligence," in *Research in Accounting Regulation,* Vol. 4, edited by G.J. Previts [JAI Press, 1990], pp. 77-97.

Lazar, F., J.M. Sievers, and D.B. Thornton, "Analysis of the Practice of Public Accounting in Ontario," working paper, Professional Organizations Committee, Attorney General of Ontario [1978].

Lipset, S.., *Continental Divide: The Values and Institutions of the United States and Canada* [Routledge, 1990].

Mason, J.B., "More Legal Steps in CGA's Claim to Public Practice in PEI," *Bottomline* [December 1990].

McKinney v. *University of Guelph Canada Law Book,* case 091002044 [December 6, 1990].

Merino, B.D., and M.D. Neimark, "Disclosure Regulation and Public Policy: A Sociohistorical Reappraisal," *Journal of Accounting and Public Policy, 1* [1982, pp. 33-57].

Peck, S.R., "An Analytical Framework for the Application of the Canadian Charter of Rights and Freedoms," *Osgoode Hall Law Journal,* 24 [1987, pp. 1-85].

Professional Institute of the Public Service of Canada v. *Northwest Territories* [*Commissioner*] *Canada Law Book,* case 090233001 [August 16, 1990].

Regina v. *Big M Drug Mart Ltd.* 18 CCC (3rd) 385 [1985].

Regina v. *Kitchen* Ontario Court (Provincial Division) [January 30, 1991].

Regina v. *Manuel* 38 OR (2d) 703 [1986].

Regina v. *Morgentaler, Smoling and Scott* 37 CCC (3d) 449 [1988].

Regina v. *Oakes* 24 CCC (3d) 321 [1980].

Regina v. *Rayner* 38 OR (2d) 336 [1987].

Regina v. *Therens* 18 CCC (#d) 481 [1985].

Regina v. *Ushkowski, Canada Law Book,* 089037001 [September 15, 1989].

Regina v. *Vaillancourt* 2 SCR 636, 81 NR 115 [1987].

Richardson, A.J., "Corporatism and Intraprofessional Hegemony: A Study of Regulation and Internal Social Order," *Accounting Organisations and Society,* 14 [1989a, pp. 415-431].

Richardson, A.J., "Canada's Accounting Elite: 1880-1930," *Accounting Historian's Journal,* 16, 1 [1989b], pp. 1-23.

Richardson, A.J., and J.B. Dowling, "An Integrative Theory of Organizational Legitimacy," *Scandinavian Journal of Management Studies,* 3 [1986, pp. 591-615].

Richardson, A.J., and B. McConomy, "Focusing on the Origins of Accounting Regulation: Three Conceptual Lenses," *CA Magazine* [May 1992].

Thornton, D., "The Case Against Government Intervention in Public Accounting Markets," paper presented to the Interprovincial Conference on Professional Regulation, Victoria B.C. [March 11, 1991].

Treilcock, M.J., "Critical Issues in the Design of Governance Regimes for the Professions," *The Law Society Gazette* [1989], pp. 349-353.

Trebilcock, M.J., C.J. Tuohy, and A.D. Wolfson, *Professional Organisations Committee Research Directorate Staff Study* [Ministry of the Attorney General, 1979].

Walker and Robertson v. *Prince Edward Island* (A-G) Supreme Court of Prince Edward Island [1992].

Weaver, R.K., "Controlling Entitlements," in J.E. Chubb and P.E. Peterson (eds), *New Directions in American Politics* [Brookings Institute, 1985].

Wilson and Maxson v. *Medical Services Commission of British Columbia, Canada Law Book,*
     case 88224019 [August 5, 1988].

Young, S.D., *The Rule of Experts: Occupational Licensing in America* [Cato Institute, 1987].

Young, S.D., "Public Accounting Licensure and Service Quality: Issues, Analysis and Evidence,"
     in *Research in Accounting Regulation,* Vol. 2, edited by G.J. Previts [JAI Press, 1988],
     pp. 107-121.

THE CENTRAL LIFE INTERESTS AND ORGANIZATIONAL PROFESSIONAL COMMITMENT OF MEN AND WOMEN EMPLOYED BY PUBLIC ACCOUNTING FIRMS

Donna L. Street, Richard G. Schroeder,
and Bill Schwartz

ABSTRACT

This research addresses resistance to the promotion of women in public accounting firms. Our results, when combined with those of other researchers, indicate that factors inherent in women, specifically their central life interests (CLIs) and organizational professional commitment (OPC), do not explain the upward mobility problems women encounter in these organizations. We propose that women perceive their opportunities in public accounting to be limited. Therefore, women are more likely than men to cast firm loyalty to the wind and pursue alternative career opportunities. Based on the current and prior research, we provide several recommendations for addressing individual, organizational, and societal gender biases which serve as barriers to the upward mobility of women. Several suggestions for future research are also outlined.

Advances in Public Interest Accounting, Volume 5, pages 201-229.
Copyright © 1993 by JAI Press Inc.
All rights of reproduction in any form reserved.
ISBN: 1-55938-496-4

The American Institute of Certified Public Accountants (AICPA) Future Issues Committee has identified the upward mobility of women as one of the 14 major issues facing the profession and appointed a special committee to study this issue. In their report to the AICPA, the Upward Mobility of Women Special Committee [AICPA, 1988] concluded that, "although many women have risen to senior levels in accounting firms, relatively few have been admitted to partnership." Research is needed which examines the factors that block the upward mobility of women. This research must address the organizational and societal factors that contribute to the problems women encounter when attempting to succeed in traditionally male-oriented professions such as public accounting.

INTRODUCTION

In 1972 and 1977, women accounted for 10 percent and 28 percent respectively of accounting graduates [Levine, 1985a, *Bowman's Accounting Report,* 1988]. Throughout the 1980s, the percentage continued to increase. By 1987, women comprised half of the accounting graduates [AICPA, 1988]. As the number of women graduates has grown, the number of women entering public accounting also has grown. In 1988, women constituted 47.2 percent of the new hires by public accounting firms [Walsh and McInnes, 1989].

In a recent survey ["Job Barriers are Falling," 1990], 43 percent of responding CPA firms reported that women comprised over half of their work force; however, the upper levels of management remain predominantly male. Although women hold approximately 16 percent of the top management positions held by accountants, few of these top positions are with the Big Six CPA firms [Berg, 1988]. According to the 1988 *Bowman's Accounting Report,* women represented 1.6 percent of the partners in Big Eight accounting firms that year.[1]

The statistics for female managers in public accounting also indicate an upward mobility problem for women.[2] The Big Six firms hold one of the worst records among the business professions for promoting women to top managerial positions [Berg, 1988]. The statistics pose some intriguing questions such as:

1. Why has there been so much resistance to the promotion of women in public accounting firms, and is this resistance evidence of organizational discrimination?

2. Does the low number of women managers and partners reflect differences in the work interests and attitudes of women and men?

3. What are the symbolic, systematic, ideological, and economic reasons for stereotyped views of women?

4. How can the public accounting industry, which has traditionally been male dominated, initiate change given the societal factors which nourish stereotyped views of women and discrimination?
5. Is partnership an adequate measure of success for women in public accounting, or should some other criteria be used?
6. If the number of women obtaining partnership status increases, will these women have the opportunity to change discriminatory practices or will they be tokens?

To address these and other important questions, the gender literature, including that addressing the accounting profession, will be reviewed in the following section.

ORGANIZATIONAL AND SOCIETAL FACTORS THAT HINDER THE UPWARD MOBILITY OF WOMEN

Organizational and societal factors contribute to the problems women encounter when attempting to climb a male-oriented career structure such as public accounting. Kanter [1977b] argues that structural constraints within organizations may result in low aspirations and lack of commitment by women. Spencer and Podmore [1987] also contend that women's aspirations and attitudes may be affected by difficulties they face in their work environment. According to Bagilole [1986], formal and informal organizational practices and procedures that are influenced by stereotyped views of women and the nature of their work can result in unequal treatment of women and affect their advancement within the organization. Women also face organizational barriers arising from theories of women's strong attachment to the home [Homans, 1987].

Organizational barriers to women's upward mobility take several forms. Discriminatory practices in the workplace are well documented and summarized by Lehman [1992]. These include management practices [Beno, 1988; Maruani and Nicole, 1987], initial job assignments [Keller, 1985], job classification schemes [Milkman, 1983; Roos, 1988], training opportunities and steretyped views of ability and productivity [Ferrao, 1984; Goldin, 1984; Kessler-Harris, 1981, 1982], wage fixing discrimination, job design [Kanter, 1980; Cockburn, 1981], and the exercise of authority [Burton 1987a, 1987b; Cook, 1983].

Contrary to stereotyped views of women, research indicates no difference in the effectiveness of male and female leaders. However, unfounded biases against female leaders still exist. Based on a meta-analysis of laboratory studies examining sex differences in leadership, Dobbins and Platz [1986] found that female leaders were viewed as less effective. But, their meta-analysis of field studies indicated no sex differences in leader effectiveness. Dobbins and Platz concluded that in laboratory settings raters do not have multiple opportunities to observe leader performance and compare this with the performance of other organizational members. Therefore, raters may be forced to rely on their implicit sex theories when evaluating the leader. These raters exhibit behavior consistent with their stereotypes.

Prior research indicates that it seems unlikely that differential behaviors or job outcomes associated with women leaders account for the sex structuring of organizations. Bartol [1978] suggests that it may be possible to explain the sex structuring of organizations through the stages and transitions which comprise the organization's filtering system. At the pre-entry level women may be filtered out due to preparation, education, and socialization for traditional female roles. Selection discrimination may filter out women at the entry level. During the training phase, women may be filtered out due to role confusion, superior-subordinate distance, and isolation. Initiation of women by the organizations may be based on the concepts of acceptance at the price of competence and/or the choice of unpalatable roles. During their first regular assignment, women may be viewed as tokens and receive less challenging work assignments. Later in their careers, women may face differential performance criteria and differential reinforcement. At the promotion or leveling off stage, women may face promotion discrimination.

Bartol argues that it is important to investigate contingencies at various career stages as they affect an individual's ability to pass to future stages. Internal and external factors that operate at various stages must be identified. Internal factors that may inhibit women from upward mobility aspirations include low self-esteem and role-conflict. External factors that may interfere with women moving into managerial positions include: attitudes of others, organizational and institutional policies and practices, differential opportunities, reinforcement of sex stereotyped behavior, family responsibilities, and limited access to inside information. Future research must focus on the specific nature of the career stage under scrutiny in evaluating the influences on movement of women through the filtering systems of organizations.

Acker and Van Houten [1974] argue that deviancy from a preferred status in the culture adds to the structuring of control within an organization. Women in traditionally male-oriented organizations may be viewed as "double deviants" because they deviate from the preferred status held by their male colleagues on two important dimensions, sex and workgroup majority [Fairhurst and Snavely, 1983]. Workgroup minorities are often viewed as tokens. One of the major problems of tokenism is that a token's perceived power in relation to a majority member's is seen to be low by both the token and the majority member. Kanter [1977b] describes several examples of token compliance to control attempts by the dominant majority. These include loyalty testing where the token is expected to reassure dominants of the token's unwillingness to turn against the dominants. For example, the token may "let slide" or join in statements defamatory to other members of minority status. Female tokens may be trapped in stereotyped female roles (e.g., mother, seductress, pet). Instead of fighting mistaken impressions and negotiating appropriate role relations, tokens may find it easier to accept the stereotyped role rather than risk social isolation and uncertain role relations.

Gender issues in the workplace must be analyzed in relation to wider issues and events in society [Ciancanelli, Gallhofer, Humphrey, and Kirkham, 1990]. Zimmer [1988] argues that sexist ideology in society plays a role in forming workplace behavior and attitudes. Several researchers [Frisbie and Neidert, 1977; Epstein, 1981; Giles, 1977; Harlen and Weiss, 1981] conclude that an increase in the number of women entering male-dominated professions may give rise to tensions and hostilities owing to men's efforts to resist upsets to the patriarchal order of things. Some fear that an increase in wage rates for women must be offset by a decrease in real wages for men [Cook, 1988; and Milkman, 1988]. Torrey [1976] argues that men are socialized to be threatened by any sign of competitiveness or lack of submission by women. Given the difficulty some men have of taking women seriously because of their sex [Collinson and Knights, 1985' Astrachan, 1986], some researchers [Homans, 1987; Fox and Hesse-Biber, 1984; Zimmer, 1988] question the effectiveness of organizational structural changes aimed at eliminating discrimination.

GENDER RESEARCH IN ACCOUNTING

Accounting researchers [e.g., Burrell, 1987; Hopwood, 1987; Kirkham, 1988; Lehman, 1988, 1990, 1992; Tinker and Neimark, 1987] have only recently begun to acknowledge the significance of a broader societal analysis of gender issues. One group of researchers argues that women's advancement in the workplace is constrained by the demand for female labor [Breguel, 1987]. Tinker and Neimark [1987] pose that closing high-paying accounting jobs to women supports the capitalist system by maintained a "reserve army" of low-paid workers. Evidence indicates that the accounting profession has had a traditional separation between bookkeepers (traditionally unqualified women) and accountants and auditors (traditionally men). This separation has been noted in the United States [Sokoloff, 1988], England [Ciancanelli et al., 1990], Australia [Dando and Watson, 1986], and Canada [McKeen and Richardson, 1988].

Reed and Kratchman [1990] studied the effects of changing role requirements on accountants. They found that female accountants, regardless of their family status, reported no less work involvement than did males with similar personal circumstances. The results also indicate that certain groups of women accountants are more committed to their profession than men. Reed and

Kratchman noted some subtle gender differences. Marriage and birth of their first child were life events that impacted significantly the demands placed upon female accountants. Males indicated considerably less change in the role mixture as their families increased in size. Based in their findings, the authors concluded than an unequal division of labor, obligations, rights, power, and rewards for men and women in accounting continues.

Reed and Kratchman argue that it is critical for accountants to raise the profession's consciousness about the presence and harmful effects of stereotyped attitudes. Women are not necessarily less committed to their jobs than their male colleagues, and men are no less committed to their families than women. Reed and Kratchman state that remedies aimed at restructuring behavior must be aimed at the personal, organizational, and societal levels. The authors also encourage individuals to consider their roles, life priorities, and work needs prior to selecting an accounting position.

A survey conducted by Reed Accountancy in England [Ciancanelli et al., 1990] revealed that 85 percent of responding women accountants viewed opportunities for women in accounting as either good or excellent. Accounting was also viewed as a very good or excellent career for young women by 70 percent of the women respondents. However, the same survey reveals high levels of discrimination being experienced by women accountants. Forty-seven percent of the women respondents believed that their sex had caused career problems; the percentage increased to 60 percent for women who had been a member of the accounting profession for more than eleven years. Although the majority of women considered accounting a career with good prospects, 86 percent believed that the opportunities were better for men. Forty-one percent of the women respondents state that clients had been surprised to find that their auditor was a woman.

Maupin [1990] examined the impact of sex role identity on the career success of public accountants. Using the Bem Sex-Role Inventory, she classified 461 CPAs as Masculine, Feminine, Androgynous (high on both Masculine and Feminine traits), or Undifferentiated. All of the 45 partners (including 13 women) participating in the study were classified as either Masculine or Androgynous. Maupin concluded that the results indicate that the majority of CPAs rising to the upper levels in public accounting exhibit androgynous behavior. Based on further analysis of the data, Maupin concluded the androgynous CPAs are more likely to experience high job satisfaction than CPAs with either Masculine or Feminine behavior.

Lehman [1990] questions Maupin's interpretation of the survey results. Lehman points out that a significant proportion of accountants achieving success (measured by partner status) and satisfaction in Maupin's sample are Masculine sex-typed. Based on statistical tests reported by Maupin, Lehman concludes that Masculinity, not Femininity or Androgynous behavior, is necessary for women to achieve job satisfaction. At the entry level, while only eight percent of the men were classified as Feminine, 46 percent of the women were sex-typed Feminine. Based on these findings, Lehman poses some important questions: Why do almost half of upper-level females exhibit masculine behavior, and why are there no Feminine sex-typed females at the partner level?

The literature reveals a broad range of issues and concerns related to women in the workplace. Additional research is needed in accounting to address many of these important issues and to isolate factors that hinder the upward mobility of women in accounting organizations. The purpose of our study is to examine work interests and attitudes of men and women employed in public accounting firms. Specifically, the study will determine if central life interests (CLIs) and organizational-professional commitment (OPC) differ by sex in these organizations. Hypotheses are based on a review of literature from numerous areas including history, sociology, and organizational behavior.

WOMEN'S WORK INTERESTS AND ATTITUDES

In the introduction, several important questions were posed including:

1. Why has there been so much resistance to the promotion of women in public accounting firms, and is this resistance evidence of organizational discrimination?
2. Or, is the low number of women managers and partners reflective of differences in the work interests and attitudes of women and men?

We will attempt to answer these questions by examining the CLI and OPC of men and women employed by public accounting firms. If our results indicate that women are not work oriented and exhibit less organizational and professional commitment than men, an argument may be made that factors inherent in women, including their work interests and attitudes, serve as barriers to their upward mobility. If our results indicate that women are work oriented and exhibit high organizational and professional commitment, an argument can follow that other factors, such as organizational discrimination and societal stereotypes, are blocking the upward mobility of women in public accounting firms.

Central Life Interests (CLIs)

Dublin [1979] defined CLI as that portion of the individual's life space in which an effective investment is made. Affective investments are defined by Dublin, Champoux, and Porter [1975] as:

Work oriented: work activities are the social experiences most valued by the individual.

Nonwork oriented: nonwork activities are the social experiences most valued by the individual.

Flexible focus: the individual does not have a preference for work or nonwork social experiences. The individual is able to adapt to various social experiences and perform effectively as he or she moves among them.

Research indicates that CLIs covary with personality traits such as need for self-actualization and job security and achievement; these findings support the argument that personality influences CLI. In addition, CLI has been found to be affected by the situation confronting an individual [Morrow, 1983].

Based on prior studies [Levine, 1985a], work is more likely to be a central life interest for professionals than it is for industrial workers. Individuals who indicate a work orientation are characterized as being upwardly striving [Goldman, 1973], more committed to the organization [Dublin, Champoux, and Porter, 1975], less alienated and indifferent [Brown, 1968], and more satisfied with their jobs [Dublin and Champoux, 1975] than non-work-oriented individuals.

Levine [1985a] surveyed senior and staff accountants in the New York City offices of large CPA firms to determine their CLIs. The primary purpose of Levine's study was to determine whether work-oriented accountants intend to remain with their firms longer than non-work-oriented accountants. Only 25 percent of the respondents were found to have a work orientation. By group, 28 percent of the seniors and 23 percent of the staff were classified as work oriented. Statistical tests indicated that work-oriented male seniors intended to stay with the firm longer than non-work-oriented male seniors (7.6848 versus 4.3867 years; significant at .05). Work-oriented male staff also intended to stay with their firms longer than non-work-oriented male staff (7.8028 versus 4.8957 years; significant at $p = .05$). Although work-oriented female staff and seniors intended to stay with their firms longer than non-work-oriented female staff and seniors, the differences were not statistically significant.

Levine noted that female accountants, regardless of their work orientation, intended to stay with their firms for a shorter period of time than their male colleagues. These findings are consistent with the literature which indicates that although attrition from the lower levels of CPA firms is high for both sexes, the problem is greater among women [Westcott and Seiler, 1986].

Based on the same survey, Levine [1985b] reported additional analyses based on sex. Twenty-nine percent of the male seniors who responded were work-oriented; 24 percent of the female seniors were work oriented. The differences by sex were not statistically significant. For the responding staff members, 25 percent of the males and 20 percent of the females were work oriented. Again, the difference was not statistically significant. Levine concluded that his findings lend no support to the argument that factors inherent in women serve as barriers to their upward mobility in public accounting firms. Additional research is needed to determine if CLIs differ by sex at other hierarchial levels in public accounting firms.

Organization-Professional Commitment (OPC)

Organizational commitment is represented by the strength of an individual's identification with and involvement in an organization [Porter, Crampon, and Smith, 1976]. Individuals high in organizational commitment possess:

1. a strong belief in and acceptance of the organization's goals and values,
2. a willingness to exert considerable effort on behalf of the organization, and
3. a strong desire to maintain membership in the organization [Mowday, Steers, and Porter, 1979].

Professional commitment is represented by the strength of the individual's identification with and involvement in the profession. Originally, the OPC model assumed that organizational and professional commitment are mutually exclusive attitudes.

More recent studies have indicated that organizational and professional commitment may not be mutually exclusive [Aranya and Ferris, 1984]. Aranya, Pollock, and Amernic [1981] state that organizational commitment actually may be dependent on professional commitment. Other studies indicate that professional commitment is developed during the period of introduction to the profession [Larson, 1977], and organizational commitment is dependent upon the ability of an organization to fulfill professional expectations [Bartol, 1979]. Recent studies indicate that individuals may be high on both organizational and professional commitment, low on both, or high on one and low on the other [Harrell, Chewning, and Taylor, 1986]. Bline, Duchon, and Meixner [1991] report that results of numerous tests indicate that the two scales are indeed measuring different constructions.

Organizational and professional commitment are influenced by an individual's position in the organization's hierarchial structure [Schroeder and Imdieke, 1977; Norris and Niebuhr, 1983; Harrell, Chewning, and Taylor, 1986]. Individuals in public accounting firms with relatively more decision-making responsibility (partners and managers) tend to exhibit a higher organizational and lower professional commitment than those individuals with relatively less decision-making responsibility (juniors and seniors).

Some organizational commitment models [Stevens, Beyer, and Trice, 1978] suggest that factors such as personal characteristics, role-related or job characteristics, and work experiences influence organizational commitment.

Additional research is needed to determine if organizational commitment and professional commitment differ by sex in public accounting firms.

Women's Work Orientations

Women's opportunities, success and behavior are embedded in ideology and consciousness of everyday experiences [Borisoff and Merrill, 1985 Gilligan, 1982; Hentoff, 1988; Illich, 1982; Keohane, 1981; Kessler-Harris, 1986; Lerner, 1986]. These factors influence the determination of commitment and have resulted in several explanations for the failure of women to advance to managerial positions; these include: (1) the person-centered explanation and (2) the organizational-centered explanation [Fagenson, 1986].

The person-centered explanation poses that factors that are inherent in women because of sex-stereotyping act as a barrier to their upward mobility. That is, evidence exists that men and women receive differential treatment in education, at the work place, in social institutions in political empowerment and in periods of economic crisis [Bouchier, 1983; Charvet, 1982; French, 1985; Keohane, 1981; and Lerner, 1986]. More recently, the accounting literature has revealed similar findings [Burrell, 1987; Crompton, 1987; Hopwood, 1987; Lehman 1990, 1992; Reed and Kratchman, 1990; Thomas, 1989; Tinker and Neimark, 1987].

According to the person-centered theory, women are socialized from birth to adopt behaviors and attitudes that are antithetical to being a successful leader. The person-centered explanation holds that women's orientations toward their families and careers are contrary to the demands placed upon executives. For example, corporate executives have been found to be highly committed to their careers and organization [Kanter, 1977a]. Whereas, women have been found to value their personal life and peer group relationships over their careers and not to have a strong sense of organizational commitment [Reitz and Jewell, 1979].

These differences in attitudes have been attributed to a differential childhood sex-role socialization [Hennig and Jardim, 1977] and differential gender identity formation [Chodrow, 1978]. The person-centered advocates hold that these differences result in different patterns of responses between men and women [Henning and Jardim, 1977].

The organizational-centered explanation holds that an individual's position in the organizational structure shapes his or her attitudes. That is, one's hierarchical position, not one's sex, determines interests and attitudes in organizational settings. Consequently, since women mainly occupy the lower positions in organizations and consider their promotions to be less likely than for men, their orientations are developed in response to these stimuli [Kanter, 1977a].

According to the organizational-centered explanation, the individuals in upper levels of organizations are in highly satisfying jobs and develop strong organizational and work commitments. In contrast, the individuals in the lower levels of organizations tend to develop attitudes that impede their progress and become more committed to their personal life than their job or organizations.

Fagenson [1986] tested the person-centered and organizational-centered explanations by sampling women attending a business conference. The subjects were analyzed with respect to their positions within their organization's hierarchy. Fagenson's results supported the organizational-centered explanation but did not support the person-centered explanation.

Chusmir's Model of Job Commitment

Chusmir [1982] states that job commitment (Chusmir defines job commitment in terms of Stevens, Beyer, and Trice's [1978] explanation of organizational commitment) is directly affected by perceived role behaviors and attitudes which include need satisfaction, work commitment, and sex-role conflict. Other variables which have a direct, as well as an indirect, effect on job commitment are intrinsic need strength (high order growth needs) and job circumstances (job satisfaction, meaningfulness of work, utilization of skills, psychological job factors, and nonmotivational job factors). Family characteristics (marital status, child responsibility, supportiveness of spouse, spouse's earnings, and satisfaction with family life) and personal influences (sex, background, and attitudes and values) indirectly influence job commitment.

Need satisfaction (i.e., need for achievement, an internalized Protestant work ethic, and need for autonomy) correlates positively with job commitment for both men and women [Hall and Schneider, 1972]. Prior research indicates that power, achievement, and affiliation needs do not differ by-sex for accountants [Street and Bishop, 1991]. However, needs and expectations are socially constructed; therefore, by-sex differences may exist for other types of needs. Perceptions of need satisfaction are problematic and may be difficult to measure. Future research is needed to address the impact of need satisfaction on job commitment.

Dublin, Champoux, and Porter [1975] have shown that a work orientation is positively associated with organizational commitment. Levine [1985b] found no significant difference in the work orientation of male and female staff and seniors employed by public accounting firms. Our study will examine the work orientation of men and women at all hierarchal levels in public accounting firms to determine if this variable differs by sex.

Job commitment also may be affected by sex-role concepts. The research literature clearly indicates that a woman's level of job commitment is strongly and negatively affected by sex-role conflict [Herman and Gyllstrom, 1977; Terborg, 1977]. Society in general and family and work colleagues in particular burden the working women with conflicting role-set and expectations [Chusmir, 1982]. Although researchers find sex-role conflict among working women (those with both traditional and nontraditional views) [Terborg, 1977], this same conflict is not found among working men [Hamner and Tosi, 1974]. Sex-role conflict exists among both single and married women but is reported to be stronger for married women and working mothers [Herman and Gyllstrom, 1977].

Although sex appears to have no biological effect on job involvement [Hall and Rabinowitz, 1977], sex does subject females to environmental pressures not placed on males. Chusmir [1982] argues that this finding implies that stereotyped assumptions are not correct in concluding that because of their sex women will be lower in commitment than men. However, a woman's sex does present her with additional environmental stress. Therefore, it is likely that the situation itself rather than the sex of the individual affects commitment. Chusmir's conclusion is consistent with social behaviorist theories such as those proposed by Mischel [1968] and Ekehammar [1974]. These social learning theorists believe that the situation causes behavior. According to Mischel and Ekehammar, men and women are likely to exhibit the same degree of turnover, absenteeism, and/or commitment given the same situation.

Job and work commitment are indirectly affected by family circumstances. Gilligan [1982] reports that women tend to describe themselves in terms of others (i.e., mother, wife) while men tend to describe themselves in terms of achievement. However, Fuchs [1971] found that a majority of married women view themselves as committed to work. Research also indicates that when compared to unmarried women, married women experience more interrole conflict [Herman and Gyllstrom, 1977] and are less satisfied with their jobs [Andrisani and Shapiro, 1978]. Fogarty, Rapoport, and Rapoport [1971] indicate that working women with children are more committed to their work then working women without children. A husband's unfavorable attitude toward his wife's employment causes conflict for many wives that reduces work commitment [Andrisani and Shapiro, 1978]. Fuchs [1971] found a strong association between family structure (the degree to which husbands and wives share household and family roles, with particular emphasis on how strong a part the father plays) and work commitment.

Job circumstances also influence both work commitment and job commitment. Andrisani and Shapiro [1978] and Thomas [1979] found that for working women job satisfaction and job commitment are positively interrelated. Research also indicates that chance for advancement [Stead, 1978], participation in decision making [Ruh and White, 1975], and goal setting [Steers, 1976] are major factors that help explain job commitment.

Several studies have determined that discriminatory practices are built into work structures through management practices and initial job assignments [Burton, 1987b; Compton, 1987; Kessler-Harris, 1986], through job classification schemes [Burton, 1987a and 1987b; Milkman, 1983], through gendered perceptions of liability and productivity and through the exercise of authority [Gilligan, 1982; Kessler-Harris, 1981, and 1982; Lerner, 1986]. These job circumstances may have a negative impact on organizational commitment.

METHODOLOGY

To determine if the work interests and attitudes of public accountants differ by sex, a sample of accountants employed by large accounting firms were surveyed using the CLI instrument developed by Dublin [1956] and the OPC instrument development by Aranya and Ferris [1984].

The Instruments

The CLI Inventory uses a forced choice design on 32 items to classify respondents. The items deal with membership in formal organizations, technological aspects of the environment, informal personal relations, and everyday experiences. Depending upon whether responses indicate that the workplace is their CLI or whether other areas of their social experiences are more important, respondents are classified as either (1) work, (2) non-work, (3) flexible focus, or (4) unclassified. Dalton and Todor [1983] reported a test-retest reliability of .78 and a gamma of .92 for the CLI instrument.

The OPC scale is based upon a definition of organizational commitment which conceptualizes the construct as having the three primary components discussed previously: (1) a strong belief in and acceptance of the organization's goals and values, (2) a willingness to exert considerable effort on behalf of the organization, and (3) a strong desire to maintain membership in the organization. Mowday, Steers, and Porter [1979] reported an average reliability coefficient for the scale of .90. Aranya and Ferris [1984] used the organizational commitment scale as the basis for constructing the professional commitment scale. Based on a comprehensive evaluation of the Porter, Crampon, and Smith [1976] measure of organizational commitment and the Aranya, Pollock, and Amernic [1981] measure of professional commitment, Bline, Duchon, and Meixner [1991] conclude that both measures possess strong internal reliability.

Sample

Juniors, seniors, managers, and partners employed by public accounting firms in the Philadelphia area served as the subjects. Subjects were selected using the "Contact person" technique reported by Schroeder and Verreault [1987]. Public accounting firms in the Philadelphia area were identified. From these a sample of 13 firms was selected (4 large, 4 medium, and 5 small), and a contact person (senior member) in each firm was identified. For each firm, the contact person was requested to designate a number of audit professionals to participate in the study. The questionnaires were delivered to the contact person, who distributed them to the individuals participating in the study. Each respondent was instructed to complete the questionnaire and return it in a sealed envelope to the contact person. After collecting all of the questionnaires, the contact person returned them to the researchers. The final sample consisted of 177 individuals (124 men and 53 women) from the 13 firms.

Hypotheses Tested

Prior research indicates that due to factors such as sex-role conflict, family interests, and job circumstances work interest and attitudes of men and women may differ. Research also indicates that hierarchial level in the organization may affect work attitudes and interest. To determine whether the CLI and OPC of accountants employed by public accounting firms differ by sex and/or hierarchial position within the firm, a series of hypotheses was tested. To test the hypotheses, subjects were grouped two ways: (1) sex and (2) hierarchical position (partners/managers or seniors/juniors).

Hypotheses 1 through 5 addressed CLI

H1: CLIs do not differ by sex.

H2: CLIs do not differ by sex at the partner/ manager level (male partners/ managers versus female partners/managers).

H3: CLIs do not differ by sex at the senior/junior level (male seniors/ juniors versus female seniors/juniors).

H4: For males, CLIs do not differ by hierarchal position within the firm (male partners/managers versus male seniors/juniors).

H5: For females, CLIs do not differ by hierarchal position within the firm (female partners/managers versus female seniors/juniors.

Hypotheses 1 through 5 were tested by first categorizing each respondent as either work, nonwork, flexible focus, or unclassified. Next, the chi-square statistic was used to test for significant differences between expected and observed frequencies.

Hypotheses 6 and 7 addressed the OPC of public accountants:

H6: Organizational commitment does not differ by sex when controlling for hierarchal level.

H7: Professional commitment does not differ by sex when controlling for hierarchal level.

Table 1. Total Respondents by Sex and Position

	Sex	
Position in the Firm	Male	Female
Partner	32	5
Manager	32	9
Senior	30	18
Junior	30	21
Total	124	53

Hypotheses 6 and 7 were analyzed by developing organizational commitment scores and professional commitment scores for each respondent. Analyses of covariance (ANCOVA) were conducted to determine if sex was significant to organizational (H6) and professional (H7) commitment when controlling for hierarchal level in the firm.

FINDINGS

Table 1 provides a breakdown of the number of respondents by sex and hierarchical position in the firm. This table reveals that cell size is not consistent across groups. However, the number of women at the manager/partner level is representative of the population, since considerably fewer women than men hold top level positions in public accounting firms.

Central Life Interests

First, Hypotheses 1 through 5 were tested based on the CLI classifications. For Hypotheses 1, a chi-square analysis was performed to determine whether

Table 2. Central Life Interests of Men and Women Employed by Large Public Accounting Firms

	Central Life Interest							
	Work		Non Work		Flexible Focus		Unclassified	
Sex	N	(%)	N	(%)	N	(%)	N	(%)
Men ($N = 124$)	30	(24)	17	(14)	53	(43)	24	(19)
Women ($N = 53$)	25	(47)	7	(13)	11	(21)	10	(19)

Notes: **H1:** Chi-Square value = 11.28.
significant at $p = .010$.

Table 3.   Central Life Interests of Partners and Managers Employed by Large Public Accounting Firms By Sex

| | Central Life Interest | | | | | | | |
| | Work | | Non Work | | Flexible Focus | | Unclassified | |
Gender	N	(%)	N	(%)	N	(%)	N	(%)
Men ($N = 64$)	17	(27)	5	(8)	33	(51)	9	(14)
Women ($N = 14$)	11	(79)	0	(0)	3	(21)	0	(0)

Notes: **H2:** Chi-Square value = 13.98.
significant at $p = .002$.

Table 4.   Central Life Interest of Seniors and Juniors Employed by Large Public Accounting Firms by Sex

| | Central Life Interest | | | | | | | |
| | Work | | Non Work | | Flexible Focus | | Unclassified | |
Gender	N	(%)	N	(%)	N	(%)	N	(%)
Men ($N = 60$)	13	(22)	12	(20)		(33)	15	(25)
Women ($N = 39$)	14	(36)	7	(18)		(21)	10	(25)

Notes: **H3:** Chi-Square value = 3.18.
significant at $p = .364$.

the CLIs of public accountants differ by sex. The results, which are presented in Table 2, indicate that the CLIs of female accountants are significantly different from those of their male colleagues. Females tended to be classified as work oriented (47%) while males tended to be classified as flexible focus (43%).

Tests also were conducted to determine if sex differences are present at the partner-manager level (H2) and at the senior/junior level (H3). Again, the chi-square statistic was used. As shown in Table 3, results of the first analysis reveal that the CLIs of female partners/managers are significantly different from the CLIs of male partners/managers. The majority of female partners/managers were classified as work oriented (79%) while the majority of male partners/ managers (51%) were classified as flexible focus. At the senior/junior level, the chi-square test, Table 4, indicates no significant differences by sex. The latter finding is consistent with Levine's [1985b] findings.

Tests were conducted to determine if CLIs differ by hierarchical level within sex. The chi-square results presented in Table 5 indicate that the CLIs of male partners/managers are significantly different from the CLIs of male seniors/ juniors. Similarly, a chi-square test indicated that the CLIs of female manager/ partners were significantly different from the CLIs of female seniors/juniors; these results are presented in Table 6.[3]

Table 5.   Central Life Interest of Males By Hierarchal Level

Hierarchal Level	Central Life Interest							
	Work		Non Work		Flexible Focus		Unclassified	
	N	(%)	N	(%)	N	(%)	N	(%)
Partners/Managers (N = 64)	17	(27)	5	(8)	33	(51)	9	(14)
Seniors/Juniors (N = 60)	13	(22)	12	(20)	20	(33)	15	(25)

Notes: Chi-Square value = 7.983.
significant at p = .046.

Table 6.   Central Life Interest of Females By Hierarchal Level

Hierarchal Level	Central Life Interest							
	Work		Non Work		Flexible Focus		Unclassified	
	N	(%)	N	(%)	N	(%)	N	(%)
Partners/Managers (N = 14)	11	(78)	0	(0)	3	(22)	0	(0)
Seniors/Juniors (N = 39)	14	(36)	7	(18)	8	(21)	10	(25)

Notes: **H6:** T value = −2.62.
significant at p = .012.

Based on our sample, the CLIs of those who advance to the level of partner/manager tend to be either work oriented or flexible focus. All of the female partners/managers in our sample were classified as either work oriented or flexible focus, and 57 percent of the female seniors/juniors were classified as either work oriented or flexible focus. Notice that at the senior/junior level 36 percent of the females are work oriented compared to only 22 percent of the males. Prior research indicates that upwardly anchored individuals are more likely to be work oriented than those who are not upwardly anchored [Bowin, 1970], and individuals with a central life interest in work are characterized as being upwardly striving [Goldman, 1973]. Therefore, our results indicate that female accountants are not less upwardly striving than their male peers.

These results pose some intriguing questions. Despite the strong work orientation of women, do organization members still hold stereotyped perceptions of their work interests and attitudes? Organizations, including those which employ accountants, must be made aware of the symbolic, ideological, and economic reasons for the stereotyped views of women. Women

Table 7.   Organizational Commitment Means by Sex and Hierarchal Level

	Sex		
Hierarchal Level	All	Men	Women
All	4.40	4.47	4.12
Partners and Managers	4.64	4.70	4.33
Seniors and Juniors	4.16	4.22	4.00

must be evaluated and promoted based on their actual work performance, not on stereotyped views.

Thirty-six percent of female seniors/juniors are work oriented, yet few females have achieved top positions in public accounting firms. Given that work-oriented individuals tend to be upwardly striving, why are there so few women partners? Do differential promotion criteria exist for men and women?

Organizational-Professional Commitment

Hypothesis 6 was tested based on the organizational commitment scores. Mean values for organizational commitment are presented in Table 7; these values indicate that the organizational commitment of male accountants is greater than that of their female colleagues. Analysis of covariance (ANCOVA) was used to test for the relationship of organizational commitment, sex, and hierarchal level. ANCOVA is useful in examining the relationship between two variables when the researcher is concerned that a categorical variable may be confounding the relationship. ANCOVA allows for the examination of the relationship in question by controlling for the confounding categorical variable. ANCOVA increases the precision of experiments by providing a statistical control for extraneous variables, when direct control through the design of the experiment is impractical or impossible [Wildt and Ahtola, 1988, p. 5]. In our experiment, organizational commitment is the dependent variable, sex is the independent variable, and hierarchal level is the covariate.

Prior to analyzing data with an ANCOVA model, it must be determined that there is no significant interaction between the covariate and the treatment. This assumption, termed the homogeneity of slopes assumption, indicates that the slope of the regression line of the dependent variable onto the covariate is the same in all cells of the design. In our model, the probability for the treatment by covariate interaction is greater than .65, so the assumption of the homogeneity of slopes is plausible. Subsequently, the ANCOVA model uses only the treatment and covariate as predictors. This test disclosed the following probabilities: sex $< .05$, hierarchal level $p < .0001$. Consequently, the variable

Table 8. Professional Commitment Means by Sex and Hierarchal Level

	Sex		
Hierarchal Level	*All*	*Men*	*Women*
All	4.27	4.29	4.25
Partners and Managers	4.27	4.29	4.19
Seniors and Juniors	4.27	4.28	4.27

sex adjusted for the covariate hierarchal level was found to be significant. These results, lend support to the rejection of Hypothesis 6.

Next, Hypothesis 7 was tested based on the professional commitment scores. Mean values for professional commitment are presented in Table 8. An ANCOVA analysis similar to that used to test for organizational commitment was undertaken. Once again, the homogeneity of slopes assumption was satisfied ($p < .85$). However, neither the treatment or the covariate were found to be significant. These results indicate that professional commitment does not differ by sex in public accounting firms.

Results of Hypotheses 6 and 7 provide some evidence that the OPC of accountants differs by sex. The results indicate no differences in professional commitment by sex, but they indicate that the organizational commitment of males is greater than the organizational commitment of females after controlling for hierarchal level in the firm. Therefore, differences in professional commitment cannot be used to rationalize differences in the upward mobility of male and female public accountants. However, organizational commitment may be a factor which helps explain the upward mobility problems of women in accounting. The discussion section will focus on the organizational commitment findings. Our results support Bline, Duchon, and Meixner's [1991] conclusion that the Porter et al. measure of organizational commitment scale and the Aranya et al. measure of professional commitment are measuring two different constructs.

DISCUSSION

During recent years, the number of men and women graduating from accounting programs and entering public accounting has been about equal. However, prior to reaching managerial levels, particularly partner, significantly more women than men are filtered out of these organizations. The literature poses numerous explanations of the sex structuring of organizations. One school of thought argues that the small number of women obtaining top managerial positions is reflective of differences in the work interests and attitudes of men and women. Our results do not support this position. Instead they indicate that other factors, such as discriminatory practices, block women from top managerial positions.

Our results indicate that women in public accounting are work oriented and reveal no significant differences in the professional commitment of men and women. However, the organizational commitment of women employed by public accounting firms is lower than that of their male colleagues. According to Chusmir [1982], job commitment is directly affected by perceived role behavior and attitudes, job circumstances, and intrinsic needs. Other factors such as family circumstances and sex indirectly affect job commitment.

While women employed by public accounting firms tend to be work oriented, men employed by these firms tend to be flexible focus. These results may indicate the strength of the socialization and screening process in public accounting firms. In order to be accepted in the work place, women may be overcompensating. They may feel that differential promotion criteria require them to focus primarily on work to survive in a male dominated industry.

Research indicates that male and female accountants exhibit similar needs for achievement, power, and affiliation [Street and Bishop, 1991]. However, needs and expectations are socially constructed, and other needs and need satisfaction affect job commitment.

In this research, job circumstances and sex-role conflict are used to explain differences in the organizational commitment of men and women. Research [Goldman 1973; Dubin, Champoux, and Porter, 1975; and Dubin and Champoux, 1975] has shown that individuals with a work orientation tend to be upwardly striving, more committed to the organization, and more satisfied with their jobs. However, in our study, female public accountants, who tend to be classified as work oriented, were less committed to their organization. Therefore, other factors, such as job circumstances and sex-role conflict, are intervening and result in lower organizational commitment among female public accountants.

Job circumstances have a negative impact on the organizational commitment of women accountants. Larson [1977] argues that organizational commitment is dependent upon the organization's ability to fulfill professional expectations. Ward, Moseley, and Ward [1986] found that female employees of large public accounting firms are basically satisfied with their jobs. However, female public accountants are less satisfied with certain aspects of their jobs than are their male colleagues. For example, Bullen and Martin [1987] found that women were less satisfied than men with aspects of their jobs related to promotion (opportunities for advancement, the manner in which promotions were determined, the availability of upper-level positions, and the extent to which women know when they would be promoted). Ward, Moseley, and Ward [1986] reported relatively low levels of satisfaction with promotions among female CPAs. Konstana and Ferris [1981] indicate that individuals (men and women) who leave public accounting are dissatisfied with the training received from their superiors and with their opportunity to grow professionally. Levine [1985a] reported positive relationships between the number of years females spend in public accounting and feelings of discrimination or actual discrimination. Levine [1985a] found that female seniors and staff employed by large accounting firms intended to remain a shorter period of time with their employers then their male colleagues.

Combined, these findings indicate that women in public accounting perceive their opportunities for advancement to be less then those of their male colleagues. Factors such as dissatisfaction with prospects for promotion may contribute to lower organizational commitment in women. As a result, female employees may leave their firms for other career options that they perceive as providing more opportunities for advancement. Kessler-Harris [1986] argues that the job market and the world of work can and does influence how young women think about themselves and how women assess their possibilities; aspirations are themselves conditioned by perceptions of available opportunity.

Chusmir [1982] states that research clearly indicates that the job commitment of women is strongly and negatively affected by sex role conflict. Reed and Kratchman [1990] found that the roles of spouse and parent placed significantly more demands on women accountants than on their male colleagues. Women in accounting face the same problems as other professionals; they must balance career and family [Westcott and Seiler, 1986]. Spouses and children must be fit into the busy schedule of working women who are striving to gain acceptance as qualified individuals. In response to the question "how can the profession strengthen the upward mobility of women in public accounting," the AICPA's [1984] Future Issues Committee states, "One reason why professional women find advancement difficult may be society's pressure on women to be the center of family units, including the role of childbearer and child raiser. If a woman is to fulfill both professional and family responsibilities at the same time, she may need flexibility in her professional work...."

Although family circumstances do exert significantly more demands on women than men, recent studies [Konstana and Ferris, 1981; Reed and Kratchman, 1990; Trost, 1990] indicate that women managers quit their jobs not for family but because of dissatisfaction with job circumstances. A study of women CPAs reveals that the primary reasons women give for leaving CPA firms are (1) long overtime hours, (2) not being developed for future responsibilities, and (3) better professional opportunities elsewhere [Wescott and Seiler, 1986].

Wick & Co. [Trost 1990] surveyed 110 professionals from Fortune 500 companies. When asked what in their personal life influenced the decision to quit their jobs[4], they [5] indicated: children (women 9%, men 26%). spouse (women 27%, men 26%), nothing in their personal life (women 55%, men 53%). These results indicate that women managers are no more likely than men, perhaps even less likely, to quit their jobs due to family circumstances. Some management specialists argue that currently many companies are emphasizing family issues, such as maternity leave and day care, to attract and retain female managers. This is desirable, but unless companies begin to accommodate women's desires for promotion and respect, employers run the risk of further increasing the already high rate of turnover among female employees.

Many would argue that a strong commitment to family is preferable. That is, there needs to be a commitment to child rearing if our society is to progress, and public accounting firms need to accommodate commitment to family for both female and male employees. However, public accounting firms need to realize that accommodating a commitment to family is not enough. Tashjian (of Wick & Co.) argues that corporate "fixation" on family issues may detract from the larger issues of women's advancement.

Two recent studies (Wick and Opinion Research Corporation) indicate that women are more likely than men to throw corporate loyalty to the wind if they feel they are not getting adequate opportunities for growth. Women managers who feel they have "hit the glass ceiling" leave their organizations to pursue opportunities elsewhere. One female participant in the Wick's study quit her job because she felt blocked as a women by "people who didn't want me to succeed in any way." After leaving her former employer, she took a managerial position with a company where employees "sink or swim on their own merits." She further states, "It's a challenge every day and I thrive on it."

CONCLUSIONS

Our findings are based on a sample of accountants employed by public firms located in a limited geographic area. The study should be viewed as a preliminary step in addressing the crucial issue of the upward mobility of women. Additional research is needed to determine if these results hold for more diverse samples. Specifically, this research should focus on questions such as: (1) do sex differences in organizational commitment exist for larger, more diverse samples and (2) how do the factors comprising Chusmir's model affect the organizational commitment of male and female accountants.

The AICPA's [1984] Future Issues Committee indicates that attitudes of members of the profession deserve consideration. Questions that need to be answered include: Are males as willing and cooperative when their manager is female as when their manager is male, and what are men's attitudes toward their professional women colleagues?

Future research must address sex structuring of accounting organizations. Although women currently face few barriers during the pre-entry (undergraduate education) and entry stages of their careers with public accounting firms, the filtering processes at higher levels must be carefully examined. This research should determine whether techniques such as tokenism, less challenging work assignments, differential performance criteria and reinforcement, and promotion discrimination are used to filter women out of public accounting.

Research should also address the status of the small number of women who have attained top managerial positions in public accounting firms. Are these women viewed as equals by their males colleagues? Or, are they viewed as tokens? According to Kanter [1977b], individuals are viewed as tokens when they enter an environment where their social category historically has been scarce. A skewed ratio of majority to minority members increases the visibility of tokens which may result in a set of performance pressures for tokens—that is, characteristics and standards applicable only to tokens. Majority members may stereotype tokens to familiar generalizations that often are at odds with work-related roles. This majority behavior produces performance pressure, social isolation, and role entrapment for tokens.

Crompton [1987] suggests that inequalities result from the difficulties women face in acquiring organizational knowledge, which is often essential for a professional's promotion prospects; therefore, CPA firms need to provide all employees with equal assess to tactic knowledge. Research is needed to determine whether men and women have difficult access to "mentors." Given the small number of female partners, research is needed to examine difficulties encountered when the mentor is a male and the protege is a female. Future research addressing these and other important issues is needed to provide female accountants with knowledge and techniques to attack barriers to their upward mobility in accounting organizations.

Roles and behavior deemed appropriate to the sexes have been expressed in values, customs, laws, and social roles that have evolved over thousands of years [Lerner, 1986]. Throughout history, metaphors for gender have expressed the male as the norm and the female as the deviant. However, lately, researchers have been discussing new interpretations. They suggest that female standards are not identical to men's and this difference does not necessarily imply inferiority [French, 1985].

Patriarchy (the institutionalization of male dominance over women) is a historic creation formed by men and women in a process that took thousands of years [Learner, 1986]. Men acquired the knowledge necessary to elevate "difference" of whatever kind into a criterion for dominance. Difference is a distinguishing mark that separates the classes, and class is not a separate construct from gender. Women are exposed to male dominance in institutions, including public accounting firms. As a result, many women may begin to lower their expectations for advancement within the organization.

The accounting profession does not operate in a vacuum. In order to restructure behavior, remedies must be aimed at the personal, organizational, and societal levels. As recommended by Reed and Kratchman [1990], individuals must consider their various roles, life priorities, and work needs when selecting an accounting position. Organizations including public accounting firms must examine their filtering processes and eliminate differential treatment based on social categories such as sex. Accounting organizations must develop plans whereby all employees, male and female, can simultaneously manage career and family thereby leading balanced lives. When family demands are at critical levels, organizations must be flexible with work hours and travel requirements. Accounting firms should reconsider their pyramid structure. Perhaps vertical retention makes more sense in today's world with its increasing number of dual career families.

Individuals and organizations are greatly influenced by society; therefore, substantial effort must be directed at identifying and modifying gender biases which have been built into our culture for generations. Economic conditions, education, the media, corporate practices, politics, and family practices all impact the behavior of individuals and organizations. Each of these factors has historically contributed to discriminatory practices; for example the media has depicted women as unable to cope with the stress of the professions, families have viewed the man as head of the household, educators have encouraged young women to be bookkeepers and young men to be accountants and auditors, and corporations have filled high-paying jobs with males.

Gender biases such as these must be recognized and modified. Individuals and organizations can contribute to change, but opportunities for women will continue to be limited as long as society clings to traditional views of women. Patriarchy has existed for generations, and change will not come easily. To obtain equality in the workplace, women must work to obtain equality in family matters, education, government, and all other components of society.

NOTES

1. In 1983, 69 women represented one percent of the principals and partners of the nine largest public accounting firms [Dahl and Hooks, 1985]. Between 1983 and 1988, the number of male partners increased by 825 while the number of female partners increased by only 88. Research indicates that the number of women promoted to partner during the 1980s is less then would be expected based on the number of women who entered the profession during the 1970s [Meredith and Brown, 1988].

2. In 1980, women represented 4.7 percent of the managers in firms with 25 or more AICPA members [Bowman's Accounting Report, 1988]. By 1985, the percentage of female managers had increased to 17.3 percent. However, in 1987, the percentage had dropped to 15.6 percent.

3. These results must be interpreted with caution because some of the cells had expected values of less than five. However, visual inspection of the data supports this conclusion.

4. Among respondents who had left jobs.

5. Two-thirds of the women in the Wick study had children; 90% of the men had children.

REFERENCES

Acker, J., and D.R. Van Houten, "Differential Recruitment and Control: The Sex Structuring of Organization," *Administrative Science Quarterly* [1974], pp. 152-163.

American Institute of Certified Public Accountants (AICPA), Future Issues Committee, "Upward Mobility of Women," *Major Issues for the CPA Profession and the AICPA Future Issues Committee,* [AICPA, 1984], pp. 17-19.

_____, Upward Mobility of Women Special Committee, *Upward Mobility of Women,* [AICPA, 1988].

Andrisani, P.J., and M.B. Shapiro, "Women's Attitudes Toward their Jobs: Some Longitudinal Data on a National Sample." *Personnel Psychology,* 31[1978] pp. 155-34.

Aranya, N., J. Pollock, and J. Amernic, "An Examination of Professional Commitment in Public Accounting," *Accounting, Organizations and Society* 4[1981], p. 271-280.

Ferris, K.R., "A Reexamination of Accountants' Organizational—Professional Conflict," *The Accounting Review* [January, 1984], pp. 1-15.

Astrachan, A., *How Men Feel: Their Response to Women's Demands for Equality and Power* [Doubleday, 1986].

Bagilole, B. "Women and Underachievement at Work: A study of the Internal Labour Market of the Civil Service," *Social Policy and Administration,* 20, 3[Autumn, 1986], pp. 253-267.

Bartol, K.B., "The Sex Structuring of Organizations: A Search for Possible Causes," *Academy of Management Review* [1978], pp. 805-815.

_____, "Professionalism As a Predictor of Organizational Commitment, Role Stress,. and Turnover: A Multidimensional Approach," *Academy of Management Journal* [1979], pp. 815-821.

Beno, B. "Job Classification Systmens and Women's Wages: The Institutionalization of Discrimination, Supported by the National Research Council," Working Paper, Vista College [1988].

Berg, E.N. "The Big Eight: Still a Male Bastion," *New York Times* [July 12, 1988].

Bline, D.M., D. Duchon, and W.F. Meixner, "The Measurement of Organizational and Professional Commitment: An Examination of the Psychometric Properties of Two Commonly Used Instruments," *Behavioral Research in Accounting* [1991], pp. 1-12.

Borisoff, D., and L. Merrill, *The Power to Communicate: Gender Differences and Barriers* [Waveland Press, 1985].

Bouchier, D., *The Feminist Challenge: The Movement for Women's Liberation in Britain and the USA* [Macmillian Press, 1983].

Bowin, R., "Career Anchorage Points and Central Life Interest of Middle Managers," unpublished doctoral dissertation, University of Oregon [1970].

Bowman's Accounting Report, "Women Are 1.6% of Partners in Big 8 Firms" [June 1988], pp. 13-14.

Breugel, I., "Bourgeois Economics and Women's Oppression," 1 [1978], pp. 103-111.

Brown, L., *Alienation from Work,* unpublished doctoral dissertation, University of Oregon, 1968.

Bullen, M., and L.M.C. Martin, "Job Satisfaction and Intended Turnover in the Large CPA Firm," *The Woman CPA* [October 1987], pp. 8-13.

Burrell, G., "No Accounting for Sexuality," *Accounting, Organizations and Society,* 12, 1[1978], pp. 89-1101.

Burton, C., *Women's Work: Pay Equity and Job Evaluation in Australia* [Australian Government Publishing Service, 1987a].

_____, "Merit and Gender: Organizational and the Mobilization of Masculine Bias," *Australian Journal of Social Issues,* 22, 2[May 1987b], pp. 424-435.

Charvet, J., *Feminism* [J.M. Dent & Sons, 1982].

Chodrow, N., *The Reproduction of Mothering* [University of California Press, 1978].

Chusmir, L.H., "Job Commitment and the Organizational Woman," *Academy of Management Review 7, 4*[1982], pp. 5955-602.

Ciancanelli, P., S. Gallhofer, C. Humphrey, and L. Kirkham, "Gender and Accountancy: Some Evidence from the UK," *Critical Perspectives on Accounting* [1990], pp. 117-144.

Cockburn, C., "The Material of Male Power," *Feminist Review* [October 1981], pp. 41-58.

Collinson, D., and D. Knights, "Jobs for the Boys: Recruitment into Life Insurance Sales," in EOC Research Bulletin No. 9, *Occupational Segregation by Sex* [EOC, 1985], pp. 24-44.

Cook, A.H., "Comparable Worth: Recent Developments in Selected States," *Labor Law Journal* [August 1983], pp. 494-504.

————, "Unions: Are They Keeping Up With Women," Opening Address: Women, Work, and Family Life Conference [April 1988].

Crompton, R., "Gender and Accountancy: A Response to Tinker and Neimark." *Accounting, Organizations and Society, 12,1*[1987], pp. 103-110.

Dahl, S., and K.L. Hooks, "Women Accountants, Today and Tomorrow," *CPA Journal* [1985], pp. 20-25.

Dalton, D.R., and W.D. Todor, "Psychometric Properties of the Central Life Interest Inventory," [1983], pp. 887-891..

Dando, C., and R. Watson, "Women in Accounting," *Australian Accountant* [November 1986], pp. 12-18.

Dobbins G.H., and S.J. Platz, "Sex Differences in Leadership: How Real Are They?" *Academy of Management Review* [1986], pp. 118-127.

Dubin, R.R., "Industrial Workers' Worlds: A Study of the Central Life Interests of Industrial Workers," *Social Problems,* 3[1956], pp. 131-142.

————, "Central Life Interests: Self-Integerity in a Complex World," *Pacific Sociological Review* [October 1979], pp. 405-426.

Dublin, R.R., and J.E. Champoux, "Workers' Central Life Interests and Personality Characteristics," *Journal of Vocational Behavior* [1975], pp. 165-174.

Dubin, R.R., J.E. Champoux, and L.W. Porter, "Central Life Interests and Organizational Commitment of Blue-Collar and Clerical Workers," *Administrative Science Quarterly* [September 1975], pp. 411-421.

Ekehammar, B., "Interactionism in Personality from a Historical Perspective." *Psychological Bulletin,* 81[1974], pp. 1026-1048.

Epstein, C., *Women in Law* [Doubleday, 1981].

Fagenson, E.A., "Women's Work Orientations: Something Old, Something New," *Group and Organizational Studies* [March-June 1986], pp. 75-100.

Fairhurst, G.T., and B.K. Snavely, "Majority and Token Minority Group Relationships: Power Acquisition and Communication," *Academy of Management Journal* [1983], pp. 292-300.

Ferrao, G., "Bridging the Wage Gap: Pay Equity and Job Evaluations," *American Psychologist* [1984], pp. 1166-1170.

Fogarty, M.P., R. Rapoport, and R.N Rapoport, *Career, Sex and Family* [Allen & Unwin, 1971].

Fox, M., and S. Hesse-Biber, *Women at Work* [Mayfield, 1984].

French, M., *Beyond Power: On Women, Men & Morals* [Abacus, 1985].

Frisbie, W.P., and L. Neidert, "Inequality and the Relative Size of Minority Populations: A Comparative Analysis," *American Journal of Sociology,* 82 [1977], pp. 1007-1030.

Fuchs, R.., "Different Meanings of Employment for Women." *Human Relations,* 24[1971], pp. 495-499.

Giles, M., "Percent Black and Racial Hostility' An Old Assumption Re Examined," *Social Science Quarterly,* 58[1977], pp. 412-419.

Gilligan, C., *In A Different Voice* [Harvard University Press, 1982].

Goldin, C., "The Earnings Gap in Historical Perspective," in *Comparable Worth: Issue for the 80's* [U.S. Commission Civil Rights, June 6-7. 1984].

Goldman, D.R., "Managerial Mobility Motivations and Central life Interest," *American Sociological Review* [February 1973], pp. 119-126.

Hall, D.T., and S. Rabinowitz, "Caught Up in Work," *Wharton Magazine*, 2, 1[1977], pp. 19-25.

Hall, D.T., and B. Schneider, "Correlates of Organizational Identification as a Function of Career Pattern and Organizational Type," *Administrative Science Quarterly*, 17 [1972], pp. 340-350.

Hamner, W.C., and H.L. Tosi, "Relationship of Role Conflict and Role Ambiguity to Job Involvement Measures," *Journal of Applied Psychology*, 59[1974], 497-499.

Harlen, A., and C. Weiss, *Moving Up: Women in Managerial Careers* [Wellesley College, Center for Research on Women, 1981].

Harrell, A., E. Chewning, and M. Taylor, "Organizational-Professional Conflict and the Job Satisfaction and Turnover Intentions of Internal Auditors," *Auditing: A Journal of Practice and Theory*, 5, 2[Spring 1986].

Hennig, M., and A. Jardim, *The Managerial Woman* [Anchor Press/Doubleday, 1977].

Hentoff, N., "Is This What They Teach in Law School?" *The Village Voice* [April 5, 1988].

Herman, J.B., and K.K. Gyllstrom, "Working Men and Women: Inter-and-Intra Role Conflict." *Psychology of Women Quarterly*, 1[1977], pp. 319-333.

Homans, H., "Man-Made Myths: The Reality of Being a Woman Scientist in the NHS," in *In a Man's World: Essays on Women in Male-dominated Professions*, edited by S. Spencer and N. Podmore [Tavistock, 1987].

Hopwood, A., "Accounting and Gender: An Introduction," *Accounting, Organizations and Society*, 1[1987], pp. 65-69.

Illich, I., *Gender* [Pantheon Books, 1982].

"Job Barriers are Falling for Women in Accounting," *Accounting Today* [March 5, 1990], pp. S3 and S11.

Kanter, R., *Men and Women of the Corporation* [Basic Books, 1977a].

_____, "Some Effects of Proportions on Group Life: Skewed Sex Ratios and Responses to Token Women," *American Journal of Sociology* [1977b], pp. 965-990.

_____, "The Impact of Organizational Structure: Models and Methods for Change," in *Equal Employment Policy for Women*, edited by R.S. Ratner and J.A. Steinberg [Temple University Press, 1980].

Keller, E.F., *Reflections on Gender and Science* (New Haven: Yale University Press, 1985).

Keohane, N., "Speaking from Silence: Women and the Science of Politics," in *A Feminist Perspective in the Academy: The Difference It Makes*, edited by E. Langland and W. Grove [University of Chicago Press, 1981].

Kessler-Harris, A., *Women Have Always Worked: An Historical Overview* [McGraw Hill, 1981].

_____, *Out to Work: A History of Wage Earning Women in the U.S.* [Oxford University Press, 1982].

_____, "Equal Employment Opportunity Commission v. Sears, Roebuck and Company: A Personal Account," *Radical History Review* [1986, pp. 57-79].

Kirkham, L.M., "Discussants' Comments: Cooking the Books: Gender Practices and Accounting Rituals," paper presented at the Second Annual Interdisciplinary Perspectives on Accounting Conference, University of Manchester [July 1988].

Konstana, C., and K. Ferris, "Female Turnover in Professional Accounting Firms: Some Preliminary Findings," *The Michigan CPA* [Winter 1981], pp. 11-15.

Larson, M.S., *The Rise of Professionalism: A Sociological Analysis* [University of California Press, 1977].

Lehman, C.R. "Cooking the Books: Gender Practices and Accounting Rituals," Second Interdisciplinary Perspectives on Accounting Conference, Manchester [July 1988].

————, "The Importance of Being Ernest: Gender Conflicts in Accounting," *Advances in Public Interest Accounting* [1990], pp. 137-157.

————, "Herstory in Accounting: The First Eighty Years," *Accounting, Organizations and Society* 17, No. 3/4 [1992], pp. 261-285.

Lerner, G., *The Creation of Patriarch* [Oxford University Press, 1986].

Levine, M., "Work as a Central Life Interest and Its Relationship with Intent to Remain With Large CPA Firms," *The Virginia Accountant* [1985a], pp. 29-34.

————, "Work as a Central Life Interest in Male and Female Senior and Staff Accountants in Large CPA Firms," *The Woman CPA*, 1, 2[January 1985b], pp. 27-29.

Maruani, M., and C. Nicole, "Can Computerization Break Down Sexual Barriers," Aston-Umist Labor Process Conference, University of Birmingham, U.K. [1987].

Maupin, R.J., "Sex Role Identity and Career Success of Certified Public Accountants," *Advances in Public Interest Accounting* [1990], pp. 97-105.

McKeen, C.A., and A.J. Richardson, "Women, Accounting Education and the Profession in Canada: A Historical Survey," Paper presented at the Canadian Academic Accountants' Association Education Conference, Montreal [November 1988].

Meredith, V., and B. Brown, "Women at the Partner Level: What Does the Future Hold?" *The Woman CPA* [October 1988], pp. 333-6.

Milkman, R. "State Power and Class Interest," *New Left Review* [March/April 1983], pp. 57-68.

————, "Organizing Women in Trade Union Leadership: New Directions for the Labor Movement," paper presented at the Women, Work, and Family Life Conference, New York City [April 1988].

Michael, W., *Personality and Assessment* [Wiley, 1968].

Morrow, P.C., "Concept Redundancy in Organizational Research: The Case of Work Commitment," *Academy of Management Review* [1983], pp. 486-500.

Mowday, R.T., R.M. Steers, and L.W. Porter, "The Measurement of Organizational Commitment," *Journal of Vocational Behavior* [1979], pp. 114-247.

Norris, D. and R. Niebuhr, "Professionalism, Organizational Commitment and Job Satisfaction in the Accounting Organization," *Accounting Organizations and Society, 9*[1983], pp. 49-59.

Porter, L.W., W.J. Crampon, and F.J. Smith, "Organizational Commitment and Managerial Turnover: A Longitudinal Study," *Organizational Behavior and Human Performance* [1976], pp. 87-98.

Reitz, H., and L. Jewell, "Sex, Locus of Control, and Job Involvement: A Six-Country Investigation," *Academy of Management Journal* [1979], pp. 72-80.

Reed, S., and S. Kratchman, "The Effects of Changing Role Requirements on Accountants," in *Advances in Public Interest Accounting*, Vol. 3, edited by M. Neimark [JAI Press, 1990], pp. 107-136.

Roos, P.A., "Hot Metal to Electronic Composition: Gender, Technology, and Social Change," in *Gendered Work and Occupational Change*, edited by B.F. Reskin and P.A. Roos [Temple University Press, forthcoming].

Ruh, R.A., and J.K. White, "Job Involvement, Values, Personal Background, Participation in Decision-Making, and Job Attitudes," *Academy of Management Journal*, 18[1975], pp. 300-312.

Schroeder, R.G., and L.F. Imdieke, "Local-Cosmopolitan and Bureaucratic Perceptions in Public Accounting Firms," *Accounting, Organizations and Society*, 2, 1[1977], pp. 39-45.

Schroeder, R.G., and K. Verreault, "An Empirical Analysis of Audit Withdrawal Decisions," in *Advances in Accounting*, Vol. 5, edited by B.N. Schwartz [JAI Press, 1987], pp. 205-220.

Sololoff, N.J., "Evaluating Gains and Losses by Black and White Women and Men in the Professions: 1960-1980," *Social Problems*, 35, 1[February 1988], pp. 36-53.

Spencer, A., and D. Podmore, (eds.), *In a Man's World: Essays on Women in Male Dominated Professions* [Tavistock, 1987].

Stead, B.A. *Women in Management.* [Prentice-Hall, 1978].

Steers, R.M., "Effects of Need for Achievement on the Job Performance-Job Attitude Relationship," *Journal of Applied Psychology,* 60[1976], pp. 678-682.

Stevens, J.M., J.M. Beyer, and H.M. Trice, "Assessing Personal, Role, and Organizational Predictors of Managerial Commitment," *Academy of Management Journal,* 21[1978], pp. 380-396.

Street, D.L., and A.C. Bishop, "An Empirical Examination of the Need Profiles of Professional Accountants," *Behavioral Research in Accountants* [1991], pp. 97-116.

Terborg, J.R., "Women in Management, a Research Review," *Journal of Applied Psychology,* 62[1977], pp. 647-664.

Thomas, P., "Role Conflicts in Public Accounting: Can Individual Vigilance Eradicate the Inequities?" working paper, Murray State University Murray, Kentucky [1989].

Thomas, S.G., "Structural and Attitudinal Factors Related to the Work Commitment of Employed Women," ERIC (ED 197-054) [April 1979], pp. 1-37.

Tinker, T., and M. Neimark, "The Role of Annual Reports in Gender and Class Contradiction at General Motors: 1917-1976," *Accounting Organizations and Society,* 12, 1[1987], pp. 71-88.

Torrey, J.W., "The Consequences of Equal Opportunity for Women," *Journal of Contemporary Business,* 5[Winter 1976].

Trost, C., "Women Managers Quit Not for Family but to Advance Their Corporate Climb," *The Wall Street Journal* [May 2, 1990], pp. B1, B4.

Walsh, M., and M. McInnes, *The Supply of Accounting Graduates and The Demand for Public Accounting Recruits* [American Institute of Certified Public Accountants, 1989].

Ward, S.P., O.B. Moseley, and D.R. Ward, "The Woman CPA: A Question of Job Question of Job Satisfaction," *The Woman CPA* [April 1986], pp. 4-10.

Westcott, S.H., and R.E. Seiler, *Woman In the Accounting Profession* [Markus Weiner Publishing, 1986].

Wildt, A., and O. Ahtola, *Analysis of Covariance* [Sage, 1988].

Zimmer, L., "Tokenism and Women in the Workplace: The Limits of Gender-Neutral Theory," *Social Problems,* 35, 1[February 1988], pp. 64-77.

AN ANALYSIS OF ETHICAL
AND EPISTEMOLOGICAL ISSUES
IN THE DEVELOPMENT AND
IMPLEMENTATION OF AUDIT
EXPERT SYSTEMS

Steve G. Sutton and J. Ralph Byington

ABSTRACT

The audit profession has shown a high interest in the development and implementation of audit expert systems. The integration of expert systems has generally been considered favorable as auditors, the profession, and researchers have all increased their consideration of expert systems. Unfortunately, these individual groups may have neglected the societal and individual impact of expert systems application in the audit environment. This paper explores several ethical and epistemological issues that shed a different light on the expert systems movement. The primary issues include: (1) the ownership of the expertise built into the systems, (2) the negative impact of improperly used expert systems, (3) the likely "de-skilling" of the audit work force, (4) the reduced experience level of auditors performing audit tasks, and (5) the potential for extinction of the small and medium size audit firm.

Advances in Public Interest Accounting, Volume 5, pages 231-243.
Copyright © 1993 by JAI Press Inc.
All rights of reproduction in any form reserved.
ISBN: 1-55938-496-4

The audit profession has shown an increasing level of interest in expert systems over the last several years. The interest in expert systems has been largely due to changes in the Professional Code of Ethics that have led to a more competitive environment. The increased competition has placed the major audit firms in the position of needing to develop and use increasingly complex audit technologies that will increase the efficiency of current audits from both cost and time perspectives [Messier and Hansen, 1987].

The audit technology receiving the most publicity and the correspondingly highest research budgets within the major international accounting firms has been in the area of expert systems. Unlike traditional auditor support tools that generally focus on performing numerical calculations and other highly structured tasks which can be performed much quicker and with more accuracy by the computer, expert systems attempt to model highly unstructured decisions that require a certain level of expert judgment during problem solution. The interest in developing expert systems is rarely to improve the accuracy of decisions by an expert, but rather to capture the expertise of a given individual to distribute this expertise to multiple auditors who will have quicker access (via the expert systems) to the expert's knowledge.[1]

The development and implementation of expert systems, however, have the potential to impact negatively the welfare of both individuals and society. Individuals may be hurt by the decrease in value of their own expertise as it is cloned by firms through the development of expert systems. Additionally, misuse or misapplication of the cloned expertise could potentially open an individual expert to litigation arising from failure of the expert system. These potential impacts on the welfare of individuals are categorized here as ethical concerns.

An additional issue is more long term and societal. If expert systems are used within the audit environment, will there eventually be a lack of human experts and a stagnation of the ultimate level of expertise (i.e., will audit practice remain at the expert system level of expertise rather than progressing in the future)? This also raises questions as to whether a de-skilled work force will be able to contend adequately with the supervision and evaluation of an expert system's performance. Will this work force apply the expert systems within the intended arena for which they were created? The final societal issue is the effect of the use, or failure to use, expert systems on the small and medium size firm.

As noted by Mitroff and Mason [1990], the ethical and epistemological issues related to the design of information systems have scarcely been noted, let alone previously discussed in the literature. The analysis presented in this paper examines both of these issues. However, to understand fully the issues at hand—such as the impact of a transfer of legal liability to an expert auditor and the environment that may force an exit of the small firm from the audit arena—a synopsis of the legal liability issues involved is first presented.

The paper is structured as follows: Following an introduction, an overview of expert systems development is presented. The third section describes the legal environment surrounding application of expert systems while the fourth and fifth sections address the ethical and epistemological issues, respectively. The manuscript concludes with an overview of the analysis and a framework for future research.

DEVELOPMENT OF EXPERT SYSTEMS

Expert systems (ES) generally model how an expert reaches a conclusion. The knowledge representation may be direct, using the same solution approach and weights as the expert. Alternatively, the system may apply the expert's rules and weights in a different manner than the expert.

Expert systems generally use a knowledge base and corresponding knowledge representation machinery to reach a conclusion or decision. For example, with a weighted rule or fact expert system each rule or fact has weight or strength of importance associated with it based on the weight the expert being modeled purports to assign to that fact when making a decision [Messier and Hansen, 1987]. This set of weights allows the system to regard conflicting data items in a relative manner—considering the importance of each. These systems' efficiency is often improved through the integration of semantic networks or frames to simplify the rule-based processing [Sutton, 1990, p. 74]. More recent developments have focused on the use of neural networks as a potentially more effective means of knowledge representation.

Messier and Hansen [1987] classify alternative decision aids by examining the amount of structure that exists within the problem domain. The management decision domain is described as a continuum with highly structured problems and highly unstructured problems at the end points and semistructured problems at the midpoint [Simon, 1960]. Expert systems are considered an appropriate decision aid for problems located at the unstructured end of the continuum because the quality of the decision for these problems is more dependent on the expertise of the decision maker than it is in more structured problem situations. Unfortunately, the increased amount of judgment required for the more unstructured decision also increases the probability of an unknown error or a difference of opinion between experts. The decision environment is rarely static leading to less repetitive judgments and more difficult measurement of error. Accounting and auditor judgments in these unstructured problem areas have often been the focus of client and third party litigation in circumstances where the plaintiffs have sought to recover financial losses attributed to the use of or reliance upon audited financial statements [Amhowitz, 1987].

The extensive research on expert systems has resulted in numerous working prototypes in the areas of accounting and auditing. The technology promises to provide a tool that can make accountants more efficient, while improving practice quality and consistency of audit judgment. For example, based on the same set of facts, two auditors might differ as to the appropriate planning state materiality levels on an audit. By contrast, a properly validated expert system will always suggest the same planning stage materiality level for a given set of facts [O'Leary, 1987], thus improving consistency of judgment. Another benefit of the expert system is that it can model a more experienced auditor than the accountant in the field who must make the decision, thus providing the potential for consistency of judgment, improved quality control, and standardization of the audit process.

THE LEGAL LIABILITY ENVIRONMENT OF AUDIT EXPERT SYSTEMS

In a recent survey, more than half of the Fortune 500 acknowledged that they were developing expert systems for internal use or for resale. Thus, the application of these systems will result in a certain level of exposure throughout the business community. The development of expert systems by the auditing profession adds additional complexities. These systems are developed based on the expertise of a relatively small group of individuals or even a single member of the firm.

The development of an expert system is based on knowledge acquisition from an expert. While systems should be based on a complete set of rules and accurately assigned weights, the nature of knowledge acquisition prohibits total understanding. During the development process, the expert may fail to consider all of the rules, or may be unable to properly allocate weights to these rules. The failure to induce certain rules may be due to the automatic response of the expert [Bailey, Hackenbrack, De, and Dillard, 1987], and improper assignment of weights may result from the failure of even the expert to understand how the relative weights are assigned in the decision process, thus, leading to the improper assignment of weight to a given rule. Of course, there is also the possibility that the expert may omit steps or assign improper weights out of fear of being replaced by the expert system [O'Leary and Kandelin, 1988]. When an audit ES fails, the results are likely to be similar to that of failure by any audit expert—that is, an increased risk of litigation.

Auditor Liability

In today's litigious society, the development of expert systems also requires consideration of potential legal ramifications. The number of product liabilities cases in 1986 was eight times the number in 1974. Within the auditing profession the development and application of expert systems contains not only the legal concept of negligence in the development of an expert system, but also of malpractice in the application of such systems. The use of expert systems in the auditing profession inevitably creates additional liabilities for the professional. The normal negligence actions—failure to act as a reasonable person would under the same circumstances—are compounded with malpractice, that is, the minimum level of competence required by a profession.

In the general area of liability, accountants can be held liable to clients and/ or third parties under contract law, common law, or various state and federal statutes. Depending on the circumstances, accountants may be liable for negligence, gross negligence (or reckless disregard of professional standards), and/or fraud. Under different jurisdictions, accountants can be liable (1) only to clients and parties in privity of contract, (2) to parties in privity and any actually foreseen or reasonably foreseeable third parties, or (3) to parties in privity and any third party including those that are unforeseen and sometimes even unforeseeable.

The effects of the expansion in liability on accounting practitioners have been significant. Although most of the attention surrounding large awards granted by the courts to successful plaintiffs focuses on the largest of accounting firms (primarily the Big Six firms), the effects on smaller practitioners have also been substantial. In November 1989, the professional liability insurance plan of the American Institute of Certified Public Accountants (AICPA) reported that, in the previous four years, there had been one claim for every twenty policies for a total payout of $258,000,000 in claims. Furthermore, a recent advertisement for professional liability insurance noted that a full 38 percent of the money expended for claims was used to pay the cost of defense. In addition to catastrophic awards and defense cost and as a direct result of the crisis in accountants' legal liability, many accounting practitioners and firms have been unable to find adequate malpractice insurance and have been forced to pay exorbitant prices for the insurance they have found [Collins, 1985].

The AICPA's Future Issues Committee has recognized accountants' legal liability and its related litigation issue as one of thirteen major issues facing the profession [AICPA, 1984]. Further, the first malpractice prevention and risk management conference sponsored by the AICPA was held in May 1986. In March 1990, the AICPA signified its continuing concern with accountants' legal liability when it upgraded the status of its Task Force on Accountants' Legal Liability by making it the Accountants' Legal Liability Subcommittee of the Government Affairs Committee. The state objective of this subcommittee is

[t]o consider the nature and extent of accountants' legal liability, to analyze its impact on the cost and availability of insurance, to select among identified options the best avenue for seeking relief and to coordinate the efforts both within the outside the Institute in designing and implementing a program of action [AICPA, 1989, p. 76].

Legal Issues Related to Expert Systems

The exposure to liability from the expert systems area creates additional concerns from a defense and liability standpoint. The exposure to liability may be classified as "low probability, high consequence" risk. While the risk of a material error may be low, the resulting financial statement effect may be high. When one considers the area of expert systems development, there is a direct relationship between development time and complexity. The dollar impact of development must be less than the benefit derived from application of the expert system. The liability issue associated with expert systems is compounded by the general litigious environment of the past few years. The professional firm will likely find an increase in costs directly related to the use of defective expert systems.

The potential for increased liability from expert systems usage creates an interesting paradox given that the initial desire for expert systems usage arose as a perceived solution to maintaining consistency in practice. By modeling an expert within the firm, it has been perceived that the expert system can be used to help maintain a consistent and high quality level. Unfortunately, a defective expert system would result in consistent application of a poor quality system and subsequent increased litigation. The identification of the defect would be difficult to identify, however, as the defect would only occur when the given audit circumstances caused the defective segment of the expert system to be applied in the system's judgment.

The failure "of" the expert system is a related issue and the primary guidance for use of expert systems in the audit environment is the first statement for fieldwork in GAAS, which states, "The work is to be adequately planned and the assistants, if any, are to be properly supervised [AICPA, 1984, p. 7]." The expert system may be viewed as essentially an "assistant" that must be properly "supervised" by a knowledgeable individual [Specht et al., 1991]. Thus, additional liability should only arise if the professional circumvents human judgment in the application of an expert system and places too much reliance on the judgments made by the expert system.

In the case of a generic expert system made available on the open market, a faulty expert system could also expose the developers of the system to significant litigation costs. If a "bug" exists in a purchased expert system and that system is distributed via normal channels, the erroneous system could impact the majority of audits completed by a firm. In the situation here, the "bug" would include both traditional type logic problems where the judgments produced by a segment of the system are erroneous and a problem where application in a domain differing slightly from the domain used in design could cause the system to provide erroneous judgments. An example of the potential in this latter problem can be seen in the parallels with a recent association of Professional Engineers and Geoscientists of British Columbia decision revoking a professional structural engineer's license for a minimum of two years. In this case, an engineer used an Alberta developed structural engineering expert system to design buildings built in British Columbia. The decision was based on the construction of 26 buildings in Vancouver that failed to meet the minimum earthquake standards—standards that are necessarily higher in British Columbia than in Alberta [Peters et al., 1992]. Essentially nonapplicable logic in an expert system could likewise be spread throughout audit applications without knowledge of the misfit in domain.

General concepts of tort and products liability law would clearly indicate responsibility on the part of the developers of the system [Specht et al., 1991]. The developers of the system would likely be defined to include both knowledge engineers and expert auditors—leaving both groups potentially liable for system failure. The limits in their liability would be based in part on what domain coverage was alleged to be covered by the distributed expert system.

Malpractice is closely related to negligence. The difference is that in malpractice the professional must demonstrate the standard of care of a reasonable professional. Professionals have been held liable for failure to use new technology, even if the use of the technology is not customary, if:

- the technology is available;
- has a reasonable cost;
- its use would minimize or reduce an extraordinary risk; and
- its nonuse is the direct cause of an injury [Turner, 1988].

Thus, the failure to develop and/or use an expert system may create a liability issue for accountants and auditors. Thus the potential liability from using an expert system that may be faulty cannot be avoided by simply not using a system.

Failure to use a given expert system may also increase a practitioner's liability through "testimony" of the expert system. Rule 702 of the Federal Rules of Evidence state:

> If scientific, technical, or other specialized knowledge will assist the trier of fact to understand the evidence or to determine a fact in issue, a witness qualified as an expert by knowledge, skill, experience, training, or education, may testify thereto in the form of an opinion or otherwise.

The rise of expert systems creates the potential for a new type of expert witness. The rules set forth for defining an expert witness parallel the objectives in developing an expert system. Expert systems are generally designed to allow the capturing and distribution of "scientific, technical, or other specialized knowledge ... " which we generally think of as an expertise [Sutton and Young 1992].

ETHICAL ISSUES IN EXPERT SYSTEMS DEVELOPMENT

Traditionally the expertise of an auditor was an asset of the auditor and the firm that currently employed the auditor. The development of expert systems raises new questions as to the ownership of the auditor's expertise [Mitroff and Mason, 1989]. In the traditional auditor/firm relationship, if an auditor resigned from a firm and elected to do his or her work elsewhere, the expertise obviously left with the auditor as it was all contained within the human capital of the individual. This expertise possessed by the auditor represents the primary bargaining chip that the auditor has in contracting with a firm through an employment relationship.

Through expert systems, audit firms now have the ability to capture the expertise of an audit expert. The knowledge acquisition process is designed to allow an expert systems developer to elicit the knowledge of an expert— in this case an audit expert. Once the knowledge of the expert has been elicited, this knowledge is then coded into the computer system via a knowledge representation method. Validation of the computer-based system subsequently focuses on assuring that the expert system arrives at similar solutions to the expert auditor. Once the validation process is complete, the firm has essentially succeeded in capturing the expert's knowledge and theoretically could supplant the expert within the domain of the expert system. At a minimum, it seems that the expertise that the auditor provides would now be of far less value to the firm. This diminished value of the expertise of the auditor should diminish the auditor's value to the firm and hence decrease the incentive of the firm to retain the expert. The degree of decrease in retention value will be a function, in part, of what other expertise the auditor brings to the firm.

Beyond the diminished value of the expertise, the auditor is also placed into a position of increased risk. Prior to the development of the expert system, the auditor was only liable for his or her failure to properly apply this expertise in the audit environment. However, as noted earlier, if the expert system fails during application either through decision failure or through misapplication of the system by the field auditor, the developers of the system may be liable for damages [Specht et al., 1991]. The net effect is that the audit expert that the system is based on will likely be held liable for damages from use of the system—despite receiving essentially no compensation for participation in the development process.

The diminished value of expertise and incurred liability via development of the expert system does not end when the auditor leaves the firm. This particular issue raises the ethical dilemma of ownership of the auditor's knowledge to another level. Now when an auditor leaves a firm, the firm can continue to use his or her expertise without compensation. Additionally, as this expertise continues to be used without compensating the auditor, the additional legal liability risk taken on by the audit expert continues to grow as the system is used. This situation can arise not only by the audit expert electing to leave the firm, but also if the firm elects to have the audit expert "leave."

Initially, it may seem that no firm would want to lose an expert in a given field. Evidence can be found, however, in the recent Big Eight down to Big Six mergers that this is not necessarily the situation. Within the recent mergers forming Ernst and Young, and Deloitte and Touche, several national partners for audit practice were asked to leave each of the firms. Indicative of this turnover are the removals of former national partners for governmental practice by both firms. These partners were asked to leave at a time when the profession is receiving intense criticism over its failures in the governmental area. Further evidence of this practice is found in KPMG Peat Marwick's announcement that they will retire 14 percent of their partners ["Deloitte Joins Growing List," 1991]. From the audit firms' perspective this is simply a matter of business that must be done to remain competitive in the current audit practice environment. This also raises epistemological issues as to the motivation of the profession to improve audit knowledge over time.

EPISTEMOLOGICAL ISSUES IN EXPERT SYSTEMS DEVELOPMENT

The epistemological issues of concern here are related to the potential limiting of audit knowledge by the development and implementation of audit expert systems. These concerns are derived from four potential directions of evolution within audit practice with the infiltration of expert systems:

1. The misuse of expert systems by users that are not knowledgeable regarding the limitations in domain for which an expert system has been designed.
2. The gradual "de-skilling" of auditors in the domains for which expert systems have been developed.
3. The reduced experience levels of the auditors providing audit tasks as expert systems help push additional audit procedures on to lower staff levels.
4. The eventual disappearance of the small firm from the audit practice environment.

The issue of misuse of expert systems evolves from the nature of the expert systems development and implementation process within auditing firms. A typical scenario involves the development of a system at the national level using one or more experts to model the system. After initial validation, the system is sent to several offices for field testing and validation. Any identified problems are rectified, the system is fine-tuned, and then the system is distributed nationally (or internationally depending on its usability) to the practice offices. Generally, one or more people in each practice office is trained on the use of the system in order to serve as a resource person for that office. Sometimes, this final stage is omitted as the practice office usually has to pay for the specialization training. At this point, the system is essentially openly available for use in an audit. The person using the system on an audit will usually have performed some combination of reading documentation on the system, received in-house instruction from the practice office specialist and/or discussed the system with others who have used the system before. From that point on the auditor is essentially on his or her own.

The chances that the person who actually uses the expert system most of the time fully understands the limitations of domain for which the system was designed are small. Yet, an expert system is neither designed nor validated for its performance outside the narrow domain for which it was developed. The net effect is that once an expert system is applied outside the narrow domain for which it was designed, the expertise of the system seriously deteriorates. The result can be a decrease in expertise in performing an audit rather than the desired increase via distributed expertise.

The risk of this problem occurring will likely be increased by a "de-skilling" of the auditor using the system. As the system takes over the decision making process, the auditor incurs less experience in making these decisions. Gal and Steinbart [1987, p. 57] note, "If expert systems take over most of the routine problem solving then how competent will the 'expert' be with the difficult problems?" Expert systems proponents argue that these systems take in the data and generate a decision with little explanation unless the auditor specifically requests information on how the decision was derived. In the intensely competitive audit environment with its time budgets, it seems unlikely that an auditor will regularly query the system on how the decision was made. Even if auditors do regularly query the system, does this provide the same learning as performing the task? If calculators are any indication, most auditors today would have far more difficulty adding a column of numbers by hand than their predecessors.

The other part of the question posed by Gal and Steinbart [1987] relates to problems outside the expert systems expertise. They note that a typical expert system might handle 90 percent of the auditing problems normally encountered in an audit. We would have to question how well an auditor would handle the 10 percent of less "common" problems if their skill level is decreasing for the 90 percent "common" problems. In addition, if the base skill level decreases for the auditors making the decisions then how is the field to advance? It seems that almost all members of the profession would argue that the level of performance and expertise in auditing, as a profession, has positively evolved over time. At the same time, continues improvement seems desirable— particularly in light of the current criticisms of the profession.

Further reduction in the user's ability to monitor the quality of decisions produced by an expert system is tied to an often stated objective of the firms to use expert systems to allow less experienced staff to perform tasks previously reserved for more experienced auditors. As lesser trained auditors are used to make audit decision via support by an expert system, the system switches from being a second opinion device to becoming the dominant judgment maker in the audit decision process. This intensifies all of the pressures previously discussed—that is, accuracy is defining the domain, "de-skilling" of work force, and so on.

The final epistemological issue of concern here takes a different slant in looking at the competitive effects of expert systems. From a cost development standpoint, expert systems may place the small to medium CPA firm at a comparative disadvantage. Because there are a few ES packages on the open market, internal development of a system may not be feasible owing to a lack of resources. Even if ES packages are available, the aforementioned problems in maintaining application within applicable boundaries of a domain would limit their feasibility.[2] The disadvantage also stems from the lack of the same economies of scale for expert systems development and application (i.e., the cost of development or purchase could not be spread over an equivalent number of engagement hours as the larger firms). Hence, the small and medium size firm is required to compete without the same cost and time advantages provided by an expert system and as a result may not be able to compete effectively for audit engagements. While small firms can counteract this problem to a certain degree through personalized service, the medium size firms in particular would seem to be at risk given the perceived market value to an auditee of having a Big Six auditor [Francis and Simon, 1987].

Beyond the cost efficiencies, another potential cost involved in not using an available expert system would be, as noted before, liability arising from malpractice based on the failure to use an available technology [Turner, 1988]. In the current litigious audit environment, litigation costs could put a firm out of business as has been seen with Kenneth Laventhol and, to a certain degree, a pre-merger Arthur Young. The eventual result will likely be further shrinking of the competition within the audit market with an increased market power being gained by the Big Six accounting firms.

Beyond any antitrust concerns and decreased competition effects, this is epistemologically disconcerting in that a specialized segment of the audit market is likely to disappear. While the major accounting firms may differ, it can be argued that a primary reason for the existence of the small and medium size firms is their ability to better serve their clients' needs. The forcing of these firms out of the market place would necessarily remove this specialized expertise from the audit marketplace.

CONCLUSIONS

The emphasis and allocation for funds for development and implementation of expert systems within the audit environment by the major auditing firms have significantly escalated in recent years. The focus within the prior research literature has been heavily oriented toward how we can more efficiently bring these systems into the audit process. The arguments provided in this paper suggest the necessity of reassessing the impact of expert systems.

The development of an audit expert system raises two primary problems in the competitive audit environment. The first issue, to a certain degree, is a matter of ownership of an auditor's expertise [Mitroff and Mason, 1989]. Traditionally, if an auditor resigned from a firm and elected to do his or her work elsewhere, the expertise obviously left with the auditor as it was all contained within the human capital of the individual. Now it is entirely possible via an expert system that the auditor's expertise can be retained by the firm when the auditor leaves—regardless of whether the auditor leaves willfully or is forced to leave by the firm. Such a situation raises several ethical, as well as legal, questions regarding ownership of the knowledge and related liability the auditor may be subject to even after leaving the firm.

The second problem is one of a more long-term and societal issue. If expert systems are used as experts within the audit environment, will there eventually be a lack of human experts and a stagnation of the ultimate level of expertise (i.e., will audit practice remain at the expert system level of expertise rather than progressing forward in the future)? Expert systems also place the existence of the small- and medium-size firm at risk. These firms may be placed at a comparative disadvantage as they lack the same economies of scale or justifying expert systems development. Yet, the potential legal costs of not using the available technology may also threaten these firms; existence. The eventual result will likely be further shrinking of competition and a loss of this specialized segment of the audit market.

Particularly from the standpoint of the epistemological issues, there exists a dire need for additional research on the effects of expert systems. While this research needs to focus on long-term effects, indications of these long-term effects could be captured via controlled experiments. Longitudinal studies, while likely to be more exact, risk discovering the costs to society too late. Regardless, gaining a better understanding of the effects of practice-oriented expert systems on auditors' knowledge acquisition and retention is necessary.

NOTES

1. In some cases, multiple experts are used during the knowledge acquisition phase. This generally is difficult, however, as it creates problems for the knowledge engineer in reconciling differences between experts in reasoning paths to be integrated into the system. Multiple experts are usually used, however, to validate and refine an expert system by comparing the answers of the expert system with other experts.

2. Most expert systems currently available on the market are tax-based systems that have relatively low liability risk. The number of ES available on the market is far fewer then advertisements might suggest as most advertised systems are essentially decision support systems marketed as expert systems.

REFERENCES

American Institute of Certified Public Accountants (AICPA), Future Issues Committee, *Major Issues For the CPA Profession and the AICPA* [AICPA, 1984].
———, *AICPA Committees Handbook 1989/90.* [AICPA, 1989].

Amhowitz, H., "The Accounting Profession and The Law: The Misunderstood Victim," *Journal of Accountancy* [May 1987], pp. 356-168.

Bailey, A., Jr., K. Hackenbrack, P. De, and J. Dillard, "Artificial Intelligence, Cognitive Science, and Computational Modeling in Auditing Research: A Research Approach," *Journal of Information Systems* [Spring-Summer 1987], pp. 23-129.

Collins, S.H., "Professional Liability: The Situation Worsens," *Journal of Accountancy* 160 [November 1985], pp. 57+.

"Deloitte Joins Growing List of CPAs Thinning Ranks," *Wall Street Journal* [April 30, 1991].

Francis, J.R., and D.T. Simon, "A Test of Audit Pricing in the Small-Client Segment of the U.S. Audit Market," *Accounting Review* [January 1987], pp. 145-157.

Gal, G., and P. Steinbart, "Artificial Intelligence and Research Issues in Accounting Information Systems: Opportunities and Issues," *Journal of Information Systems* [Fall 1987], pp. 54-62.

Messier, W.F., Jr., and J.V. Hansen, "Expert Systems in Auditing: The State of the Art," *Auditing:: A Journal of Practice and Theory* [Fall 1987], pp. 94-105.

Mitroff, I. and R. Mason, "Deep Ethical and Epistemological Issues in the Design of Information Systems," *Expert Systems Review* [Fall 1989], pp. 21-25.

O'Leary, D., "Validation of Expert Systems—With Applications to Auditing and Accounting Expert Systems," *Decision Science* [Summer 1987], pp. 468-486.

O'Leary, D., and N. Kandelin, "Validating the Weights in Rule-Based Expert Systems: A Statistical Approach," Presented at American Accounting Association National Meeting, Orlando [August 1988].

Peters, F.E., "Court of Enquiry, The Association of Professional Engineers and Geoscientists of the Province of British Columbia, January 13 and 14, 1992," *B.C. Professional Engineers* [March 1992].

Simon, H.A., *The New Science of Management Decision* [Harper & Row 1960].

Specht, L.B., S.G. Sutton, R.C. Trotter, and R. Young, "The Public Accounting Litigation Wars: Will Expert Systems Lead the Next Assault?" *JURIMETRICS: Journal of Law, Science, and Technology* [Winter 1991], pp. 247-257.

Sutton, S.G., "Toward a Model of Alternative Knowledge Representation Selection in Accounting Domains," *Journal of Information Systems* [Fall 1990], pp. 73-85.

Sutton, S.G., and R. Young, "An Analysis of Potential Legal Liability Incurred Through Audit Expert Systems," Working Paper, Arizona State University West [1992].

Turner, J.H., Accountants Liability," *CPA Journal* [February 1988], pp. 62-65.

UNOBSERVED COSTS OF REGULATION:

THE CASE OF FIRM-SPECIFIC TAX LEGISLATION

Charlotte J. Wright and Bud Lacy

ABSTRACT

The Tax Reform Act of 1986 had many unique features, one of which was extensive use of firm-specific or "rifle-shot" transitional rules. Theoretically, transitional rules are utilized in the tax legislative process in an attempt to avoid penalizing taxpayers for decisions made in the course of operating under current tax law whose outcomes will be taxed differently under newly enacted tax law. The authors of the rifle-shot provisions included in the Tax Reform Act of 1986 designed the legislation to limit the scope of the rules to specific companies. This study examines the tax policy implications of granting tax relief to specific firms. The capital markets are examined utilizing the seemingly unrelated regressions methodology in order to detect wealth shifts resulting from the targeted tax relief provided to 62 sample companies. The concept of horizontal equity in tax reform dictates that equals be taxed equally. The results of this study indicate that this

Advances in Public Interest Accounting, Volume 5, pages 245-265.
Copyright © 1993 by JAI Press Inc.
All rights of reproduction in any form reserved.
ISBN: 1-55938-496-4

was not accomplished in the 1986 act. Significant positive abnormal returns for the firms benefiting from rifle-shot transitional rules were detected at three event dates during the legislative period preceding the passage of the 1986 act. A control group of similarly situated firms did not have observable abnormal returns during the same test period. These results appear to indicate that targeted tax legislation was not overlooked by the capital markets and, indeed, the legislation induced the allocation of resources toward the tax beneficiary firms.

INTRODUCTION

The Tax Reform Act of 1986 had many unique features, one of which was extensive use of firm-specific or "rifle-shot" transitional rules. Traditionally, transitional rules have been included in new tax legislation to lessen the adverse impact on taxpayers who, having relied on existing law, entered into transactions whose tax consequences have not been fully realized. Firm-specific transitional rules are transitional rules that, by design, apply only to a specific taxpayer or narrowly defined group of taxpayers. While transitional rules appear to be a necessary component of equitable tax policy, targeted transitional rules which provide tax relief to only a specific few actually appear to create inequity. The use of targeted transitional rules raises nontrivial concerns regarding such issues as tax equity, capital resource allocation and overall economic welfare.

Not only did the Tax Reform Act of 1986 contain numerous rifle-shot transitional rules, these rules were written in such a way as to obscure the identities of the beneficiaries to anyone outside of Congress. Because the Tax Reform Act of 1986 contained more firm-specific transitional rules than any previous major piece of tax legislation and firm-specific transitional rules will likely accompany the next major piece of tax legislation [Bennett, 1990], a better understanding of how beneficiary companies were affected relative to nonbeneficiary companies and examination of the timing of any capital market effects appears to be in order.

The remainder of this paper is organized as follows. The next section discusses the motivation for the study and implications for policymakers. This is followed by a discussion of relevant previous research, a description of the methodology employed, the empirical results and a discussion of their implications.

MOTIVATION FOR THE STUDY

Transitional rules are special provisions added in the ordinary course of the tax legislative process. The alleged concept behind these rules is to mitigate adverse effects that may be suffered by taxpayers who entered into specific contracts or transactions prior to enactment of the new law. These rules are designed to allow taxpayers who made decisions prior to Congressional consideration of a new provision to be protected from increases in their tax liabilities that would result from the new legislation. Thus, managers making operating decisions under one set of tax laws would not be penalized by newly legislated changes in the law.

Theoretically, transitional rules are written in such a way that relief is provided equally among all parties who are similarly situated [Musgrave and Musgrave, 1976]. However, the legislative process necessary to enact tax legislation is frequently subject to extreme political forces. Because elected representatives (often pressured by lobbyists) must represent their constituents, sound tax policy may take a back seat to narrower parochial interests. Similarly, because committee chairpersons must gain consensus to ensure passage of any legislation, special relief for constituents in a key Congress member's district may be necessary to "buy" general agreement. Indeed, many participants in the tax legislative process defend the use of targeted transitional rules as a relatively minor cost of ensuring passage of broader tax legislation whose benefits outweigh the inequities resulting from these special tax provisions.

Prior to the 1986 act, rifle-shot transitional rules were seldom used and there was comparatively little controversy. The 1986 act however, was one of the most massive overhauls of the tax laws in recent history. In order to accommodate considerable decreases in tax rates, the 1986 act substantially broadened the tax base by eliminating billions of dollars of tax incentives. Some of the more significant changes included substantial reductions in depreciation deductions, repeal of the investment tax credit, and elimination of the preferential treatment for long-term capital gains. The extent of these changes and the considerable controversy accompanying passage of the 1986 act undoubtedly contributed to the inclusion of over 650 rifle-shot transitional rules included in the final bill.

During Senate debate on the 1986 act, the flood of these provisions and the mystique surrounding the identities of their beneficiaries provoked Senator Metzenbaum to demand publication of a list of the beneficiaries and the government's estimated revenue loss associated with each provision. Never before had Congress been forced to divulge the names of constituents on whose behalf they sought special tax relief. Some two years later, in a Pulitzer Prize winning series of articles, the *Philadelphia Inquirer* presented an exhaustive analysis which traced the origins, beneficiaries, and estimated dollar impact of relief granted under many of the rifle-shot provisions. According to the *Philadelphia Inquirer*, these rules resulted in the granting of an estimated $10 to $30 billion in tax relief to specific individuals or companies [Bartlett and Steele, 1988].[1] This series of articles resulted in much debate regarding the legislative policy of targeted versus generic transitional relief.

The following examples are indicative of the language used by Congress to limit the scope of the transitional rules to specific firms or individuals while at the same time obscuring the identities of the beneficiaries. (Note that in the 1986 act, section 201 amended prior law by substantially increasing the depreciable lives of assets thereby dramatically reducing depreciation deductions.)

> **The amendments made by section 201 shall not apply** to two new automobile carrier vessels which will cost approximately $47 million and will be constructed by a United States-flag carrier with an American crew, to transport foreign automobiles to the United States, in a case where negotiations for such transportation arrangements commenced in April 1985, formal contract bids were submitted prior to the end of 1985, and definitive transportation contracts were awarded in May 1986 (P.L. 99-514 Sec. 204(a)(24)(c)).

The beneficiary of this provision was identified by the *Philadelphia Inquirer* as Central Gulf Lines with the estimated tax break amounting to approximately $8 million [Bartlett and Steel, 1988].

> **The amendments made by section 201 shall not apply** to any property placed in service pursuant to a master plan which is clearly identifiable as of March 1, 1986 for a project which involves a port terminal and oil pipeline extending generally from the area of Los Angeles, California, to the area of Midland, Texas (P.L. 99-514 Sec. 204(a)(5)(F)(i)).

The beneficiary of this provision was identified by the *Philadelphia Inquirer* as Pacific Gas & Electric with the estimated tax break amounting to approximately $500 million [Bartlett and Steel, 1988].

From a macroeconomic standpoint, the policy of granting specifically directed tax relief raises a number of questions regarding horizontal equity and capital resource allocation. According to Feldstein [1976a] the fundamental concept of horizontal equity requires that the government does not treat equals unequally. Horizontal equity in tax reform requires that:

> ... if two individuals would have the same utility level if the tax remained unchanged, they should have the same utility if the tax is changed [Feldstein, 1976b, p. 124].

Feldstein [1976b] and Summers [1981] suggested that the stock market should be studied when considering the effects of tax reform. Feldstein [1976b] indicated that changes in tax law that result in wealth shifts among similarly positioned taxpayers are inequitable and a violation of basic property rights. Break and Pechman [1975, p. 49] concluded that "[a] neutral tax ... would not lead anyone ... to invest in certain securities and not in others."

In the case of firm-specific transitional rules, beneficiary companies are placed in the enviable position of being allowed to retain resources (e.g., cash) that would otherwise be payable to the federal government—a privilege which similar, competing firms do not share. These resources can then be used to enhance the productive position of the beneficiary firm or paid to stockholders in the form of dividends. Additionally, beneficiary firms may be perceived as being in a politically favored position. These factors will likely not go unnoticed by the capital markets. The enhanced cash flow and/or political positioning of the beneficiary firms may result in additional capital resources being allocated to the beneficiary firms but not to similarly situated firms. Unfortunately, this reallocation of capital may not be induced by the typical supply and demand forces but rather by successful political lobbying. Concern for these issues and the lack of empirical evidence as to the implications of granting targeted transitional tax relief provide the motivation for this research study.

RELATED RESEARCH

When market efficiency exists, new information significant to the decisional behavior of capital markets agents is reflected by changes in the equilibrium price of the firm's equity securities [Fama and Laffer, 1971]. In their seminal studies, Ball and Brown [1968] and Beaver [1968] examined the concept of market efficiency as it relates to accounting information. These authors concluded that accounting earnings and other announcements containing new information resulting in revisions of expectations regarding future cash flows of a firm are immediately impounded in the firm's stock price. This phenomena is detectable by observing the pattern of security return behavior on or near the date of the information release. Since the publication of these studies, numerous articles assessing the efficiency of capital markets and/or evaluating the effects of different types of announcements have appeared in the research literature [for example, see Brennan, 1991; Ball and Kothari, 1991; Ou and Penman, 1989].

Schwert [1981] advocated the use of market data to measure the wealth transfer effects of legislation and Summers [1981] suggested using market data to measure the incidence of tax legislation. Nonetheless, research efforts utilizing capital market information to examine the economic implications of tax legislation have been infrequent. Courtenay, Crum, and Keller [1989] studied the capital market reaction to information produced during the legislative process preceding the Economic Recovery Tax Act of 1981 and the Tax Equity and Fiscal Responsibility Act of 1982. Using a traditional market model methodology, they reported finding evidence of differential price reactions within and across portfolios of firms with varying levels of capital intensity.

Madeo and Pincus [1985] studied capital market behavior surrounding the issuance of IRS Revenue Procedure 80-55 disallowing certain interest deductions previously claimed by banks. Manegold and Karlinsky [1988] examined the market behavior related to changes in the tax laws relating to possessions corporations. Schipper and Thompson [1983, 1985] studied the impact of changes in merger-related regulations and tax laws on a group of firms that were engaged in acquisition programs. All of these studies cited two fundamental concerns with the use of a traditional market model approach when evaluating the economic impacts of legislative events: (1) multiple announcement events typically occur for any given legislated policy change and (2) cross-sectional correlation in the security returns of the affected firms resulting from announcement events occurring on the same calendar day for each firm.

Madeo and Pincus [1985], Manegold and Karlinsky [1988], and Schipper and Thompson [1983] noted that during lengthy deliberation periods, market agents have the opportunity to assess the income effects of the impending legislation, revise their prior assessment of the firms, and redirect their resources. Additionally, the traditional market model methodology assumes that firms' returns are random over time. In studies where time randomization is not possible the sample firms' returns are likely to be cross-sectionally correlated thus making use of the traditional market model unreliable. Because both of these conditions exist in capital markets studies investigating legislative-type events, these authors suggested the seemingly unrelated regressions methodology (SUR). Unlike the market model, the SUR methodology combines the estimation period and the event period(s) into a single run. The method focuses on estimating the event parameters rather than on the return residuals [Madeo and Pincus, 1985, p. 416]. Assumptions regarding cross-sectional and serial independence of the error terms are relaxed, thus eliminating the concerns cited earlier [Schipper and Thompson, 1983].

RESEARCH METHODOLOGY

Capital markets are assumed to be made up of forward-looking, rational investors. These investors are assumed to incorporate the anticipated cash flow effects of tax legislation into their investment decision making as soon as they can reliably predict the outcome of the legislative process [Courtenay, et al, 1989]. Thus the capital markets provide a metric for studying the effects of rifle-shot transitional rules. If the stated congressional intent of legislative equity is actually achieved, there should be no difference in the return behavior of transitional rule beneficiary companies and a sample of similar, nonbeneficiary firms. Accordingly, the following hypothesis is tested:

H_0:   There was no difference in the security return behavior of a group of rifle-shot transitional rule beneficiary companies and a group of similarly situated nonbeneficiary companies during the legislative period preceding the enactment of the Tax Reform Act of 1986.

Sample Selection and Data Collection

The first step in identification of firms to be included in the study was to examine the lists of transitional rule beneficiaries released by Congress on September 25, 1986. These lists contained the names of over 650 beneficiaries along with the Senate Finance Committee's estimate of the tax benefit provided to each beneficiary. A large number of these beneficiaries were individuals, estates, partnerships and other entities that are not publicly traded. The selection of the test sample began with the identification of 93 beneficiaries that are publicly traded companies. Nineteen of these were dropped since they do not appear on the Center for Research in Securities Prices (CRSP) Tape for the period November 15, 1985, through October 30, 1986. An additional 12 firms were eliminated as a result of the estimated tax benefit from their transitional rule being omitted from the report. The final sample consisted of 62 firms who, according to the Senate Finance Committee's estimates, received an aggregate estimated tax benefit of $1.9 billion. These companies, along with their estimated tax savings and the congressional origin of their transitional tax rules, are listed in Table 1.

Next, a control sample of firms was identified. Noting that the most substantial tax law changes included in the 1986 act were related to the investment tax credit, depreciation rates and capital gains, we assumed that the most critical elements in identifying "match" firms were industry membership, total assets, and net sales. Accordingly, firms constituting the control sample were selected according to the following procedure. First, all firms listed on the 1991 Compustat Annual Industrial Tape in each beneficiary firm's industry (based on their 4-digit SIC code) were identified. Next, a match company was selected by identifying an industry member whose 12-31-86 total assets and 1986 net sales were the fewest standard deviations from the beneficiary company's 12-31-86 total assets and 1986 net sales. Finally, if the potential match company did not appear on the CRSP Tape during the test period it was dropped from consideration and the next closest (as described earlier) industry member appearing on the CRSP Tape was selected. The final sample of control group firms and their beneficiary company counterparts appear in Table 2.

Earnings announcements as well as all other types of announcements relating to the 62 sample firms and the 62 control group firms were identified by examination of the *Wall Street Journal Index*. The chronology of events relating to the targeted transitional rules contained in the 1986 act appears in Table 3.

The Model

Seemingly unrelated regressions is a methodology that facilitates the assessment of firms' return behavior over a period of time during which

Table 1.   List of Companies Receiving Targeted Transitional Relief
in the Tax Reform Act of 1986

Company	Congress's Estimate of Tax Benefits (*in millions*)	Origin of Targeted Transitional Rule
Aetna Life & Casualty Co.	15	CC
Allegheny Power Systems Inc.	10	SFC
Aloha Inc.	16	COMB
American International Group Inc.	10	CC
Atlantic Richfield Co.	5	CC
Avon Products Inc.	50	SFC
Ball Corp.	1	SFC
Baltimore Gas & Electric Co.	11	SFC
Bear Stearns Cos. Inc.	8	CC
Beneficial Corp	67	CC
Brunswick Corp.	61	CC
C I G N A Corp	10	CC
Campbell Soup Corp.	12	CC
Catalyst Energy Corp.	1	COMB
Caterpillar Inc. Del.	35	CC
Chris Craft Inds. Inc.	1	CC
Chrysler Corp.	136	*COMB & CC
Control Data Corp. Del	25	SFC
Crown Cork & Seal Inc.	5	CC
Deere & Co.	212	SFC
Delta Air Lines Inc. Del.	46	SFC
Dexter Corp.	8	CC
Disney Walt Co.	33	COMB
Dominion Resources Inc. Va.	1	COMB
Dresser Inds. Inc.	12	CC
Duke Power Co.	4	*COMB & CC
Eastern Utilities Assoc.	12	SFC
Federal Express Corp.	1	SFC
Fort Howard Corp.	39	CC
General Mills Inc.	9	SFC
Great Northern Nekoosa Corp.	16	SFC
Integrated Resources Inc.	43	CC
International Paper Co.	14	CC
Johnson & Johnson	38	CC
Kansas City Southern Inds. Inc.	4	CC
Kellogg Co.	7	UD
L T V Co.	1	COMB
Leggett & Platt Inc.	2	CC
Lilly Eli & Co.	5	CC
M C A Inc.	33	COMB
Media General Inc.	1	CC
Merrill Lynch & Co. Inc.	4	COMB

(*continued*)

Table 1   (Continued)

Company	Estimate of Tax Benefits (*in millions*]	Congress's Targeted Transitional Rule
Monsanto Co.	2	CC
Morgan J P & Co. Inc.	32	CC
Murphy Oil Corp.	5	COMB
Navistar International Corp.	2	CC
P P G Industries Inc.	4	COMB
Pacific Gas & Electric Co.	4	CC
Pan Am Corp.	26	SFC
Pennzoil Co.	9	SFC
Philadelphia Electric Co.	113	SFC
Phillips Petroleum Co.	126	*SFC
Seagram Ltd.	40	CC
Temple Inland Inc.	3	CC
Texaco Inc.	85	SFC
Texas Air Corp.	57	*SFC & CC
Transamerica Corp.	1	CC
United Telecommunications Inc.	234	COMB
Valero Energy Corp.	1	CC
Weyerhauser Co.	6	CC
William Cos.	6	SFC
Zimmer Corp.	71	CC

Notes: HWMC = House Ways and Means Committee
　　　SFC　 = Senate Finance Committee
　　　CC　　= Conference Committee
　　　COMB = HWMC or HWMC and SFC
　　　UD　　 = Unable to determine

　　　* These companies had more than one transitional rule.

information affecting a group of firms becomes publicly available. As noted earlier, SUR has been used in a number of studies examining legislative-related issues in an attempt to alleviate problems which may occur since announcement dates are the same calendar dates for all companies in the sample and the results of the legislative process may be gradually impounded into the market over some period actually preceding the final passage of the legislation [Parks and Teets, 1991].

The following system of 62 equations was estimated over the 218 day trading period from November 15, 1985, through September 29, 1986.

Table 2. List of Beneficiary Companies and their Control
Group Matched Companies

Beneficiary Company	Control Group
Aethna Life & Casualty Co.	CNA Financial Corp.
Allegheny Power Systems Inc.	New England Electric Systems
Aloha Inc.	HAL Inc.
American International Group Inc	General Re Corp.
Atlantic Richfield Co.	Amoco Corp.
Avon Products Inc.	Revlon Group Inc.
Ball Corp.	Van Dorn Co.
Baltimore Gas & Elec. Co.	Northern States Power Co.
Bear Stearns Cos. Inc.	Hutton (EF) Group Inc.
Beneficial Corp.	Household International Inc.
Brunswick Corp.	Cummins Engine
CIGNA Corp.	Continental Corp.
Campbell Soup Corp.	CPC International Inc.
Catalyst Energy Corp.	Central Louisiana Electric
Caterpillar Inc. Del.	CMI Corp.
Chris Craft Inds. Inc.	Taft Broadcasting Co.
Chrysler Corp.	Ford Motor Co.
Control Data Corp. Del.	Wang Laboratories
Crown Cork & Seal Inc.	Triangle Industries Inc.
Deere & Co.	Kubota Ltd.
Delta Air Lines Inc. Del.	Trans World Airlines Inc.
Dexter Corp.	Nalco Chemical Co.
Disney Walt Co.	Ramada Inc.
Dominion Resources Inc. Va.	Houston Industries Inc.
Dresser Inds. Inc.	Dorer Corp.
Duke Power Co.	Ohio Edison Co.
Eastern Utilities Assoc.	Nevada Power Co.
Federal Express Corp.	Consolidated Freightways Inc.
Fort Howard Corp.	Stone Container Corp.
General Mills Inc.	Sara Lee Corp.
Great Northern Nekoosa Corp.	Westvaco Corp.
Integrated Resources Inc.	Edwards (AG) Inc.
International Paper Co.	Champion International Corp.
Johnson & Johnson	Pfizer Inc.
Kansas City Southern Inds. Inc.	SOO Line Corp.
Kellogg Co.	Quaker Oats Co.
LTV Co.	Bethlehem Steel Corp.
Leggett & Platt Inc.	Mahasco Corp.
Lilly Eli & Co.	Smith Kline Beckman Corp.
MCA Inc.	Warren Communications Inc.
Media Gen. Inc.	Belo (A.H.) Corp.
Merrill Lynch & Co. Inc.	First Boston Inc.
Monsanto Co.	Union Carbide Corp.
Morgan J P & Co. Inc.	Bankers Trust New York Corp.
Murphy Oil Corp.	American Petrofina Inc.

(continued)

Table 2.   (Continued)

Beneficiary Company	Control Group
Navistar International Corp.	American Motors Corp.
P P G Inds. Inc.	Grace (W.R.) Co
Pacific Gas & Electric Co.	Consolidiated Edison Co. N.Y. Inc.
Pan Am Corp.	US Air
Pennzoil Co.	Maxus Energy Corp.
Philadelphia Elec. Co.	Public Services Enterprises
Phillips Petroleum Co.	Sun Co. Inc.
Seagram Ltd.	Brown Forman Inc.
Temple Inland Inc.	Domtar Inc.
Texaco Inc.	Chevron Corp.
Texas Air Corp.	AMR Corp.
Transamerica Corp.	Loews Corp.
United Telecommunications Inc.	Contel Corp.
Valero Energy Corp.	Sonat Inc.
Weyerhauser Co.	Georgia Pacific Corp
William Cos.	Consolidatd National Gas Co.
Zimmer Corp.	Silvercrest Corp.

$$R_{it} = \alpha_i + \beta_{it-1}R_{mt-1} + \beta_{it}R_{mt} + \beta_{it+1}R_{mt+1} + \gamma_1 ANN1 + \gamma_2 ANN2 + \gamma_3 ANN3$$
$$+ \gamma_4 ANN4 + \gamma_5 ANN5 + \delta_{qit}EARN_{it} + \delta_{oit}OTH_{it} + \lambda_i IMP_1 + \epsilon_{it}$$

.

.

$$R_{nt} = \alpha_n + \beta_{nt-1}R_{mt-1} + \beta_{nt}R_{mt} + \beta_{it+1}R_{mt+1} + \gamma_1 ANN1 + \gamma_2 ANN2 + \gamma_3 ANN3$$
$$+ \gamma_4 ANN4 + \gamma_5 ANN5 + \delta_{qnt}EARN_{nt} + \delta_{ont}OTH_{nt} + \lambda_n IMP_n + \epsilon_{nt}$$

where:

R_{it} = The return of security i on day t;

R_{mt-1} = the equal weighted return of the market on day t-1;

Rm_t = the equal weighted return of the market on day t;

R_{mt+1} = the equal weighted return of the market on day t+1;

$ANN1_t$ = December 16, 17, 18, 1985: HR 3838 passed by House of Representatives;

$ANN2_t$ = June 23, 24, 25, 1986: HR 3838 passed by Senate;

$ANN3_t$ = August 15, 16, 17, 1986: HR 3838 passed out of conference committee;

$ANN4_t$ = September 15, 16, 17, 1986: List of beneficiaries compiled;

$ANN5_t$ = September 26, 27, 28, 1986: Final version of bill passed by House and Senate;

$EARN_{it}$ = earnings announcements made by firm i;

OTH_{it} = any announcement (other than earnings) made by firm i;

Table 3. Chronology of Legislative Events Resulting in Passage
of the Tax Reform Act of 1986

Date	Event
September 18-November 23	House Ways and Means Committee Deliberations of HR 3838
December 3	HR 3838 favorably reported out of House Ways and Means Committee
December 7	House Ways and Means Committee report filed (HRpt 99-426)
December 10	House Rules Committee approved modified closed rule (HRes 336) on HR 3838
December 11	Vote on HRes 336 failed
December 16	House Rules Committee approved modified closed rule (HRes 343) on HR 3838
*December 17	HR 3838 passed by House
March 19-May 5	Senate Finance Committee deliberations of HR 3838
May 6	HR 3838 favorably reported out of Senate Finance Committee
May 29	Senate Finance Committee report filed (SRpt 99-313)
June 2	Senate Finance Committee released bill text
June 4	HR 3838 brought up on Senate Floor
June 9-23	Senate debate
*June 24	HR 3838 passed by Senate
July 17-21	Conference committee deliberations
*August 16	Conference committee agreement approved
September 8	Congress reconvened
*September 16	Date of first list of targeted transitional rule beneficiaries
September 18	Conference committee report filed (HRpt 99-841)
September 25	Conference committee agreement approved by the House of Representatives and lists of all targeted transitional rule beneficiaries officially released
September 26	Senate debated conference committee report
*September 27	Conference committee report approved by the Senate
October 18	Session ended
October 22	President signed HR 3838

Note: *Event date for SUR analysis.

IMP_i = the estimated \$ impact of the transitional rule/market value of firm i's equity at 12/31/85 relative to the event dates and zero otherwise

β_is = estimated betas for lagged, contemporaneous, and lead market returns, for firm i;

γ_is = estimated dummy coefficients for legislative event periods;

δ_{qi} = estimated dummy coefficient for quarterly earnings announcements made by firm i;

δ_{oi} = estimated dummy coefficient for other than quarterly earnings announcements made by firm i;

λ_i = estimated value impact coefficient for firm i;

ϵ_{it} = estimated residuals;

n = number of firms in the sample (62);
t = 1 to 218.

Control Variables

Three-day market returns, for the movement of the market as a whole as well as lead and lag variables (R_{mt-1}, R_{mt}, R_{mt+1}) were included in the model in order to adjust for possible nonsynchronous trading [Scholes and Williams, 1977].[2] A second control variable, IMP_i, was included since the estimated dollar impact of transitional rules varied dramatically across firms. IMP_i was calculated by dividing the estimated dollar benefit of the transitional rule (as provided by the Senate Finance Committee's listing) for firm i by the market value of firm i's common equity as of December 31, 1985. A third set of variables, $EARN_{it}$ and OTH_{it}, were included in order to control for earnings and other firm-specific announcements appearing during the test period. $EARN_{it}$ is a dummy variable denoting the day before and the day earnings announcements regarding a sample firm appeared in the *Wall Street Journal*. Similarly, OTH_{it} is a dummy variable denoting the day before and the day any other-than-earnings announcements regarding a sample firm appeared in the *Wall Street Journal*. For any given date, each of these variables was assigned a value of 1 if an announcement appeared or zero if no announcement was detected.

Event Parameter Estimates

The focus of the testing was on the estimates of the tax-related event parameters, $ANN1_t$, $ANN2_t$, $ANN3_t$, $ANN4_t$, and $ANN5_t$. These variables were coded as dummy variables with 1 being assigned to the day before, the day of and the day after a significant vote or announcement was made in the passage of the 1986 act.[3] Significance of any of these variables indicates that abnormal returns accrued to sample firms during one of more of the stages of the passage of the 1986 act. The sign of the coefficients (γ's) gives an indication as to how the market perceived the event relative to the firms in the sample.

The model was run for the beneficiary companies then the procedure was repeated for the sample of control companies. For the control group one modification of equation 1 was necessary. Since the companies in the control group, by definition, did not have transitional rule-related tax benefits, the variable IMP_i was deleted from the model. Accordingly, for the control group of companies the following system of 62 equations was estimated over the 218-day trading period from November 15, 1985, through September 29, 1986.

$$R_{it} = \alpha_i + \beta_{it-1}R_{mt-1} + \beta_{it}R_{mt} + \beta_{it+1}R_{mt+1} + \gamma_1ANN1 + \gamma_2ANN2 + \gamma_3ANN3$$
$$+ \gamma_4ANN4 + \gamma_5ANN5 + \delta_{qit}EARN_{it} + \delta_{oit}OTH_{it} + \epsilon_{it}$$

.

.

$$R_{nt} = \Lambda_n + \beta_{nt-1}R_{mt-1} + \beta_{nt}R_{mt} + \beta_{nt+1}R_{mt+1} + \gamma_1ANN1 + \gamma_2ANN2 + \gamma_3ANN3$$
$$+ \gamma_4ANN4 + \gamma_5ANN5 + \delta_{qnt}EARN_{nt} + \delta_{ont}OTH_{nt} + \epsilon_{nt}$$

where each of the variables is defined earlier.

RESULTS

The first procedure performed involved using the SUR methodology to examine security returns around key dates in the legislative period preceding the passage of the 1986 act. In this step the SUR procedure was applied to all companies in the beneficiary group for the entire legislative period. The procedure was repeated for the control group. No significant event date variables were detected for the control group, however, for the beneficiary companies significant positive returns were detected at two of the event dates.[4] Estimates of the event-related parameter coefficients are presented in Table 4 for the beneficiary group and in Table 5 for the control group. $EARN_{it}$ (the quarterly earnings announcement variable) was significant at the .05 level for the both groups. This result is consistent with the accounting earnings-related literature cited earlier. OTH_{it} (the other announcement variable) was not significant for either group of companies.

A variable representing the estimated size of each company's tax relief (IMP_i) was included in Equation (1) for the beneficiary companies. As reported in Table 4, this variable was not significant. The lack of significance could result from a number of factors the most likely being error in estimates of amounts. A comparison of the listing of the estimated tax benefits which was prepared by Senate Finance Committee and the amounts estimated by and published in the *Philadelphia Inquirer* series revealed a wide disparity in the amounts. Rerunning the model using the *Philadelphia Inquirer's* estimated tax benefits in the calculation of IMP_i would not be helpful since the *Philadelphia Inquirer* articles included estimates for only 17 of the 62 beneficiary companies. The lack of significance of this variable could also result from the market's assessment of the amounts of the tax relief simply not corresponding with those published by Congress. This variable was not critical to the analysis of the results since significance did not affect the testing of the null hypothesis.

The variables of interest in the evaluation of H_0 are the event-date variables. None of the event-date variables was significant for the control group. For the beneficiary companies, $ANN1_t$, $ANN3_t$, and $ANN5_t$ were not significant

Table 4. All Beneficiary Firms' Control and Event Parameter Estimates from Seemingly Unrelated Regressions

	Parameter Estimate	Standard Error	t-Statistic	$p > t$
Quarterly Earnings Announcement Variable:	δ^{qi}			
$EARN^{it}$	0.00084	0.000415	2.014	0.044
Other than Earnings Announcement Variable:	δ^{oi}			
OTH^{it}	−0.00080	0.001071	−0.753	0.451
Impact Variable:	λ^{i}			
IMP^{i}	2.969E-9	1.9391E-9	2.014	0.126
Deliberation/ Announcement Variables:	γ^{i}			
$ANN1^{t}$ (December 16-18,1985)	0.00164	0.001628	1.006	0.314
$ANN2^{t}$ (June 23-25,1986)	0.00319	0.001624	1.964	0.049
$ANN3^{t}$ (August 15-17,1986)	−0.00251	0.002788	−0.901	0.367
$ANN4^{t}$ (September 15-17,1986)	0.00283	0.001633	1.731	0.083
$ANN5^{t}$ (September 26-28,1986)	−0.00062	0.001631	−0.383	0.702

Table 5. All Control Firms' Control and Event Parameter Estimates from Seemingly Unrelated Regressions

	Parameter Estimate	Standard Error	t-Statistic	$p > t$
Quarterly Earnings Announcement Variable:	δ^{qi}			
$EARN^{it}$	0.00871	0.003455	1.719	0.100
Other than Earnings Announcement Variable:	δ^{oi}			
OTH^{it}	−0.00881	0.020124	0.438	0.661
Deliberation/ Announcement Variables:	γ^{i}			
$ANN1^{t}$ (December 16-18,1985)	0.01689	0.061475	0.275	0.783
$ANN2^{t}$ (June 23-25,1986)	0.00575	0.061308	0.094	0.925
$ANN3^{t}$ (August 15-17,1986)	−0.01406	0.105696	0.133	0.894
$ANN4^{t}$ (September 15-17,1986)	−0.00080	0.061652	−0.014	0.988
$ANN5^{t}$ (September 26-28,1986)	0.00787	0.061589	0.128	0.898

Table 6. Beneficiary Firms Included in Bill by the HWMC or SFC Control
and Event Parameter Estimates from Seemingly Unrelated Regressions

	Parameter Estimate	Standard Error	t-Statistic	$p > t$
Quarterly Earnings Announcement Variable:	δ^{qi}			
$EARN^{it}$	0.00031	0.000530	2.908	0.004
Other than Earnings Announcement Variable:	δ^{oi}			
OTH^{it}	−0.00132	0.001534	−0.859	0.391
Impact Variable:	λ^{i}			
IMP^{i}	3.971E-9	8.553E-9	0.464	0.624
Deliberation/ Announcement Variables:	γ^{i}			
$ANN1^{t}$ (December 16-18,1985)	0.00423	0.002427	1.771	0.077
$ANN2^{t}$ (June 23-25,1986)	0.00491	0.002420	2.029	0.043
$ANN3^{t}$ (August 15-17,1986)	−0.00149	0.004128	−0.362	0.717
$ANN4^{t}$ (September 15-17,1986)	0.00222	0.002433	0.914	0.361
$ANN5^{t}$ (September 26-28,1986)	−0.00151	0.002431	−0.619	0.536

Table 7. Control Firms Matched with Firms with Transitional Rules
Added in the HWMC or SFC Control and Event Parameter
Estimates from Seemingly Unrelated Regressions

	Parameter Estimate	Standard Error	t-Statistic	$p > t$
Quarterly Earnings Announcement Variable:	δ^{qi}			
$EARN^{it}$	0.00160	0.00898	1.178	0.084
Other than Earnings Announcement Variable:	δ^{oi}			
OTH^{it}	−0.00173	0.038869	0.444	0.656
Deliberation/ Announcement Variables:	γ^{i}			
$ANN1^{t}$ (December 16-18,1985)	0.03555	0.122951	0.289	0.772
$ANN2^{t}$ (June 23-25,1986)	0.01068	0.122615	0.087	0.931
$ANN3^{t}$ (August 15-17,1986)	0.03088	0.211407	0.146	0.883
$ANN4^{t}$ (September 15-17,1986)	−0.00292	0.123312	−0.024	0.981
$ANN5^{t}$ (September 26-28,1986)	0.01409	0.123183	0.114	0.908

Table 8. Beneficiary Firms Included in Bill by the CC Control and Event Parameter Estimates from Seemingly Unrelated Regressions

	Parameter Estimate	Standard Error	t-Statistic	$p > t$
Quarterly Earnings Announcement Variable:	δ^{qi}			
$EARN^{it}$	0.00202	0.000559	3.611	0.0003
Other than Earnings Announcement Variable:	δ^{oi}			
OTH^{it}	−0.00077	0.001378	−0.557	0.578
Impact Variable:	λ^i			
IMP^i	3.073E-9	1.9199E-9	1.601	0.110
Deliberation/ Announcement Variables:	γ^i			
$ANN1^t$ (December 16-18,1985)	0.00014	0.002038	0.069	0.945
$ANN2^t$ (June 23-25,1986)	0.00207	0.002032	1.017	0.309
$ANN3^t$ (August 15-17,1986)	−0.00331	0.003488	−0.949	0.343
$ANN4^t$ (September 15-17,1986)	0.00445	0.002043	2.180	0.029
$ANN5^t$ (September 26-28,1986)	−0.00016	0.002041	−0.081	0.936

Table 9. Control Firms Matched with Firms with Transitional Rules Added in the CC Control and Event Parameter Estimates from Seemingly Unrelated Regressions

	Parameter Estimate	Standard Error	t-Statistic	$p > t$
Quarterly Earnings Announcement Variable:	δ^{qi}			
$EARN^{it}$	0.00151	0.003784	1.348	0.109
Other than Earnings Announcement Variable:	δ^{oi}			
OTH^{it}	−0.00084	0.000704	1.197	0.231
Deliberation/ Announcement Variables:	γ^i			
$ANN1^t$ (December 16-18,1985)	−0.00179	0.002068	−0.868	0.385
$ANN2^t$ (June 23-25,1986)	0.00023	0.002063	0.115	0.908
$ANN3^t$ (August 15-17,1986)	−0.00258	0.003555	−0.726	0.467
$ANN4^t$ (September 15-17,1986)	0.00106	0.002074	0.515	0.606
$ANN5^t$ (September 26-28,1986)	0.00110	0.002072	0.532	0.594

while $ANN2_t$ and $ANN4_t$ were positive and significant at the 0.05 and 0.10 levels, respectively. Therefore, H_0 was rejected. These results appear to indicate that the capital market did behave as if the transitional rules were perceived as providing economic advantage to beneficiary firms.

In order to determine if these results were due to a subset of companies, the timing of the observed significant abnormal returns was examined. A check was made to determine when during the legislative process each beneficiary company's transitional rule(s) was added to the bill. This information is reported in Table 1. This procedure revealed that, for our sample of companies, transitional rules affecting 30 companies were initiated either in the House Ways and Means Committee (HWMC) or the Senate Finance Committee (SFC) or both, while 34 companies were affected by provisions initiated in the Conference Committee (CC). For one firm the source of the transitional rule was not clear and three of the beneficiary firms had transitional rules added in a combination of both the HWMC/SFC and the CC.

The sample of beneficiary firms was subdivided into two groups: the firms affected by transitional rules which were included by either the HWMC or the SFC or both and the firms affected by transitional rules introduced in the CC. (The three companies with transitional rules introduced in both stages were included in both groups.) The control firms were likewise subdivided. The SUR methodology was repeated for each group.[5] The results of testing the HWMC/SFC subgroup and their matched firms are reported in Tables 6 and 7, respectively. The CC subgroup and their matched firms' results are reported in Tables 8 and 9, respectively.

For the beneficiary firms that had transitional rules introduced in the HWMC/SFC, $ANN1_t$ (which was not significant when the procedure was run over the total beneficiary sample) was positive and significant at a .10 level. $ANN2_t$ (which was significant for the total beneficiary sample) was also positive and significant at a .05 level.[6] None of the event date parameters were significant for the subgroup of control firms. These results indicate that significant positive abnormal returns did accrue to the firms benefiting from the firm-specific transitional rules introduced at this stage of the legislative process, a phenomena which was not observed for the similarly situated firms. $ANN4_t$ which was significant for the undivided sample of beneficiary firms was not significant for the subgroup. This result was not surprising since these firms were not affected by rules introduced after $ANN2_t$.

Next the results from the beneficiary firms having transitional rules introduced in the CC were examined. Here, $ANN4_t$ (which was also significant when the procedure was run over the total beneficiary sample) was significant at a .05 level. $ANN3_t$, which represents the date that CC agreement was actually approved was not significant. Once again, none of the event date parameters were significant for the subgroup of matched firms. These results are consistent with the previous results in indicating that significant positive abnormal did accrue to the firms benefiting from the firm-specific transitional rules introduced at the later stage of the legislative process.

The results of the subdivided groups are especially interesting when one considers Congress's argument that, in the absence of special relief, the firms benefiting from the firm-specific transitional rules would be disproportionately disadvantaged. There is no evidence that the capital market perceived this to be the case. The provisions of the 1986 act which would have negatively affected these companies were included in the bill by the dates denoted as $ANN1_t$ and $ANN2_t$. Absent any special relief, one would expect to observe negative abnormal returns accruing to the affected companies. This was not the case for either subgroup of beneficiary companies or for the control companies.

CONCLUSIONS

The results of this study have important tax and public policy implications. According to tax theory, when legislating tax policy, Congress should act in such a manner as to maintain horizontal equity (i.e., equals should not be taxed unequally). This study provides empirical evidence that the rifle-shot transitional rules contained in the Tax Reform Act of 1986 resulted in a significant shift in the capital markets with positive abnormal returns accruing to firms benefiting from the targeted tax relief. Capital appears to have been shifted toward companies which were efficient at lobbying and not necessarily the most efficient employers of resources. These results appear to indicate that the use of firm-specific tax relief is not sound tax reform policy. Using the capital market as a metric, it appears that the use of such tax provisions has serious horizontal equity and resource allocation implications.

Finally, this research also yields an interesting side note. Lawmakers apparently go to a great deal of effort to write rifle-shot transitional rules such that the identities of beneficiary companies are obscured. Congress should be aware that these efforts accomplish little. Apparently, capital market agents are quite efficient at identifying the targeted firms.

There are limitations associated with any empirical research. The most prominent limitation, which results from legislative-type events, is identification of relevant announcement dates. The research design should help to reduce the likelihood of confounding events. Another limitation is the inability to reliably determine the dollar value of the tax benefits accruing to beneficiary firms.

NOTES

1.   A transitional rule's dollar impact may be a one-time occurrence, as in the case of investment tax credit, or there may be long-term effects, as in the case of depreciation deductions.

2. The system was estimated without the lead and lag variables and the results were essentially identical.

3. The use of three-day event windows appears to be acceptable in a SUR model when it is assumed that the information is impounded gradually (rather then instantly) into the security returns [Parks and Teets 1991].

4. Additionally, a traditional markets model methodology was employed in testing for significant abnormal returns around the legislative event dates ($ANN1_t$, $ANN2_t$, $ANN3_t$, $ANN4_t$ and $ANN5_t$. The conclusions reached by analysis of those results were identical to those resulting from application of the SUR methodology.

5. We were concerned with the small sample sizes which resulted from subdividing the sample. Schipper and Thompson [1983] indicated that their sample size of 34 firms was adequate. The results of the SUR procedure over the sample sizes of 30 and 34 are consistent with the results obtained with a sample of 62.

6. In the tests of the subgroups, the statistics for the control variables were consistent with the previous results.

REFERENCES

Ball, R., and P. Brown, "An Empirical Evaluation of Accounting Income Numbers," *Journal of Accounting Research,* 6, 2[1968], pp. 159-178.

Ball, R., and S.P. Kothari, "Security Returns Around Earnings Announcements," *Accounting Review*, 66, 4[1991], pp. 718-738.

Bartlett, D.L., and J.B. Steele, "The Great Tax Giveaway," *The Philadelphia Inquirer* [April 10-16, 1988].

Beaver, W.H., "The Information Content of Annual Earnings Announcements." *Empirical Research in Accounting: Selected Studies, 1968 Journal of Accounting Research*, supp. [1968], pp. 67-92.

Bennett, R., (U.S. Department of the Treasury). "Waiting For the Next Transitional Rule Expose," *Tax Notes* [September 24, 1990], pp. 1693-1694.

Break, G., and J. Pechman, *Federal Tax Reform: The Impossible Dream?* [The Brookings Institutional, 1975].

Brennan, M.J., "A Perspective on Accounting and Stock Prices, *Accounting Review*, 66, 1[1991], pp. 67-79.

Courtenay, S.M., R.P., Crum and S.B. Keller, "Differential Reactions to Legislative Signalling During the Enactment of ERTA and TEFRA: An Empirical Investigation of Market Returns and Volume," *Journal of Accounting and Public Policy* 8, 4[1989], pp. 283-321.

Fama, E.F., and A.B. Laffer, "Information and Capital Markets," *Journal of Business* 44, 3[July 1971], pp. 289-298.

Feldstein, M., "Compensation in Tax Reform," *National Tax Journal*, 29, 2[1976a], pp. 122-130.

————, "On the Theory of Tax Reform" *Journal of Public Economics*, 6, 1[1976b], pp. 77-104.

Manegold, J.G., and S.S. Karlinsky, "The Security Market Impact of a Tax Law Change: Possessions Corporation Revisions," *The Journal of the American Taxation Association*, 9, 2[1988], pp. 65-83.

Madeo, S.A., and M. Pincus, "Stock Market Behavior and Tax Rule Changes: The Case of the Disallowance of Certain Interest Deductions Claimed by Banks," *Accounting Review*, 60, 3[July 1985], pp. 407-429.

Musgrave, R.A., and P.C. Musgrave, *Public Finance in Theory and Practice*, 2d ed. [McGraw-Hill, 1976].

Ou, J.A., and S.H. Penman, "Financial Statement Analysis and the Prediction of Stock Returns," *Journal of Accounting and Economics*, 11, 3[1989], pp. 295-329.

Parks, R., and W. Teets, "A Simulation Investigation of Seemingly Unrelated Regression as Used in Accounting Information Event Studies," Working paper, University of Illinois at Urbana-Champaign [December 1991].

Schipper, K., and R. Thompson, "The Impact of Merger-Related Regulations on the Shareholders of Acquiring Firms," *Journal of Accounting Research*, 21, 1[1983], pp. 184-221.

Schipper, K., and R. Thompson "The Impact of Merger-Related Regulations Using Exact Distributions of Test Statistics," *Journal of Accounting Research*, 23, 1[1985], pp. 408-415.

Scholes, M., and J. Williams, "Estimating Betas From Nonsynchronous Data," *Journal of Financial Economics* 5, 3[1977], pp. 309-327.

Schwert, G.W., "Using Financial Data to Measure Effects of Regulation," *Journal of Law and Economics*, 24, 1[April 1981], pp. 121-158.

Summers, L.H., "Taxation and Corporate Investment: A Q-Theory Approach," *Bookings Papers on Economic Activity*, 1[1981], pp. 67-140.

PUBLIC INTEREST COMMENTARY

THE ENACTMENT OF SHARK REPELLENTS MAY BE A VIOLATION OF THE DUTY OF CARE

Nancy Meade and Dan Davidson

ABSTRACT

Corporate takeovers in the 1980s and the accompanying threat to the job security of corporate management have led to the enactment of antitakeover devices, or shark repellents, by many corporations. Whether shark repellents benefit stockholder welfare or protect corporate management is examined from ethical and public interest perspectives. Analysis of recent research and of court cases reveals that management's support of some types of shark repellents may be a violation of the business judgment rule.

INTRODUCTION

Recent research has examined the relationship of antitakeover devices, or shark repellents, to stockholder welfare. Shark repellents are enacted to protect the

Advances in Public Interest Accounting, Volume 5, pages 269-280.
Copyright © 1993 by JAI Press Inc.
All rights of reproduction in any form reserved.
ISBN: 1-55938-496-4

firm from the takeover market. Whether the management of these firms enact shark repellents to promote shareholder welfare or to promote and protect the interests of the management is the object of this examination.

Ethical issues are also a concern in the use of such devices by management. Willcox [1988] suggests that certain types of shark repellents (i.e., corporate charter amendments) may be an abuse of power by the firm's management. Willcox goes on to state that the question of whether stockholders should empower management with devices to ward off corporate raiders depends on the circumstances. We suggest that such empowerment should rest on the relationship of the devices to both corporate interests and shareholder welfare. The purpose of this paper is to examine the use of shark repellents from an ethical perspective. The examination will compare prior research concerning different types of shark repellents and their effect on shareholder welfare with several recent court opinions determining the validity of management's actions in enacting such devices. Results of the analysis suggest that management's actions in promoting some types of shark repellents amount to a violation of the business judgment rule by the board of directors

THE TAKEOVER MARKET

Corporate takeovers have occurred with sufficient frequency to cause commentators to view them separately from other securities market transactions. The desire to effect corporate takeovers, and the methods used to carry them out, have led to the development of a "takeover market." Among other things, the takeover market provides a way to protect shareholder interests by providing a method to replace management teams that are not acting in the best interests of the shareholders. Jensen [1986]calls the takeover market a "court of last resort" for shareholders. Congress was convinced as early as 1967 "that takeover bids should not be discouraged because they serve a useful purpose in providing a check on entrenched but inefficient management" [Senate Report No. 550, 1967, pp. 3-4]. Congress also did not want to deny the shareholders "the opportunities which result from the competitive bidding for a block of stock of a given company" [Congressional Record, 1967, p. 24666].

The threat of the takeover market leads to the enactment of shark repellents. The literature suggests that the enactment of shark repellents may promote shareholder interests, management interests, or both. From an ethical perspective, neither the desire to promote shareholder interests nor the desire to promote the interest of both management and shareholder is unethical, and should not violate the business judgment rule. The area of concern is action by management that promotes management's own interest at the expense of the shareholders. Such action is normally "justified" by management's reference to and reliance on the business judgment rule.

The literature discusses whether shark repellents promote shareholder interests or management interest. Arguments that shark repellents promote shareholder interests fall into two board categories. Grossman and Hart [1980] suggest that shark repellents afford management the power to hold out for the best offer during a takeover attempt, thus protecting the shareholders and ensuring that each shareholder receives the greatest possible price for his or her securities. Carney [1986] states that shark repellents provide a way to solve communal resource problems by affording management with a way to bind stockholders into one cohesive unit to repel an attempted takeover. The uniting of the shareholders against an external threat is seen as a benefit, and thus as an enhancement of shareholder interests.

The arguments that shark repellents promote management interests are presented in three variations; management entrenchment, managerial welfare, and "improved management." Despite differences in the approach, all three seem to refer to the same concept, protecting management interests at the expense of the shareholder. Collectively the three state:

1. management interests may diverge from shareholder interests;
2. because monitoring by shareholders is imperfect, management makes decisions that benefit themselves at the expense of the shareholders; and
3. the takeover market limits managerial discretion.

As a result, management may enact shark repellents to insulate themselves from the takeover market and possible job displacement (management entrenchment). They may be protecting their personal interests and advantages since managers who are insulated from the takeover market can more easily usurp resources and opportunities for their own ends, and so forth, consuming perquisites or allocating corporate funds to pet projects (managerial welfare). If the management fears that an inefficiently managed firm will become a takeover target, they may enact shark repellents to prevent such a takeover effort ("improved management").

TYPES OF SHARK REPELLENTS

The Appendix contains a description of some of the common types of shark repellents as identified by the Investors Responsibility Research Center. An important distinction among types of shark repellents can be drawn based on the mode of enactment. Some types of shark repellents may require the approval of the shareholders before they can be enacted, while others may be instituted merely by the action of the board of directors. For example, corporate charter amendments require shareholder approval, while poison pills do not. Poison pills are usually enacted unilaterally by the board of directors.

Some shark repellents take the form of bylaw amendments. The Model Business Corporation Act provides that the initial bylaws of the corporation are adopted by the board of directors, and that the power to alter, amend, or repeal bylaws or to adopt new bylaws shall be vested in the board of directors unless specifically reserved to the shareholders in the articles of incorporation. In those states that follow the MBCA, it is quite likely that the articles of incorporation do not reserve amending power for the shareholders, allowing the directors to determine the contents of the bylaws without shareholder input or interaction.

If the articles of incorporation do reserve the power to amend the bylaws for the shareholders, or if the state of incorporation does not follow the MBCA, the shareholders have the right to propose amendments to the bylaws, and they also have the right to approve any/all amendments to the bylaws. In these circumstances, it would seem less likely that the directors could successfully propose amendments that would serve as shark repellents to the disadvantage of the corporation or to the detriment of the shareholders. Thus, it would appear that, if the shareholders must approve amendments to the bylaws, any enactments in the bylaws that serve as shark repellents are more likely to be ethical, at least in so far as the shareholders are concerned. Any benefits or protections provided to the board of directors would seem to be merely incidental.

Another form of shark repellent can be found in amendments to the Articles of Incorporation. Amendments to the Articles of Incorporation are normally initiated by the board of directors in a resolution setting forth the proposed amendments. This resolution is then communicated to the shareholders in a manner that complies with the notice requirements of the bylaws. The shareholders vote on the proposed amendments at either the regular meeting or at a special meeting.

Because the amendments to the Articles of Incorporation must be approved by the shareholders, it would appear that any amendments to the articles which are intended to serve as shark repellents are more likely to be ethical, at least from the perspective of the shareholders. The protection thus afforded to the management would again seem to be merely incidental. Realistically, however, a strongly entrenched board might be in a position from which it could dominate the vote, and the election may be purely pro forma. In such a situation, the shareholders may well ratify the amendments that contain shark repellents without being truly aware of the effect that such ratification will have on any proposed takeovers, or on the continued status of the directors to retain their positions.

THE BUSINESS JUDGMENT RULE

The officers and directors of a corporation are obligated to perform their duties on behalf of the corporation with the amount of diligence and due care that a reasonable and prudent person would exercise in the conduct of his or her own personal affairs in the same or similar circumstances. Such a standard of conduct is difficult, at best, to measure, and any attempts to measure it are going to arise after the point in time at which the conduct occurred. As a result, the legal system has developed the "business judgment rule." The business judgment rule excuses the officers or directors from liability for any errors in judgment, provided that the error was made in good faith in the course of conducting business and based upon the sound business judgment of the officer or director. Thus, conduct by either the officers or directors that results in losses for the corporation will not result in liability, if the conduct was undertaken in good faith, and if the loss was occasioned by an honest mistake in judgment. However, conduct that has as its primary purpose self-advancement, and that is undertaken for personal, as opposed to corporate motives, would not fall within the protection afforded by the business judgment rule. If such conduct, for example, the creation of a shark repellent, was harmful to the corporation or to the interests of the shareholders, the officers and directors responsible for the conduct would face potential liability for the actions taken.

The courts have articulated the scope of the business judgment rule in numerous cases over the years. As viewed and applied by the courts, the judgment rule is a "presumption that in making a business decision the directors acted on an informed basis, in good faith, and in the honest belief that the action taken was in the best interests of the company" [*Aronson* v. *Lewis,* 1984]. One hallmark of the application of the business judgment rule is that the court will not substitute its judgment for that of the board, if the decision of the board can be "attributed to any rational business purpose" [*Sinclair Oil Corp.* v. *Levien,* 1971]. The board's power to act derives from its fundamental duty and obligation to protect the corporate enterprise, which includes stockholders, from harm reasonably perceived, irrespective of its source" [*Unocal Corporation* v. *Mesa Petroleum Co.,*].

Other court opinions (e.g., *Smith* v. *Van Gorkom,* 1985] have redefined the business judgment rule to some extent. These opinions have insisted that, in order to rely on the defense of the business judgment rule, a board of directors must make a reasonable investigation of the relevant facts in the case, and must make a reasoned decision based on these facts.

The business judgment rule still carries with it a presumption that the directors acted in good faith, and with the best interests of the corporation in mind [*Aronson* v. *Lewis,* 1984]. Where the business judgment rule is properly invoked the decision of the board of directors will be upheld by the court unless there is a showing of abuse of discretion. "However, the protection of the business judgment rule will not be afforded to directors who fail 'to inform themselves, prior to making a business decision, of all material information readily available to them ' " [*Aronson* v. *Lewis, 19844, p. 812*]. The *Smith* v. *Van Gorkom* court stated that "directors have an affirmative duty to protect the financial interests of the stockholders, and must proceed with a critical eye in acting on their behalf.

The Courts have also specifically extended the business judgment rule and its provisions to the area of takeovers [*Pogostin* v. *Rice,* 1984]. However, in the case of a takeover, there is an "omnipresent specter that a board may be acting primarily in its own interests, rather than those of the corporation and its shareholders, there is an enhanced duty which calls for judicial examination at the threshold before the protections of the business judgment rule can be conferred" [*Unocal Corp.* v. *Mesa Petroleum Co.,*1985, p. 954] so that the directors must establish that they have reasonable grounds for believing that a danger to corporate policy and effectiveness exists before any antitakeover devices may be established. Even if the directors meet this test, they may only choose those defensive measures that are reasonable in relation to the threat posed by the takeover.

This two-tier proportionality test, referred to by courts as the *Unocal* test, is applied any time the management enacts a shark repellent and that enactment is challenged by any interested parties. The management must first show that they had reasonable grounds for supposing that there was a danger to corporate policy or effectiveness. The standard here is a mere showing that a reasonable investigation was made before the device was enacted. The second test is that the board must establish that the measures taken were reasonable in relation to the threat posed. The court imposes this two-tier test because "when managers are busy erecting obstacles to the taking over of a corporation by an investor who is likely to fire them if the takeover succeeds" a conflict of interests exists, and this conflict cannot be cured by "vesting the power of decision in a board of directors" [*Dynamics Corp. of America* v. *CTS Corp.,* 1986].

The business judgment rule and the resulting immunity from liability for decisions that do not turn out well are a basic and significant aspect of corporate law. The rule ensures that directors do not have to guarantee their decisions in advance, so that the directors can take the chances that corporate growth and development so often require. However, the business judgment rule also provides management with considerable freedom to enact shark repellents [Easterbook and Fischel, 1981]. In the early 1980s when many of the shark repellents first appeared, there was little or no evidence that these devices were harmful to the shareholders, and the business judgment rule shielded the directors who were challenged for enacting shark repellents. Empirical studies since then show that some of the shark repellents are not in the best interests of the shareholders. Table 1 summarizes the results of these studies.

ANALYSIS OF EMPIRICAL STUDIES

The types of shark repellents classified as poison pills do not appear to be in the best interests of the shareholders. Malatesta and Walking [1988]

Table 1.   Empirical Stuidies on Shark Repellents

Type of Shark Repellents	Study	Results
Supermajority, Classified Board, and Both	DeAngelo and Rice [1983]	CAR < 0, n.s.
Supermajority, Classified Board, and Fair-Price	Linn and McConnell [1983]	Weekly CAR, n.s. Monthly CAR > 0, sig.
Fair-Price, Supermajority, Classified Board, and Authorized Preferred	Jarrell and Poulslen [1987]	n.s. CAR < 0, sig. n.s. n.s.
Dual Class Recapitalization	Partch [1987]	no effect
	Jarrell and Poulsen [1988]	CAR < 0, sig.
	Cornett and Vetsuypens [1989]	CAR > 0, sig.
Eliminate Cumulative Voting and enact a Classified Board	Bhagat and Brickley [1984]	CAR < 0, sig.
Supermajority (Non-Fair-Price)	Meade and Brown [1990]	ROA less than matched firms without Supermajority
Greenmail	Holderness and Sheehan [1985]	CAR > 0, sig.
	Mikkelson and Ruback [1985]	CAR > 0, sig.
Anti-Greenmail	Eckbo [1990]	Mixed Results
Corporate Restructuring	Dann and DeAngelo [1988]	CAR < 0, sig
Poison Pills	Malatesta and Walkling [1988]	CAR < 0, sig. ROA < industry average
Poison Pill Flip Over Flip In	Ryngaert [1988]	n.s. CAR < 0, sig.

Notes: n.s. = Results were not statistically significant.
      sig. = Results were statistically signigicant.
      CAR = Cumulative Average Returns.
      ROA = Return On Assets.

find that the enactment of poison pills results in a significant negative reaction by investors. Ryngaert [1988] finds similar results in his study, but posits that the negative reactions are to a particular type of poison pill, the flip-in pill. Flip-in pills provide shareholders with rights to purchase common or preferred stock or corporate debt in the event that a triggering event occurs, usually a tender offer for the company's stock. If a tender offer is made, the rights "flip-in" to allow the holders of the right to purchase stock at a substantial discount. The rights are valid only for the original holder, not for the would-be acquirer. Such a poison pill makes it difficult for an acquirer to obtain a majority interest in the firm.

The corporate charter amendments that require supermajority voting to approve a merger without a fair-price clause, and the elimination of cumulative voting, especially when coupled with classified boards, also do not seem to be in the best interests of the shareholders. The announcements of an intent to enact a non-fair-price supermajority charter amendment results in negative market reactions [Jarrell and Poulsen, 1987]. Meade and Brown [1992] also find that firms with this type of amendment are less profitable when compared with similar firms without these types of amendments. When cumulative voting is eliminated in conjunction with adoption or retention of classified boards, the market reaction is negative [Bhagat and Brickley, 1984] Corporate restructurings are also viewed negatively by the market [Dann and DeAngelo, 1988]. The corporate restructurings evaluated in the study were all in response to hostile takeover attempts.

The announcement of a firm's intention to enact an anti-greenmail amendment has been tested both directly and indirectly. Eckbo [1990] finds mixed market reactions to announcements of anti-greenmail amendments. Results depend on whether the firm was a takeover target at the time of the announcement. If the firm was a target, the announcement resulted in a negative reaction. If the firm was not a target, the proposal received a positive market reaction. There is also evidence that repurchases resulting in greenmail are associated with significant positive increases to shareholder wealth [Mikkelson and Ruback, 1985; Holderness and Sheehan, 1985].

The effect of dual class recapitalization on shareholder interests is not clear from the research. Partch [1987] concludes that they have no effect on shareholder wealth. Jarrell and Poulsen [1988] conclude that recapitalizations are not in the best interests of the shareholders. Cornett and Vetsuypens [1989] find a positive market reaction in these situations, and conclude that such actions promote shareholder wealth and interests.

Two types of corporate charter amendments, the classified board and fair-price supermajority voting requirements, appear neutral to shareholder interests [DeAngelo and Rice, 1983; Jarrell and Poulsen, 1987]. The Linn and McConnell study looked at supermajority, fair-price supermajority, and classified board amendments as a group. The results they found vary depending on whether weekly or monthly cumulative average returns (CARs) are used. Weekly CARs are not significantly affected, but monthly CARs were affected significantly.

CONCLUSIONS

The management of a corporation has a fiduciary duty to the corporation and to its shareholders. When the management is considering any antitakeover defenses there is a potential for self-serving motivations, so that the management will be held to a heightened fiduciary standard, the *Unocal* analysis. Any actions that have the effect of reducing the wealth of the shareholders, especially when made to solidify the position of the managers, is a violation of the business judgment rule, a violation of the legal duty of the management, and is unethical conduct.

When managers spend time and energy seeking to entrench themselves rather than seeking to further the interests of the corporation, the managers are violating their duty to the corporation, and they are acting in an unethical manner. Entrenchment of management at the expense of shareholder welfare is an example of management's abuse of power [Willcox, 1988] and is also a conflict of interests.

Any actions by the board of directors that discourages takeovers can be challenged ethically. The burden then shifts to the board to show that the action was reasonable, and made to further corporate goals and interests and/or to protect the shareholders. Many of these actions have been found to be not in the best interests of the shareholders, and they appeal to be self-serving on the part of management.

Some of the antitakeover conduct undertaken by various boards of directors have resulted in legislative reactions in a number of states. For example, Maryland was the first state to enact a "fair-price" statute to regulate takeovers. At least thirteen other states have subsequently adopted similar statutes. Ohio enacted a "control share acquisition" statute that was subsequently adopted in fourteen other states, four of which also adopted a "fair-price statute. Finally, Pennsylvania, Maine, and New York have enacted legislation designed to protect both the target company and the minority shareholders of that corporation.

The courts have stated that "a corporation does not have unbridled discretion to defeat any perceived threat by any Draconian means available" [*Unocal Corp.*, 1985, p. 955]. The restriction placed on the directors is to ensure that they do not act purely or primarily from a desire to perpetuate themselves in office. The directors must only take actions that are "designed to ensure that a defensive measure to thwart or impede a takeover is indeed motivated by a good faith concern for the welfare of the corporation and its stockholders, which in all circumstances must be free of any fraud or other misconduct" [*Cheff* v. *Mathes,* 1964].

Board conduct to prevent takeovers raises serious questions of propriety. The conduct is likely to be challenged on ethical and legal grounds. The directors have a heightened fiduciary duty in the antitakeover area, and there is an increase in state regulation in this area. The potential for abuse has also led to a strong push for federal regulation,perhaps even federal pre-emption, of this topic. Finally, directors can no longer simply hide behind the immunity of the business judgment rule in this area, since the conduct itself is often an alleged violation of the business judgment rule.

APPENDIX

Antitakeover Devices

Bylaw Amendments

State law allows shareholders the right to propose amendments to a company's bylaws unless the company charter prohibits such action. One antitakeover measure is for firms to adopt provisions to severely limit or prohibit shareholders from taking such action.

Classified Boards of Directors

A classified board of directors is one in which directors are divided into separate classes for staggered terms of office. In this way, only a fraction (one half or one third) of the board members are eligible for election each year.

Redemption Rights

Holders of common stock redemption rights may require the firm to redeem their shares at a premium if any shareholder acquires a substantial amount of stock through a hostile tender offer. Rights are intended to discourage hostile tender offers through possible distribution of the firm's assets to shareholders before a would-be acquirer could seize control of the firm. Common stock redemption rights are similar to poison pills.

Dual Class Capitalization and Unequal Voting Rights Plans

Several types of unequal voting rights plans are identified by the Investors Responsibility Research Center [1988]. One type, *Dual class capitalization,* creates a second class of common stock possessing either superior or inferior voting rights to existing voting stock. The second and third types both involve *unequal voting rights plans.* The second type grants *super voting rights* to the long-term stockholders, while the third type, the *substantial shareholder provision,* reduces the voting power of the holder when a prespecified amount of ownership is reached. The Investors Responsibility Research Center study [1988] states that: "The effect of these measures is to reduce the voting power of public shareholders and enhance the control of management, making hostile takeovers almost impossible."

Fair Price Requirements

Fair price provisions require a would-be acquirer to pay a prespecified price for all tendered shares. The provision usually does not apply if an offer is approved by the target's board of directors or if the bidder obtains a specified supermajority level of approval from the target's shareholders.

Lock-In Provisions

Lock-in provisions make it more difficult to rescind provisions already in place. A supermajority lock-in provision requires a supermajority level of approval to change an existing antitakeover charter of bylaw provision. The level is often set at 75 or 80 percent and sometimes even higher.

Nonfinancial Effects of Mergers

This provision requires the board of directors to evaluate a proposed merger from the perceived ensuing effect on employees, host communities, suppliers, and others.

Pension Parachutes

Pension parachutes are designed to prevent would-be acquirers from using existing target company pension funds to help finance an acquisition.

Poison Pills

Poison pills are intended to deter a hostile bid by triggering actions that make the target financially unattractive or by giving target shareholders rights to demand conversion into securities of the bidder on terms attractive to the target company but not to the bidder.

REFERENCES

Bhagat, S., and J.A. Brickley, "Cumulative Voting: The Value of Minority Shareholder Rights," *The Journal of Law and Economics* [October 1984], p. 339-365.

Carney, W.J., "Two-Tier Tender Offers and Shark Repellents," *Midland Corporate Finance Journal* [Summer 1986], p. 48-56.

Congressional Record, No. 113 Remarks of Senator Javits [1967], p. 24666.

Cornett, M.M., and M. R. Vetsuypens, "Voting Rights for Shareholder Wealth," *Managerial and Decision Economics* [September 1989], pp. 175-188.

Dann, L.Y., and H. DeAngelo, "Corporate Financial Policy and Corporate Control," *Journal of Financial Economics* [January-March 1988], pp. 87-127.

DeAngelo, H., and E.M Rice, "Antitakeover Charter Amendment and Stockholder Wealth," *Journal of Financial Economics* [April 1983], pp. 329-359.

Easterbook, F.H. and D.R. Fischel, "The Proper Role of a Target's Management in Responding to a Tender Offer," *Harvard Law Review* [April 1981], pp. 1161-1204.

Eckbo, B.E., "Valuation Effects of Greenmail Prohibitions," *Journal of Finance and Quantitative Analysis* [December 1990], pp. 491-505.

Grossman, S.J. and O. Hart, "Takeover Bids, the Free Rider Problem, and the Theory of the Corporation," *The Bell Journal of Economics* [Spring 1980].

Holderness, C.G. and D.P. Sheehan, "Raiders or Saviors? The Evidence on Six Controversial Investors," *Journal of Financial Economics* [December 1985], pp. 555-579.

Jarrell, G.A., and A.B. Poulsen, "Shark Repellents and Stock Prices: The Effects of Antitakeover Amendments Since 1980," *Journal of Financial Economics* [September 1987], pp. 127-167.

————, "Dual-class recapitalization as Antitakeover Mechanisms: The Recent Evidence," *Journal of Financial Economics* [January-March 1988], pp. 129-152.

Jensen, M.C., "The Takeover Controversy: Analysis and Evidence," *Midland Corporate Finance Journal* [Summer 1986], pp. 6-32.

Linn, S.C., and J.J McConnell, "An Empirical Investigation of the Impact of 'Antitakeover' Amendments on Common Stock Prices," *Journal of Financial Economics* [April 1983], pp. 361-399.

Malatesta, P.H., and R.A. Walking, "Poison Pill Securities: Stockholder Wealth, Profitability, and Ownership Structure," *Journal of Financial Economics* [January-March 1988], pp. 346-376.

Meade, N.L., and R.M. Brown, "Corporate Antitakeover Amendments and Firm Performance," Working Papers, Virginia Tech [1992].

Mikkelson, W.H., and R.S. Ruback, "An Empirical Analysis of the Interfirm Equity Investment Process," *Journal of Financial Economics* [December 1985], pp. 523-553.

Partch, M.M., "The Creation of a Class of Limited Voting Common Stock and Shareholder Wealth," *Journal of Financial Economics* [June 1987], pp. 314-339.

Ryngaert, M., "The Effect of Poison Pill Securities on Shareholder Wealth," *Journal of Financial Economics* [January-March 1988], pp. 377-417.

Senate Report No. 550, 90th Congress, 1st session [1967], pp. 3-7.

Willcox, T.L., "The Use and Abuse of Corporate Powers in Warding Off Corporate Raiders," *Journal of Business Ethics* [1988], pp. 47-53.

Cases

Airline Pilots Association, International v. *UAL Corporation*, 717 F.Supp. 575 [N.D. Ill 1989].

Barkan v. *Amsted Industries, Inc.*, 567 A.2d 1279 [Del. Supr. 1989].

Cheff v. *Mathes*, 199 A.2d 548, 554 [Del. 1964].

Dynamics Corp. of America v. *CTS Corp.*,794 F.2d 250,256 [7th Cir. 1986].

Edgar v. *Mite Corp.*, 457 U.S. 624 [1981].

Moran v. *Household International, Inc.*, 500 A.2d 1346 [Del. Supr. 1985].

Pogostin v. *Rice*, 480 A.2d 619 [Del. 1984].

Revlon, Inc. v. *MacAndrews & Forbes Holding, Inc.*, 506 A.2d 173 [Del. Supr. 1986].

Shamrock Holdings, Inc. v. *Polaroid Corporation*, 559 A.2d 257 [Del. Ch. 11989].

Sinclair Oil Corp. v. *Levien*, 280 A.2d 717,720 [Del. 1971].

Smith v. *Van Gorkom*, 488 A.2d 858 [Del. 1985].

Unocal Corporation v. *Mesa Petroleum Co.*, 493 A.2d 946 [Del. Supr. 1985].

THE FOREIGN CORRUPT PRACTICES ACT OF 1977 AND ITS AMENDMENTS IN 1988

Zabihollah Rezaee

ABSTRACT

The Foreign Corrupt Practices Act (FCPA) of 1977 made it illegal for U.S. firms to pay bribes. Since its passage, the FCPA has received numerous criticisms. Problems with the FCPA can be classified into two categories: (1) the law's ambiguous language on antibribery provisions; and (2) impractical record-keeping and internal control requirements. In response to the problems and criticism of the FCPA, the FCPA Amendments of 1988 were enacted. While the Amendments maintained major parts of the 1977 Act, several significant changes were made which eased U.S. restrictions on foreign trade. This article presents the provisions of the FCPA, explores the impact which this law has had on U.S. companies, compares the new law (Amendments of 1988) to the original FCPA, and discusses what the act means for corporations, management, and the accounting profession.

Advances in Public Interest Accounting, Volume 5, pages 281-295.
Copyright © 1993 by JAI Press Inc.
All rights of reproduction in any form reserved.
ISBN: 1-55938-496-4

INTRODUCTION

During the 1970s, some 450 U.S. corporations, including more than 100 of the Fortune 500 companies, under a program of voluntary disclosures, confessed to previously undisclosed and improper payments to political figures and parties both overseas and at home.[1] In response to a large amount of corruption scandals, including investigations by the Office of the Watergate Special Prosecutor, Congress passed the Foreign Corrupt Practices Act (FCPA) in 1977.[2] In legislating the FCPA, Congress intended to require corporations to establish and maintain internal accounting control systems sufficient to signal illegal payments and to enhance reliability of financial statements. By inflicting fines, the law hopes to decrease the number of dishonest business incidents, such as bribes.

The primary purpose of the Act was to stop U.S. corporate involvement in bribing foreign officials in order to upgrade the image of the U.S. government overseas. After the act's passage, the FCPA received numerous criticisms promoting amendments to the act on August 23, 1988 [see Seitzinger, 1988; Fremantle and Shermarkatz, 1988]. The amendments can be found in Title V of the Omnibus Trade and Competitiveness Act of 1988[3]. The purpose of this paper is to discuss the provisions of the FCPA and examine its impacts, problems, and amendments.

PROVISIONS OF THE FCPA

The FCPA was enacted as Title 1 of Public Law 95-213[4] and is composed of four sections: Section 101 states the title of the Act; Section 102 covers accounting standards; and Sections 103 and 104 deal with foreign corrupt practices. Based on the antibribery provision of the Act, it is unlawful for Securities and Exchange Commission (SEC) registrants, both domestic and foreign, and domestic nonregistrants to influence foreign governments, officials, political parties, or political candidates through payments of gifts (bribes). The FCPA does not prohibit so-called grease or facilitating payments to clerical government employees to expedite government processing of shipments through customs. Therefore, there is some confusion as to what constitutes a legal facilitating payment and what constitutes an illegal bribe.

The accounting standards provisions of the Act are composed of the record-keeping and internal accounting control requirements. These provisions are amendments of Section 13 (b)[5] of the SEC Act of 1934[6] and, accordingly, apply only to SEC-registrant entities. The intent of the record-keeping provision is to enhance reliability and credibility of financial statements and to enable preparation of accurate and fairly stated financial reports. The intent of the internal accounting control provision is to provide reasonable assurance for detecting and preventing illegal payments to ensure that transactions are executed as authorized and recorded in compliance with Generally Accepted Accounting Principles (GAAP), and to maintain accountability for assets.

WHAT THE FCPA MEANS FOR CORPORATIONS, MANAGEMENT, AND THE ACCOUNTING PROFESSION

The FCPA represents one of the most significant entries of government into corporate affairs. Corporate accountability and social responsibility have become important issues, not only to the image of a nation but also to its social well-being. The discussion of the impact of the FCPA on corporations', managements', and accountants' behavior is clearly of major significance in public interest and social accounting. The FCPA was an important attempt by Congress to (1) enforce corporations to realize their social responsibilities; (2) place management in the position to report on corporations' social activities; and (3) encourage public accountants to audit public companies' social behavior other than financial behavior. Activists and researchers [e.g., Parker 1986;] have examined these issues regarding the social behavior and performance of corporations.

Corporations

The FCPA resulted from a public scandal. Millions of dollars were paid in kickbacks, bribes, or other questionable payoffs to foreign officials by some of the biggest companies in the United States such as Gulf Oil Corporation and Exxon Corporation. Some payments were even made with the apparent authorization of chief executive officers from general corporate funds or from secret "such funds" maintained off the books. The litany of corporate misdeeds shocked the public and substantiated the fact that companies do not realize their social responsibilities. The FCPA provided a legislative solution to this public scandal, which according to Tinker [1984, p. 182], "destablized the governments of Japan, South Korea, the Netherlands, Indonesia, and other nations."

The FCPA encouraged corporations while operating in a free market system to realize their social responsibility by recognizing the impact of their private production activities and affairs on the social environment and public interest. Illegal payments paid to foreign officials by U.S. corporations were considered to have jeopardized abroad the image of American democracy, impaired public confidence in the financial integrity and objectivity of U.S. corporations and most of all affected·adversely American foreign policy.[7] The FCPA has placed a social responsibility on the corporation to exercise control over its officers, directors, and employees to ensure that corporate assets are not used in bribing foreign officials.[8] According to Briloff [1984, p. 45], the FCPA was enacted to "put an end to what President Carter described as ethically repugnant conduct by American enterprise."

The FCPA has brought about many changes in corporate structure and it has had positive impacts in many business and accounting areas [see Aggrawal and Kim, 1982; Baird and Michenzi, 1983; Pastin and Hooker, 1980; Tipgos, 1981]. First, Codes of Conduct have been adopted by many companies to aid compliance with the FCPA. According to the antibribery provision of the act, corporate management is responsible for vouching that corrupt practices do not occur in the conduct of their business.[9] To fulfill this responsibility, many firms have developed their own corporate code of conduct to serve as a guide for officers and employees who conduct business in the United States and in foreign countries as well.

The passage of the FCPA made the United States the first country to enact a law that prohibits its business enterprises from bribing a foreign official even outside its territorial limits. Because bribery is likely acceptable business conduct in many nations, the FCPA put U.S. firms doing business abroad in a difficult competitive position. Thus, the Act has encouraged U.S. firms to be overly cautious either by foregoing what would have been legitimate business or by simply not competing for foreign sales in the global market. Some critics of the FCPA have stated that the antibribery provision of the Act have cost up to $1,000,000,000 annually in lost U.S. export trade [Seitzinger, 1988]. However, Graham [1983] concludes that U.S. exports to "bribe-prone" countries have increased faster than those "nonbribe-prone" countries. This indicates the U.S. corporations have either not stopped bribing despite the requirement of the Act or bribes were not a significant factor in the global market competitiveness.

One of the negative impacts of the Act has been to put U.S. corporations in competitive disadvantage in the global market by imposing restrictions that their foreign competitors do not have to face, in most cases. However, U.S. corporations, in coping with the antibribery provision of the Act, have established strategies to export through a distributorship overseas or to form newly established companies to be used as conduits. For example, Boeing Corporation is currently selling aircraft to the ultimate users through a distributorship or Grumman Corporation recently sold two Gulfstream IIs to the Saudi Arabian National Airline through a Leichtenstein corporation created as a conduit [Park, 1990].

Another criticism of the FCPA is that of exporting morality, specifically, the United States was more interested in exporting its cultural biases than its products. The unilateral effort of the U.S. Congress to upgrade the ethical standards of international business is considered by some as delineating large portions of the globe as unsafe areas for U.S. companies to solicit business [Northam, 1980]. For example, in a nation in which acceptance of such payments is customary and not unlawful, the FCPA is likely to offend many citizens of that nation. Thus, the impact of the antibribery provision of the Act on the globalization of U.S. corporations is likely to be negative, encouraging businesses of other countries to gain an unfair and harmful competitive advantage over U.S. businesses.

Critics have argued that a multinational agreement prohibiting businesses of all the world's industrialized nations from bribing foreign officials is the best solution to the problems of the FCPA. However, such an agreement may not be easy to obtain because: (1) many countries may not find such an agreement in their financial interest, and (2) there is lack of proper enforcement procedures even if those countries sign such an agreement. If a multilateral agreement for the adoption of an antibribery law is not signed, U.S. firms will bear an additional cost which is not shared by foreign competitors who are not subject to comparable regulation. Fortunately, the United Nations General Assembly approved a Code of Conduct in 1980 to restrict business practices as formulated by the U.N. Conference on Trade and Development. This code of conduct prohibits illicit payments by multinational corporations outside the borders of their home country [Aggarwal and Kim, 1982].

Management

The increased competitiveness of our business environment, the complexity as well as diversity of today's business activities, and the globalization of the economy have provided impetus to the increased social and oversight responsibilities of management. These responsibilities are shared by a board of directors and top executive management. Those who have oversight responsibilities in the organization should be aware of provisions of the FCPA. The Act helps deter management override and enhance control systems. Although the FCPA is directed at prohibiting companies making illegal payments to foreign officials, it includes a requirement that public companies establish an adequate internal control system. The rationale of the FCPA was that controls will ensure against illegal payments or at least will facilitate the detection of illegal payments.

The Act made management more aware of controls because they can be held liable for illegal payments. Furthermore, system security controls are required to ensure compliance with the provisions of the Act. Failure to provide adequate system security controls could place a company in violation of the Act's requirements for an adequate system of internal control. Management could be subject to exposures of violations of the FCPA including significant loss of revenues and business opportunities, business interruption, and excessive costs of doing business. As a result of the passage of the FCPA, many companies now voluntarily include in their annual reports to shareholders a management report on internal control. According to Root [1983], private and publicly held companies voluntarily evaluate the adequacy of their systems or internal control on a continuing basis.

The FCPA is directed at company management. The Act requires that management be responsible for compliance with provisions of the FCPA and, accordingly, the SEC should require management to certify the company's compliance with the FCPA. One of the outcomes of the FCPA was the interest in the management report to shareholders published in annual reports. The purpose of the management report is to improve communication with users of financial statements and management's response to corporate social responsibilities. In this report management should assume responsibility over the content of financial statements as well as the effectiveness of the internal control system. Management should further acknowledge its responsibility for compliance with provisions of the Act, improve the veracity of financial reporting, and prevent abuses from occurring.

The use of the management report is evidence of positive impact of the FCPA and the response to the public concern about companies' social responsibility. Management should recognize its responsibility for conducting the company's affairs in an ethical and socially responsible manner. The commitment to ethical and social responsibility should be reflected in key written policy statements communicated to all affected employees. These policy statements should cover, among other subjects, code of business and ethical conduct, resolution of potential conflict of interests, compliance with applicable laws and regulations, especially antitrust laws and the FCPA, and proper conduct of domestic and international business practices. However, critics of the Act have argued that the "reason to know" standard concerning liability for actions of a firm's agent in a foreign country places unrealistic and unjustifiable responsibility on management and, accordingly, it should be removed from the FCPA.

The Accounting Profession

The FCPA is directed at company management. Independent auditors have no direct responsibility under the Act. In compliance with provisions of the FCPA, independent auditors should study and evaluate the established internal controls systems to detect illegal payments and to advise their clients about weaknesses and faulty control systems, but they are not required to report on deficient systems. The independent auditor, according to the AICPA rule[10] is expressly forbidden from providing any type of assurance that an entity is in compliance with provisions of the FCPA. The AICPA believes that such an opinion is a legal determination and, accordingly, beyond the auditor's expertise. However, accountants should realize the responsibility presumed to have been vested in them by the FCPA. The Act has encouraged accountants to realize their public interest and social responsibilities and, accordingly, has had the following positive impact on the accounting profession.

First, in reaction to the FCPA and in response to the perceived "expectation gap," the American Institute of Certified Public Accountants (AICPA), in 1979, issued *Statement on Auditing Standards* No. 16 and No. 17 titled, "The Independent Auditor's Responsibility for the Detection of Errors and Irregularities" and "Illegal Acts by Clients," respectively. *SAS 16* stated that auditors should search for material errors and irregularities in financial statements. *SAS 17*, while disclaiming auditor responsibility to detect illegal acts, clearly required that auditors be alert to the possibility that illegal acts may have occurred and required reporting them. Recently, the expectation gap has grown not only wider but in a different direction as users of financial statements began to equate business failure with audit failure. In January 1988, in response to the Commission for Fraudulent Financial Reporting's recommendations for the accounting profession, the Auditing Standards Board (ASB) issued nine new SASs as part of the expectation gap agenda. The nine new SASs can be summarized into four general groups: (1) standards to enhance the auditor's responsibility and capability to detect fraud and illegal acts; (2) standards to provide for more effective audits; (3) standards requiring improved external communications; and (4) standards requiring improved internal communications. Two of them, *SAS 53* and *SAS 54*, replaced *SAS 16* and *SAS 17*, respectively, and address the auditor's responsibility for discovering and reporting client errors and irregularities as well as responsibilities related to illegal acts by clients.

Second, as a result of the FCPA, an adequate system of internal accounting controls for presenting and detecting illegal payments is no longer a matter of management preference or technical proficiency, it is a matter of law.[11] Therefore, *SAS 20*, as amended by *SAS 30*, was adopted by the AICPA in providing the vehicle whereby auditors can perform an audit of the client's system of internal accounting controls more thoroughly. *SAS 30* states that examinations in accordance with this statement can help the management of the company evaluate it own compliance with the FCPA. *SAS 30* also requires the auditor to inform the client of material weaknesses in internal accounting control detected during the audit. Furthermore, two AICPA auditing interpretations, "Material Weaknesses in Accounting Control and the Foreign Corrupt Practices Act" and "Compliance with the Foreign Corrupt Practices Act" require that if the auditor finds a material weakness in internal accounting control, the matter should be discussed with the client's management and legal counsel to determine if the weakness violates the Act.

Third, internal auditors' responsibilities have been increased since the passage of the FCPA. The Act has focused management and public attention on the internal control system and mandated that a business must show evidence of an effective internal control system. One element of the internal control system of a company is an internal auditor. Therefore, internal auditing has become increasingly oriented toward operational control, oversight, and

protection and has moved further away from financial auditing. In fact, after
the passage of the Act, many internal audit departments have received larger
budgets and expanded staffing authorization [Mautz, 1980]. In addition, the
National Commission on Fraudulent Financial Reporting [Treadway, 1987,
p. 4] recommended a far more prominent role for internal auditors and
recognized that internal auditors pay a crucial role in detecting and deterring
fraudulent financial reporting.

Finally, since the passage of the FCPA, the audit committee has become
the main party responsible for overseeing compliance with the Act [see
Neumann, 1981]. To enhance auditors' independence, the Act recommended
the establishment of a standing audit review committee made up of independent
members of the board of directors to whom the external and internal auditors
report. As a result, the New York Stock Exchange required all listed domestic
companies to establish audit committees by June 30, 1978 [AICPA, 1979]. The
audit committee operates as a liaison between the independent auditor and
the board of directors and, accordingly, can reenforce auditor independence
while opening lines of communication between external auditors.

PROBLEMS WITH THE FCPA

Since its passage, the FCPA has led to many complaints by U.S. companies,
and there have been attempts by the business community and the accounting
profession to convince Congress to revise the law [see Benjamin, Dascher,
and Morgan,1979; Fanning, 1987; Seidel, 1981]. Problems with the FCPA can
be classified into three broad categories: (1) The Law's ambiguous language
on antibribery provisions; (2) impractical record keeping and internal control
requirements; and (3) liability for actions of a firm's agent in a foreign country.

The Law's Ambiguous Language on Antibribery Provisions

The FCPA has failed to distinguish between a facilitating payment and an
illegal bribe. A bribe can be defined as money paid for making a decision, while
"grease" is money paid to facilitate cutting through red tape.[12] Grease payments
are gifts to foreign officials whose duties are essentially clerical and,
accordingly, should not involve substantial amounts. Facilitating payments
involving a large amount could be considered as a corrupting influence. Note
that grease payments are not necessarily unethical while bribes are always
unethical by definition. Because the Act has failed to outlaw grease payments,
there is some confusion as to what constitutes a legal facilitating payment and
what constitutes an illegal bribe.

Perhaps, it is unrealistic attempting to place U.S. standards of business on foreign countries that incorporate facilitating payments into their way of conducting business. There are dangers of losing business by eliminating these payments. Pastin and Hooker [1980] concluded that economic losses come from construction of the ability of U.S. corporations to do business abroad and political losses have occurred due to this holier-than-thou image of the FCPA. Critics (i.e., Fanning, 1987; Maher, 1981; Johnston, 1983) have argued for precise and specific guideline as to what is permitted and what particular conduct is prohibited by the Act. Specifically, they have argued for precise statutory languages to enact Congress's original intent in permitting "facilitating" payments.

Impractical Record Keeping and Internal Control Requirements

The law's ambiguous language has led to impractical record keeping that has caused wide-ranging application of it provisions to virtually any deficiency in internal accounting controls, regardless of materiality. The FCPA states that books and records should be kept in reasonable detail.[13] This would vary with different companies. To determine reasonableness, management would have to perform a cost-effective analysis and take into consideration judgment factors such as the diversity of the firm, its size and degree of centralization.

The SEC has concluded that there is no limit of materiality in the internal control provision of the Act.[14] One June 6, 1980 in its Release No. 3-16877, the SEC stated that "The Commission wishes to reemphasize the fact that the internal accounting provisions of the FCPA are not limited by a standard of materiality."[15] The SEC holds that all transactions must be accurately recorded on the company's books—not just material transactions. The position held by the SEC is offset by legislative history and administrative releases that provide for a cost/benefit relationship. In the report issued by the National Commission of Fraudulent Financial Reporting [Treadway, 1987, p. 40], the commission, while supporting both antibribery and accounting standards provisions of the Act, criticized that "the provisions of the FCPA are not limited by a standard of materiality."

The Act failed to distinguish between an honest, unintentional accounting error and an intentional act of fraud or irregularity. As a result, U.S. companies have been compelled to apply large resources and effort in complying with this provision of the Act. The Act violates the principle that criminal sanctions should be defined with narrow specificity. According to Daniel Peller, an attorney at the New York firm of Paul, Weiss, Rifkind, Wharton and Garrisson, "Criminal statutes should be crystal clear since liberty is at stake;; [see Fanning, 1987]. The FCPA is not crystal clear regarding the criminal liability provision for unintentional accounting errors as opposed to intentional acts of fraud and circumventions of internal controls. Because the FCPA is not limited to international acts and does not include a scienter (intentional misconduct) requirement, it could impede communication between a company's management and its independent auditors because management may fear unintentional violations of the Act.

Liability for Actions of a Firm's Agent in a Foreign Country

The FCPA is not clear with regard to the "reason to know" standard concerning liability for actions of a firm's agent in a foreign country. U.S. companies are required to use their influence to encourage their agents in foreign countries not to use funds, payments, or commissions to bribe foreign officials. Critics [see Seidel, 1981; Seitzinger, 1988] of the Act argued for the removal of the "reason to know" standard. This would eliminate the legal responsibility of management of a domestic firm over the unauthorized and undirected actions of foreign agents. This implies that: (1) U.S. firms should not have to bear the responsibility of playing detective concerning the independent actions of persons that they retain as agents in foreign countries; and (2) the United States should attempt to export its products, not its cultural biases. Many foreign firms incorporate these payments into their way of conducting business and, therefore, placing U.S. standards of business on these foreign companies is unfair. Seitzinger [1988] argued that there should be an international agreement among the world's industrialized nations prohibiting businesses of all those countries from bribing foreign officials.

AMENDMENTS OF THE FCPA

In response to the problems and criticism of the FCPA, Congress has deliberated on reforming, modifying, and simplifying the Act. After a great deal of debate, the FCPA Amendments of 1988 were signed into law as Title V of the Omnibus Trade and Competitiveness Act of 1988[16] on August 23, 1988. While the amendments maintained the major parts of the FCPA, some significant changes were made in the 1977 Act.

First, the amendments manifested what constitutes a legal facilitating payment and what constitutes an illegal bribe by widening the range of what is considered a "grease payment" to foreign officials and certain others.[17] For example, the amendments permit any facilitating or expediting payment to a foreign official or political party, if the payment was made to expedite or to secure the performance of a routine governmental action by a foreign official or political party. Furthermore, the antibribery provisions shall not apply to the payment of a gift, or the offer or promise of anything of value, which was lawful under the written laws and regulations of the foreign officials or political party. However, the amendments prohibit payments made to foreign officials that induce them to do any act in violation of the lawful duties of such officials.

In sum, according to the provisions of the amendments, a U.S. business or citizen may use one of the following "affirmative defenses" in arguing that no violation of the FCPA has occurred:[18] (1) payments, gifts, or offers of anything of value, which were lawful under the written laws and regulations of the providers; (2) those payments, gifts, or offers of anything of value were reasonable and bona fide expenditures, such as travel and lodging expenses, and were directly related to the promotion, demonstration, or explanation of products or services, or the execution or performance of a contract with a foreign government or agency; and (3) any payment for routine governmental action is permissible without consideration of the status of the official who performs the action. According to the amendments, "routine governmental action" is defined as "only ordinarily and commonly performed by a foreign official in obtaining permits, licenses, or other official documents to qualify a person to do business in a foreign country."[19] Indeed, the attorney general is required to issue guidelines describing:[20] (1) types of conduct that would fit within the "affirmative defenses," and (2) general precautionary procedures that issuers may use in compliance with provisions of the amendments.

Second, the amendments substantially altered the accounting standards provisions of the FCPA. The amendments eliminated the criminal liability provision of the Act for unintentional accounting errors and omission as opposed to intentional acts of fraud, irregularities, and circumventions of internal accounting controls. The amendments state:[21] (1) no criminal liability should be imposed for failing to comply with the accounting standards provisions, unless a person knowingly falsifies books, records, or accounts; (2) no person shall knowingly circumvent or knowingly fail to implement a system of internal accounting controls or knowingly falsify any books, records, or accounts. According to the SEC's Release No. 34-15570, the falsification-of-records provision covers not only journals and ledgers but also correspondence, memorandums, papers, tapes, and other documents, whether expressed in ordinary or machine language; and (3) a U.S. company that holds 50 percent or less of the voting power of a foreign or domestic firm is required to proceed in good faith to use its influence to encourage the majority interest holder to devise and maintain an adequate and acceptable system of internal accounting controls. An insurer who demonstrates good faith efforts to use such influence shall be conclusively presumed to have complied with the requirements of the Act.

Third, related to the accounting standards of the FCPA, is a new definition of "reasonable detail" and "reasonable assurance" described in the 1988 amendments. The reasonable detail requires that an issuer maintain adequate and sufficient books, records, and accounts. The reasonable assurance requires that an issuer must safeguard corporate assets at such level of detail and degree of assurance as would satisfy prudent officials in the conduct of their own affairs considering a materiality standard of comparing benefits to be obtained and cost to be incurred in obtaining such benefits.

Fourth, in the 1988 amendments, Congress changed the "knowing" standard of the FCPA. This standard applies to criminal and civil liabilities of firms or individuals who make payments to third parties "knowing or having reason to know" that payment would be used by a third party for purposes prohibited by the FCPA. The "knowing" requirement includes the standards of "conscious disregard," "willful blindness," or "deliberate ignorance" in finding violations of the FCPA. However, businesses or individuals will not be held liable under the Law for "simple negligence" or "mere foolishness."

Finally, The amendments increased penalties for violations of the FCPA. The maximum fine for a firm or domestic concern is raised from one million to two million dollars and for individuals from \$10,000 to \$1000,000.[22] In addition to the fine paid by a firm or domestic concern, an individual fine of up to \$10,000 may be imposed for civil penalty. The maximum potential imprisonment is still five years.

CONCLUSION

The Foreign Corrupt Practices Act is one of the most significant legislations enacted concerning corporate governance and responsibility as well as corporate obligation to maintain accurate books, records, or accounts to prevent illegal payments. The Act makes it illegal for SEC registrants or domestic nonregistrants to influence foreign governments or officers through gifts or payments and also requires that the SEC registrants comply with certain records-keeping and internal control requirements to prevent or detect such payments. The 1977 Act has apparently increased the prevalence of corporate code of conduct, the budgets of internal audit departments, the importance of the corporate audit committee, the time spent by internal auditors in reviewing internal controls, and firms' resource consumption. Perhaps the most glaring weakness for the FCPA has been its ambiguous language on antibribery provisions and impractical record-keeping and internal accounting control requirements, and assumption of liability for actions of a firm's agent in a foreign country.

Almost eleven years after passage of the FCPA, with much persistence and in response to numerous criticisms, and August 23, 1988, the President signed into law the Omnibus Trade and Competitiveness Act of 1988, of which Title V is known as the FCPA Amendments of 1988. While the amendment maintained major parts of the 1977 act, several significant changes were made, including: (1) the enactment of a "knowing" standard in order to find violations of the act and to eliminate the criminal liability provision for unintentional accounting errors and omission as opposed to intentional acts of fraud, irregularities, and circumventions of internal accounting controls; (2) increased clarification on what constitutes a legal facilitating payment and what constitutes an illegal bribe by widening the range of what is considered grease payments to foreign officials and by providing certain defenses against finding violations of the FCPA (e.g., the gift is lawful under the law or the foreign country); and (3) the establishment of a new definition of "reasonable detail" and "reasonable assurance" as a basis for a materiality standard (cost/benefit test) as to the justification of both the record-keeping and internal control provisions.

The FCPA and its amendments are a product of the cultural and political environment of the early 1970s and, accordingly, should be evaluated in that context. The Act was an important attempt by Congress to: (1) enforce corporations to realize their social responsibilities; (2) place management in the position to report on corporations' social activities; and (3) encourage public accountants to audit public companies' social behavior other than financial behavior. The FCPA has placed a social responsibility on the business community and the accounting profession to ensure that corporate assets are not used in bribing foreign officials. Critics argue that by enacting the FCPA, the U.S. government finds itself in a catch 22—pioneering international ethical business conduct and seemingly losing the competitive edge in the global market. In the short run, the FCPA and its amendments may be deemed unfavorable to U.S. exports, but in the long run some benefits may be derived as discussed in this paper.

NOTES

1. U.S. General Accounting Office, Report to Congress, Impact of Foreign Corrupt Practices Act on U.S. Business, Washington, [March 4, 1981].

2. P.L. 95-213, Title 1; 91 Stat. 1494, Dec. 19, 1977 (codified as amended at 15 U.S.C. §778dd-1 to-2 [1982].

3. P.L. 100-418, 102 Stat. 1107.

4. P.L. 95-213, Title 1; 91 Stat. 1494 [Dec. 19, 1977].

5. 15 U.S.C. §78m(b).

6. 15 U.S.C. §§78a *et seq.*

7. S. Rept. 95-114, 95th Cong., 1st Sess., at 3 [1977].

8. S. Rept. 95-114; at 1.

9. 15 U.S.C. §§78dd-1 and 78dd-2.

10. AICPA Auditing Interpretation No. 5, "Compliance with the Foreign Corrupt Practices Act of 1977," Question 1a, Au §9642.10 issued October 1978, modified August 1980.

11. 15 U.S.C. §78m(b) (2) (B).

12. Rept. No. 95-114, at 10.

13. FCPA, Supra note 1 §102, 15 U.S.C. §78m (b) [1982].

14. Statement of Policy Concerning the Foreign Corrupt Practices Act, Exchange Act Release No. 17,500, 21 SEC Docket 1466, 1471, reprinted in the Fed. Reg. 11,544 [1988]

15. 21 SEC Docket at 1467.

16. P.L. 100-418, 102 Stat. 1415 [1988]
17. H.REP, Supra note 2, at 8.
18. P.L. 100-418, Supra note 5, §5003 (c) (1).
19. 15 U.S.C. §§78dd-1, -2.
20. 15 U.S.C. §78dd-1, Supra note 5, §5003 (a).
21. CONF. REP., Supra note 36, at 916.
22. FCPA, Supra note 4, §104 (g).

REFERENCES

Aggrawal, R., and S.H. Kim, "Should the FCPA Be Abolished?" *The Internal Auditor* 39 [April 11982], pp. 20-23.

American Institute of Certified Public Accountants (AICPA), *Professional Standards* Vol. A&B [Commerce Clearing House, 1990]

————, "Report of the Special Committee On Audit Committee" [AICPA, 1979].

Baird, B., and A. Michenzi, "Impact of the Foreign Corrupt Practices Act," *The Internal Auditor*, 40[June 1983], pp. 20-22.

Benjamin, J., P. Dascher, and R. Morgan, "How Corporate Controllers View the Foreign Corrupt Practices Act," *Management Accounting* [June 1979], pp. 43-49.

Cooper, D.J., "A Social Analysis of Corporate Pollution Disclosures: A Comment," in *Advances in Public Interest Accounting*, Vol. 2, edited by M. Neimark [JAI Press, 19988], pp. 179-186.

Fanning, D., "Am I My Brother's Keeper?" *Forbes* [May 4, 1987], p. 66.

Fremantle, A., and S. Katz, "The Foreign Corrupt Practices Act Amendments of 1988," *The International Lawyer* [Fall, 1989], pp. 755-767.

Graham, J.L., "Foreign Corrupt Practice Act: A Manager's Guide," *Columbia Journal of World Business* [Fall 1983], p. 90.

Heinz B., "Easing FCPA Violation Penalties Gains SEC Support," *Journal of Accountancy*, 133 [April 1983], p. 12.

Johnston, W. "All in Favor of Bribery Please Stand Up," *Across the Board* [June 1983], pp. 3-5

Maher, M.W., "The Impact of the Regulation on Controls: Firms' Response to the Foreign Corrupt Practices Act," *The Accounting Review* 56[October 1981], pp. 751-768.

Mautz, R.K., *Internal Control in U.S. Corporations: The State of Art* [Financial Executive Research Foundation, 1980].

Neumann, F., "Corporate Audit Committees and the Foreign Corrupt Practices Act," *Journal of Accountancy*, 155 [March 1981], pp. 78-80.

Northam, R.E., "Corporate Accountability and the FCPA," *The Accounting Forum* [May 1980], p. 23.

Okcabol, F., and T. Tinker, "The Market for Positive Theory: Deconstructing the Theory for Excuses," in *Advances in Public Interest Accounting*, Vol. 3, edited by M. Neimark [JAI Press, 1990], pp. 71-96.

Parks, J.H., "Time to Remove Self-Imposed Barriers to Export Trade," *The Journal of Business Strategy* [November/December 1990], pp. 57-60.

Parker, L.D., "Polemical Themes in Social Accounting: A Scenario for Standard Setting," in *Advances in Public Interest Accounting*, Vol. 1, edited by M. .Neimark [JAI Press, 1986], pp. 67-94.

Pastin, M. and M. Hooker, "Ethics and the Foreign Corrupt Practice Act," *Business Horizons* [December 1980], pp. 43-47.

Puxty, A.G., "Social Accounting as Immanent Legitimation: A Critique of a Technicist Ideology," in *Advances in Public Interest Accounting,* Vol. 1, edited by M. Neimark [JAI Press 1986], pp. 95-112.

Root, S.J., "FCPA: Where do We Go From Here?" *The Internal Auditor* [April 1983], p. 28.

Seidel, G.J., "Corporate Governance Under the Foreign Corrupt Practices Act," *Quarterly Review of Economics and Business* [Autumn 1981], pp. 43-48.

Seitzinger, M.V. "Foreign Corrupt Practices Act Amendments of 1988," *CR's Report for Congress* [August 30, 1988], pp. 1-13.

Tinker, T., *Social Accounting for Corporations* [Markus Wiener Publishing, 1984].

Tipgos, M.A., "Compliance with the Foreign Corrupt Practices Act," *Financial Executive,* 38 [August 1981], pp. 38-48.

Treadway, J.C., Jr., *Report on the National Commission on Fraudulent Financial Reporting* [National Commission on Fraudulent Financial Reporting, 1987].

TRUTH OR TRUISM:

WHAT DO ACCOUNTING RESEARCHERS WANT?

Dan Subotnik

ABSTRACT

Accounting practitioners have long bemoaned the irrelevance (to them) of academic research. This article not only validates their complaint, but it also shows the intellectual bankruptcy of much of this work. Starting with an examination of some recent academic work in auditing, casting primary focus on the *Accounting Review,* and continuing with a review of other products of contemporary accounting scholarship, "Truth or Truism" demonstrates that too frequently researchers devote time and energy to proving what we already know through common sense. Public acknowledgment of this phenomenon would seem to be essential if the efficiency of accounting research is to be maximized. Recognizing that challenges to received wisdom are not invariably unprofitable, this paper examines the issue of the standard by which academics ought to be guided when operating in what appears to be terra cognita. A test is proposed to help accounting scholars distinguish between projects likely to be worthwhile and those that are not. Finally, the problem of framing worthy research projects

Advances in Public Interest Accounting, Volume 5, pages 297-312.
Copyright © 1993 by JAI Press Inc.
All rights of reproduction in any form reserved.
ISBN: 1-55938-496-4

is placed in the context of a recently developed philosophy of science. Drawing on work initiated by Professor Freeman Dyson [1988], the author locates accounting on the unification-diversification continuum and analyzes the significance of such placement for the field.

INTRODUCTION

When asked over the phone recently for a reference to a comprehensive study of contemporary accounting research, an ex-president of the American Accounting Association was at a loss to name one. And without a navigational guide of this nature, of course, any broad-based critique of accounting scholarship, such as attempted here, is especially risky. Yet so great are the resources that we commit to our research in accounting, that an attempt to come to some general, if tentative, conclusions about our work would seem highly useful, if not urgent.

This paper can be seen as the product of a contradiction. On the one hand the Bedford Committee[1] could point with pride to the payoffs of academic accounting research such as statistical sampling, information economics, artificial intelligence, mathematical financial modeling, behavioral budgeting, and stock market efficiency concepts. These benefits alone, it concludes, "would justify requiring accounting faculties to conduct research as a condition for their teaching" [Bedford Committee, 1986, p. 184].

On the other hand, and at the same time that some of these developments were taking place, Abe Briloff, a leading accounting academic, was expressing a far different opinion:

> In our research endeavors the academic community finds our presumptive first-rate accounting intellects constrained to demonstrate their competence as second-rate financial analysts, applying third-rate mathematical methodology to fourth-rate data contained in various computerized data banks compiled by fifth-rate accounting drones. As a consequence, the leading journals ... demonstrate intensified mathematical sophistication, with diminished contact with the real world [Briloff, 1984, pp. 509-510].

Articulating what is surely a similar critique, Accounting Hall of Famer and Harvard Professor Emeritus Robert Anthony has written: "Most issues of *The Accounting Review* don't contain one useful article, and I have even given up looking at *Journal of Accounting Research* and similar publications" [letter to author, June 25, 1990].

It is not only accounting research that is vulnerable to these charges but also business research generally. "I happen to be an old quantifier—going back 60 years," writes Peter Drucker," ... so I can hardly be accused of being opposed to quantification. But what goes on now is a gross abuse," He goes on to say that "nobody seems to teach or to learn the basic specifications for the use of figures and the limitations of quantitative methods" [letter to author, September 5, 1990]. Richard West, Dean at the New York University Graduate School of Business, underscores this notion when, discussing business research, he writes: "[I]t's often crap. They say nothing in these articles and they say it in a pretentious Way. If I [weren't] the Dean I would write on the bankruptcy of American management education" [Is Research in the Ivory Tower 'Fuzzy,' 1990, p. 62].

Briloff, Anthony, Drucker, and West, highly qualified analysts of business education, have not elaborated on their striking critiques. It is, perhaps, for this reason that the AAA, the journals, the American Assembly of Collegiate Schools of Business, and business school deans have not felt compelled to face head-on the painful issue they raise. In this article, empirical support is offered for the critics' views. At the same time a notion is advanced that might help reconcile their views with those of the Bedford Committee in some limited respects.

The central thesis of this paper is that far from overvaluing academic rigor—a charge recently leveled against business school academics by the Graduate Management Admissions Council [1990]—and to the substantial detriment of the field, many (most?) North American accounting researchers actually undervalue it. This is because too often they attempt to prove propositions that, in the end, are self-evident and thus, even under the best circumstances, cannot add anything to our understanding. A necessary, if insufficient, condition for an article of high quality, it is suggested here, is that the article's thesis, if proved, should lead to a substantial change of behavior or provide confirmation of a practice or theory that has been called into question in the area of activity under study.

One might perhaps expect undeveloped or lax editorial standards in a field where there has been such a proliferation of journals in recent years. What is surprising—and deeply disturbing—is that the issue of empty scholarship is frequently, if unintentionally, raised by works found even in the *Accounting Review* (*AR*), a journal that was recently rated number two overall by accounting educators [Hull and Wright, 1990]. In the auditing subfield, an area that will receive special attention here, in fact, *AR* runs neck and neck with the overall leader, the *Journal of Accounting Research*. It is precisely because of its great prestige that *AR* has been made into the primary focus of this paper.

Over the last few years editorial policies of journals such as *AR* have been called into question. Articles found in *Accounting, Organizations and Society, Critical Perspectives in Accounting,* and *Advances in Public Interest Accounting* have highlighted the severe limitations of our positivistic and social research ideologies [see, e.g., Williams, 1989; Arrington and Francis, 1989; Briloff, 1990]. This author hopes he has contributed to that debate through his prior articles on the impact of the mathematization of the field.[2] This article continues the tradition of challenging those who would appear to be too mesmerized by quantitative research to evaluate it properly.

PART I

Consider a recent article on the relationship between audit structure and role stress by Bamber, Snowball, and Tubbs [1989], "Audit Structure and Its Relation to Role Conflict and Ambiguity: An Epistemological Investigation." First, let's define the article's key terms, some of which are borrowed from Cushing and Loebbecke [1986]. "Structure," say the authors, is "the arrangement of people, tasks and authority to achieve more calculable and predictable control over organizational performance." "Role conflict" refers to the "simultaneous occurrence of two (or more) sets of pressures such that compliance with one would make difficult or impossible compliance with the other." "Role ambiguity" is defined "in terms of [1] the predictability of the outcome or responses to one's behavior ... and [2] the existence or clarity of behavioral requirements, often in terms of inputs from the environment, which would serve to guide behavior and provide knowledge that the behavior is appropriate" [pp. 286-287]. "Role stress," though not formally defined, is measured as the aggregate of role conflict and role ambiguity.

What were the *findings* of this study? "Structured firm seniors perceived their tasks as more analyzable than did seniors in unstructured firms" [p. 292]. The former also "perceived their work to be characterized by greater formalization of rules and procedures" [ibid.]. Moreover, "Work flow coordination, adequacy of authority, communication adequacy and adaptability all contributed significantly to role conflict.... Work flow coordination, violations in the chain of command and communication adequacy contributed significantly to role ambiguity ... " [p. 294].

But if one starts with the definition of structure set forth above, it is virtually inevitable that a statistical comparison of seniors in structured and unstructured firms will "reveal" that those in the former group will describe their task as "more analyzable." No more surprising will be the finding that in structured firms stress is associated with violations in the chain of command and inadequate work flow coordination, whereas in unstructured firms, stress is associated with the lack of perceived authority to make necessary decisions.[3] Indeed, it is difficult to see how conclusions such as these can be said to offer any information beyond the kind explicit in a tautology.[4]

There is admittedly a point at which this article comes close to telling us something new. It involves the authors' finding of a lack of parallelism between role conflict and role ambiguity (categories which are ordinarily affected in similar ways by a number of organizational features) at structured relative to unstructured firms. Instead of pursuing this surprising discovery, however, the authors mechanically lump together the findings with regard to role conflict and role ambiguity, drawing the broad conclusion that structured firm seniors report less role stress overall that do seniors in unstructured firms. This conclusion may not have the total redundancy of a tautology; but it is difficult to see how it tells us anything that is not already known.

Other Evidence from Audit Research

The criticism can be applied to a recent piece by Wand and Weber [1989]. The issue here is how auditors should go about structuring "their search space so they can identify those system locations where controls and audit procedures must be modified when system changes occur" [Wand and Weber, 1989, p. 87]. The findings: "[A]uditors need examine only those subsystems where changes made to the system alter the events that occur within the subsystem.... When the events that can occur do change, however, auditors must examine the subsystem to determine whether controls are in place and working to correctly designate each event as either 'lawful' or 'unlawful' " [p. 88].

That these findings could have been anticipated is openly acknowledged by the authors themselves. "The model presented here," the authors write, "provides formal support for an intuitively appealing idea; namely, auditors should not have to reexamine *all* controls within a system when the system is modified" [Want and Weber, 1989, p. 105]. No investigation, it is true, starts out in a vacuum; many end up confirming the expectations of their authors. In this case, however, the conclusion was virtually foregone right at the outset.

And, again, the same holds for a recent article by Abdolmohammadi and Wright [1987] on the relationship between audit experience and auditor judgment. In this study the authors took a number of audit tasks, and, with the help of experienced practitioners, classified them as structured, semistructured, or unstructured in nature. Then, based on these tasks and classifications, they administered a questionnaire to different auditors at varying stages of their careers. The authors' hypothesis: "Experience effects in auditing are positively related to the level of task complexity."

Here are their findings: While *structured* tasks elicited no differences in test-takers' responses,

> [t]he results support the central hypothesis in that significant decision differences were consistently found between experienced staff and other subjects for unstructured and semi-structured tasks ... The significant experience effects found for unstructured and semi-structured tasks suggest that accounting students or less experienced staff are dubious surrogates in such audit decision settings [Abdolmohammadi and Wright, 1987, p. 12].

Can anyone seriously doubt that audit partners and manager usually exhibit more refined judgment than do accounting novices, a category here that includes students (and that it is through unstructured tasks, rather than, say, reconciling ordinary bank statements, that judgment difference is most manifest)? If it were otherwise, would a marketplace providing major firm partners ten times the income of juniors be *rational?*[5]

The authors conclude their article by saying that "we are only in the embryonic stages of understanding" the nature and effects of experience. Not all that embryonic, thankfully.[6]

In an effort of this nature the charge is to be expected, and indeed it has been leveled at the author, that articles have been picked selectively to demonstrate the point sought to be made. Conceded. The author is not condemning all *AR* auditing articles. He is merely hoping that by taking a fairly abbreviated time period in the recent past (1987-1991), and highlighting a number of the most egregious examples of the identified problem, he can convince readers that reform is appropriate, if not urgent.

Still More Evidence

On the assumption that one more illustration in this series is necessary, we turn now to a recent piece by Vicky Heiman [1990]. "This study," she writes, "provides evidence that consideration of alternative explanations affects auditors' likelihood assessments of an initially hypothesized cause in analytical review, and that a discounting model is descriptive of this process. When auditors had at least two alternative explanations available to them," she continues, "their initial likelihood assessments of the hypothesized cause were reduced" [p. 888]. Another finding in this piece will be discussed later. For the moment, need anything more be said?[7]

Nonauditing Evidence

The phenomenon under review can be observed in areas other than auditing. Consider the article "Pretest Reviews in Intermediate Accounting: An Empirical Analysis" by Richard L. Ott. Here is an excerpt from the conclusion:

> The objective of this study was to determine the effects of a structured review on student exam scores in intermediate accounting. The results suggest that structured review does make a difference in student performance .... Students like structured reviews for various reasons—time on task holistic learning, and identification of weaknesses before the exam ... [Ott, 1988, p. 386].
> Students surely have never doubted this. Have faculty?

And a similar problem lies at the heart of a related study, "Empirical Evidence on the Effectiveness of Quizzes as a Motivational Technique " by Faromorz Elikai and J. Baker [1988]. The study concludes that final exam scores in accounting can be improved through periodic quizzes when, and only when, quiz grades are an important factor in the overall grade.

Finally, let's look at "Factors Motivating Academic Research in Accounting," which concludes: "[T]he clearly important motivating factors ... were financial.... " The implication of this finding, the authors announce, "is that faculty must be rewarded financially in salary and have their research specifically supported if they are to be motivated researchers [Abdolmohammadi, Mennon, Oliver, and Umpathy, 1988].[8] One wonders: What response did the authors expect from a survey of academics? Should business school deans open up the purse strings in the wake of this article?[9]

Interestingly, there was another finding that emerged from this study, one that, to this critic, has the makings of a real bombshell. In their questionnaire the authors asked whether satisfaction of intellectual curiosity was a factor in motivating research. The response: Except for assistant professors, No. What does this say about the accounting research environment today?

PART II

What If Anything, Is Really Known?

In attempting to prove what to many of us, at least, is self-evident, the authors of the articles under review unwittingly raise a fundamental academic issue: To what extent should researchers accept the accumulated body of wisdom and intuition, and when should this body be reexamined?

Pursuant to a longstanding Western tradition, nothing called knowledge is beyond challenge. "Students," writes Bronowski [1973, p. 360], [should] bring a certain ragamuffin, barefoot irreverence to their studies [because] they are [at the university] not to worship what is known but to question it." Allan Bloom [1987 pp. 252-253] makes the same point in admitting that even the teaching of his beloved Aristotle "ought always to be approached with questions and doubts, not faith."

Does this mean that we should not be able to rely on anything in our scholarship, that our assumptions should always be challenged? Is every imaginable question a mountain that legitimately justifies attempts to scale it "because it's there." Should we still be devoting resources to prove that debits and credit are equal?

Let's explicitly consider what our attitude should be toward projects which seem merely to defend intellectual territory which, on the surface, is already secured. Clearly projects where a tautological conclusion seems unavoidable because it is logically implicit in the relationship between the premises and problem are relatively easy to reject on principle. On the other hand, in cases not involving logical tautology, even putting aside consideration of technically sophisticated kinds of received knowledge, it is equally clear that examining what is accepted as undisputed knowledge can be immensely useful. Conventional wisdom and common sense are, after all, terms that are often used as smokescreens for what is really cultural prejudice. How then, as a practical matter, can we be efficient in selecting our research projects?

A Proposed Research Criterion

There is a criterion to be offered that could help assess the value of our research. What is specifically indicated here is the concept of doubt, a concept that has been accepted in the modern West as a test of intellectual value at least as far back as Descartes.

This is not to advocate that accounting scholars should have to design their research in terms of a principle anywhere near as sophisticated or systematic as Cartesian doubt. What does seem reasonable is that before embarking on an inquiry to which the probable answer seems obvious in advance, we ought to be able to attach at least the possibility of doubt to *some* aspect of the inquiry as we envision it. Or if we cannot find a problem that involves us in *active* doubt, which is surely one of the least arguable indications of a need for research, then at least the problem should hold out the prospect of offering some *conceivable* doubt.[10]

"But who," asks a well-meaning, but unabashedly frank early critic, "applies the criterion, you?" The answer is simple: perhaps even the same folks who currently enforce editorial policies and who now, we can hope, have more carefully considered the implications of prevailing practice.

Again, a requirement that doubt precede intellectual activity does not imply that some projects offering no apparent reason for prospective doubt might turn up some surprises. However, simply to plunge into any imaginable research venture without stopping to consider whether anything about it is open to doubt, seems on the whole an unpromising way to accomplish work that yields high intellectual value. At the very least every such project drains resources for other projects where outcomes are subject to doubt.

To return to the article about structure and role stress, surely we will all agree that there is no intellectual advance in a finding that those working in an environment which lacks rules of behavior will tend to feel at sea. Does an article that arrives at such a conclusion not owe its readers at least some minimal reason for suspecting the possibility of a different result?

The Power of Negative Thinking

The authors of the articles discussed give no evidence of having doubted anything in the professional literature on which they rely. On the contrary, the authors refer to their predecessors' work in tones that are almost reverential.

Nor do these authors doubt their own findings. Consider Heiman's piece [1990]. Added to the first finding, that "varying the number of alternative explanations influenced the degree of reduction in likelihood assessments," was a second, this one not so intuitively appealing: "varying the strength of alternatives had no effect.... The presentation of strong versus weak errors [as alternatives] did not differentially affect auditors' likelihood assessments" [p. 889].

Now who among us can even begin to accept the extraordinary proposition, generalized for us by the author, that accounting graduates ultimately make judgments based on the quantity of ideas rather than on their quality? If the statement is true we would obviously have to reduce our accounting programs to rubble and begin from scratch. But does the author, who we have to assume accepts her own findings, provide any evidence of doubt by acknowledging the absolutely revolutionary impact of her message?

How have we come to a state of affairs where researchers take prior work and their own findings as conclusive and, consistent with this, design projects that do not seek to confront doubt but to avoid it? For one of my reviewers the answer would seem to lie in the kinds of people attracted to the field and Ph.D. training of graduate students. This, while not a completely satisfying hypothesis, is one a psychologist might well find worth pursuing. For our purposes here let us consider the phenomenon of the computer.

One of the things computer technology was designed to do is handle massive amounts of data with such a high degree of mathematical certainty (assuming a correct program and inputs) as to virtually remove the specter of doubt from the researcher's results. This seems a positive state of affairs; yet after reading literature of the sort reviewed here one is sorely tempted to suspect that the very possibility of mathematically indisputable results may actually have the effect of discouraging authors from creating an intrinsically ambitious design for their project.

If the foregoing speculation is correct, what an irony confronts us! The computer, which in theory allows us to gather and process information from the ends of the earth, induces us in actuality to look no further than the end of our noses. While this line of argument cannot be definitively proved here, some promising new work in the philosophy of science seems to support this disturbing notion.

PART III

Unity and Diversity

In 1988 Freeman Dyson, the physicist and cosmologist (who speaks to us from the top of the ivory tower, the Institute for Advanced Study), published a book titled *Infinite in All Directions*.[11] In the first chapter of this work, a paean to the complexity of the world, Dyson provocatively claims that "[d]iversity is the great gift which life has brought to this planet" and "[s]cience has as many competing styles as painting or poetry" [pp. 5, 11].

In a subsequent and stunning chapter titled "Manchester and Athens," Dyson contrasts two principal styles of science. The one, corresponding to Manchester, "emphasizes ideas and theories; it tries to find unifying concepts which tie the universe together" [Dyson, p. 40]. Dyson elaborates, "Unifiers are people whose driving passion is to find general principles which will explain everything" [p. 44].[12] Such people, according to Dyson, "believe that nature can be reduced to a finite set of equations.... " [p. 36]. Likewise, "[t]hey are happy if they can leave the universe a little simpler than when they found it." Insofar as the computer is used to determine and measure relationships of disparate pieces of data in the universe, the unifiers inevitably gravitate toward it.

The other style "emphasizes facts and things; it tries to explore and extend our knowledge of nature's diversity." "Diversifiers," by Dyson's definition, are people whose passion is to explore details. They are in love with the heterogeneity of nature ... " [p. 45]. Such people, in his view, "believe that nature is inexhaustible" or, as he elsewhere puts it, "They are happy if they leave the world a little more complicated than they found it" [p. 45].[13]

Nothing Old Under the Sun

In his review of Dyson's book, distinguished biologist Stephen J. Gould [1988] expands on the distinction between the schools while openly holding himself out as a Mancunian (i.e., from Manchester). As opposed to the "quantifiers" who constitute the first school, members of the second school work "more as historians than as guardians of 'the scientific method' ... because our empirical world is a temporal sequence of events so unrepeatable by the laws of probability and so irreversible by principles of thermodynamics, that everything interesting happens only once in its meaningful details" [p. 32].

Building on Gould's vivid evocation of contingency and uniqueness, the eminent political scientist George Kennan takes the analysis a step further. "If this [condition] is true of the natural sciences," he writes, "how could it be otherwise in the social and political ones?" [Kennan, 1989, p. 22]. How indeed? Whether we are talking about prices of securities, auditor behavior, agency costs, or the accuracy of financial statements, human motivation and behavior determine what we see. But since human motivation and behavior are caused by an unlimited, undeterminable, and probably unrepeatable number and *balance* of factors—and because the operative mode in these matters is change, not stasis—the utility of combining data on the items just mentioned will always be limited. The fundamental problem facing the researcher in the social sciences, in short: *Plus c'est la même chose, plus ça change.*

Is this all too abstract? If so, let us consider for a moment the possibility of quantitive methods being used to explain results in law. One might suppose that mathematics would make an ideal partner of law on a theory that it could help standardize the process of judicial decision making. There are, after all, hundreds of thousands of cases and thus millions of pieces of data just waiting to be processed by a computer. Here, however, Dyson Gould, and Kennan's observations seem telling. To illustrate by way of contract law, much of what lawyers do in contract litigation case is to advocate an interpretation of the language used by the parties in a way that is most favorable to their clients. But by law the meaning of any words or terms must be derived from examination of the entire agreement between the parties, the relationship between the parties, and frequently the oral communications of the parties at the time of the signing of the contract. Is it likely that these factors will prove identical in any two cases? And are not tort cases equally individualized, though for different reasons? In any event unifiers have been singularly unsuccessful in explaining results (as opposed to arguing policy) in the field of jurisprudence.

In time the Dyson, Gould, and Kennan view will have to be refined to deal with, among other things, differences in unification and diversification as they affect differences in the physical and social sciences. For the present let us explore the connection between DGK and contemporary accounting research. It would seem that it is their incomplete understanding of science that has led mainline researchers to suppress doubt about their own and others' work and thus to concentrate on projects where everything is known in advance. One looks in vain, however, for evidence of Dyson's diversitarian mode in the articles we have looked at or in the broad range of accounting scholarship. One longs for a concluding statement such as: "This is my finding, but there is much evidence pointing the other way."

There are hundreds, indeed thousands, of macro research projects around, all grist for our computer mills, tying factor A to factor B, exchange rates to wars, gold production expectations to inflation, recession, or what have you— all counting on the technology of the computer to help organize (and freeze) the actual world. Maybe what is needed in accounting is the very thing that Dyson suggests physics needs: a better balance between the two scientific modes.

Dyson, Gould, and Kennan help remind us that we should never suspend disbelief in our work or that of our colleagues, that no model can stand for all of reality—that indeed, the part of reality that is not explained by, and even contradicts, the model is potentially the most valuable source of information and ought not to be papered over in the name of unification or simplification.[14]

As for a topic such as the relationship between the structure and the efficiency of an audit, the implications are clear. Authors of a piece of this nature would not limit themselves to the closed-ended process of the questionnaire, as did the authors in "Audit Structure...." Rather, in the tradition of say a Freud (or even a Studs Terkel), if they were not satisfied with the existing state of knowledge they would go out and exhaustively interview some seniors and managers about their job experience (not unlike Cushing and Loebbecke, on whose work these particular authors rely) in an attempt to elicit and assess the full range of operative psychological factors and the various conditions that affect perceptions. And when an unexpected finding was made—that structure did not lead to inflexibility in the atypical audit, for example—far from ignoring it, auditors would seek to know why, since the answer might shed light on the entire project.

Would we be better off tiling the current balance in our field in the direction of diversitarianism? Dyson, who is surely no methodological innocent, would no doubt say yes. "The history which I find illuminating," he writes, "is the kind which the professionals call 'anecdotal'. I am interested in individual people, not in social and economic statistics" [Dyson, p. 35].

CONCLUSION

Until recently, for a period of 12 years, Ed Koch served as mayor of New York City. In an attempt to be responsive to the needs of his constituency, His Honor would periodically ask the public and the media: "How'm I doing?"

In the accounting research field, as in some others, the big questions are too infrequently posed. Without even beginning to claim that "Truth or Truism" provides a comprehensive answer to this question for accounting research generally, the author does attempt a response here that cuts across research lines.

There is no way to mathematically prove the central thesis of this paper, that too much research is not sufficiently imaginative because the results obtained are essentially implicit in the question raised. There are going to be differences about the meaning of "insufficiently imaginative" and especially, "too much." Readers will ask whether the entire literature has been examined. Two observations attend the thesis here: First, this article's success will ultimately depend on the reader's ability to accept an argument that is not mathematical in nature; work of this sort is frequently dismissed out-of-hand as insufficiently rigorous. The problem with this criticism is that mathematics, as a tool, is, in the end, of limited utility. It can prove something is wrong. It cannot prove something is silly.

Second, payoffs from this paper (if any) will not take the form of nailed-down truth, but rather of better focused questions about the purpose and utility of our future research. If Bronowski's earlier quoted opinion of the function of the university is accepted, such a contribution will be more than payoff enough for the work involved in this analysis.

It may take a long time for all of us to get to the point where we recognize that mathematics cannot substitute for the rigorous thinking that social scientists engaged in prior to the advent of the computer. But with increasing pressure by those of us who are deeply concerned, change will happen. And when it does, this author predicts it will come fast. For when we all come to realize that so much energy, time, and money has been wasted, tenure standards, teaching methods, Ph.D. training will change, which will encourage academics in the field to research not the easy but the difficult problems. Articles will then be welcomed for the importance of questions they raise and not because they give play to methods that happen to be available.

Support for the shift to a truly productive research environment may well come from the accounting firms. Consider this: Staggering as it may seem, many of the articles in the high prestige journals cited here were subsidized by the accounting profession. Imagine what will happen when the funding organizations come to the realization that important work in areas such as ethics, intellectual history, and the collapse of the S & L industry, is not being done because of biases endemic in the field for which, in no small measure, they are responsible.

The discussion here leads to a final, narrow and scientific question. Inasmuch as the evidence presented is drawn essentially from audit and educational research, as opposed to, say, market research, one wonders: Is research in the former areas especially vulnerable to the kind of criticism leveled against the pieces reviewed in this article? Intuitively speaking, we would probably say no. But there is something intriguing here that might point the other way. Bear in mind that the very developments adduced by the Bedford Committee as evidence of the social value of accounting research do not have as their principal focus problems in the area of measurement and analysis of individuals' thought processes.

Is this significant?

NOTES

1. The Bedford Committee, known also as the Committee on the Future Structure, Content and Scope of Accounting Education, published a report in *Issues in Accounting Education* [Bedford Committee, 1986].

2. In particular see "Wisdom or Widgets" [Subotnik, 1988], which attempts an explanation of the drive to "scientize" academic accounting. This research for the most part cannot be effectively summarized here. The article does point out that if accounting research were limited to the quantitative variety little if any useful work could be done in such important areas as intellectual history and ethics.

3. The piece itself makes clear that virtually all the earlier "findings" could have been anticipated.

4. Am I forgetting that the point of Bamber et al.'s article was to verify the work of Cushing and Loebbecke? I don't believe so. Though Bamber and his coauthors imply a need to confirm empirically Cushing and Loebbeck's work, they never provide, or even suggest a basis for questioning the latter's definitions in the first place.

5. An early reviewer asked, "If you believe in rational labor markets, why don't you believe in rational markets for ideas?" Do all markets have to be rational? A friend in industry claims that there is nothing to concentrate the mind like the knowledge that a particular judgment may result in millions of dollars of income or the same amount of expense. It is not a pleasant thought, but perhaps there is nothing comparable to concentrate our minds on in academia.

6. My view has been disputed by a colleague who claims that the point of the Abdolmohammadi paper is not to show that experience differences exist with respect to unstructured projects, but to capture those differences in an experimental setting so they can be analyzed and understood. Through this process, he argues, we will be better able to train future auditors.

The problems with their paper, however, as the authors themselves admit, is that the findings have limited value "due to any one (or a combination) of intelligence, design or choice phases of the decision process." To remedy the situation the authors offer the usual nostrum of articles that provide little to chew on that "future research" be done in this area. But, of course, different groups will always have different responses to value-laden materials of this nature, and if different materials are used, responses will be yet more disparate. As a result the benefits will continue to be limited. The tendency of academics in their attempts at useful generalizastion to ignore the uniqueness or even the differences of the events and conditions that make up our world is the subject matter of much of Part III.

7. If so, consider one of the findings of Eric Spire's "Audit Evaluation of Test-of-Control Strength" [1991]: "For practitioners, the study provides evidence that firm wide policies do affect judgments made by auditors: thus, setting policies may be effective in influencing judgments on individual audits ... [T]his study shows that auditors from firms providing caution that inquiry and observation are relatively weak derive less assurance from inquiry and observations than auditors from other firms" [p. 274].

8. To give the researchers their due, they do show that assistant professors do not view promotion and tenure as substitutes for financial rewards.

9. Before moving on we can briefly consider "An Experiment Testing the Behavioral Equivalence of Strategically Equivalent Employment Contracts" by Stanley Baiman and Barry L. Lewis [1989]. This study in the principal-agent area (a field I know little about) deals with the problem of employees lying to employers and raises what may be an important question.

Baiman and Lewis state that their findings were consistent with the idea that the tendency to lie for monetary [gain] is different across individuals; that is, different people have different ethical standards. The accounting models of communication ... assume that all agents are identical and would lie for monetary advantage. Our results show that these models might be improved by expanding them to discriminate between agents of different 'ethical types' " [p. 15]. Here then is the question: Can any benefit be expected from a (much celebrated) line of research having as its premise that everyone is equally prone to lie?

10. A reviewer would recast the requirement of doubt into a proposition that no proposed study is worth doing where the outcome may not cause authors to change their minds.

11. Is Dyson the only major thinker who has something to say about contemporary applications of the scientific method? Hardly. But his statement is perhaps the latest on the subject and, more important, it has already been accepted and then refined, as will be noted shortly, by scholars such as Stephen J. Gould and George Kennan. This would seem to be sufficient reason to hitch a ride for a while with Dyson-Gould-Kennan.

12. Reference must be made to the pathbreaking work done in this area by Arthur Lovejoy in *The Great Chain of Being* [1964]. Lovejoy persuasively shows that the "uniformitarian"-diversitarian dichotomy lies at the heart of the difference between the Enlightenment and Romantic periods of Western history. Lovejoy concludes that unformitarianism, which is devoted to "the simplification and the standardization of thought and life" and suppresses the "*differentness* of men," "is the history of a failure" [pp. 292, 293, and 329].

13. The distinction drawn by Dyson may have an analog in the field of decision theory. Perhaps unifiers are ones who tend to look for confirmation of their thinking while diversifiers focus on disconfirming elements.

14. The notion that extreme examples yield more insight into a body of work than do so-called normal ones was asserted by the noted critic, Walter Benjamin [see Rosen, 1977, p. 33].

A similar principle lies at the heart of deconstruction, in Jacques Derrida's notion of the "supplement" and the "frame" [see Culler, pp. 102-106, 193-199].

REFERENCES

Abdolmohammadi, M., K. Mennon, T.W. Oliver, and S. Umapathy. "Factors Motivating Academic Research in Accounting," in *Advances in Accounting*, Vol. 6, edited by B.N. Schwartz [JAI Press, 1988].

Abdolmohammadi, M., and A. Wright, "An Examination of the Effects of Experience and Task Complexity on Audit Judgments," *Accounting Review* [October 1987], pp. 1-13.

Arrington, C.E., and J. Francis, "Letting the Chat out of the Bag: Deconstruction, Privilege, and Accounting Research," *Accounting, Organizations and Society*, 14, 1/2 [1989], pp. 1-28.

Baiman, S., and B.L. Lewis, "An experiment Testing the Behavioral Equivalence of Strategically Equivalent Employment Contracts," *Journal of Accounting Research* [Spring 1989] p. 1-20.

Bamber, E.M., D.A. Snowball, and R.M. Tubbs, "Audit Structure and its Relation to Role Conflict and Role Ambiguity," *Accounting Review* [April 1989], pp. 285-299.

Bedford Committee, "Future Accounting Education: Preparing for the Expanding Profession," *Issues in Accounting Education* [Spring 1986], pp. 168-195.

Bloom, A., *The Closing of the American Mind* [Little Brown, 1987].

Briloff, A., "Corporate Governance and Accountability Malaise," *Journal of Corporation Law* [Spring 1984], pp. 473-511.

Briloff, A., "Accounting and Society: A Covenant Desecrated," *Critical Perspectives in Accounting*, 1[1990], pp. 5-30.

Bronowski, J., *The Ascent of Man* [Little Brown, 1973].

Culler, J. *On Deconstruction: Theory and Criticism after Structuralism* [Cornell University Press, 1982].

Cushing, B.E., and J.K. Loebbecke, *Comparison of Audit Methodologies of Large Accounting Firms* [American Accounting Association, 1986].

Dyson, F., *Infinite in All Directions* [Harper & Row, 1988].

Elikai, F., and J. Baker, "Empirical Evidence on the Effectiveness of Quizzes as a Motivational Technique," *Issues in Accounting Education* [Fall 1988], pp. 248-254.

Gould, S.J., "Mighty Manchester," *New York Review of Books* [October 27, 1988], pp. 32-35.

Graduate Management Admissions Council, *Leadership for a Changing World, The Future Role of Graduate Management Education* [1990].

Heiman, V., "Auditors' Assessments of the Likelihood of Error Explanations in Analytical Review," *Accounting Review* [October 1990], pp. 875-890.

Hull, R., and G. Wright, "Faculty Perception of Journal Quality: An Update," *Accounting Horizons* [March 1990], pp. 77-87.

"Is Research in the Ivory Tower 'Fuzzy, Irrelevant, Pretentious'?" *Business Week* [October 29, 1990], pp. 62-66.

Kennan, G.F., "The History of Arnold Toynbee, "*New York Review of Books* [June 1, 1989], pp. 21-23.

Lovejoy, A. *The Great Chain of Being* [Harvard University Press, 1964].

Ott, R.L., "Pretest Reviews in Intermediate Accounting: An Empirical Analysis," *Issues in Accounting Education* [Fall 1988], pp. 378-387.

Rosen, C., "The Origins of Walter Benjamin," *New York Review of Books* 24 [November 10, 1977], p. 33.

Spire, E., "Audit Evaluation of Test-of-Control Strength," *Accounting Review* [April 1991], pp. 259-276.

Subotnik, D., "Wisdom or Widgets: Whither the School of Business?" *Abacus* [September 1988], pp. 95-106.

Wand, Y., and R. Weber, "A Model of Control Change and Audit Procedure Change in Evolving Data Processing Systems," *Accounting Review* [January 1989], pp. 87-107.

Williams, P., "The Logic of Positive Accounting Research," *Accounting, Organizations and Society,* 14, 5/6[1989], pp. 455-468.

Advances in
Public Interest Accounting

Edited by **Cheryl Lehman,** *Hofstra University.*

Associate Editors: **Marilyn Neimark,** *Baruch College, The City University of New York* **Barbara D. Merino,** *North Texas State University,* and Tony Tinker, *Baruch College, The City University of New York*

Volume 1, 1986, 227 pp. $73.25
ISBN 0-89232-516-X

CONTENTS: Editorial. **Accountancy and the Public Interest,** *Abraham J. Briloff.* **Reexamining the Rules of the Game: The Dingell Hearings and Beyond,** *Roberty Chatov.* **Fantasies of Information,** *Richard J. Boland, Jr..* **Polemical Themes in Social Accounting: A Scenario for Standard Setting,** *Lee D. Parker.* **Social Accounting as Immanent Legitimation: A Critique of a Technicist Ideology,** *Anthony G. Puxty.* **The Befuddled Merchant of Venice: More on the "Misuse" of Accounting Rates of Return Vis-a-Vis Economic Rates of Return,** *Robert E. Jensen.* **Hazardous Waste Disposal, Corporate Disclosure, and Financial Performance in the Chemical Industry,** *Joanne Rockness, Paul Schlachter, and Howard O. Rockness.* **An Analysis of the Impact of Corporate Pollution Disclosures Included in Annual Financial Statements on Investors' Decisions,** *Martin Freedman and Bikki Jaggi.* **Action Research: Public Utility Regulation—An Opportunity for Research and Service in the Public Interest,** *Ralph Estes.*

Volume 2, 1987, 197 pp. $73.25
ISBN 0-89232-698-0

CONTENTS: Preface. **Professional Value System of Academic Accountants: An Empirical Inquiry,** *Ahmed Belkaoui and James L. Chan.* **Of Gods and Demons, Science and Ideology,** *Wai Fong Chua.* **Risk, Financial Self-Discipline and Commodity Relations: An Analysis of the Growth and Development of Life Insurance in Contemporary Capitalism,** *David Knights.* **Accounting Ethics: Surviving Survival of the Fittest,** *Cheryl R. Lehman.* **Directions for Social Accounting Research: A Survey of Potential Data Sources,** *Joanne W. Rockness and Paul Schlachter.* **Case Study Research in Accounting: Methodological Breakthrough or Ideological Weapon,** *Chris Smith, Richard Whipp, and Hugh Willmott.*

J A I P R E S S

Waving Goodbye to the TWA Bus: "Paper Prophets" and the Sraffian Critique of Marginalism, *Tony Tinker*. Towards a "Real" Value Accounting, *James F. Becker*. The Dingell Hearings and Related AICPA Initiatives, *Thomas P. Kelley*. The Reagan Administration, A New Issue with Warmed Over Ingredients, *John E. Ullmann*. A Social Analysis of Corporate Polution Disclosures: A Comment, *David J. Cooper*. An Analysis of the Impact of Corporate Pollution Disclosures: A Comment, *In-Mu Haw and Byung T. Ro*. An Analysis of the Impact of Corporate Pollution Disclosures: A Reply, *Martin Freedman and Bikki Jaggi*.

Volume 3, 1990, 275 pp. $73.25
ISBN 0-89232-784-7

CONTENTS: Editorial. Accounting Dosen't Matter, Does It? Intellectual Tyranny and the Public Interest: The Quest for the Grail and the Quality of Life, *Ed Arrington*. Talking About Accounting: A Comment on Arington's Paper, *Paul F. Williams*. Publica or Privatus: Pro Whose Bono?, *Ralph Estes*. The Debate on Whether Client Management Should Negotiate Audit Contracts: Yuppies Versus Puppies Versus Guppies Versus Suppies, *Robert E. Jensen*. The Market For Positive Theory: Deconstructing the Market for Excuses, *Fahrettin Okcabol and Tony Tinker*. Sex Role Identity and Career Success of Certified Public Accountants, *Rebekah J. Maupin*. The Effects of Changing Role Requirements on Accountants, *Sarah A. Reed and Stanley H. Kratchman*. The Importance of Being Ernest: Gender Conflicts in Accounting, *Cheryl R. Lehman*. Corporate Social Disclosure Practice: A Comparative International Analysis, *James Guthrie and Lee D. Parker*. The State and Political Theory in Corporate Social Disclosure Research: A Response to Guthrie and Parker, *Patricia J. Arnold*. The Association Between Environmental Performance and Environmental Disclosure in Annual Reports and 10Ks, *Martin Freedman and Charles Wasley, Washington University*. The Accountant in the Class Structure, *Robin Roslender*. The Relevance of Weberianism to Class Analysis of Accounting: A Reply to Roslender, *Trevor Hopper*.

Volumes 1-3 of Advances in Public Interest Accounting were edited by Marilyn Niemark, Baruch College, City University of New York

Volume 4, 1991, 261 pp. $73.25
ISBN 1-55938-254-6

CONTENTS: **Accountability, Corporate Social Reporting and the External Social Audits,** *Rob Gray, David Owens, and Keith Maunders.* **External Social Accountability: Adventures in a Maleficent World,** *Lee D. Parker.* **Social Accountability and Universal Progmatics,** *Anthony G. Puxty.* **Toward a Better Understanding of the Underreprestantion of Women and Minorities in Big Eight Firms,** *Michael C. Knapp and Soon-Yong Kwon.* **Role Conflicts in Public Accounting: Can Individual Vigilance Suffice?,** *Paula B. Thomas.* **The Context of the Contemporary Accounting Profession,** *Ahmed Riahi-Belkauoui.* **The Internal and External Validity of Wealth Exchange Ratios in Mergers,** *Robert P. Crum, Charles R. Enis, and J. Edward Ketz.* **Regulators and Economic Benefits: The Case of Occupational Health Standards,** *Martin Freedman and A.J. Staglinao.* **Theorizing Accounting Regulation in a Global Context: Insights From a Study of Accounting in the Federal Republic of Germany,** *Sonja Gallhofer, James Haslam, and Tony Lowe.* **Accounting's Panopticon: The ICC's Bureau of Statistics and Accounts and the Public Interest,** *Paul J. Miranti, Jr.* **Exploring the Deterrent Effect of the Foreign Corrupt Practices Act,** *Pekin Ogan, Yaw M. Mensah, and Michael Gift.* **Public Interest Commentary, What's in a Name? Big Eight, Seven, Six...** *Lawrence A. Ponemon and David R.L. Gabhart, Bentley College.*

JAI PRESS INC.

55 Old Post Road - No. 2   P.O. Box 1678
Greenwich, Connecticut 06836-1678
Tel: (203) 661-7602   Fax: (203)661-0792

Advances in Accounting Information Systems

Edited by **Steven G. Sutton,**
Faculty of Management, The University of Calgary

Volume 1, 1992, 209 pp. $73.25
ISBN 0-89232-575-1

JAI PRESS INC.

55 Old Post Road - No. 2   P.O. Box 1678
Greenwich, Connecticut 06836-1678
Tel: (203) 661-7602   Fax: (203)661-0792

Advances in Accounting

Edited by **Bill N. Schwartz,** *Chairperson, Department of Accounting, Virginia Commonwealth University*

Volume 10, 1992, 318 pp. $73.25
ISBN 1-55938-416-6

CONTENTS: Decision Aids for Error Quantifications in Attribute Sampling: Circumvention, Efficiency, and Experience Effects, *Mohammad J. Abdolmohammadi.* An Empirical Investigation of the Effects of Presentation Format and Personality on Auditor's Judgment in Applying Analytical Procedures, *John C. Anderson and Philip M.J. Reckers.* The Association Between Auditors' Uncertainty Opinions and Business Failures, *H. Perrin Garsombke and Seungmook Choi.* Educational Preparation for Auditors, Promotion Time, and Turnover: A Survival Analysis, *J. David Spiceland, Philip H. Siegel, and Carolyn R. George.* Audit Disclosure of Consistency: An Analysis of Loan Officer Reaction to SAS No. 58, *Marshall A. Geiger.* The Incorporation of Ethics into the Accounting Curriculum, *James H. Thompson and Timothy L. McCoy.* Noisy Performance Measures in CEO Compensation Contracts: An Empricial Analysis, *Susan Pourciau.* A Re-Examination of the Relative Importance of CPA Firms' Performance Evaluation Criteria, *John M. Hassell, Harry W. Hennessey, Jr., and James E. Rebele.* An Analysis of the Relative Contribution of Experience/Education to the Professional Development of Auditors, *Philip H. Siegel, John T. Rigsby and John Leavins.* The Effects of Mode of Information Presentation and Cognitive Style on Bond Rating Change Decisions, *Michael C. Nibbelin, Charles Bailey. and Robert W. Zmud.* The Impact of Audit Technology Approach on Organizational-Professional Commitment in Large Public Accounting Firms, *Richard G. Schroeder and Alan Reinstein.* The Interactive Effect of Humor and Type A Behavior: Accounting Perspective and Evidence, *Freddie Choo.* An Investigation of Lending Decisions in the Oil and Gas Industry, *Linda Nichols.* Start-Up Costs and the Cpomparability of Financial Statements, *Richard A. Samuelson.* The Sensitivity of Failure Prediction Models to Alternative Definitions of Failure, *Paul R. Bahnson and Jon W. Bartley.* An Alternative Graphical Intuitive Extrapolation Procedure: Evidence Concerning the Accuracy of Forecasts, *Roger G. Holland, Kenneth S. Lorek, and Allen W. Bathke, Jr.* The Relation Between Earnings Impact and Timing of Mandatory Accounting Standards Adoption — The Case of SFAS 2 Adoption, *Emeka Ofobike.*

Also Available:

Volumes 1-9 (1984-1991)
  + Supplement 1 (1989) $73.25 each

Advances in Management Accounting

Edited by **Marc J. Epstein**, *Graduate School of Business Administration, Harvard University*

Volume 1, 1992, 242 pp. $73.25
ISBN 1-55938-420-4

CONTENTS: Introduction. Managerial Accounting: Yet Another Retrospective, *Jacob G. Birnberg.* **Relevance Regained: Management Accounting: Past, Present, and Future,** *Eric G. Flamholtz.* **From Cost World to Throughput World,** *Eliyahu M. Goldratt.* **Management Information and Accounting Information: What Do Managers Want?,** *Sharon M. McKinnon and William J. Bruns, Jr.* **How Activity-Based Cost Systems Help Managers Implement New Strategic Directions,** *Robin Cooper.* **Social Accounting Past and Future: Should the Profession Lead, Follow — or Just Get Out of the Way?,** *Ralph Estes.* **Whistle-Blowing or Whistle-Swallowing: Understanding the Motivation to Report Organizational Wrongdoing,** *Marcia P. Miceli and Janet P. Near.* **An Alternative Formulation for Activity-Based Cost Functions,** *Scott K. Jones and Kay M. Poston.* **An Empirical Investigation of the Effect of Negotiation Strategy and Risk-Taking Behavior on Transfer Pricing Outcomes,** *Ralph E. Viator, C. Douglas Poe, and Jerry R. Strawser.* **Strategic Goals and Objectives and the Design of Strategic Management Accounting Systems,** *Richard J. Palmer.* **How the Effect of Company Growth Can Reverse the Lifo/Fifi Decision: A Possible Explanation For Why Many Firms Continue to Use Fifo,** *James R. Martin.* **Supervision: A Significant Dimension of Ethics For Management Accountants,** *Richard E. Coppage.*

JAI PRESS INC.

55 Old Post Road - No. 2   P.O. Box 1678
Greenwich, Connecticut 06836-1678
Tel: (203) 661-7602   Fax: (203)661-0792